W9-CJG-059

THE
SHADOW
OF THE
PANTHER

THE
SHADOW
OF THE
PANTHER

HUEY NEWTON AND THE PRICE OF BLACK POWER IN AMERICA

HUGH PEARSON

 Addison-Wesley Publishing Company

Reading, Massachusetts • Menlo Park, California • New York •
Don Mills, Ontario • Wokingham, England • Amsterdam •
Bonn • Sydney • Singapore • Tokyo • Madrid • San Juan •
Paris • Seoul • Milan • Mexico City • Taipei

Many of the designations used by manufacturers and sellers to distinguish their products are claimed as trademarks. Where those designations appear in this book and Addison-Wesley was aware of a trademark claim, the designations have been printed in initial capital letters.

Library of Congress Cataloging-in-Publication Data

Pearson, Hugh.
   The shadow of the panther : Huey Newton and the price of black power in America / Hugh Pearson.
      p. cm.
   Includes bibliographical references and index.
   ISBN 0-201-63278-0
   1. Black power—United States—History. 2. Black Panther Party—History. 3. Newton, Huey P. 4. United States—Race relations.
I. Title.
E185.615.P38 1994   94-666
973′.00496073—dc20   CIP

Jacket design by Lawrence Ratzkin
Jacket photograph by *The Oakland Tribune*
Text design by Jean Hammond
Set in 10.5-point Janson by DEKR Corporation, Woburn, Mass.

2 3 4 5 6-MA-97969594
Second printing, July 1994

This book is dedicated to the memory of my mother, the late Edith Richardson Pearson; my father, Dr. Huey L. Pearson, whose importance to my life I can never repay; and to the memory of the late Robert C. Maynard, who invited me to join the staff of his newspaper, which inspired me to move to the San Francisco Bay Area, making this book possible.

Contents

THE
SHADOW
OF THE
PANTHER

1

Murder in the Early Morning

WILLIE PAYNE, JR., IS A BEARDED, MIDDLE-AGED, AFRICAN American male of medium height who wears dirty, disheveled clothes. He looks as though he is homeless, even though he isn't. His light brown skin has a faint reddish hue. His handsome face is weathered, but friendly. You might run into Willie if you live in the San Francisco Bay Area and take the BART train to work from the West Oakland station on Seventh Street. Or you may encounter him as you exit the station on your way home. He's the man pushing the large shopping cart filled with empty, crushed soda cans, checking to see if you have one you're about to discard which he can add to his pile, to redeem for money to help pay his rent and support his crack addiction.

Like many other African American men whose formal educations ended after high school, in an earlier era Willie might have worked in a factory, or as a longshoreman at the port of Oakland, or in the sprawling Southern Pacific rail yards only blocks away. But in postindustrial America most of those jobs have dried up. Technology has streamlined work at the docks. Most of the factories in the area are now closed. Southern Pacific has adjusted to the jet age.

Thus many of the black men in West Oakland have become unemployment statistics who don't even look for work. They collect redeemable cans, sell odds and ends, stand idly on the neighborhood street corners, or engage in something far more lucrative—the sale of drugs.

Just east of where these men live is the gleaming, burgeoning Oakland skyline, composed of buildings in which many college-educated black men enjoy far different lifestyles. To the north is the city of Berkeley and its University of California campus. In the office buildings of Oakland and Berkeley, as well as at UC Berkeley—one of the nation's premiere universities—successful black men such as Landon Williams can be found.

In the 1960s, when radical change in American society seemed possible, men like Williams worked to transform the lives of the Willie Paynes they had left behind in West Oakland. They were inspired by the atmosphere in a metropolitan area that defined the radicalism of the decade. White college students at UC Berkeley spurred and shaped campus activism for white college students nationwide. Across the bay in San Francisco, young people transformed that city into the national symbol of resistance to everything the American dream stood for.

One of the most important influences on young blacks in the San Francisco Bay Area, and eventually across the nation, was the group Williams chose to join in October 1967 while he was a student at San Francisco State University. The Black Panthers first met in a clubhouse in 1966 on Peralta Street in West Oakland, only four blocks from where Willie Payne lives today. Party cofounder Huey Newton would never make the transition from political activist to an effective operator within the system the way Landon Williams would. Newton developed severe cocaine and alcohol addictions and siphoned much of the funds earmarked for the very Panther programs designed to benefit poor African Americans—the free health clinics, the free breakfast programs for children, and the free school. In 1989 Huey Newton, like Willie Payne, was a crack addict. And on the night of August 21, no man was more important to Newton than Willie Payne.

According to Payne, he encountered Newton that night at the

corner of Ninth and Center streets in front of Payne's apartment. They had known each other since 1967. Newton asked Payne if he had a pipe to smoke some crack with. Payne answered yes. Newton said he would stop by Payne's apartment after he got some crack from the dealers operating out of a house at Tenth and Cypress streets. He and Payne could then take turns smoking hits of it from Payne's pipe.

Newton approached a dealer standing on Twelfth Street and said, "I'm Huey Newton. I just got out of jail and I want a dove." A dove was a $20 piece of crack. Because of Newton's long-established legend as cofounder of the Panthers and a force to be reckoned with on the Oakland streets—a true elder of sorts—the dealer gave him the dove of crack, free of charge. Allegedly, Newton had been relying on this method of securing drugs for some time. He had become a severe cocaine addict in 1970 after his release from prison following the reversal of his voluntary manslaughter conviction in the 1967 death of Oakland police officer John Frey.

At that time the Oakland police force was nearly all white with a reputation for brutality among Oakland's black populace. Hence, the Panthers began as a group who monitored the police, carrying guns and advising black citizens being arrested by them of their rights. The police were determined to rid the streets of the Panthers as soon as possible.

On that October night in 1967, Officer Frey stopped Newton and a companion at Seventh and Willow streets. After checking in on his police radio, Frey radioed for help. Officer Herbert Heanes came to his aid. When Heanes arrived, Frey made Newton get out of his car and led him toward the police cars. While standing between the cars, Newton overpowered Frey and shot him. Officer Heanes returned fire, wounding Newton. Heanes also was wounded, although he couldn't identify Newton as the gunman who wounded him. John Frey died; Newton and Heanes survived.

Newton's arrest in the shooting death of Officer Frey was treated as an outrage by radicals and liberals of the day, because, at that time, Newton claimed to be innocent. Consequently, a national "Free Huey" campaign ensued, consuming most of the energy of the Black Panther Party, creating a welter of sympathetic publicity, and attracting a massive number of new party recruits and the financial backing of the chic rich. As a result of the campaign, the Black Panther Party drew the interest of people such as Landon Williams and Mary Kennedy. Landon became a weapons expert for the party, while Mary performed the ordinary duties of a rank-and-file member.

A young, intelligent Oakland high-school student named Sheeba Haven would also be drawn to the party. On her graduation from high school she received a full scholarship to UC Berkeley, but soon dropped out to join the Panthers. Haven met Newton the day after he emerged from jail in 1970 after his conviction was overturned on a technicality. She remained a dedicated Panther soldier who worked in the trenches, while Newton resumed his place at the head of the party.

Huey became a favorite of the "beautiful people" eager to turn him on to their expensive, recreational, mind-altering drugs. At that time, inexpensive crack hadn't yet been invented. And snorting cocaine hardly stigmatized people as it would after the drug became cheap and available to the desperate, demoralized people of West Oakland with whom Newton, by August 1989, was regularly keeping company. Cocaine was "in," and Newton took to it readily.

But between 1970 and 1989, economic changes profoundly altered the city of Oakland. The mid-1970s marked the beginning of a rapid transformation of urban areas from manufacturing to service-based economies. Working-class blacks saw more and more job opportunities dry up at the Oakland port, in the factories, and in the rail yards. Increasing numbers of the demoralized and unemployed began sinking first to heroin and then to cocaine use, as that drug became cheaper and cheaper, thanks to drug traffickers prowling the streets of East and West Oakland, the two neighborhoods with the highest concentration of low-income blacks. One such trafficker was a former member of the Young Panthers named Felix Mitchell. (The Young Panthers were an auxiliary group that the party organized for young people from the community; they were not actual party members.) He became head of the 69 Mob, an outfit reputed to gross between $12 and $50 million per year from its drug-dealing activities. Mitchell quickly became the most notorious and vicious drug kingpin in the city.

But it was said there was one man Mitchell feared—Huey Newton. Allegedly, Newton had once been instrumental in driving some of Mitchell's dealers from an East Oakland neighborhood. It was also alleged that in 1977, Mitchell ordered the murder of a nineteen-year-old Oakland youth, because he believed the victim was part of a Black Panther assault team sent to extort money from his gang. Further rumors that some Panthers were involved in drug activities in the city circulated in 1981. It was said that Newton had a plan to continue financing the Panthers' free school in East Oakland by establishing a cocaine distribution network through his connections in Cuba, the nation to which he had fled in 1974 in order to beat indictment for the murder of a prostitute and the pistol whipping of a tailor. He had returned to Oakland in 1977, whereupon he had paid off the tailor to drop charges against him, and eventually had beaten the prostitute murder rap after two juries were unable to reach a verdict.

After those incidents, the Black Panther Party suffered an even greater decline in respect. By then Landon Williams, Mary Kennedy, and Sheeba Haven were no longer in the party. And the life of Huey Newton became one of the demoralizing reasons that increasing numbers of young blacks stopped demanding, "Power to the People!" Just as instrumental were breakthroughs in affirmative action for college-educated African Americans and the simultaneous rightward turn of formerly radical white youths. It all translated into increased abandonment of Newton and the remaining Panthers.

By 1982, records of the Panther-run Oakland Community Learning Center were being scrutinized for possible charges of embezzlement of state and federal funds. And Newton's alleged notion of keeping the school in operation through a cocaine connection turned into a classic rumor used to confirm his nearly complete disintegration.

Shortly thereafter, a change occurred in Oakland's drug trafficking hierarchy. In 1985 Felix Mitchell was found guilty of racketeering and sentenced to life in prison with no possibility of parole. According to law enforcement agencies, his gang, as well as the gangs of rival dealers, disintegrated in the face of massive sustained federal raids. The following year Mitchell was murdered in prison. Then Daryl Reed, a twenty-year-old nephew of Mitchell, allegedly put together a new gang, which by 1988 had established a crack empire in Oakland. Crack became the dominant drug dealt on the streets, and the prison-based Black Guerilla Family (BGF) became involved in dealing it.

Some former Panthers who were serving prison sentences in San Quentin were part of the BGF. Rumors circulated that Newton and remnants of the old Panthers were extorting money and free drugs from the BGF. It was also said that disenchanted former Panthers who were part of the BGF had old scores to settle with Newton because of the fratricide that had occurred within the party, and because of Newton's abandonment of many Black Panthers serving jail sentences after he took full command of the party following his release from jail in 1970. In any case, by the wee hours of the morning of August 22, 1989, a contract was waiting to be carried out on the life of Newton.

The dealers who gave Newton crack in the late-night hours of the previous day (August 21) and the early-morning hours of the day he was killed (August 22), were among the approximately twenty BGF dealers operating in West Oakland. After securing the dove from the dealer, Newton returned to the house at 902 Center Street in which Willie Payne had a ground-floor apartment. Payne was standing outside with a woman. Newton took the small chunk of crack and broke it in half, giving one half to Payne and keeping the other for himself. He told Payne he would see him later and then made his way over to a group of four people, with whom he began to argue.

They went into a house to continue their argument. Payne and the woman accompanying him entered Payne's apartment, where Payne retrieved his crack pipe to smoke the half dove of crack Newton had given him. About a half hour later, Newton emerged from the other house and returned again to Payne's apartment. When Payne let him in, Newton had a piece of crumpled magazine paper with more crumbs of crack—about five or six doves altogether. He, Payne, and Payne's female visitor began smoking the doves. It took about one hour for them to smoke all of them. Then Newton left Payne's apartment to try to get more crack free of charge.

Payne wasn't the only person in the neighborhood Newton knew. He had another friend who lived nearby. Newton went to her place to get a bottle of Seagram's gin. Then he went back to the people who had given him the six doves of crack free of charge.

When Newton returned to Payne's apartment, in addition to the bottle of gin he had a sandwich bag full of free crack cocaine. At that point Newton, Payne, and Payne's female guest decided to have a crack-smoking party. People from the surrounding houses received word that Newton and Payne were giving crack away. About sixteen people showed up at Payne's apartment.

But the small party was suddenly ruined when someone arrived with news that "there are people looking for Huey." The guests left rapidly, but Payne and Newton remained. Both men were nervous. Newton began talking about his life as though he sensed imminent death. He reminisced with Payne about the Newton family moving to Oakland from Monroe, Louisiana. He admitted killing Officer John Frey. He said that before he killed Frey, the police and the power structure could just come down to the black community and do anything they wanted. But after he shot Frey, much of that changed. He talked about once being famous and looked up to as a hero by people everywhere. He remembered hobnobbing with other celebrities, debating eminent scholars such as Erik Erikson at Yale, and being on television programs such as David Frost's talk show. He spoke of living in Cuba, what he liked about it and what he didn't like about it. He talked about pistol-whipping a tailor for calling him "baby," insisting that the tailor just happened to be in the wrong place at the wrong time after Newton had a telephone argument with a Black Panther member on the East Coast. He talked about a melee he had with Ike and Tina Turner at a benefit concert they gave for the Black Panther school in 1973. He said that in 1974 the prostitute was murdered because she had insulted him. He then grew calm and said he figured he was going to get killed. He placed his arm around Payne.

Payne grew very nervous. He asked Newton why he was talking that way, and then he began trying to figure out a way to protect him. Payne offered to barricade his door and hide Newton inside. Then at 5 A.M., when commuters began making their way to the BART station three blocks away, Newton could elude his pursuers in that commuter rush. But Newton refused to cooperate with the plan. In a sudden burst of his legendary bravado, Newton shouted, "I'm Huey Newton! I'm not afraid of anyone! If anyone tries to hurt me, I'll go up to that house and kill everything in there!" He was referring to the crack house at Tenth and Cypress. Newton told Payne that he had a gun, although Payne didn't see one on him.

Then Newton decided he wanted some more crack. He asked Payne to go with him to get it, thinking that if Payne was with him, he'd be safer. But Payne refused. So Newton left Payne's apartment by himself, heading toward the crack house at Tenth and Cypress.

Shortly after Newton's departure, Payne also left his apartment. If someone really was after Newton, why be where Newton was last seen by a number of people? Payne walked in the opposite direction of Newton, toward a housing project called Cypress Village. He bummed a cigarette from someone and then began to walk back toward home, figuring that it was probably safe by then. As he passed a convenience store he noticed a number of discarded bottles and cans he could add to his pile redeemable for money to support himself. So he picked them up and then continued toward home. As he walked up Ninth Street, he noticed someone's feet sticking out up ahead on the right sidewalk. The rest of the body was hidden by hedges. Payne thought it was a neighborhood man who lived around the corner from him. The man he thought it was often got into arguments with some of the neighborhood young people, and Willie figured they had beaten him up. On second thought, he wondered if it was someone else.

Too nervous to go and look, Payne instead knocked on the door of an upstairs neighbor. "There's someone laying outside," Willie told him. "I think it's Big Hank." The neighbor said he thought he had heard some shots. Willie said that well, then, maybe there was someone shot outside. The neighbor brushed the shots off as someone probably shooting in the air. Willie said no. If the neighbor heard shots and Willie saw someone lying down outside, put two and two together.

The neighbor peeped outside and said he didn't see anything. They got the neighbor's girlfriend out of bed and asked her to look. At first she didn't see anything either. Willie told her to stick her head out and look real good. The woman stuck her head out and finally saw what Willie was referring to. They called 911. But it was too late to save the life of the man lying on the sidewalk. At 6:10 that morning, Huey Percy Newton was pronounced dead on arrival at Highland Hospital, from three bullet wounds to the head.

2

Genesis

I**F A PERSON HEADS WEST FROM WHERE** H**UEY** N**EWTON'S** body lay, turns right onto Wood Street, and travels seven blocks to the corner of 16th Street, an ornate, beige, empty train station rises on the left with numerous railroad tracks behind it. The current condition of the station does no justice to its historic significance, just as Huey Newton's predicament before he died did no justice to the historic significance many people attached to him. It was on the passenger trains berthed at such stations that Negro men triggered the social earthquake that inspired most of the activism of the 1960s—activism that eventually led to the Black Panthers' being exalted far beyond anything Huey Newton and Bobby Seale originally envisioned. It was the Pullman porters who first organized to gain guaranteed citizenship rights denied to Negroes. It was somehow fitting that they played such a vital role in the mass movement that followed, since their jobs involved conveying people from one place to another.

During the first decades of the twentieth century, Pullman porters were held in very high esteem in Negro communities across America. The work was usually steady, and it paid relatively well compared with other jobs available to Negro men. To say your father was a Pullman Porter was to invite instant respect from other Negro children. Particularly in the south, even Negro men with college educations sought jobs as Pullman porters. The families of Pullman porters gained entrée to the best Negro social clubs. At one time in West Oakland the Negro Pullman porters were kings among men who had little reason to feel kingly.

However, these "kings" among the least kingly of men were treated like serfs by their employers. Southern Pacific railroad owned the impressive station at 16th and Wood streets. In the 1920s, when the Negro population in the Bay Area was so small that it was barely noticeable, except when you traveled through West Oakland, even the "kingly" Negro Pullman porters were expected to conform to certain ingrained notions about Negroes.

"You're not the type the Pullman Company employs for porters," a white man working for the company told the tall man with light brown skin known as C. L. Dellums. Dellums was in desperate need of a job to keep his room rent paid in a house only blocks from the station. "You speak good English, but you say 'yes' and 'no.' You said 'yes' and 'no' to Mr. Wells. That's why he wasn't going to hire you." Dellums was supposed to say "yes *sir*" and "no *sir*" to Mr. Wells. A person would have thought he knew better, since he had recently arrived from East Texas. The only thing that saved him was that he was a Free Mason and he had flashed his Mason ring in front of Mr. Wells in a desperate, last-ditch effort to get a job. Mr. Wells was a Mason too. And although the Negro and white Masons were separate groups, the white Mason allowed Free Masonry to supersede Dellums's "transgression." He hired Dellums as a Pullman porter.

Dellums immediately noticed that the Pullman porters were being exploited. Some were working as many as 485 hours per month, or approximately 16 hours per day, yet receiving the same $60 per month as if they worked 335 hours, the minimum number of hours allowed. Many porters couldn't even make $60 per month because the Pullman Company had devised all sorts of schemes to get the most work out of them for the least pay. One rule was that the company didn't pay P.M. time. That meant a porter could be ordered to report to his train by noon but not get clocked for pay until after midnight. The porters commonly reported to the trains by three or four o'clock in the afternoon, prepared the berths to receive passengers, received passengers by eight o'clock in the evening, and did not get paid for any of it. When forced to discard this method, the company set up a "mileage month," ensuring continuance of the exploitation by starting pay only after the train moved, which usually wasn't until midnight or later, meaning the company obtained as much as eight hours of free labor from the porters at every port of call.

Deciding the situation was intolerable, the audacious Dellums helped another audacious Negro man, A. Philip Randolph, to form a union called the Brotherhood of Sleeping Car Porters. Randolph, with his dark skin and commander's bass-baritone voice, was the very incarnation of what many whites then considered to be an arrogant Negro who didn't know his place. So audacious was Randolph that he once challenged the Premier Negro Leader of the time. When W. E. B. Du Bois called for Negro soldiers to serve in World War I, Randolph begged to differ, asking why they should fight for a country that didn't grant them their rights at home. His question was to no avail, as he probably knew it would be. Eventually, more than 360,000 Negro men served in the war. But in speaking out against Du Bois and the war, Randolph established himself as a voice to be reckoned with. He attempted to do, among the Negro leadership, something classical playwrights noticed about men centuries ago: sons, in one way or another, must always try to slay their fathers. In the African American version of this tradition, Premier Negro Leaders (fathers) were continually sniped at by new aspirants to the title (sons) who had previously admired and followed them.

Du Bois had "slain" Booker T. Washington, who had inherited the mantle of Negro leadership from Frederick Douglass, the man most responsible for influencing Abraham Lincoln to sign the Emancipation Proclamation. Washington was considered an accommodator of white racism, although a shrewd observer of his politics might conclude that he was simply more pragmatic than Du Bois. At the time of his rise at the turn of the century, white Americans, particularly in the South, were erecting strong racial

barriers—even theorizing about the innate inferiority of Negroes—so Washington called for less emphasis on Negro political
rights and more emphasis on gaining training in highly marketable
vocations. Then Negroes could open businesses such as sawmills,
which over time would become too valuable to local economies for
white racism to make much of a difference. He felt the same would
apply if Negroes accumulated land.

Du Bois, however, demanded immediate political rights for
Negroes, and the development of a highly educated, talented tenth
of professionals (doctors, lawyers, Ph.D.'s), which would serve as a
locomotive engine, pulling the rest of Negro America out of de-
spair and poverty. He cofounded an integrated organization that
would exist for the express purpose of fighting, primarily through
the courts, for the political rights of Negroes—the National Association for the Advancement of Colored People (NAACP).

Then along came A. Philip Randolph to "slay" Du Bois.
Shortly after Randolph called for a Negro boycott of World War
I, Marcus Garvey, a short, rotund, dark-skinned Jamaican festooned in military attire, began fascinating the American Negro
masses with his call for not only complete separation from whites
but a Pan African nation located in Africa itself. Garvey's notion
was that all Negroes in the Americas would eventually travel to the
Pan African nation on a shipping line he was developing called the
Black Star line. Like Washington, Garvey stressed economics over
politics. But his platform contained a strong message of pride in
African roots, which neither Washington nor Du Bois emphasized.
The first phase of his program called for trade between Negroes
in the Americas and Negroes in Africa. He established "Buy Black"
campaigns in Negro communities throughout the nation. He liked
to dress his followers—primarily the poorest and least skilled Negroes (the same socioeconomic class that constituted most of the
Black Panthers about forty years later)—in elaborate military attire
and hold parades that amounted to extravagant pageants. Garvey's
movement would founder, however, after he was convicted of mail
fraud in 1925.

By then, A. Philip Randolph's star was rising as he feverishly
organized the sleeping car porters. In the beginning, the porters

who trudged back and forth between the Southern Pacific railroad station in West Oakland and the trains berthed behind it were hesitant to join his Brotherhood of Sleeping Car Porters—hesitant, but proud that someone was speaking up for them.

That was the way it was when you were a Negro, especially a Negro man. You wore a mask, a mask that C. L. Dellums had forgotten to adjust properly before leaving his room on the day he applied for work as a Pullman porter—and had to flash his Mason ring to obtain the job. You put on the mask and simply ate for breakfast your anger at having to face another day of humiliation. And when you returned home, or, in the case of a working porter, to your bunk on the train, rifling through that day's humiliation, you might pound your mattress in frustration. Or you could release steam accumulated from the humiliation with a glass of liquor in front of you at an illegal card game on Seventh Street, the Negro commercial hub of West Oakland. You released it with fellow Negro men at places like a club on the corner of Seventh and Wood streets owned by Slim Jenkins, right down the street from the spot where, years later, Huey Newton would release steam by shooting officer John Frey. Jenkins had been smuggled in from Louisiana by train, by C. L. Dellums, for the express purpose of providing a place where Negro men could let off steam, and perhaps get lucky enough to win some money to pay the rent they owed in rooming houses, if they weren't lucky enough to have jobs as Pullman porters.

At first, Negro porters were likely to pay their dues to the Brotherhood but ask that their name not be listed on the membership rolls. When C. L. Dellums and A. Philip Randolph first tried to negotiate away the exploitation of the porters, the Pullman Company thought the organization was much smaller than it actually was and didn't take the Brotherhood's demands seriously.

But the Brotherhood would eventually gain recognition as a union and eventually gain concessions from the Pullman Company. Those accomplishments would allow A. Philip Randolph to "slay" W. E. B. Du Bois, replacing him as the Premier Negro Leader. And C. L. Dellums would become a local Negro leader. Fired for his organizing efforts, he no longer rode the trains. Instead he served as West Coast president of the Brotherhood, maintaining an office on Seventh Street, the growing Negro commercial hub of Oakland. His office was above the club of the man he had smuggled in from Louisiana to provide gambling action, drinking, and laughter to the Negro men of Oakland. And Pullman porters felt a bit more like the "kings" they were among most Negro men, while men like Randolph and Dellums, who didn't have to serve white passengers, mounted speaker's platforms across the nation. Wearing suits and ties, they spoke not only for the porters but for all Negro men who had to swallow humiliation. Dellums effectively established his family name in the Oakland/Berkeley area, to the eventual benefit of his nephew Ron Dellums, who would one day rise to become a powerful U.S. congressman. But that would happen in the 1970s. Now the country was suffering through the Great Depression. A. Philip Randolph's Brotherhood of Sleeping Car Porters became part of a national labor alliance, the Congress of Industrial Organizations (CIO), which successfully called for non-discrimination against Negroes, opening the door to Negro participation in Works Progress Administration (WPA) projects, relief programs, and public housing. Then the nation entered World War II.

Wartime industries began gearing up to bring the nation out of the Great Depression by churning out millions of pieces of armaments. But Negroes weren't to be included in churning them out. Responsibility for building the ships, guns, tanks, jeeps, helmets, and everything else to be used in the war was to go to whites. President Franklin Roosevelt swore there was nothing he could do about that. So A. Philip Randolph, the Premier Negro Leader, made plans to bring hundreds of thousands of Negroes to Washington, D.C., for a great march designed to embarrass the nation that claimed to be preparing for war to make the world safe for democracy. And when President Roosevelt heard that, he suddenly decided there *was* something he could do about all the industries contracted to manufacture armaments which were planning to bring only white citizens out of the Great Depression into the factories.

Roosevelt issued executive order 8802, outlawing racial discrimination by any wartime industry receiving federal contracts. And A. Philip Randolph had never looked better before his followers. And the Brotherhood of Sleeping Car Porters had never felt prouder of their union leader as they traveled to and from the trains at 16th and Wood streets, berthed behind the ornate Southern Pacific railway station in West Oakland. For in bringing Negroes out of the Great Depression, executive order 8802 would precipitate a flood of approximately 50,000 Negro migrants from Louisiana, Arkansas, and East Texas, via the trains the porters worked on, to the Bay Area, so that the men and women in the families could work in the shipyards that constructed Navy destroyers and other vessels on the San Francisco, Oakland, Richmond, and Sausalito docks—ships to be used to defeat the Japanese and Germans. The Negro populations of Oakland, Berkeley, and San Francisco grew to very noticeable sizes. And among those migrants would be a man named Walter Newton, who would scout for work before sending for his family, including a little boy named Huey, who, years later, would be murdered only blocks from the station.

The Negro Pullman porters couldn't be prouder of the president of their union, couldn't think of any man who was more shrewd or dignified, or who better called the lie to the notion that they were inferior, than this Premier Negro Leader named A. Philip Randolph. And among those proud, beaming porters was E. D. Nixon, based in Montgomery, Alabama, and head of the Alabama branch of the Brotherhood. Nixon worshiped Randolph and did his best to emulate him, although his diction wasn't nearly as refined. Nixon, a large man with a very dark brown complexion, was determined to do as much politically as a Negro man could do in Montgomery. Until the end of World War II, that didn't amount to much.

In the meantime, Randolph, the Premier Negro Leader, would find himself "slain" by a flamboyant young Negro man named Adam Clayton Powell, Jr. Powell, with his very light brown skin and straight hair, could have passed for white but chose instead to inherit the Negro church, Abyssinian Baptist in Harlem, which his father had built into the largest Protestant congregation in the nation. Powell used the church as a dynamic platform to fight for the rights of Negroes in the nation's largest, most visible city. And Powell fought for those rights far more loudly than Randolph had, turning the heat up one more notch on white America, usurping a newly created Harlem congressional seat that everyone was certain would go to Randolph.

Despite Powell's emergence, Randolph would not be forgotten. He remained revered for some time after being usurped by Powell and held a permanent place in a cabinet of Negro leaders with whom the white power structure consulted whenever it was deemed necessary. And no one revered him more than the president of the Alabama chapter of his union, E. D. Nixon.

In Montgomery, Nixon was the "go to" man for Negroes with problems. A person didn't go to the Negro teachers, or handful of Negro doctors and lawyers, or Negro ministers, or Negro professors at Alabama State College, although they were all members of professions more prestigious than that of Pullman Porter. You went to unrefined E. D. Nixon, who spoke a diction that made whites feel comfortable around Negroes. He used words such as *mens* instead of *men*, and *womens* instead of *women*. Yet he exhibited more daring than the refined Negro professionals of Montgomery, who were a bit embarrassed by him. It was Nixon, the unrefined Pullman porter, rather than the refined Negro professionals, who approached the white police officers, the white judges, the white government officials in Montgomery, who even once pushed his way into the governor's office on behalf of Montgomery Negroes with grievances. And it was Nixon, the unrefined Pullman porter, rather than the refined Negro professionals, who got his name on ballots for local offices he had no chance of winning.

On December 1, 1955, when a Negro woman named Rosa Parks boarded a Montgomery bus in which the Negro section was filled, Nixon got his chance to do even more than he normally did for local Negroes. Parks made her way to no-man's-land, a neutral zone between the front and the back of the bus that allowed the bus driver some discretion in drawing the line separating the races. One day the line might be drawn in row 8 of no-man's-land. Another day it might be drawn at row 10. Parks refused to get up when the driver decided that the line would be drawn in back of where she was seated, so she was arrested. The first call she made was to her mother, who in turn called the "go to" man, E. D. Nixon.

Nixon went to the jail to make bond for Parks, who was a seamstress and a valued member of the local chapter of the NAACP. After conferring with a friendly lawyer, Nixon decided that Parks's case was the one that Negroes in Montgomery had been waiting for to challenge segregation on the buses. He asked Parks if she was willing to take the case as far as it had to go. She said yes. Nixon made calls notifying all of the Negro professionals in Montgomery of what had happened. A group of women among their ranks suggested that Montgomery Negroes hold a one-day boycott of the city's bus lines to show support for Parks. One woman called Nixon, who was preparing to make his Pullman porter passenger train run, and asked his blessing on the idea. Nixon readily agreed to it, telling her that he had also thought of something along those lines.

To spur support for the boycott, the proud Pullman porter assembled an ad hoc committee of prominent Montgomery Negroes, including the newly arrived minister of Dexter Avenue Baptist Church. The one-day boycott was successful beyond all their imaginations. But they were still hesitant, still timid about pressing on. That evening they met to plan a larger mass meeting. Courage alternated with years of fear that if Negroes pressed too hard, vented their feelings of humiliation too much out in the open, it would mean loss of much-needed jobs to pay rent, buy clothes, and eat. White Montgomery would be scrutinizing the mass meeting; reporters would cover it, and they could print quotes and the names of those who vented their frustration out in the open instead of saving it for the social clubs, barrooms, pool halls, and illegal card games, or to contemplate late at night before falling off to sleep. As a result, many prominent Montgomery Negroes thought it best to print the set of demands for the people attending the mass meeting and to ask them to vote in secret ballots.

But to the proud Pullman porter, the man who regularly turned down berths for white passengers, the man who regularly said plenty more "yes sirs" and "no sirs" to whites in the course of fulfilling his duties than were said by the more refined Negro professionals at the meeting—the ministers, undertakers, school-teachers, and handful of doctors, lawyers, and college professors—this secret, hesitant methodology would not do. Nixon got up from his seat and demanded to know how they expected to run a boycott in secret. "Let me tell you gentleman one thing," he intoned. "You ministers have lived off of these wash-women for the last hundred years and ain't never done nothing for them!" He told all the others they were cowards. He told them that they allowed the women to bear the brunt of the one-day boycott. "We've worn aprons all our lives," declared Nixon. "It's time to take the aprons off. . . . If we're gonna be mens, now's the time to be mens." As Nixon said that, the new minister in town walked into the meeting late. "Brother Nixon," he said, "I'm not a coward. I don't want anybody to call me a coward."

So the new minister was elected to head the committee spear-heading an extension of the boycott, which would last for close to one year. The boycott was eventually a success—and the civil rights movement was born. Premier Negro Leader Adam Clayton Powell, Jr., was "slain" by the head of the Montgomery boycott committee, the Reverend Martin Luther King, Jr.

The success of the boycott led to other successful bus boycotts, which spread like wildfire throughout southern cities to the point where eventually municipal buses in the South were no longer segregated. And Martin Luther King, the new "kingliest" man among the least "kingly" of men, the new Premier Negro Leader, who was only in his late twenties, rode higher and faster than any of the previous Premier Negro Leaders. In privacy some would-be Premier Negro Leaders sniped at him, as did the man he had most recently deposed. Roy Wilkins, head of the NAACP—the legacy of earlier Premier Negro Leader W. E. B. Du Bois—would grow both irritated with King's rise and fearful that it would signal the demise of the NAACP. When a Negro couldn't call a local "go to" man like E. D. Nixon, there had always been the local branch of the NAACP, which amounted to a massive, multimembered organism that set the slow wheels of courtroom justice grinding in hundreds of lawsuits throughout the nation.

King's success would cause disciples to flock to him. One cadre of disciples would be composed of an alliance of Negro ministers who joined the Southern Christian Leadership Conference (SCLC), the organization King founded to further the budding civil rights movement. Another cadre would be composed of younger admirers—primarily college and graduate-school students—who would follow their own path, as they tried to carry King's success to the next level. Among such young disciples would be John Lewis, a seminary student; Bob Moses, a schoolteacher from Harlem; James Forman, a schoolteacher from Chicago; and Stokely Carmichael, an undergraduate at Howard University.

Lewis spoke in monosyllables instead of in the cadences of King. The contrast between King and Lewis virtually paralleled the contrast between Randolph and Nixon. Proud and unrefined, Lewis was from a remote rural section of Alabama, whereas King was from Atlanta's black bourgeoisie.

Bob Moses was far more refined than Lewis. He had a master's degree in philosophy from Harvard and believed that there should be not one Premier Negro Leader but many leaders sharing the top spot. To that end he became involved in the budding movement by first allying himself with Martin Luther King's important right-hand man, Bayard Rustin, also an important right-hand man to A. Philip Randolph.

Forman, a Korean War veteran, had been an undergraduate student at Roosevelt University in Chicago when the Montgomery boycott took off. His chief impression was that at long last Negroes had evolved beyond talking about what needed to be done to get rid of racism. At long last, rather than flee north, away from the basest demonstration of racism as manifested in the Jim Crow South, Negroes had successfully confronted it. He knew that the next level of struggle required physical confrontation. Like Moses, he was intellectual. He was also an aspiring writer, and almost a year older than King. And although he admired King, as did Bob Moses, he didn't idolize him. He thought King's inspirational ability showed what could be done by an entire host of leader-heroes.

The same would hold true for the young Carmichael, who was

about to begin studies at the Bronx High School of Science—one
of three exclusive New York City public secondary schools—when
the Montgomery boycott took place. His family had emigrated
from Trinidad. On enrolling at Howard University in Washington,
D.C., Carmichael became involved in the budding activism on
campus. The success of the Montgomery movement, and the attempt to integrate all-white Central High in Little Rock, Arkansas,
had generated much excitement. In September 1957, nine Negro
students stood their ground against Little Rock's whites, who did
their best to ensure that the students would not successfully test
the courtroom victory won by the legal arm of the NAACP.

A year before the Montgomery boycott, the NAACP Legal
Defense Fund had successfully argued before the U.S. Supreme
Court the case of *Brown* v. *Board of Education of Topeka*, outlawing
school segregation. Under the protection of National Guard
troops, the brave young students in Little Rock, led by a woman
named Daisy Bates, successfully faced down the white racists—
withstanding their taunts, their spit, their kicks—and integrated
Central High. Many Negro women like Daisy Bates would play
important roles in the movement, women such as Diane Nash, Ella
Baker, and Fannie Lou Hammer. But the day had yet to arrive
when their importance as leaders would be recognized as much as
that of the men. With the success of Little Rock, the disciples of
the Premier Negro Leader, Martin Luther King, Jr., were galvanized to an even greater extent.

However, to King's philosophical left, another development
was taking place. Whenever a Premier Negro Leader established
himself, which usually occurred with the blessing of the mainstream press, someone was waiting to knock him from the pedestal.
Such challengers did not try to carry the established leader's overall
program farther, disagreeing only with a few particulars, as when
Randolph opposed Du Bois on the issue of Negroes fighting in
World War I; instead, they completely opposed everything the
Premier Negro Leader stood for. Du Bois had done this to Wash-
ington. Marcus Garvey had tried to use the same method to unseat
Du Bois. And by the close of the 1950s, a man in New York City

would gain increasing attention for views that totally opposed King's.

On July 2, 1958, the FBI identified Malcolm X, head of the New York City chapter of the Nation of Islam, as a key Negro leader. Malcolm called whites "greedy, irredeemable devils." He called for complete separation of the races and a homeland for Negroes in separate states of the United States. One year later, attention to Malcolm X would increase substantially after reporter Mike Wallace aired a five-part series on a local New York City television station, "The Hate That Hate Produced."

One of the first things Wallace noted during the program were the criminal records of both Malcolm X and Elijah Muhammad, founder of the Nation of Islam. By doing so, Wallace cast doubt on their credentials for legitimate leadership. Fear of this type of discrediting was a major reason that mainstream Negro leaders were careful to follow the letter of the law in all areas except where their civil rights were being violated. It was also a major reason that they pursued cases of discrimination and outright harm only against the most upstanding Negroes in the community. Such a tradition had been followed during the Montgomery bus boycott. Rosa Parks had not been the first Negro arrested for refusing to sit in the back of the bus. Claudette Colvin had been arrested before Parks. But E. D. Nixon decided Colvin would not do as the person to rally around in challenging bus segregation, since she was pregnant but unmarried.

Still, in the North the mainstream Negro leadership realized that it had to maintain some type of dialogue with the most popular of the militant leaders, no matter what their backgrounds. In "The Hate That Hate Produced," Wallace showed footage of Manhattan borough president Hulan Jack, who at that time occupied the highest municipal office of any Negro in the nation, conversing with Malcolm X. He showed footage of NAACP head Roy Wilkins conversing with him too, carefully noting that neither Jack nor Wilkins was a black separatist, but both found it necessary to dialogue with leaders like Malcolm X because such leaders spoke for a substantial minority of Negroes.

Malcolm X's popularity among Negroes was rising in the North. But in the South, King was still undisputed. The Montgomery and Little Rock victories were still reverberating a refreshing optimism about race relations that had never been felt before. King and his disciples were also considered to be fighting on the front lines of the most vicious racism, while Malcolm X was safely ensconced in Harlem. However, at the end of the 1950s there were Negro men in the thick of matters in the Jim Crow South, providing an alternative philosophy to nonviolence.

Throughout southern history, Negro men could occasionally get away with defending themselves. Most such incidents were isolated and never caught on among a large number of Negroes. Negro self-defense on a mass scale had been wiped out at the turn of the century, the era of America's most virulent racism. In many areas of North Carolina, South Carolina, Georgia, Florida, Alabama, Mississippi, and Louisiana, Negroes outnumbered whites, precipitating white fear of Negro domination. At that time there were many armed confrontations between whites intent on economically and politically disenfranchising Negroes, and Negroes determined to defend their newfound rights gained during the post–Civil War Reconstruction era. By the 1880s, while northern soldiers, carpetbaggers, and politicians looked the other way, southern whites gained the cooperation of local police and militia, and so that eventually, instances of Negro resistance became isolated (usually in counties where whites felt less threatened, because whites made up a clear majority).

At that point, white violence against Negroes became so sadistic that the most grisly incidents (to be included among the killings classified as lynchings) were called "Negro barbeques." During such gruesome events, over time, the rope gave way to kerosene burnings, blow torchings, dragging to death behind automobiles, usually before a small crowd of whites who would then take "souvenirs" from the corpse's body. (A 1904 edition of the Vicksburg, Mississippi, *Evening Post* desribed how one Negro couple, accused but never convicted of murdering a white planter, was tortured before being burned to death by a crowd who chopped off their fingers and ears, gouged out their eyes, and extracted "big pieces of raw, quivering flesh" from their bodies with a gigantic corkscrew before setting them afire.)

Thus, by the 1950s, the cautious manner in which Negro men challenged southern racial traditions—the habit criticized by E. D. Nixon at the first Montgomery bus boycott meeting—had become a tradition. The nascent civil rights movement spurred by men like Nixon, and carried on by Martin Luther King, Jr., and his disciples, was considered a cunning, revolutionary answer to the years of oppression rained down on Negroes since the turn of the century. It was believed that to try and gain rights any other way was to invite the worst kind of trouble. At the close of the 1950s, it was just this type of "trouble" that was invited not only by the Louisiana Deacons of Defense and Justice, but also by a man named Robert Williams, who lived in the town of Monroe, North Carolina.

The story of Monroe began one day in the summer of 1957 at the whites-only public swimming pool. A boy from Newtown, the Negro section of Monroe, swam in the pool and was intentionally drowned. Dr. Albert Perry investigated the incident. True to the tradition of southern Negro professionals usually pressing their demands only so far, Perry did not insist on immediate integration of the facilities. Instead he demanded that the town reserve a separate day for Negroes to swim at the pool, since the money of all the townspeople paid for the pool. The city's answer was that if it did that, the pool would have to be drained too often, since whites would never agree to swim in water that was used by Negroes. At that point Perry decided to try to settle the incident in the manner Negroes throughout the country were used to settling such matters—by contacting the NAACP. Local NAACP chairman Robert Williams took a group of youngsters to the pool. They were refused its use. Williams then decided to file a lawsuit. What happened next sent Williams down the road of a radicalism that eventually led to his ostracism by the national leadership of the civil rights movement.

As punishment for filing the suit, the local Ku Klux Klan began nightriding through Newtown, targeting Dr. Perry with threats. The Klan held meetings, then paraded through Newtown in as many as eighty cars, blowing their automobile horns, firing guns into the air, and calling Negro women "whores." In response to the threats they specifically made against Perry, Robert Williams organized an armed guard of Negro men to stand vigil twenty-four hours a day around Perry's home. They became known as the Deacons for Defense. They stood vigil for three months.

The Negroes of Newtown tried to inform the national press of the nightriding. But instead of investigating on its own, the press relied on the town's police department to confirm the reports, and the police denied that anything was happening. Neither would they do anything about the nightriding. Fed up with this, on the night of October 5, 1957, the Deacons for Defense decided to do something on their own. The Klan came through Newtown in its usual manner: horns blaring, guns firing, insults frothing from their mouths. But this time they were met by a loud, disciplined, sustained barrage of return gunfire. The guns were being fired into the air. The KKK motorcade scattered. Some of the Klansmen abandoned their cars and fled on foot. One car turned up a dead-end street and, on turning around, was met by Robert Williams himself and a detail of men.

"What are you fellows doing over here?" asked Williams.

"Oh, Mr. Williams, we just didn't know what we were doing," answered the driver. "If you just let us out, I promise we'll never do it again."

"Well, you fellows want to be more careful next time," admonished Williams. "You could get killed."

"Oh yes, sir, we know."

"Then get the hell out of here!"

After that, there were no more Klan caravans through Newtown. But more than ever, Dr. Perry, Robert Williams, and the rest of the Negro community were marked for revenge.

Important members of the white community pressured a white woman into falsely accusing Dr. Perry of performing an illegal abortion. Perry vehemently denied the charge but was convicted and sent to jail for nearly three years. The following year, two Negro boys aged seven and nine were playing house with a group of white kids their age, including two little white girls. One of the white girls and one of the Negro boys kissed. The little girl told her parents. Joined by his neighbors, the girl's father went looking for the boy and his family with a gun. Both boys were located, arrested, and sent to reform school indefinitely. As head of the local chapter of the NAACP, Robert Williams was asked to intervene. On investigating the case, Williams called in the national office of the NAACP. There followed a classic case of alienation between the Negro middle class and the Negro poor.

The national office discovered that the two boys were the products of poor homes and that their mothers had never been married to their fathers. Since the boys were deemed illegitimate, the national office had reservations about any further involvement in their case, feeling that the boys' families just weren't the type of Negroes to shine a national limelight on. Robert Williams was pressured to withdraw the local chapter from pursuing the case any further.

But an English reporter got wind of the case and decided to visit the boys in reform school. She brought their mothers and a photographer along, and the photo of the reunion between the boys and their mothers was shown in newspapers around the world. Huge demonstrations in support of the boys were held in Paris, Rome, Vienna, and Rotterdam. A committee was formed in Europe to support the boys. Fifteen thousand signatures were collected demanding their release. The petition was sent to President Eisenhower and the governor of North Carolina. The boys were released on February 13, 1959.

The same year the boys were released, a Negro man in Monroe was arrested and charged with the attempted rape of a white woman. Shortly afterward, a white man was arrested and accused of attempting to rape a pregnant Negro woman in front of her six-year-old son, then chasing the woman across an open field. Because a Negro man had been lynched earlier in another county not far away, some members of Robert Williams's Deacons for

Defense wanted to do the same thing to the white man. Williams
dissuaded them. But Williams himself would become enraged by
the verdicts that were handed down in the two cases.

On May 4, 1959, the Negro man accused of attempted rape
was convicted and sentenced to two years in jail. That same day
the white man was freed by a grand jury investigating his case. At
that point Robert Williams issued a statement that alarmed the
national NAACP. "We cannot rely on the law," Williams said from
the courthouse steps. "We can get no justice under the present
system. If we feel that injustice is done, we must right then and
there, on the spot, be prepared to inflict punishment on these
people. Since the federal government will not bring a halt to
lynching in the South, and since the so-called courts lynch our
people illegally, if it's necessary to stop lynching with lynching then
we must be ready to resort to that method. We must meet violence
with violence."

Roy Wilkins immediately disavowed Williams's statement and
moved to suspend Williams from the NAACP for six months.
Williams drifted farther and farther left. By now, he had launched
a newsletter, *The Crusader*, to further his views. Later he would
publish a book, *Negroes with Guns*, that would fascinate Huey
Newton. In 1960 Williams illegally visited newly communist
Cuba—a grave mistake in the eyes of the civil rights establishment,
which steered clear of socialist and communist organizations because segregationists said that communists were the real brains
behind any Negro effort to gain rights. And at no time in the
nation's history was communism more of an anathema than during
the 1950s and early 1960s.

The young disciples of Martin Luther King would ignore
Williams for the time being (the older disciples would always be
opposed to him). As the 1960s began, all of King's disciples were
eager to see what else could be accomplished through nonviolence.
After the victories in Montgomery and Little Rock, over the course
of a little more than two years, King and his disciples honed their
nonviolent philosophy, borrowing from Mahatma Gandhi. They
also developed platoons of civil rights troops who would not fight
back when hit by racists. That was how John Lewis initially became

involved in the movement. He began appearing at classes on non-violence given in Nashville by King disciple James Lawson, through the auspices of an organization called the Fellowship for Reconciliation. Lewis was sent for even more intensive training to Tennessee's Highlander Folk School, somewhat of a Paris Island for nonviolent protesters. At Highlander, would-be nonviolent troops of all colors were pummeled with abuse by stand-ins for racists. And Lewis passed with flying colors.

After a few false starts, the movement found its feet once again in January 1960. Four Negro college students from North Carolina A&T sat down at a "whites only" Woolworth's lunch counter in Greensboro, and their protest electrified the nation. The next series of battles, lunch counter sit-ins, was on. John Lewis was charged with leading the lunch counter confrontations in Nashville. On February 26, 1960, Lewis led a column of protesters to the designated stores. A small crowd developed, composed primarily of white teenagers who taunted Lewis and the other sit-in participants by calling them "chicken" and "nigger." Knowing that the protesters wouldn't fight back, some in the crowd threw rocks at them, burned them with lighted cigarettes, and kicked them. As they sat at counters they were spit on, cursed, hit up side the head, and then finally arrested.

To young Negro college and seminary students, being willfully arrested was a major psychological divide to cross, even though their arrests resulted from intentionally breaking an unjust law. The Montgomery bus boycott had only slightly altered certain rules of etiquette among middle-class and honest, working-poor Negroes, which had been established by earlier Premier Negro Leader Booker T. Washington. Only *one* woman actively broke any law to initiate that boycott. Everyone else simply needed to stay off the buses, or, if they normally never rode the bus, as was the case with most members of the Negro middle class, they provided a support network of auto caravans for those who did.

There was a difference, too, with what happened in Little Rock. In Little Rock the Negro students bravely withstood the taunts, spit, and kicks of racists in order to do what the U.S. Supreme Court guaranteed was their right—to enroll in a desegregated school. Thus they weren't violating any law, but instead were demanding that the existing law be enforced.

The first nonviolent protesters at the segregated lunch counters had to overcome that little voice drummed into their heads by fine, upstanding middle-class or working-poor parents, or single mothers who were washerwomen who had worked for years in white homes to ensure a better life for their children. That voice scolded its children every time they even hinted they were veering from the "right path," a path that needed to be clean of a criminal record so that they could gain entry to the best Negro colleges and universities, such as Booker T. Washington's own Tuskegee Institute. Time and time again the collective voice warned its children, "Now don't you go shaming the family by being thrown in jail like some ignorant no 'count nigga!" Continuously going to jail on purpose meant disobeying that voice for an existence behind bars that was at the same level as the "uncouth, embarrassing" Negroes who shamed the "race."

To be sure, such "uncouth, embarrassing" Negroes who became entangled in the southern criminal-justice system prior to the civil rights movement were treated with an overwhelming degree of unfairness. They made up the majority of southern prisoners, largely because of their skin color. They were often railroaded into confessing to crimes against whites that they hadn't committed. They spent an inordinate amount of time in jail before they were formally charged with any crime and given a trial. And when their cases were tried, virtually never did the trials occur before juries with any Negroes on them.

But included among the ranks of such men were those who would be criminals even without the existence of Jim Crow. Every community had such criminals, and the middle- and working-class Negroes wanted no connection to them—the ones who cut each other up inside and outside of pool halls and barrooms, or stole from and killed other people, primarily other Negroes. As the movement gained ground, the line separating such criminals from Negroes who were unjustly imprisoned would become blurred beyond recognition by the increasingly radicalized Negro college students spending time in jail for their civil rights activities. And later, their young northern white allies would further help blur the line. This blurring would eventually have unfortunate consequences not yet foreseeable in 1960.

The movement progressed from lunch counter sit-ins, to movie theater pickets, to an even more audacious tactic. The success of the primarily student-led sit-ins spurred creation of a potent new organization. The loose collection of college students who had been holding lunch counter and theater protests in North Carolina, in Tennessee, and throughout the South met over Easter weekend 1960, at Shaw University in Raleigh, North Carolina. They had been organized primarily by Ella Baker, who worked for Martin Luther King's SCLC. In a private meeting with King and his SCLC chief of staff, Wyatt T. Walker, Baker refused to urge the students to become the youth branch of the SCLC. Instead the students organized themselves into the Student Nonviolent Coordinating Committee (SNCC).

SNCC joined with an older civil rights organization called the Congress of Racial Equality (CORE), which obtained a new lease on life after the success of Montgomery and the student lunch counter sit-ins. CORE had been founded in the early 1940s. It held sporadic sit-ins, usually outside the South, in service to the idea of racial equality, events that didn't garner nearly as much publicity as such protests would after the success of Montgomery. In the spring of 1961, CORE's president, James Farmer, approved the idea of CORE staffer Gordon Carey that CORE should try to desegregate interstate bus waiting rooms and eating facilities on one Greyhound and one Trailways bus a piece, riding from Washington, D.C., to New Orleans, using Negro and white volunteers. John Lewis and one other member of the newly formed SNCC decided to join in, and the group was called Freedom Riders. None of the volunteers realized what they were in for once they reached Alabama.

Their Greyhound bus pulled into the station in Anniston, only to face a mob of angry whites ready to beat the Freedom Riders senseless. After one look at the mob, the bus driver turned the engine back on and left the station without letting passengers out. But the mob had slashed the bus tires. Not far outside the town the vehicle began veering from side to side. The driver pulled the bus over, turned off the engine, and dashed for the woods, leaving the Freedom Riders at the mercy of a convoy of automobiles carrying angry racists who were in hot pursuit. The racists pounced on the bus, smashed its windows, ripped open the luggage compartment, and threw a firebomb inside. They tried to force the Freedom Riders to remain in the vehicle. It was only through the efforts of an undercover officer, who unholstered his gun, that the riders escaped the bus. Once outside they were pummeled by the mob. Then the attackers got into their cars and drove off, leaving the Freedom Riders to be rescued by Alabama state troopers.

The Freedom Riders on the Trailways bus that followed would also taste mob fury. But it would be in Anniston proper, rather than on the outskirts of town. As the Trailways bus sat at the Anniston Trailways station, a white Freedom Rider was beaten because he came to the defense of a Negro Freedom Rider whom white toughs, who had boarded the bus in Anniston, were forcing to move to the back. After everyone was seated, the bus driver drove out of Anniston and headed for Birmingham, where Klansmen, the media, and other white bystanders were waiting. In Birmingham, when the Freedom Riders left the bus and made their way to the white waiting room, a full-scale riot broke out. The Freedom Riders and several of the newsmen covering the carnage were kicked and repeatedly beaten with lead pipes and other weapons. CORE abandoned the ride, noting the worldwide publicity that the beatings had already created.

On learning this, Diane Nash, a young Negro woman who could have passed for white and was part of the Nashville cadre of student activists in SNCC, asked Farmer if the Nashville students could take up the Freedom Ride from Birmingham and finish it. Farmer gave his consent. Nineteen Nashville students—including John Lewis, who had had to abandon the original run because of a previous commitment—made their way to Birmingham. Before resuming the ride, the students endured a week of haggling among federal government officials, who wished to ensure that the governor of Alabama would protect them; the Greyhound

Company, which couldn't find a driver brave enough to drive the bus from Birmingham to Montgomery; and local racists, who did their best to intimidate the riders. On May 20 the Freedom Ride resumed. Little did anyone know what awaited the bus in Montgomery.

Montgomery whites had been shamed by the success of the municipal bus boycott five years earlier. Their city had been the capital of the Confederacy. And now the nation viewed the Negro population of Montgomery to be a strong inspiration to Negroes throughout the nation, who desired to rise above the lot so many whites deemed their natural place. Montgomery racists were determined to show the world that they knew how to put "niggers" back in their place.

The Greyhound bus containing the Freedom Riders rolled into the Montgomery station. The entire place appeared to be virtually deserted, except for a bevy of reporters. John Lewis alighted from the bus first, followed by the other riders. He began his press briefing and then suddenly fell silent. Coming up behind the reporters, who were from such prestigious news outlets as Time-Life and NBC News, were twelve white men brandishing baseball bats, bottles and lead pipes, making their way to the riders and newsmen. Soon the twelve men were joined by several other whites. They began beating the reporters, photographers, and Freedom Riders with impunity. Racists grabbed their victims, holding them in place while their accomplices repeatedly pummeled their bodies with pipes, or their faces with fists, brass knuckles, every imaginable object. Spectators stood on the side egging them on with shouts of "Kill the niggers!" White Freedom Rider Jim Zwerg was smashed with his luggage, and held between the knees of one rioter while his teeth were knocked out. John Siegenthaler, an aide to Attorney General Robert Kennedy, who had been sent to Montgomery as an observer, was knocked unconscious, requiring days of hospitalization.

The Freedom Ride ground to a standstill while a legion of civil rights leaders, as well as the federal government, sought a way out of the impasse. Martin Luther King rushed to the scene, as did

James Farmer of CORE. The Freedom Riders who didn't require hospitalization found refuge in the church of King's assistant, the Reverend Ralph D. Abernathy. A rally was to be held at the church that night, attracting Montgomery Negroes who supported the Freedom Riders. On receiving word of this, white racists gathered outside of Abernathy's church, their numbers growing to ever more menacing proportions, until they became a full-scale mob encircling the entire sanctuary. Attorney General Robert Kennedy held tense negotiations with the governor of Alabama to ensure that the people inside would be accompanied by the Alabama National Guard when they left the church. Martin Luther King and James Farmer of CORE were the featured speakers at the rally.

Meanwhile, reinforcements for the original Freedom Riders rushed in. Among them was Stokely Carmichael, then an undergraduate active in the SNCC chapter at Howard University. Unbeknownst to the Freedom Riders, a deal was being cut between the federal justice department and the governors of Alabama and Mississippi, to allow their safe exit from Montgomery by bus. Their bus was to be accompanied by an armed convoy of guardsmen and helicopters, all the way to Jackson, Mississippi, where the Freedom Riders were to be arrested and the Freedom Ride was to end. Once they reached Jackson and were arrested, many decided to serve the jail sentences handed down to them rather than accept bail. They served their time in Jackson's Parchman Penitentiary, where they were exposed to the sights and sounds of subtle and overt tortures leveled on Negro men. Some of those men were genuine criminals who had engaged in petty crime and murder, while others had been unfairly ensnared in the fiercely racist criminal "injustice" system of Mississippi. The Freedom Riders shared space with the men, joined them on the prison chain gangs, and introduced them to freedom songs as they all worked. Philosophically, the Freedom Riders over time fell into two groups—those who believed profoundly and deeply in nonviolence, and those who were no longer so sure about the tactic. The former group eagerly sang spirituals, while the latter abstained, derisively referring to the others as the "de lawd" group. John Lewis, who would later serve as chairman of SNCC, was among the true believers in nonviolence, while Carmichael, who would one day oust Lewis as chairman in a bitter election, was among those having second thoughts.

After reading about the Freedom Rides, James Forman decided to make a trip south from Chicago to observe what was happening in the movement firsthand. He had been to the South before, because his family hailed from Mississippi where he still had relatives. This would be the second time one of his southern trips involved investigating civil rights activities, the first time being when he went to Little Rock, Arkansas, to observe the integration of Central High. On this trip, he traveled under the auspices of the National Freedom Council, a Chicago support group for the civil rights movement which he was instrumental in starting. Forman's idea was to write about what was taking place. On a stop in Tennessee he met former Freedom Rider Paul Brooks, who had been trying to drum up support for more Freedom Rides, but without success. Brooks then had another idea. He told Forman that he wanted to investigate what was happening to a man in Monroe, North Carolina, who had decided that Negroes should defend themselves rather than withstand the savage abuse of white racists.

Even though he had been suspended by the national office of the NAACP for his 1960 statement in support of violent retribution against racists, Robert Williams was reelected president of the organization's Monroe chapter. In 1961 he was even more bold and outspoken. During the height of the United Nations debate over the Bay of Pigs invasion in Cuba, Williams sent a telegram to Cuba's U.N. ambassador, Raul Roa, who interrupted a speech by America's U.N. ambassador, Adlai Stevenson, to read what Williams had written:

> Please convey to Mr. Adlai Stevenson: Now that the United States has proclaimed military support for the people willing to rebel against oppression, oppressed Negroes in South urgently request tanks, artillery, bombs, money, and the use of American airfields and white mercenaries to crush the racist

tyrants who have betrayed the American revolution and Civil War. We also request prayers for this noble undertaking.

By the summer of 1961, Williams had reinstated picket lines demanding a Negro public swimming facility in Monroe, or at least a day for Negro children to swim at the current pool. One day on the way to the pool, his car was repeatedly rammed and run off the road. Both he and his wife tried to get help from the local police, the Justice Department, and the FBI, but to no avail. Two days later his car was hit again, this time next to the pool picket lines. A large crowd of whites gathered. Williams and a detail of men from his Deacons of Defense held them off with their guns.

By the latter part of the summer, the Negro community drew up a list of demands to complement its demands for a pool. The list called for the reinstatement of Dr. Albert Perry's license to practice medicine in the county. (Since his release from prison on the abortion charge, Perry had been practicing in nearby Charlotte.) The list also called for desegregation of all public facilities in the town.

To observe what was happening in Monroe, Forman and Brooks boarded a train from Atlanta, where they encountered a Negro Pullman porter who would prove to be one more example of a Negro connected to the railroad, ready to help push the movement along. The porter asked them if they were going to Monroe.

"I'm from Monroe," he told them. "I get off at Monroe. Y'all know anybody in Monroe?"

"A few people," Forman answered.

"Monroe's a rough town," said the porter.

"Hear Robert Williams has been having a little trouble," Forman interjected.

"Y'all know Robert Williams?" the porter asked.

"We heard of him," replied Brooks.

"Y'all going to Monroe to see Robert Williams?"

"Maybe," Forman answered.

"Kinda figured y'all was going to see him."

When they arrived in Monroe, the Pullman porter drove them to the home of Robert Williams.

After investigating the situation in Monroe, James Forman and Paul Brooks presented the idea of a trip there to the Freedom Riders newly released from jail in Jackson, Mississippi. The visit was to be a nonviolent show of support for the Negro community of the town. The Freedom Riders could join Brooks and Forman or become part of a new project in Mississippi.

Bob Moses, who had recently joined SNCC, had just initiated efforts to register Negro voters in that state, which had the most notoriously racist voter-registration laws of any state in the nation. The number of Negroes registered in Mississippi had been reduced from 190,000 in 1890 to 8,600 by 1892, and had hardly budged. More than any other young disciple of King, with the possible exception of John Lewis, Bob Moses would discover the mental limits of patience with nonviolence. The U.S. Department of Justice had already urged the young civil rights enthusiasts to concentrate on registering voters in lieu of engaging in any more direct action. The choice between voter registration and direct action caused a searing, often acrimonious debate within SNCC. Voter registration would eventually win. And Bob Moses would eventually spearhead voter registration efforts, the results of which would have profound consequences on the morale of both young Negro and white activists engaging in those efforts over the next three years. But in August 1961, Moses only wanted Negro Freedom Riders to work with him in Mississippi.

While some Negro Freedom Riders left for Mississippi, Paul Brooks and James Forman gathered an integrated group of former Freedom Riders for the trip to Monroe. On arriving in town, the group set up a picket line at the Union County courthouse. The mayor also happened to be a dentist, so they set up a picket line outside of his dental office as well. Although he was happy to see support for the cause of Monroe's Negro community, Robert Williams declined to participate in the pickets set up by the Freedom Riders because of his increasingly differing views on nonviolent direct action.

When the white citizens of Monroe saw the integrated picket lines, they went into a frenzy. They taunted white Freedom Riders with shouts of "Your mama's at home sleeping with a nigger!" They drove by with signs on their cars; one read, "Coon Season Open!" They told the Freedom Riders they wouldn't live to see the following day. James Forman called the home of Robert Williams requesting that he send four cars to pick up the Freedom Riders by 5 P.M. But the Monroe police blocked streets, preventing any cars from picking them up. Violence broke out. Forman was hit over the head by one racist with the barrel of a gun, which inflicted a deep bloody gash. A few whites fired guns directly at the Freedom Riders. The bullets missed them but wounded one white police officer. Instead of arresting the racist rioters, the police officers arrested the Freedom Riders for inciting a riot.

The experience radicalized James Forman, a process that would take hold of more and more young civil rights activists in the following years. While in jail, Forman and the Freedom Riders sang freedom songs to each other and the Negro prisoners jailed for other charges. Although Forman didn't know why the other prisoners were in jail, his increasing radicalism drew him to conclude that they "had, no doubt, been put there for other unjust causes."

In September 1961, Forman and the Freedom Riders were convicted of inciting a riot, but were given suspended sentences with the understanding that all they had to do was leave Monroe and never return. After learning that they would get no more legal support from SCLC, the NAACP, or any other civil rights group that had money, because their activities were associated with Robert Williams, they accepted the sentence and left.

While the riot had been going on at the courthouse square, the Negroes in the Newtown section of Monroe had listened to the gunfire and become increasingly angry, increasingly ready to do something. They began gathering in crowds. Robert Williams remained at his home. To try to prevent an armed revolt among Negroes in the town, a highway patrolman drove to Robert Williams's home and urged him to give up his arms. Williams refused, citing his right to protect his family and his property. Angered by the request of the patrolman, in light of what was happening at the courthouse square, the crowd urged Williams to hold the patrolman hostage. But he allowed the patrolman to leave. Minutes later a middle-aged white couple drove by. The crowd converged on the couple, forcing their car to a halt. The man was pulled from the car as the crowd shouted, "Kill him!" because it thought the Freedom Riders were being killed at the courthouse square.

There would be conflicting accounts of what happened next. According to the mainstream press, Robert Williams arrived on the scene and held the white couple hostage at gunpoint. But according to eyewitness Julian Mayfield, a writer, Williams arrived on the scene to save the white couple from the mob's fury because the mob had no intention of allowing the couple back inside their car to leave. Williams allegedly led them inside his house, even allowing them to make a phone call. Nevertheless, he would be charged with kidnapping and a warrant would be issued for his arrest. Rather than face the charges, Williams fled Monroe for good, heading first to New York City by bus, then to Cuba, and then to China.

The example set by Williams in Monroe planted the first real seeds of militancy in the southern civil rights movement, a militancy that would grow rapidly among younger Negro activists in the next five years. But first they had to taste more atrocity at the hands of white racists. That atrocity would be directed against the nonviolent work initiated by Bob Moses.

Moses had been urged to start a voter registration campaign in Mississippi by a Mississippian named Amzie Moore. But where would the experimental work begin? Fittingly, a Negro man working for the railroad provided the answer. C. C. Bryant was employed by the Illinois Central railroad. He was also head of the Pike County, Mississippi, chapter of the NAACP. Bryant invited Moses to come to the Pike County town of McComb to start the project. Like C. L. Dellums in Oakland, Bryant was a Mason. He offered the facilities of the all-Negro Masonic Temple in the town as a place for Moses to teach Negroes the ins and outs of the arcane Mississippi voter registration laws. The voter registration experiment would grow to encompass the counties of Pike, Amite, and Walthall.

At the end of the summer of 1961, Moses was arrested under trumped-up charges of interfering with a police officer, as he tried to register three potential Negro voters. After his arrest, voter registration work acquired much greater appeal in the eyes of the young SNCC workers. Moses was released from jail after the national office of the NAACP reluctantly paid his fine. The NAACP was exasperated. Bob Moses and local chapter leaders like C. C. Bryant and Robert Williams were considered troublemakers. The attitude of the national office was still, "Leave the civil rights fight to us and our courtroom litigation!"

SNCC shifted all of its activity to Bob Moses's Mississippi project. However, young volunteers, including a local high-school student named Hollis Watkins, wanted to engage not only in canvassing for volunteers for SNCC's voter registration school but also in some form of direct action, like their SNCC heroes. On August 29, the high-school students engaged in a sit-in at a Woolworth's lunch counter in McComb and were arrested. On going to jail, Hollis Watkins found himself surrounded by twelve white men in a room, including a police officer. He answered every question the police officer put to him with a "yes" or a "no," making a "mistake" similar to the one C. L. Dellums had made with the railroad dispatcher in Oakland, California, nearly forty years earlier.

"When you answer me, boy, you say 'yes sir' or 'no sir'!" the officer instructed. The consequences of disobeying such an order in Mississippi could be far more dire than of disobeying it in California. To keep from saying "yes sir" and "no sir," Hollis answered the questions in sentences. The twelve white men drew closer, surrounding him as if they were about to beat him within an inch of his life. Luckily, Hollis survived this "transgression." But the whites in Mississippi would find themselves getting angrier and angrier at the civil rights revolution in their state. Soon they would express that anger in the grisliest ways imaginable.

SNCC's voter registration activity in the three-county area worried not only the ordinary white citizens but also the white elected officials. They sweated at the prospect of significant numbers of Negro voters. Among them was a state assemblyman, E. H. Hurst. Hurst knew Herbert Lee, a Negro farmer in Amite County who was attending SNCC's voter registration school. One morning Hurst followed Lee to the local cotton gin to confront him about his efforts to become a registered voter. Pulling up next to Lee's pickup truck, Hurst decided that the best way to convince Lee to cease his voter education activity was to pull out his .38-caliber pistol while talking to him. Lee slid out of the passenger side of his pickup truck, telling Hurst that he refused to talk with him as long as the gun was out. Hurst ran around to the passenger side of Lee's truck, shouting at Lee, "I'm not playing with you this morning!" Then he aimed the gun point blank at Lee's head and pulled the trigger.

Lee's murder would be ruled a justifiable homicide after Hurst lied, insisting that he pulled the gun because Lee had confronted him with a tire iron. Witnesses, including a Negro logger who depended on whites to help him stay in business, backed up the Hurst account.

At Lee's funeral, Lee's widow had something searing to say to Bob Moses. She approached him and began beating her chest, shouting, "You killed my husband!" Moses could at least find solace in the fact that he wasn't asking the Negroes of Mississippi to risk anything he wasn't willing to risk himself. Before the murder of Herbert Lee, in an earlier registration effort, Moses had accompanied a farmer named Curtis Dawson and a man named Preacher Knox to the Amite County, Mississippi courthouse, twenty-five miles from McComb. They were blocked from entering the courthouse by three young white men. One of the white men then struck Moses in the head with a knife handle, slapped him, and hit him in his temple. As Moses cowered on the ground from the blows, his assailant struck him in the head again, driving Moses's face into the pavement. The three white men left, and Moses, Dawson, and

Knox proceeded to the courthouse. On seeing the bloody Moses and his companions, the white registrar announced that he was closed for the day.

The beating of Moses and the killing of Herbert Lee would be only the tip of the iceberg. Over the next couple of years, racist violence would be tasted by Mississippi Negro citizens and SNCC workers such as Travis Britt, Ivanhoe Donaldson, Bob Zellner, Sam Block, and Jim Travis. Lewis Allen, the Negro logger who had backed up state assemblyman Hurst's lie as to why he had killed Herbert Lee, would be shot dead by white racists three years later in his own front yard. NAACP Mississippi field secretary Medgar Evers would be shot and killed by a white racist as he emerged from his car in the driveway of his home. Seeing her husband dying in the driveway left Myrlie Evers with a temporary profound hatred of even the most well-meaning whites. Witnessing and enduring so much violence would cause James Forman, now executive secretary of SNCC, to suffer a bleeding ulcer that would nearly take his life. And all of the white perpetrators of the violence would get off scot-free.

The movement spread: to Albany, Georgia; to Martin Luther King's 1963 Birmingham campaign, with its searing images of Negro children enduring the hungry fangs of German shepherds and clothes-ripping cascades of water from fire hoses; to the 1963 March on Washington, organized by early Premier Negro Leader A. Philip Randolph. By 1963 Randolph had become an elder statesman. This march would witness the new Premier Negro Leader, Martin Luther King, making his most memorable and stirring speech of all, telling the world, "I have a dream. . . ." The rush of shocking images and stories would slowly awaken a profound sense of guilt within white Americans, mainly in the North, and would increasingly fuel debates among both northern and southern Negroes about the best way to gain liberation from racism.

3

Feeling the Southern Earthquake from a Distance

IN THE EARLY 1960S, A YOUNG JEWISH MAN NAMED JOE Blum felt a certain empathy with Negroes. This was a common sentiment among Jews at the time who watched everything that was happening to Negroes in Montgomery, Little Rock, Greensboro, and Birmingham, and in the state of Mississippi, coming across television screens and being splashed across newspapers. Many of them couldn't help but feel, "There, but for the grace of God, go I." Wise Jewish Americans knew that every society had to have its "niggers." In the United States, Jews weren't exactly niggers, but neither were they well loved by others who considered themselves white. Jewish Americans, for the most part, were one notch above being niggers. But in Europe, Jews had historically been the niggers. And to see vivid examples of other people suffering atrocities similar to what Jews suffered in Europe struck a raw nerve.

In 1961 Joe Blum left New York City for California. He arrived in the San Francisco Bay Area intent on gaining admission to the undergraduate division of one of the top state universities in the nation—the University of California at Berkeley. But first he had to attend a junior college for a semester and obtain at least a 3.0 grade point average. Blum chose Oakland City College (later renamed Merritt College), an institution with a large number of Negro students. By 1960, Oakland's Negro population had swollen to about one-quarter of the city's total, thanks to the steady stream of Negroes that had been arriving in the Bay Area in large numbers since 1942, when A. Philip Randolph had pressured President Franklin Roosevelt into issuing executive order 8802.

The young Negro students at Oakland City College were also pondering media images of the struggle in the South. But since they were in the urban North, as well as in the West, they were influenced by the same factors then taking hold of other northern Negroes. Vicious Jim Crow was at a distance. Northern Negroes suffered from de facto segregation—that is, segregation of the housing market, the employment office—but not the type that kept them off the voter registration rolls, or prevented them from sitting at lunch counters downtown, or forced them to use separate public water fountains and restrooms. Negro youths could watch what was happening in the South, something their parents had gladly escaped, and indulge in the luxury of being armchair quarterbacks.

And like their counterparts in places such as New York City, by 1961 the young California Negroes were just as likely to be influenced by a Malcolm X as by a Martin Luther King, Jr., or King disciples such as Bayard Rustin and the many ministers affiliated with his movement. They would go to hear Malcolm X speak on a swing through San Francisco or Oakland just as quickly as they would go to hear King or anyone he might send to the West Coast to speak on his behalf. Among liberal politically aware Bay Area white college students, however, Martin Luther King, James Farmer of CORE, and the young activists from SNCC held their undivided attention.

While attending classes at Oakland City College, Joe Blum noticed the mood of the Negro students. There were large swinging doors at the entrance to the buildings on campus. The doors whacked back and forth menacingly for the person immediately behind whoever opened and went through one. It was considered courteous to hold the door open for the next person, but with the rise in nationalist sentiments among Negro students, most refused to hold doors open for whites. Not a student named Huey Newton, though: Newton held the door open for whoever was behind him because he felt it was the system, and not white people, that was the enemy. Many other Negro students chided him for doing so. Most were enthralled by Donald Warden, a Negro lawyer at UC Berkeley and a popular radio talk show host who had started the Afro-American Association and opened it to all Negro college students in the Bay Area. "It was Donald Warden who was the most articulate spokesperson for black nationalism," recalls Blum. "And Huey Newton was the spokesperson for the other position." Newton's position caused Blum some measure of relief and optimism. So Blum decided that he liked Huey Newton.

But at the time Joe Blum knew nothing of another side to Newton. Newton, too, had once been a follower of Donald Warden. In fact, he had arranged a security detail for Warden's trips into the Negro communities of Oakland, San Francisco, and Berkeley to proselytize about Afro-American nationalism. Newton had introduced into Warden's organization Negro men from the streets. Many could barely read but were looking for someplace to channel their anger and frustration about life. Huey Newton was of two minds. On the one hand, he liked the intellectual challenge presented by his classes at Oakland City College. His favorite class was in philosophy. He also liked the intellectual challenge of involvement in Warden's organization, where he read books by authors like earlier Premier Negro Leaders W. E. B. DuBois and Booker T. Washington. On the other hand, he had no taste for the kind of future that Oakland City College, or any other college for that matter, was designed to prepare its students for—a future to which most students in Warden's organization eagerly aspired.

Newton liked the streets, and he liked the men who hung out on the streets. He had grown up in West Oakland and North Oakland after his father, Walter, moved the family to California from Monroe, Louisiana, in 1945, when Huey was three years old, amid the growing tide of Negroes flowing into the state on the issuance of executive order 8802. Huey was the youngest of Walter and Armelia Newton's seven children. His mother's and father's formal educations didn't extend beyond high school. Walter Newton worked a variety of jobs to support the family—longshoreman, handyman, truck driver. "As a youngster, I well remember my father leaving one job in the afternoon, coming home for a while, then going to the other," Huey later recalled, although he also noted that his father found time for the family. Walter Newton refused to let his wife work. He also became a volunteer assistant minister at Antioch Baptist, a small church in Oakland.

Huey had been named in honor of Louisiana governor Huey P. Long. Although Long was a racist, he avoided the typical race-baiting politics of southern politicians of the 1920s and 1930s. Walter Newton had been impressed by that and by Long's populist efforts on behalf of the state's ordinary citizens, which brought free schools, paved roads, and jobs to Negroes as well as to whites.

During Huey's childhood, the Newton family moved frequently throughout West and then North Oakland. By the time Huey entered high school, they had settled in North Oakland. Because he was light brown in complexion and had a baby face, and his name was Huey and he had a squeaky unmasculine voice, Newton learned to fight early in life. He was taught by his older brother Sonny, who became a street hustler. Sonny taught Huey to go for the jugular, the quick knockout, since Huey wasn't physically imposing enough to intimidate potential rivals.

Friends and acquaintances say that because he had such a funny name, was considered a pretty boy, and was of medium height, Newton often jumped first rather than wait to defend himself against potential adversaries. He became a delinquent and was kicked out of every public high school in Oakland. (He managed to graduate from Berkeley High, later claiming that he did so without knowing how to read. His brother Melvin disputes that claim.) As a teenager and young adult, he often entered a pool hall, an after-hours club, or a house party, or walked up to a street corner where a group of guys were hanging out, picked an argument with the biggest person there, got into a fight with him, and "kicked his ass" just to establish himself. Eventually, he acquired a reputation for being so bad, so quick to the draw, that others on the rough streets of Oakland respected him, and he developed friendships with the same young men he would physically whip.

Newton developed unique qualities. On straightening himself out enough to gain admission to Oakland City College, he began holding his own with students there. Yet he remained comfortable on the street corners with young Negro men who drank wine all day, wolf-whistled at women, gambled all night, and fought one another—young men whom most college-bound Negroes shied away from. He could stay up for hours at a time, days on end, arguing with his college friends over the intellectual fine points to be gleaned from books by Camus, Sartre, Kierkegaard, or the four volumes of Mao Tse-tung. Or he could use his budding intellectualism on his street buddies, shaming them so much with his superior intellect that they would want to fight. They would get into a fight with Newton, get whipped by him, and end up respecting him, if not following him wherever he would go.

Newton often led them in burglarizing white homes in the Oakland and Berkeley foothills, sometimes in broad daylight; they camouflaged themselves as gardeners. Newton became an expert at running shortchange scams on convenience-store clerks, and running phony credit schemes on stores as well. He used his apartment as a gambling den, serving as the house and taking a cut of the money that exchanged hands. In fact, Huey Newton never worked a legitimate, nine-to-five job.

Before falling out with Donald Warden, Huey Newton had developed a security detail for Warden's organization. And, true to his budding nature, his falling out with Warden wasn't purely political. Sometimes Newton and the other members of the security detail got into fights with young whites who didn't like what Warden had to say about whites. Rather than "throw down" along with the security detail, Warden refused to fight. Seeing that Warden was unwilling to engage in physical confrontation, Newton lost respect for him. Thus Newton's break with Warden had as much to do with Warden's lack of relish for using his fists as with anything else. The ability to use your fists was the first step to gaining honor with people like Newton and his street buddies. Not using your fists implied that you were a punk.

And, simply put, the socialist theories that Newton studied at Oakland City College—theories stating that capitalism is an altogether vile system—were far more amenable to the lifestyle he preferred than Afro-American nationalism was. Most nationalist theories among Negroes merely sought to replicate capitalism. Communist and socialist philosophy deemed most jobs to be sophisticated forms of labor exploitation. Newton could burglarize homes, shortchange convenience-store operators, engage in other scams, and assure himself that all of it was okay because he was getting over on a system that needed to be dismantled. Communism was a popular topic in 1961, because of Fidel Castro's overthrow of Batista and the related Bay of Pigs fiasco. "Fair Play for Cuba" societies sprouted like weeds among liberal college students at the same time that the civil rights movement and Negro nationalism were in the news. The Bay Area would soon become a key epicenter of activism among both Negro and white students.

In 1961, Huey Newton was still active among the Negro students at Oakland City College and among Negroes in the Oakland streets. Joe Blum gained admission to UC Berkeley that fall after a successful semester at Oakland City College. Blum arrived on a campus where many in the white student body viewed the shocking scenes of Freedom Riders being pummeled in Birmingham and in Montgomery the previous spring with increasing concern. They turned their attention to the plight of Negroes locally.

By the end of World War II, more than 10,000 Negroes had been employed by the firms Kaiser Industries, Moore Drydock, and Bethlehem Steel, building Navy destroyers and gunboats at the shipyards. The approximately 50,000 Negroes who had migrated to the East Bay during the war were augmented by returning Negro World War II troops who chose to settle in the area after being discharged from the service. They were also followed by relatives from East Texas, Louisiana, and Arkansas who heard the proverbial fanciful stories that all immigrants tell on returning to the "old country"—that they left home and found a pot of gold the likes of which could never be obtained unless you followed them to where they were newly settled. Of course, the stories were somewhat exaggerated. For after the war, most of the Negro shipyard workers, who had been segregated into AFL Jim Crow auxiliaries with no union democracy and no job security, were left to fend for themselves.

Oakland whites had not expected Negroes to stay after the war, much less continue to arrive from the South in large numbers. They panicked in much the same way that earlier white settlers panicked when white Oakies poured into California during the Great Depression after disastrous dust storms forced them off their land, and greedy Central Valley canneries enticed them to the state with promises of an abundant amount of work picking fruit and vegetables.

In Oakland, the white powers-that-be, just like their counterparts in other urban areas, decided that a Maginot Line must be drawn to confine most of the Negro community to one segregated area. It was to be the flats west of the neighborhoods that rose up into the hills providing views of the entire San Francisco Bay. By 1961 the Negro community comprised a black belt in the flats of the East Bay that stretched some 200 blocks from South Berkeley into East Oakland. The farther you progressed toward the bay, the poorer the residents. And to further contain and intimidate the masses of Negroes confined to the flats, the white powers-that-be decided that shock troops were necessary—that is, a tough and unyielding police force. In the years immediately following World War II, Oakland police recruiters traveled to the American South and recruited whites to join the police force to keep the Negroes "in line."

"On Fridays, the police would regularly lie in wait outside West Oakland bars that served as banks for cashing paychecks, arrest those emerging on charges of drunkenness, and in the privacy of their prowl cars beat them and rob them of their week's pay en route to the West Oakland police station," recalled Jessica Mitford in her autobiography, *A Fine Old Conflict*. So bad were the Oakland police in the years immediately following World War II that in 1950 the California legislature launched an investigation that resulted in the resignation of Oakland's police chief and the sentencing of another officer to jail at San Quentin.

The city of Oakland was run by its business cartel, which

included the very powerful heads of Kaiser Industries and Clorox, the William Knowland family (owners of the city's daily newspaper, the *Oakland Tribune*), and a handful of others. The city government was composed of a city manager (who for all intents and purposes ran the city to the satisfaction of the business community), a weak mayor, and a city council that was elected at large rather than district by district. All of this effectively diluted Negro voting power in Oakland so that, unlike in Mississippi, whites didn't need to intimidate Negroes who wished to register and vote.

By 1961 the unemployment rate in Oakland was 9 percent, twice the national average. Estimates placed the rate in the Negro community at 25 percent. And at least one out of three Negro youths was said to be unemployed and a high-school dropout. In 1961 the school districts of the city were gerrymandered to create all-white Skyline High. Every Negro high school had a police patrol.

As the politically aware white students at UC Berkeley began to look at the lives of Negroes in Oakland, the whites of Oakland began to look at the students. The college was considered a bastion of wrongheaded liberalism, beatniks, and communists. The latter conclusion was directly due to the fact that in 1952, at the height of the national red-bait scare, the faculty of UC Berkeley had been a principal target of Senator Joseph McCarthy's powerful House Un-American Activities Committee (HUAC), which called on prominent citizens to take loyalty oaths. Large numbers of the faculty had refused. And when HUAC came to San Francisco City Hall in 1961 to hold hearings, the students at UC Berkeley played no small role in the massive demonstrations and sit-ins that resulted in the San Francisco fire department washing the demonstrators off the steps inside the building.

So, by 1961, primed by what they saw from the civil rights movement in the South—the lunch counter sit-ins, then the Freedom Rides—increasing numbers of UC Berkeley students wanted to do something locally to improve race relations. But through which organization could they do so? The NAACP was oriented toward courtroom litigation. The Urban League concentrated on securing corporate philanthropy. Neither SNCC nor SCLC had any real organization outside the South. The sole national direct-action civil rights organization with any local branches was CORE. So the students began signing up with CORE's Oakland and Berkeley chapters. With the enthusiastic aid of newly interested white students, the Bay Area CORE chapters began to picket the local branches of national dime and department store chains, as a complementary activity to the lunch counter sit-ins taking place at those chains' southern facilities.

Since its inception in the early 1940s, CORE had been a thoroughly integrated organization, committed to nonviolent Gandhi-style picketing. Although CORE gained its first real dose of national attention in 1961 after initiating the Freedom Rides, the organization's modus operandi *while picketing* remained the same as it had been since the 1940s. To appear as "gentlemanly" and "ladylike" as possible, the picketers were required to conform to a strict code. Men wore suits and ties on line, while women wore dresses. Talking and smoking were forbidden. Everyone was re-quired to be properly spaced apart, holding their signs in a precise manner. With the increased involvement of the Bay Area students, however, this style of picketing would see its final days.

In 1963, the year of Martin Luther King's Birmingham civil rights campaign, the assassination of Medgar Evers, the historic March on Washington, and the bombing of a Birmingham church that killed four little Negro girls, direct-action campaigns among Bay Area students gained a full head of steam. Oakland and Berkeley CORE began documenting specific cases of employment discrimination and then picketing companies that practiced it, most notably Montgomery Ward in Oakland.

In a city with a Negro population that was over 25 percent of the total, Montgomery Ward had a work force that was only 2 percent Negro. CORE prepared a seventy-page booklet defending its right to demand that the company engage in more than just token employment of Negroes. After two weeks of picketing by CORE, Montgomery Ward reached an agreement that was to be the prototype of future fair employment agreements for companies in the Bay Area. The company was to provide statistical reports, institute special recruitment drives, and set goal projections, all of which eventually opened up hundreds of jobs to nonwhites.

By the time the agreement between Montgomery Ward and CORE was reached, the jarring scenes emanating from Martin Luther King's 1963 Birmingham civil rights campaign were resulting in jam-packed lecture halls and gymnasiums featuring prominent Negroes on speaking tour to the Bay Area. "I'm not going into the details of police dogs, fire hoses, and paddy wagons [in Birmingham]," the writer James Baldwin told 9,000 students that May, filling UC Berkeley's Harmon Gymnasium to the rafters. "You people already know about such things."

Indeed they did. After King's Birmingham campaign, statisticians counted 758 racial demonstrations and 14,733 arrests in cities across the nation. More and more, Bay Area students were pacesetters in those efforts. Their next direct-action activity took place that June as they added their presence to a monthlong sit-in at the state capitol in Sacramento, successfully demanding passage of a fair-housing law for the state of California.

In the middle of the Sacramento demonstrations, Medgar Evers was murdered in Mississippi, on the same night that President Kennedy made his first speech unequivocally supporting civil rights. That August saw the March on Washington. That September brought the church bombing that killed four little Negro girls in Birmingham. Bay Area students steadily grew more troubled, more restless, and filled with guilt over what they saw and read; they determined to make their feelings count for something locally.

By September 1963 enough students had joined CORE to start a separate CORE chapter (to be called Campus CORE) at UC Berkeley. The stage was set for a radical change in CORE's methods of protest. That November, Campus CORE students led action against CORE's next local target—Mel's Drive-In restaurant, the place that later would be turned into an icon of the late 1950s and early 1960s, via the film *American Graffiti*. The students accused Mel's (actually a thirteen-restaurant chain) of hiring Negroes only for menial behind-the-scenes positions, rather than as waitresses, countergirls, carhops, and bartenders. Hundreds of

Campus CORE students descended on the Berkeley Mel's outlet. This time they refused to be polite, maintaining only a picket line that didn't interfere with business—the modus operandi of previous protests. They also refused to wear suits and ties and dresses and to carry signs at precise heights. They wore all sorts of casual clothing as they engaged in sit-ins inside the restaurant and blocked customers from coming through the entrances. They sang, shouted, clapped, and walked two abreast outside of the facility, rather than single file. Ninety-two demonstrators were arrested in the first wave of activity. After two large demonstrations, an agreement was reached with Mel's management to hire Negroes in up-front positions.

In December, John Lewis, now chairman of SNCC, came to the Bay Area to talk about the organization's activities. Like King, he had given a speech to the nation at the March on Washington the previous summer. Speaking to a raptly attentive audience on the UC Berkeley campus, Lewis described SNCC as an organization of students who were "part domestic Peace Corps and part guerilla warfare," trying to help southern Negroes rise above the atmosphere of hate and fear in a nonviolent overthrow of segregation. To the students' laughter, he said that most other civil rights organizations were composed of middle-class Negroes and whites who engaged in a "tea and cookie" approach to the issues: "The white people drink all the tea, and the Negroes eat all the cookies." Lewis called instead for a grassroots movement like that of SNCC, and then he announced plans for a window of opportunity through which they could become an active and significant part of SNCC. Eventually, it would pave the way to a very important turning point in the tone, direction, and philosophy of the entire movement. Lewis announced that in the coming year, 1964, SNCC planned to saturate one or two southern states with 500 to 1,000 field workers who would help register massive numbers of Negroes to vote for the first time.

What Lewis described in only a peripheral manner was a calculated new plan designed by Bob Moses. Lewis, Forman, Moses, and the other SNCC workers had certainly noticed the increased interest in the movement on the part of young northern whites, particularly by 1963. Between the fall of 1961, when he was arrested on trumped-up charges related to his voter registration activity in McComb, Mississippi, and the end of 1963, Moses had become the recognized expert on registering Negro voters in the rural South. In 1962 the Kennedy administration decided to heavily back up such registration efforts by mobilizing the Democratic Party and sympathetic foundations to create the Voter Education Project (VEP).

The directors of VEP called a meeting of all the principal civil rights organizations active in the South—the NAACP, SCLC, SNCC, CORE—at which SNCC outlined exactly how it intended to go about increasing its registration activities. The other civil rights groups, most notably the NAACP, balked at SNCC playing the major role in such a controversial campaign. The NAACP wanted nothing to do with trying to register Negro voters in the rural South and thought the entire idea was suicidal. But the director of VEP, Wiley Branton, insisted the project was a sound one, that SNCC should take the lead in it, and that Bob Moses should be appointed field director of the effort, which was supposed to be a combined activity on the part of all the organizations under an umbrella organization called the Council of Federated Organizations (COFO).

COFO began by concentrating most of its efforts in Mississippi. By the middle of 1962, the dangerous work that Moses and the other SNCC workers had started in McComb and its surrounding counties was transferred, with a new infusion of funds, to other parts of the state. Predictably, violence broke out. There were more cold-blooded killings, more beatings. By the fall of 1963, COFO had decided to hold a Freedom Vote in Mississippi, as the next logical step in building its voter registration movement. What better way to encourage people to vote, the reasoning went, than to give them appealing candidates to vote for, helping them to imagine what life might be like if they had real political power? Officially registered voters, as well as those not officially registered, were declared eligible to participate. They cast their votes for candidates on a "freedom ballot" over a three-day period in the first week of November 1963.

The Freedom Vote would rate the front page of the *Daily Californian*, the student newspaper at UC Berkeley. During three days of balloting at designated areas throughout Mississippi, 80,000 votes were cast. Aaron Henry, a Negro pharmacist in Clarksdale who also happened to be vice president of COFO, ran for governor. Bob Moses served as his campaign manager. Approximately sixty white students from Yale and Stanford universities, recruited by a man named Allard Lowenstein, aided the SNCC workers in mobilizing Negroes to participate in the vote. Although SNCC workers would later become suspicious of Lowenstein, viewing him as someone sent to infiltrate SNCC on behalf of more moderate civil rights interests (the "tea and cookie" set Lewis referred to in his Berkeley speech), the SNCC workers were impressed by the willingness of the Yale and Stanford students to travel that far to help out. Because they were so impressed, they saw it as all the more evidence that trying to mobilize 500 to 1,000 students for the summer would work; hence, John Lewis's December 1963 speaking tour in the Bay Area.

The students at UC Berkeley were deeply impressed by what Lewis had to say. So were many UC professors, twenty-six of whom took out a full-page ad in the *Daily Californian*, urging students to pass a referendum on the ballot of the student government association, which would donate a large portion of student funds to SNCC. The referendum would be defeated in a close vote. But John Lewis's trip had hardly been in vain. A loose network of auxiliary groups called the Friends of SNCC had been established among sympathetic northerners throughout major cities. They raised the much-needed funds required to keep SNCC's work going. Lewis's trip helped strengthen SNCC's very important beachhead in the Bay Area. In fact, so strong would SNCC's Bay Area connection become that the only official newspaper connected to SNCC, *The Movement*, would be published out of the Bay Area and eventually edited by the same man who was favorably impressed by Huey Newton during his short tenure as a student at Oakland City College—Joe Blum.

As 1964 began, interest in direct-action activities in the Bay Area reached a fever pitch. The activities of the students involved in civil rights protests were beginning to garner for the Bay Area the reputation for activism by which the rest of the nation would know it for years to come. After November's demonstrations at Mel's Drive-In, the Ad Hoc Committee to End Discrimination was formed. Spearheaded by a young Negro senior from Berkeley High named Tracy Sims, Roy Ballard of San Francisco CORE, and Mike Myerson, a UC Berkeley student who was part of a radical student party called Slate, the committee mostly comprised young white students from places like UC Berkeley. Now there were two key local direct-action groups to which students, affected by what they saw and read of happening in the South, could devote their time and energy. And both CORE and the Ad Hoc Committee would raise their tactics to new heights of civil disobedience.

CORE struck first. In February it began regional protests against the Lucky grocery-store chain. Of a work force of approximately 1,000, Lucky employed only 50 Negroes. CORE claimed the chain's record was due to racial discrimination. At the corner of Haste Street and Telegraph Avenue, not far from the UC Berkeley campus, sat a store that was part of that chain—Lucky Store No. 18. Campus CORE activists hit on their most daring tactic of all.

They set up the usual picket lines outside of the store. But demonstrators also entered the supermarket under the pretext of being regular customers. They took shopping carts and filled them to the brim with every conceivable grocery item. Then they proceeded to the checkout counter. The clerk would check through all the goods and present the total tab. At that point the demonstrator would pull out his wallet and declare that he forgot to bring his money, so he couldn't purchase the groceries. This tactic tied up all of the checkout lanes and largely emptied the shelves. In addition, demonstrators simply filled carts with groceries and left the carts in the lanes. They took particular relish in placing loaves of bread at the very bottom, then piling canned goods on top, rendering the loaves unsalable when store clerks placed the goods back on the shelves.

This tactic, known as the shop-in, precipitated the first real divisions among students on campus and the first real tension between the campus and the local community. Large numbers of pro–shop-in demonstrators picketed outside the store, while their cohorts emptied the shelves and tied up the checkout aisles. Soon, anti–shop-in demonstrators (most notably members of the campus fraternities) staged counterdemonstrations. They also followed the demonstrators inside the store, reshelving their groceries as fast as the demonstrators placed them in the carts or on the checkout counters. Between four and six o'clock, Lucky Store No. 18 looked like the set of a farcical situation comedy or television game show.

Two weeks after the shop-ins began, Mayor John F. Shelley of San Francisco stepped in to mediate an agreement between the regional CORE chapters and the management of Lucky. The grocery chain agreed to establish a program specifically geared toward hiring more Negroes. Little did Mayor Shelley know that within four days, San Francisco itself would become the next target of massive direct action in a dramatic act that would draw more attention than the shop-ins. This time the Ad Hoc Committee to End Discrimination would be responsible.

The Sheraton Palace Hotel had been a San Francisco landmark since the late eighteenth century. It hosted presidents, kings, queens, and every manner of California's glitterati. The hotel's ornate Palm Court atrium was a fixture among postcards displaying tourist sites in San Francisco. It was precisely because of the prestige of the Sheraton Palace that the Ad Hoc Committee chose to make an example of it, for all the other hotels in the city. The complaints against the San Francisco hotels were the same as those against all other demonstration targets—there were not enough Negro employees in positions of importance. Never before in the entire civil rights movement had there been a demonstration like the one to come at the Sheraton Palace, where the grievance was related to hiring practices rather than to an establishment's refusal to serve Negro customers.

The Ad Hoc Committee began peaceful negotiations with hotel management. Conflict between the committee and the Sheraton Palace representatives began when 123 demonstrators were arrested outside the hotel for violating an injunction imposed at the hotel's request, limiting the number of pickets to nine. The arrests sparked the wrath of Bay Area civil rights activists. That Friday evening at about six o'clock, approximately 1,500 chanting pickets, including many college professors and other working adults in addition to students, showed up and surrounded the Sheraton Palace in a double line extending along three sides of the hotel. The demonstrators were controlled every fifteen feet by Ad Hoc monitors with white armbands. Thomas Irwin, a demonstrator, carried a Nazi sign in an apparent attempt to draw an analogy between the American Nazi party and the hotel's management. Angry bystanders ripped the sign from his hands. Daryl Bishop, another demonstrator, carried eight confederate flags up and down the lines in an attempt to compare the hotel management to southern racists.

Although their chants were quite bland, like Bishop, the demonstrators compared the situation to that in the South, shouting, "Jim Crow must go! Segregation must go!" Realizing that hotel management had no intention of asking for arrests, they filed into the ornate lobby. Hotel staff held up two signed injunctions, one requiring the Ad Hoc Committee to show cause for their demonstration, the other restricting the committee to 100 demonstrators. But the hotel made no arrests. At midnight Ad Hoc leaders asked the demonstrators to sit down. They filled the hotel lobby, leaving a small passageway for reporters and television cameramen, who were out in full force covering the event.

The demonstrators were kept informed of the progress of negotiations while they withstood the heckling of hotel guests. Then Saturday morning at three o'clock, eighteen-year-old Ad Hoc leader Tracy Sims mounted a marble lobby table. "The Sheraton Palace has once again shown bad faith," she told the demonstrators. "They have refused to sign an agreement they themselves proposed. Are you ready to go to jail for your beliefs?"

Demonstrators roared their approval, then began to sing "We Shall Overcome." At four o'clock, they decided to block all of the hotel doorways, automatically causing a fire hazard. If they didn't remove themselves, police officers told them, they would be arrested for trespassing and disturbing the peace. Willie Brown, who would one day become the very powerful Speaker of the California assembly, was one of two attorneys for the Ad Hoc Committee. Brown urged the demonstrators to switch from blocking the doorways to holding a sleep-in in the lobby, so that they could avoid arrest. The leaders took a vote. To the roaring approval of the demonstrators, they announced, "We are going to jail."

At that point the police moved in, beginning the difficult task of trying to unlink the demonstrators, who had joined themselves arm to arm. A total of 167 of them were placed in paddy wagons and sent to jail, including Mario Savio, future leader of Berkeley's Free Speech Movement. Because not enough bail money was available for everyone to be arrested, approximately 600 demonstrators remained inside the hotel to hold a sleep-in in the lobby. At 9:30 Saturday morning they began to march and chant in the lobby, not stopping until 3:00 P.M., when Tracy Sims appeared to announce that Mayor Shelley had engineered a pact that was signed by the Sheraton Palace management and binding with all the major hotels in the city. Demonstration leaders projected that the pact would pave the way for 1,500 to 2,000 jobs to be opened up for nonwhites.

Hard on the heels of the Sheraton Palace demonstration, while Saturday's negotiations were still in progress, came San Francisco's next civil disturbance. Every progressive activist seemed determined to hold some sort of local civil rights action. This one was led by the president of the San Francisco NAACP, proving once again that the organization's national office didn't have the degree of control over branch members that it desired. Although the NAACP could claim its first civil rights martyr in Medgar Evers, who when he died was simply carrying out instructions to do something in Mississippi so that the NAACP wouldn't appear too conservative, the national office still lived in the dinosaur age. The list of dissident branch members now included Dr. Thomas Burbridge, president of the San Francisco NAACP.

The Cadillac dealership on Auto Row on Van Ness Avenue was targeted by Burbridge. Large numbers of demonstrators and bystanders blocked traffic on busy Van Ness, while 200 protesters, led by Burbridge, entered the Cadillac showroom to protest the dealership's hiring policy. Student activists from UC Berkeley made up one-fifth of the 107 demonstrators arrested for sitting in at the showroom.

"For eighteen months I was able to see no hope at all, anywhere, until I hit San Francisco last March," commented comedian-activist Dick Gregory, on observing the Sheraton Palace and Auto Row sit-ins. "I think the answer to the Negro problem lies here—in the San Francisco formula. Seventy-four percent of the civil rights demonstrators are white. . . . There can't be any race riots here or bloodshed because there are too many whites working for us."

San Francisco power brokers had had enough. Of all the cities in the country, why, city fathers and key business leaders wondered, had theirs been targeted for the most embarrassing civil rights protests above the Mason-Dixon Line? Although many Negro citizens would disagree (particularly those affected by a seeming conspiracy on the part of the city to drive Negro residents across the bay to Oakland), San Francisco thought of itself as perhaps the most racially liberal major city in the country. In the early part of the century, none other than James Weldon Johnson, prominent Negro leader and composer of "Lift Every Voice and Sing"—the song widely regarded as the Negro national anthem—declared that racially speaking, San Francisco was the most hassle-free American city he had ever been in. And because San Francisco was one of the premier tourist destinations in the country, there was that revenue to protect.

So Mayor Shelley moved swiftly from putting out the "fire" at the Sheraton Palace to putting out the "fire" on Auto Row. That same Saturday evening he called a meeting of top local civil rights leaders. In exchange for a two-week moratorium on civil disobedience in the city, Shelley agreed to appoint a committee for the peaceful settlement of all racial disputes by "conciliation and mediation."

But conciliation and mediation were ideas rapidly falling by the wayside for increasing numbers of young Negro and white activists. In fact, 1964 was to be the year that pronounced fragmentation within the civil rights movement really began. This was a watershed year, because that spring the Civil Rights Act was passed, outlawing all forms of segregation in public facilities. Passage of the act was achieved largely as a legacy to the recently assassinated president, John F. Kennedy. As a result, the direct-action front of the civil rights campaign could pull up its tent. The sole remaining theater of war for the civil rights movement in the South was the effort to secure voting rights for Negroes. From that point on, former direct-action activists would divide into different philosophical camps, groping for a way to further advance the lives of American Negroes, while the voting rights activists would raise the ante of risk involved in methods for bringing down the final legal barrier to Negro advancement.

/ "We felt that it was high time for the United States . . . to feel the consequences of its racism," recalled James Forman of Mississippi Freedom Summer. "We could not bring all of white America to Mississippi. But by bringing some of its children as volunteer workers, a new consciousness would feed back into the homes of thousands of white Americans as they worried about their sons and daughters confronting the 'Jungle of Mississippi,' the bigoted sheriffs, the Klan, the vicious White Citizens' Councils. We recognized the result might be great pain and sorrow, but we were not asking the whites to do any more than we had done."

By June 1964, from all over the north, close to 1,000 mostly white volunteers landed in Mississippi. A virtual Who's Who of future activists in the upcoming anti–Vietnam War protests, the hippie movement, and Berkeley's Free Speech Movement—such as Tom Hayden, Abbie Hoffman, and Mario Savio—headed to Mississippi. Fay Stender, the attorney who six years later would discover the legal caveat that would result in the overturning of Huey Newton's manslaughter conviction in the shooting death of Officer John Frey, headed to Mississippi for Freedom Summer. Such volunteers weren't even settled in before the predictable tragic violence struck.

The story of the murder of James Cheney, Andrew Goodman, and Mickey Schwerner just outside of Philadelphia, Mississippi, is a well-known one. As SNCC workers predicted, because the murders involved two whites (Goodman and Schwerner), they attracted far more publicity than they would have had the victims all been Negroes. This fact caused quite a bit of resentment among those Negro workers in SNCC who had vetoed the idea of inviting so many young white volunteers to Mississippi for the summer. Other tensions started brewing as well.

Everyone selected to participate was explicitly required to work under the direction of Negroes who in many instances were less skilled than the northern volunteers at reading, spelling, using typewriters, and so on. For the first time, young white volunteers realized the distance between their ideals and the reality of inter-acting with poor Negroes in the South (something that many of the young Negro volunteers from such colleges as Howard University, Morehouse, and elsewhere also had to confront), as well as working with the proud Negro SNCC volunteers resentful of so many whites joining their efforts. "Suddenly, in an instant, in our town are five or six brightly scrubbed white kids from the North," recalled SNCC veteran Bob Zellner. "Here's Jesse (Negro) labo-riously doing the stencil. Sally (white) from Rutgers comes along and says, 'Here, I type 120 words per minute, let me do it.'" Both the college Negroes in SNCC and the rural southern Negroes who were relatively unskilled feared that their feelings of inferiority (and by extension much of the theoretical basis for white racism) were confirmed whenever the young whites proved more knowledgeable than they.

The fears of white men and feelings of guilt and resentment in Negro women were smoked out as well, when "interracial" romances developed among some of the volunteers, most notably Negro men and white women. Negro women and white men had been sexually active since slavery. And a noticeable minority of Negro women maintained discreet relationships with white men throughout Jim Crow. Such relationships (most notably those dur-ing slavery), resulted in offspring who became categorized as "light-skinned Negroes." As long as such relationships remained discreet, they were acceptable under the rules of slavery, then Jim Crow. But relationships between Negro men and white women, discreet or otherwise, were another matter.

For Negroes and whites alike, Mississippi Freedom Summer smoked out all of the implications of America's racial sickness: IQ fears, sexual fears, white guilt over valuing white lives over Negro lives, guilt among liberal and radical whites over the realization that others classified as white Americans could be evil to a degree they had never before imagined. Although the Freedom Rides, the 1963 violence in Birmingham, the prior deaths of many Negroes trying to register to vote in the rural South, and so many other incidents had vividly dramatized white evil in the South, the execution of Andrew Goodman and Mickey Schwerner was the biggest wake-up call of all for the idealistic northern white students who converged on Mississippi.

At that point, in the eyes of the young whites (particularly the young Jewish activists among them, since both Goodman and Schwerner were Jewish), Mississippi Freedom Summer was transformed from a domestic Peace Corps opportunity into an apparent request to die in a vast concentration camp masquerading as one of the fifty states. That this was true was demonstrated by the reaction of UC Berkeley Campus CORE members, who, on hearing that Cheney, Goodman, and Schwerner were missing, immediately held a sit-in at the office of Cecil Poole, the U.S. district attorney for northern California. Poole was a Negro. But because he was part of the federal government, which at that point was the enemy because it had not provided adequate protection to the missing Cheney, Goodman, and Schwerner, protesters declared that Poole "used to be a Negro," demonstrating the first signs of a habit that would become common among liberals and radicals—connecting being a "real" Negro with one and only one way of seeing the world. Five Campus CORE members were in Mississippi for the summer, and chapter members wanted assurance that the Justice Department would beef up protection for the summer workers. They refused to leave Poole's office in San Francisco until he placed a call to Washington on his private line. Yet after he did this they were still disappointed. "The country was not ready to get angry, even at the blatant murder of three of its most selfless people," wrote Campus CORE newsletter reporter David Friedman. "Like the Germans during Hitler's regime, the American people will not accept their collective responsibility for the atrocities committed in their name."

At that point, advocates of nonviolence, such as Martin Luther King, looked less like disciples of Mahatma Gandhi and more like disciples of British prime minister Neville Chamberlain, the man who had appeased Hitler. Consequently, more than ever before, the stage was set for a generational split within the movement. Older progressive Negroes and their liberal white allies would stick with King and his more moderate coterie. Younger Negroes and their idealistic young white allies would search for a new Premier Negro Leader to shape a concrete direction for their changing attitudes. Nothing dramatized this split more than the emotions wrought after the bodies of Cheney, Goodman, and Schwerner were finally discovered buried in an earthen dam on a farm outside of Philadelphia, Mississippi, on August 4. Although all three workers had been shot, the magnitude of injuries suffered by Cheney was greatest of all. Before receiving the bullet that was to be the coup de grace, Cheney had been savagely beaten, his bones broken. And although the entire nation was shocked by this added fact, it galvanized something of an Old Testament mentality—that is, an inadvertent respect for Judaic principles like "an eye for an eye"— among the young Negro workers as they marched headlong toward their growing militancy.

CORE's national office approached David Dennis, a CORE field secretary who codirected COFO (the official sponsors of Mississippi Freedom Summer) along with Bob Moses, to give a eulogy at the funeral of James Cheney. CORE headquarters, like the headquarters of the NAACP, was proving to be far more moderate than many of its branches. It instructed Dennis to use his eulogy to help cool things off for an angry nation. Dennis agreed. He walked to the pulpit of the Baptist church in Meridian, Mississippi where the funeral was held, but found he couldn't be Christian. "When I got up there . . . I saw little Ben Cheney [James's eleven-year-old brother], [and] things just sort of snapped," recalled Dennis:

To be sitting up there talking about things were going to get better, and we should do it in an easy manner, and with nonviolence and stuff like that [seemed like being in a fantasy world] . . . this country operates, operated then and still operates, on violence . . . it's an eye for an eye, a tooth for a tooth. That's what we respect. So I just stopped and said what I felt . . . there was no need to stand in front of that kid Ben Cheney and lie to him.

The attitude represented by Robert Williams and his Deacons for Defense had finally come full circle and enveloped the same young civil rights workers who had been dazzled by the accomplishments of Martin Luther King during the time Williams was active in Monroe, North Carolina.

The fait accompli to the generational split was just down the road. It would be prompted by what happened later that month in Atlantic City at the Democratic National Convention, when the Mississippi Freedom Democratic Party (MFDP)—the organization created among the newly registered Negro voters—attempted to replace the official Mississippi delegation to the national convention, which had been chosen through racist exclusion. After hearing Fannie Lou Hammer's heartrending account of her life as a sharecropper, it appeared that the national convention might just seat all of the MFDP delegates. But President Johnson wouldn't stand for that. Hubert Humphrey was to be Johnson's running mate. So Johnson blackmailed him into galvanizing support for the compromise proposed by the Credentials Committee, calling for the seating of just two MFDP delegates, to augment the regular Mississippi delegation.

The compromise proposal raised the ire of the Freedom Summer workers and MFDP, not only because the regular Mississippi delegation had been chosen through a segregated system but also because that delegation didn't even pledge unconditional support to the Democratic presidential ticket in November. They threatened to support the Republican nominee. By contrast, the MFDP delegates pledged their unconditional support for the Democratic

presidential ticket. And now here was the Democratic party telling
MFDP that it would rather seat a full slate of racist delegates who
threatened disloyalty, and give MFDP just two at-large seats at the
convention. Moderate national Negro leaders met with Mississippi
Freedom summer workers and the MFDP delegates, to get them
to accept this watered-down remedy to years of voting discrimination. But the realities behind backroom-engineered, back-slapping,
cigar-chomping politics were lost on the workers and delegates in
the thick of their emotions over dangers they had endured, murders they had witnessed, and rural livelihoods they had risked, all
in service to the belief that they could make freedom ring. August
of the previous year, during the March on Washington, Martin
Luther King had demanded that freedom ring, among other places,
"from every hill and molehill in Mississippi. . . ." Now here were
the originators of the March on Washington telling the MFDP
delegates and Freedom Summer volunteers, who had worked so
hard to make that dream come true, about *certain realities.*

"Yes . . . there is a difference between protest and politics,"
Bayard Rustin told them during the caucus meeting. "The former
is based on morality and the latter is based on reality and compromise. . . ." "You're a traitor, Bayard, a traitor!" shouted Mendy
Samstein of SNCC. "Sit down!" To Samstein, Rustin must have
sounded like Neville Chamberlain, newly returned from his meeting with Hitler in 1939. The fact that Rustin had earned his spurs,
enduring beatings in nonviolent demonstrations all over the world
as far back as the 1940s, while Samstein was still in diapers; that if
it hadn't been for the mapping out and advising Rustin did for A.
Philip Randolph and Martin Luther King, there would have been
no foundation for Mississippi Freedom Summer; that it was Rustin
himself who taught Bob Moses—undisputed sage among freedom
workers—the ropes when it came to entering hostile territory and
organizing by himself, was perhaps lost on the young SNCC volunteer. The Premier Negro Leader spoke next.

"I'm not going to counsel you to accept or reject [the com-
promise]," intoned King. "But I want you to know I have talked to
Hubert Humphrey. He promised me there will be a new day in
Mississippi if you accept this proposal. . . ."

MFDP refused the compromise, for a reason best summed up by Fannie Lou Hammer: "We didn't come all this way for no two seats!"

Voting rights remained on the agenda in the South, but with an increasingly militant tone. At the same time, with the passage of the 1964 Civil Rights Act outlawing Jim Crow public facilities, the energy of the rest of the movement shifted north, concentrating on the plight of Negroes in urban ghettos. This was Malcolm X's bailiwick, the place from which he had continuously heckled nonviolent southern movement workers. Malcolm symbolized that the North was a different animal from the South. Harlem, his base, was the most renowned Negro community in the world. Malcolm's background spoke leagues about the northern street corner blues: he had once been a street hustler, hobnobbing with the same types of people Huey Newton enjoyed. And although by 1964 Malcolm had broken with the nation of Islam and no longer preached racial hatred, in the eyes of most Americans he still symbolized an approach to the rights of Negroes that was 180 degrees different from that of the civil rights establishment.

As a result of what they saw and heard about during Mississippi Freedom Summer and the treatment of MFDP at the Democratic National Convention, young northern whites began to understand, even encourage, increasing militancy among Negroes, as the movement headed north. "A new leadership is emerging which reflects the aspirations of the urban Negro," wrote Charles Leinenweber of Berkeley's Campus CORE. "Yesterday's militants—like King and Rustin—are the new Uncle Toms. . . ." In the same issue of the Campus CORE newsletter, Jack Weinberg declared, "An Uncle Tom is a Negro who has the ear of the white power structure."

Of course, Negroes who were educated and middle class usually had the ear of the white power structure. They also supported organizations like the NAACP, the Urban League, and, increasingly, SCLC—particularly in 1964, after Martin Luther King earned the imprimatur of the Nobel Peace Prize. Although educated, middle-class Negroes were not always of one mind, as evidenced by the petty squabbling among Roy Wilkins, Martin

Luther King, and Whitney Young of the Urban League, they could call up the most prominent white philanthropists and politicians and get an audience. It was educated, middle-class Negro leaders who stood up at the Mississippi Freedom Democratic caucus at the Democratic National Convention, urging acceptance of compromise on all those poor rural Negroes who had been brought into the system by all those young Negro and white college volunteers. The Negro middle-class establishment looked like sellouts, while the poorer Negroes looked like noble heroes. So, naturally, as the movement began casting its main thrust northward, these same young, idealistic Negro and white college students sought out the poorest and most disenfranchised northern Negroes they could find, to match the nobility they attached to the poor rural Negroes in Mississippi.

If the men in those ghettos who sang the street corner blues didn't have jobs, then the young white activists newly returned from Mississippi were certain it was *always* because there were no jobs available. The fact that the plight of the urban poor in the ghettos was a complex mix of lack of opportunity and lack of desire on the part of many such poor to pursue opportunities that did exist was lost on the young idealistic whites. They knew nothing of the young Negroes on the streets of Oakland, for example, who ridiculed anyone serious about a college education. If those same denizens of the street corner drank all day long, the young idealistic, guilt-ridden whites were certain that they were *always* drowning their blues, because of the lack of opportunity. If they burglarized homes or cut each other up, it was explained the same way. So when, in the same year as Mississippi Freedom Summer, Huey Newton got into an argument at a party in Oakland with a guy named Odell Lee and ended up stabbing him repeatedly with a steak knife, Newton was more than just a cunning, intellectual street brawler. He was one of the poor, downtrodden, misunderstood residents of the ghetto.

Newton's knifing of Odell Lee would earn him his first substantial jail sentence. Lee had no weapon during the altercation. Choosing to represent himself at trial, Newton was convicted of felonious assault with a deadly weapon and sentenced to six months in prison. But Newton realized the tenor of the times: "A jury of my peers would have understood the situation and exonerated me," he insisted. "But the jurors of Alameda County [where Oakland is located] come out of the big houses in the hills to pass judgment on the people whom they feel threaten their 'peace.'" That Odell Lee was also Negro and a resident of the city's flatlands, rather than white and a resident of the big houses in the hills and thus not a member of the jurors' race and class whom they needed to protect, made no difference to Newton. That had he appeared in court with a lawyer, rather than given jurors the impression that he was beyond needing representation, things might have turned out differently, didn't occur to Newton. That a jury of twelve Negroes from the flatlands—a jury Newton certainly deserved— could just as easily have found him guilty of felonious assault with a deadly weapon was unimaginable to Newton. In this new day, every Negro in the proverbial ghetto had an excuse for every criminal act he or she committed, even if it was committed against another Negro: it was the result of suffering under oppression.

The times, they were a-changin'. So when Newton was sent off to Santa Rita—a minimum-security county prison farm—to serve his six-month sentence, and a Negro inmate tried to prevent him from dipping in the mess hall line for more than the allotted share of food given to every inmate, Newton could feel comfortable reacting as he did: "I called him for protecting the oppressor's interests and smashed him with a steel tray."

While Newton was proceeding through the criminal justice system, the fall semester rolled in on college campuses in the Bay Area. Fresh from either participating in or closely following the events related to Mississippi Freedom Summer, many white college students redoubled their efforts to improve race relations locally. Students for a Democratic Society (SDS) held its first meeting in the Bay Area on September 28, 1964, at UC Berkeley, and informed students of its plans to organize deprived residents of East and West Oakland the following summer. That same fall, students were solicited for door-to-door canvassing in Bay Area neighborhoods, to try to prevent passage of a constitutional amendment that would overturn the Rumford Fair Housing Act, which had been approved the previous year by the California legislature. In October and November, Campus CORE began to gather statistics regarding the scarcity of nonwhite waiters, waitresses, and cashiers at designated first-class restaurants in Oakland (most notably a prestigious dining area known as Jack London Square), in preparation for demonstrations that would begin that winter. And the Ad Hoc Committee to End Discrimination continued recruiting students for its demonstration campaign against the *Oakland Tribune*—already begun by the end of the summer—protesting the low numbers of nonwhite employees at that newspaper.

By now, many establishment whites in the Bay Area had had enough of the frenzy of civil rights activity there. The first signals of their impatience had come that summer, at the July trials for those arrested in the demonstrations against the Cadillac dealership on San Francisco's Auto Row. Although civil rights demonstrations had opened the door to hundreds of jobs for nonwhites, the courts decided to send demonstrators a strong message: causing widespread unrest in the South was fine, but not in the urban area that thought of itself as the nation's most liberal. Negroes were systematically excluded from the juries that heard evidence against the demonstrators. Dr. Thomas Burbridge, leader of the Auto Row demonstration, was sentenced to nine months in prison, leading James Farmer, national director of CORE, to observe, "As far as the civil rights sentences in San Francisco are concerned, San Francisco is the worst city in the country." Wrote *San Francisco Chronicle* columnist Art Hoppe: "Never have the injustices of our courts been so flagrantly obvious."

In Oakland that fall, establishment whites attempted to stifle civil rights activities altogether, by pressuring UC Berkeley administrators into preventing students from setting up recruitment tables on campus. Most notable in this attempt was California U.S. Senator and *Oakland Tribune* publisher Bill Knowland, who grew increasingly irritated over the magnitude of demonstrations against his newspaper—demonstrations sponsored by the Ad Hoc Committee to End Discrimination. A brick walkway just outside the university's Sather Gate, measuring approximately sixty by twenty-six feet, was being used by all campus groups to recruit students for political activities. It was the best place from which to recruit civil rights demonstrators, volunteers to circulate petitions seeking protection for the state's fair-housing legislation, and volunteers to work in Mississippi the following summer. Since demonstrators were arrested every day that demonstrations took place at the *Tribune*, the university realized it was facing possible charges of aiding and abetting illegal activities on the part of its students. Administrators panicked. The first thing they attempted was selling, renting, and leasing the space outside Sather Gate to the city of Berkeley. But the city wouldn't go for it.

Eventually, the university decided it had no alternative but to extend to the strip of walkway outside Sather Gate the same ban on political activity that existed on the rest of the campus. On September 14 a letter was circulated by the dean of students, outlining the university's intention to ban political activities on the walkway. The following night, a meeting was held by students representing Campus CORE, Friends of SNCC, the W. E. B. Du Bois Club, the Young People's Socialist League, the Young Socialists Alliance, Campus Women for Peace, Slate, the Young Democrats, and the Young Republicans—all organizations that had set up tables on the sixty- by twenty-six-foot brick walkway. The students decided to resist the ban and continue their political activities on the walkway. They did so, and eight students were suspended.

Protests immediately erupted. Students active in the civil rights organizations set the tone and tactics of the protests. The student organizations banned together, calling themselves the Free Speech Movement (FSM). Campus CORE's Jack Weinberg became one of the leaders (Weinberg would later coin one of the most memorable phrases of the 1960s: "Don't trust anyone over thirty"). One day in October, Weinberg was busy on the banned brick walkway soliciting funds for CORE, when the university had him arrested. Angry students immediately converged on the squad car Weinberg was placed in, preventing it from moving. Approximately 2,000 students gathered as Mario Savio, president of Campus Friends of SNCC, mounted the top of the trapped squad car and galvanized the cause. "I spent the summer in Mississippi,"

Savio would later say in explanation of his motives. "I witnessed tyranny. I saw groups of men in the minority working their will on the majority. Then I got back here and found the University preventing us from . . . getting people to go to Mississippi to help."

Six weeks later the university's Board of Regents finally gave in to the student demands and rescinded the ban on political activities on the walkway. However, still frightened of the potential wrath of powerful people such as Bill Knowland, the university insisted on its right to discipline students engaged in soliciting for activities resulting in off-campus arrests—in other words, anyone participating in demonstrations against the *Oakland Tribune*. By November it looked as though the university's concession would end the student revolt. But the school still insisted on disciplining Savio and the other leaders of the October demonstrations. At that point, even students who had been indifferent to the Free Speech Movement accused the university of overkill, and the movement was born anew, bigger than ever.

Savio and his cohorts began organizing the students for a demonstration tactic that would be used by campus protest groups of all persuasions for years to come: occupying the university administration building. Wednesday, December 2, at noon, approximately 1,000 students marched into Sproul Hall as folksinger queen Joan Baez strummed a guitar and sang "We Shall Overcome." Secretaries and administrators abandoned ship. The demonstrators set up a message center, commissary, temporary infirmary, recreation center, study hall, rooftop lookout posts, classrooms, a walkie-talkie network, and a speaker's rostrum. Students snuggled down for the night in sleeping bags, as Mario Savio issued the statement, "We intend to stay in here for a long time."

At midnight, California governor Edmund Brown, Sr., instructed state police to remove the students, by force if necessary. At 3 A.M. Chancellor Edward W. Strong, accompanied by a police lieutenant, forced his way through the mass of student humanity inside Sproul Hall and read a statement to the students that concluded with the plea, "Please go!" When the students didn't budge, 600 state police officers and matrons moved in to begin the largest mass arrest of college students in American history, effectively opening the door to a new era and propelling Berkeley into the epicenter of the 1960s.

Officers dragged 814 demonstrators off to jail, which turned out to be Santa Rita, the county's minimum-security prison farm. Joe Blum was among the last group of sit-in demonstrators arrested. At about 7 A.M. he was handcuffed and hauled off by bus to Santa Rita. Blum was sitting next to the bus window, exhausted from the vigil, when, as the bus pulled into the prison compound, he heard an amazed voice screaming at him from the prison yard. "Hey, Joe!" the voice said. "How many of you motherfuckers are coming out here?" It was Huey Newton, still at Santa Rita serving his six-month sentence for assaulting Odell Lee, and still remembering, to Joe's astonishment, Joe's face and name from their days at Oakland City College when Huey had held the doors on campus open for Joe and other white students. The sight of Joe and the mass of students confirmed to Newton more than ever before that, indeed, the times were a-changin'.

4

A Large Cat Leaps
Out of Alabama

BY THE TIME "AULD LANG SYNE" RANG OUT 1964 AND ushered in 1965, Joe Blum and the other student protesters from UC Berkeley were no longer at Santa Rita prison. Huey Newton remained, although he would be released later that year. The student demonstrators at UC Berkeley were winning the Free Speech Movement. Their action caught the imaginations of students nationwide and opened the door to the liberalization of rules at college campuses across the nation. It also caused a migration to Berkeley of young whites from around the country who were disenchanted with the nation's establishment and anxious to be in the vicinity of the campus that symbolized their dissatisfaction to America as a whole. During the upcoming summer, heading south to engage in "domestic Peace Corps work" would remain a popular activity among UC Berkeley students. Branching out into similar involvement in northern ghettos would become popular too, as SDS began its program to organize ghetto residents in East and West Oakland.

The Free Speech Movement also paved the way for a second cause that would consume the energy of white students and become even more popular among them than working in civil rights. That spring, UC Berkeley became one of the first sites of teach-ins against America's involvement in the Vietnam War. The teach-ins both expanded the base of student activism and provided an outlet for white students who felt either uncomfortable interacting with Negroes or unwanted in the quest for racial justice, because of the increasing militancy of young Negroes.

Such militancy was getting a firmer grasp on young Negroes in the Bay Area. By the time Huey Newton emerged from prison later that year, an organization called the Revolutionary Action Movement (RAM) had established a chapter in Oakland. Bobby Seale, Newton's friend from Oakland City College, had joined the chapter. RAM was a small organization whose members looked up to Robert Williams, naming him honorary chairman. Williams was still in exile from the United States after fleeing Monroe, North Carolina, to escape kidnapping charges. From Cuba, and then Red China, he continued to publish *The Crusader*, the newsletter he had started before leaving Monroe. He also began a radio broadcast from Cuba called "Radio Free Dixie." Williams became ever more strident in both media. While John F. Kennedy was president, issues of *The Crusader* featured passages reading, "The slick John Kennedy gang is operating one of the greatest sham governments in the entire world." Turning around the racist stereotypes whites held of Negroes and using the stereotypes on whites, Williams described the United States as "a jungle filled with wild beasts and savages presided over by an impotent witchdoctor, Slick John Kennedy." He urged Negroes across America to engage in armed revolt.

Founded in 1963, RAM saw itself as taking up Williams's challenge—hence its name, meant to distinguish it from all the other militant groups who huddled together and talked of revolution and yet did nothing truly revolutionary. Acting on their commitment to move rather than sit around and theorize, in February 1965 three East Coast RAM members were arrested and charged with conspiring to blow up the Statue of Liberty, the Liberty Bell, and the Washington Monument. But the RAM members in Oakland, who were mainly students at Oakland City College, were really no different from their counterparts in other militant organizations. They talked about the oppression of the white man, but did nothing so extreme as to plan bombings of public buildings. At the time, most young militants weren't ready for that type of action, which irritated Huey Newton, who was always ready to "throw down," always ready to take a risk. RAM didn't like Newton any more than he liked RAM. Both Newton and Seale were considered too street. Soon they dropped out of RAM and continued searching for something they felt was more meaningful to the lives of the "brothers on the block."

In reality, all the young Negroes who were dissatisfied with the concept of nonviolence felt rudderless. These included the people Newton derided as well as the man they had looked up to since the beginning of the 1960s—Malcolm X. As 1965 began, Malcolm had just returned from his pilgrimage to Mecca. He was still sharpening his new theories in the new organization he had started, the Organization of African American Unity (OAAU). The young people who had looked up to him since the start of the decade still consulted him, even as he was getting his bearings straight. He was also feeling the pressure of death threats from the Nation of Islam. Most prominent among the disenchanted young Negroes looking up to Malcolm were the members of SNCC, which would play the most important role of any organization in shaping and directing the growing dissatisfaction of young Negroes after Malcolm was assassinated. SNCC's journey to that crucial role was born from its continuing voter registration activities in the Deep South.

Although SNCC still had a bitter taste in its mouth from the game of political horsetrading it had been encouraged to play at the 1964 Democratic National Convention, the organization still had faith in the ballot. It was determined to find a way for Negroes at the grassroots to use the ballot to bypass the handful of men in the Democratic National Convention's smoke-filled rooms. SNCC found it repulsive that the regular civil rights establishment was willing to play the games of such men. So SNCC did its best to be the antithesis of Martin Luther King's SCLC, its principal rival in southern activism.

As SNCC's alienation from leaders such as King grew, its

members searched for a way to incorporate the teachings of Malcolm X into their work. In December 1964 they took a group of Mississippi youths to Harlem so Malcolm X could speak with them about the interconnectedness of their struggle with the Negro's struggle in the North, as well as with the struggles of oppressed people throughout the world. In February 1965, just weeks before his assassination, Malcolm X was invited by SNCC to speak in Selma, Alabama, where it had an ongoing voter registration drive in progress.

By the time Malcolm spoke in Selma, the Negro community of that town had grown impatient with the lack of progress in the SNCC program. That January they had invited SCLC to lead a new registration drive, although SNCC remained active as well. The registration campaign still faced constant resistance from Selma's white establishment, who rebuffed Negroes every time they showed up to register at the Dallas County Courthouse. Often they were arrested or beaten, sometimes by Selma's notorious sheriff, Jim Clark. Clark's viciousness was caught on national television when he was confronted by the Reverend C. T. Vivian, a King lieutenant. One day Vivian led a line of potential voters up Selma's courthouse steps. Clark and his deputies shooed them away with the display of repulsion and disdain a person would demonstrate if a herd of cattle showed up at the dinner table. Vivian led the potential voters right back up the steps, all the while disparaging Clark and his deputies for refusing to treat Negroes as human beings. Clark decided he finally had enough after Vivian followed him back up the courthouse steps, excoriating him with the words, "You're a racist, the same way Hitler was a racist!" At that point, Jim Clark turned around and punched C. T. Vivian so hard that Clark required treatment for a fractured bone in his left hand. Vivid scenes of the incident on national television pounded one more nail into the coffin of nonviolence as a philosophy among Negroes.

By the month of March, SCLC made plans to hold one of its infamous marches. As an organization, SNCC refused to participate in the march, both because it was growing increasingly militant and because it thought of SCLC as built around the worship and elevation of Martin Luther King above and beyond any real commitment to people at the grassroots level. Only John Lewis and three other SNCC members participated in the march, and they did so as individuals rather than as representatives of SNCC. Lewis, in fact, was asked to lead the march while King remained in Atlanta. The outcome of the march drove even more nails into the coffin of nonviolence.

Lewis and the rest of the marchers left Selma, heading for the Edmund Pettus Bridge just outside of town, only to encounter hundreds of Alabama police and state troopers waiting on the bridge with billy clubs, police dogs, and cattle prods. Some of the troopers were on horseback. National television cameras were at the ready to record the event. The troopers warned the marchers to cease and desist. The marchers remained on the bridge. They knelt and prayed. When the marchers got up, the troopers waded into them, attacking them with billy clubs, cattle prods, and tear gas, and trampling them with horses. "I felt like it was the last demonstration, the last protest on my part, like I was going to take my last breath from the tear gas," recalled John Lewis, who sustained a skull fracture. "I saw people rolling, heard people screaming and hollering . . . we were beaten back down the streets of Selma." The nation watched in horror. ABC television cut in on a program about Nazi racism to show viewers the carnage in Alabama.

Predictably, the shocking scenes prompted a second march from Selma, this time led by Martin Luther King and attended by supporters of nonviolence of all colors from throughout the nation, including the wife of a U.S. senator. But as if in a symbolic show of respect for the first marchers, the march would proceed no farther than the Edmund Pettus Bridge. Because of a federal court order prohibiting the march, King had agreed ahead of time to march as far as the bridge and then turn around. This action would occasion an even greater riff between SNCC (which would derisively refer to the second march as Turn Around Tuesday) and leaders like King. The militancy of SNCC workers would be sharpened even more after what happened next.

The first martyr of the Selma registration movement had been a young Negro named Jimmy Lee Jackson. During a February nighttime rally in support of a jailed voter registration worker, Jackson's grandfather had been physically attacked by Alabama state troopers trying to prevent the rally. When Jimmy came to his grandfather's aid to try and take him to the hospital, he too was savagely beaten, then shot at close range by the troopers, only to die one week later. Jackson died only days after Malcolm X was assassinated in New York City, which may have had something to do with the fact that the nation virtually ignored his death. However, the nation didn't ignore what happened to a white worker right after the second Selma march.

Jim Reeb, a white Unitarian minister who had answered Martin Luther King's call for thousands to join him in that second march, went out to eat with two other white Unitarian ministers at the conclusion of Turn Around Tuesday. One of the ministers was from Berkeley. On returning from their meal, all three ministers were physically attacked by white racists who were angry about the civil rights activities in Selma. Reeb received the worst blows of all and, days later, died of his head injuries. The entire civil rights movement mourned his death. Both President Johnson and Vice President Humphrey placed calls to the Reeb family. SNCC workers such as Stokely Carmichael grew furious at the difference between the nation's reaction to Reeb's death and its lack of reaction to the death of Jimmy Lee Jackson.

Two days after Reeb's death, President Johnson appeared on national television and made one of his most famous civil rights speeches, to introduce a voting rights bill designed to strike down all the archaic registration laws and applications used for so long to keep Negroes off of southern registration rolls. At the end of his speech, Johnson intoned, "It is not just Negroes, but all of us who must overcome the crippling legacy of bigotry and injustice. And we *shall* overcome." The speech brought tears to the eyes of Martin Luther King, confirming that perhaps his belief in nonviolence hadn't been in vain.

But those were hardly the sentiments of SNCC workers, especially Stokely Carmichael. Six days after Reeb's death, the federal judge who had placed a ban on any march from Selma to

Montgomery lifted his ban, leading to King's last great march—a third one from Selma, this time all the way to Montgomery, cherished by many as the most glorious march of the entire movement. A bevy of national celebrities performed at a rally along the route. At the culmination of the march, thousands cheered one of King's most memorable speeches on the steps of the state capitol in Montgomery. Although they participated in the march, most SNCC workers demonstrated far less enthusiasm. Because SNCC had a plan.

SNCC decided that after the Selma to Montgomery march it would organize Negro residents in Lowndes County, Alabama (which was along the march route). Lowndes County's population was overwhelmingly black. And, still licking its wounds from the SCLC takeover of its voter registration efforts in Selma, but realizing that a new day was about to arrive with the easing of voter registration restrictions via the Voting Rights Act, SNCC was anxious to select a locale in which the conditions among Negroes were abominable. As the Selma to Montgomery march wended its way through Lowndes County, Carmichael recorded the names and addresses of a few of the approximately 12,000 Negroes in a total county population of 15,000. Ninety percent of the county land was owned by eighty-six white families. Over half of the Negro population lived below the poverty line. And at the beginning of 1965, not one Negro in Lowndes County was registered to vote.

SNCC moved into Lowndes County the day after the murder of one more white civil rights worker shocked the nation. It happened in Lowndes County. Viola Luizzo, a Detroit housewife who took part in the historic Selma to Montgomery march, drove some marchers back to Selma after the march was over. Returning to Montgomery, Luizzo was traveling with a Negro man sitting next to her in the front seat. Seeing this, four Klansmen pulled alongside Luizzo's vehicle in their car and shot Viola Luizzo twice in the face.

Before the murder of Luizzo, Lowndes County had developed a reputation for subjugation and brutality against Negroes that brought shivers to Negroes and whites even in the rest of the state.

That such an archaic situation could exist in a county so close to Montgomery, ten years after the success of the bus boycott led by Premier Negro Leader Martin Luther King, was difficult to believe. That the notorious county was also so close to Tuskegee, the place that had been home base to earlier Premier Negro Leader Booker T. Washington—where his college was located, built by former slaves, including a veterinary school and very impressive farm that had served as the base of the brilliant Negro scientist George Washington Carver—seemed ironic.

But perhaps it was fitting. SNCC had entered Lowndes County and joined forces with John Hulett, who, just before the Selma to Montgomery march, had become the first Negro registered to vote in the county. Hulett then became a founding organizer and chairman of the church-based Lowndes County Christian Movement for Human Rights. Ten months into its organizing efforts with Hulett, SNCC workers would transform the Christian movement into an independent political party called the Lowndes County Freedom Organization (LCFO), with the goal of seizing political power in the county. This was a symbolic transfer of the keys in more ways than one. It symbolized that the movement was no longer to be based in the church. It would now be secular. And although Hulett would become LCFO chairman too, he would share power with Carmichael and the others in SNCC who detested the singing and praying and carrying on in the church. The decision to launch the LCFO was made after SNCC researchers discovered a little-known Alabama law enabling groups to organize independent political parties on a countywide basis. SNCC's decision to complement its voter registration drive by establishing an independent political party in Lowndes County would have far-reaching consequences for Negroes throughout the country. Ultimately, it would mean that south central Alabama could be recorded in history as the birthplace of three different movements used to guide the lives of all African Americans at one time or another.

At the turn of the century, there had been Booker T. Washington's notion to accommodate the Jim Crow laws, which rapidly reempowered southern whites and marked the end of the liberal reconstruction period. Washington turned his Tuskegee base into an example of how Negroes could learn the value of property ownership and gain vocational skills, under his theory that if they took what they learned from Tuskegee and implemented the lesson throughout the South, Jim Crow would eventually come tumbling down. In the mid-1950s came the idea for King's nonviolent resistance to Jim Crow, precipitated by the peaceful desegregation of Montgomery buses and culminating first in the Civil Rights Act of 1964 and then in the Voting Rights Act of 1965. And now in the mid-1960s, when Negroes were growing impatient with the concept of nonviolence, this same area was to be the birthplace of a new philosophical and cultural dictum. And it would be the result of what SNCC was doing in Lowndes County.

At an SNCC staff meeting in November 1965, SNCC worker Courtland Cox, who had been working in Lowndes County, decided to illustrate SNCC's aims in that area on the blackboard. According to James Forman he wrote on the board that SNCC was trying to "get power for black people." From that staff meeting onward, increasing numbers of SNCC workers began using the word *black* to describe Negroes, initiating the first sparks of a shift in the name used to describe Americans of sub-Saharan African descent, which would sweep the entire nation by the end of the 1960s. The workers also increasingly referred to the concept of power for black people, particularly once they started their independent party, the LCFO, in January 1966, and began feverishly organizing potential voters for the party's May 1966 primary election slate.

Talk of power for black people accelerated among SNCC workers, particularly as 1966 began, when one more black person was murdered, this time an SNCC worker. Sammy Younge, Jr., was a student at Booker T. Washington's Tuskegee Institute. He had only recently joined SNCC when one day, on stopping at a white-owned gasoline station, he was murdered by the attendant for trying to use the "white" toilet. The murder of Sammy Younge occurred a year and a half after the passage of the Civil Rights Act outlawing Jim Crow public facilities nationwide. James Forman was particularly shaken by Younge's murder, no doubt because eight years before passage of the Civil Rights Act, before there was an SNCC, Forman, emboldened by the Montgomery bus boycott in progress at the time, stopped for gas on a trip through the South and defied Jim Crow by using the "white" toilet at the station. Although the white attendant yelled and glowered at him, Forman had gotten away unharmed. And now when it was legal to ignore this southern tradition, here was a new young SNCC worker dead for doing the same thing Forman had gotten away with. "For myself, Sammy's murder marked the final end of any patience with nonviolence—even as a tactic," concluded Forman. The executive secretary of SNCC was officially on board with the new ideology SNCC was developing and driving like a fast locomotive through the entire movement.

But SNCC chairman John Lewis, who along with Bob Moses probably held the record among SNCC workers for withstanding physical beatings at the hands of southern racists, was still a loyal believer in nonviolence. By the spring of 1966, Lewis, who had entered SNCC as a seminary student, was among the last of the religious-based SNCC workers: those who not only stuck with the concept of nonviolence but also still believed that blacks could work with whites to advance the national racially. By the spring of 1966, Lewis was far outnumbered by the nonreligious-based SNCC members such as Forman, who had been executive secretary of SNCC almost from the beginning; Stokely Carmichael, who gained increasing responsibility within SNCC after graduating from Howard University in 1964; and others such as Courtland Cox, Cleveland Sellers, and Ivanhoe Donaldson. By this time, Bob Moses had voluntarily assumed an ever-lowering profile within SNCC, because of the awe others had held him in since 1962. So self-conscious had Moses become about the aura attached to him that he temporarily changed his name from Bob Moses to Bob Parris.

By May 1966, Stokely Carmichael, field director of the Lowndes County campaign, was riding high within SNCC. He and the workers under his direction had increasingly popularized use of the word *black* as they galvanized the black residents of Lowndes

County. They increasingly talked up the idea of black people seizing power in the county by voting for the Lowndes County Freedom Organization. They also figured out the solution to an obstacle they foresaw to many blacks in the county recognizing their party's slate on a ballot.

Even as late as 1966, many of the black people in Lowndes County could not read. But with the signing of the Voting Rights Act in August 1965, that was no longer a problem when a person went to register. So LCFO needed a way for illiterate voters to distinguish its candidates from those of the regular white-dominated state Democratic organization. The regular organization already had its symbol, which was a white rooster. To distinguish LCFO candidates from the candidates represented by the white rooster, Carmichael and his organizers chose the symbol of the black panther.

The LCFO effort energized SNCC like it had not been energized since Mississippi Freedom Summer, but now with a different aim. SNCC workers were relieved that the long process of organizing in Lowndes County would not culminate in the need to bargain with powerful whites. The Lowndes County campaign was designed to be a demonstration project—a demonstration of how black citizens could empower themselves without giving white people a second thought. Even the white workers within SNCC became suspect, simply because they were white.

The new mood among SNCC workers prompted drastic changes in the organization at its annual meeting that May in Kingston Springs, Tennessee. The struggle was on between those who still believed in nonviolent interracial cooperation and those who wanted to turn SNCC into an all-black organization stressing black self-empowerment. It wasn't so much that those who believed that SNCC should become all black hated the whites in SNCC; they appreciated their support, but thought it best that they organize to change attitudes in white communities. Black people, the all-black faction felt, needed to see they could do everything for themselves. This was the mood sweeping young blacks across the nation, now that they believed nonviolence was obsolete, now that it appeared the direct-action battles in the South were over.

With the end of southern civil rights campaigns, no longer would the lack of opportunity among so many blacks be seen primarily through the image of inferior southern environments. It would now be symbolized by the plight of those in crowded, desperate conditions in the urban North and West. The method of calling attention to such plights was to riot. Riots in places like Harlem had already made news the summer of 1964. But they garnered attention in the most frightening manner of all in August 1965, the day after the Voting Rights Act was signed into law, rendering the nonviolent southern civil rights campaign extinct. And of all places for that to occur, it happened in one of the "ghettos" that didn't look at all like what was deemed a ghetto in cities like Chicago and New York. Unrest of a previously unheard of magnitude occurred in a black Los Angeles neighborhood filled with bungalows. The Watts section of Los Angeles exploded in the largest, most unsettling racial disturbance the nation had yet seen.

Although the vast majority of Watts residents didn't partici- pate in the upheaval, it started in the manner typical of riots in the 1960s—with a police incident. Los Angeles police officers stopped a black youth and accused him of driving drunk. The youth's mother and a crowd gathered at the spot. More police officers arrived. The crowd and police exchanged angry words, rocks flew, and the unrest escalated. Youth gangs roamed the streets of Watts at night, pelting anyone in their path, black or white, with bricks and bottles. They shattered windows of stores, set a mobile televi- sion station wagon aflame, torched entire blocks, and turned back fire fighters who attempted to put out blazes. They sacked stores, and fired guns at many of the 900 police officers attempting to squelch the disturbance. Whites in the area were beaten. Black comedian-activist Dick Gregory was wounded in the leg by snipers as he attempted to walk the streets and help restore peace. The unrest spread over a four-day period across a twenty-four-square- mile area of South Los Angeles. Ten thousand National Guards- men were called in, and when calm was finally restored, almost thirty people (mostly black) were dead, hundreds of people were wounded, more than 1,800 were jailed, and property damage totaled over $100 million.

After the Watts upheaval, King was increasingly discredited. He was even booed on a visit to Watts. Outside the South, particularly among young blacks, Malcolm had been the man. But Malcolm had just died. Someone was needed to replace Malcolm, to cajole, inspire, stand on King's philosophical left, perhaps even replace King altogether. But who would that be? Earlier Premier Negro Leader Adam Clayton Powell, Jr., the man King had deposed by the close of the 1950s, saw an opportunity to fill that void. On the elevation of the Democrats to power in the White House with the election of Kennedy, Powell had already risen to become the most powerful black politician in the country. In King's celebrated days, Powell exercised tremendous influence in Washington as chairman of the House Education and Labor Committee. While King seared the hearts and minds of the nation with his speeches and direct-action campaigns, Powell was busy moving the legislation proposed as a response to King's activities. Powell had remained jealous of King throughout King's heyday. And now that King was on the ropes, particularly with younger blacks, Powell was taking advantage of the situation, denouncing King. He even drew a verbal line around Harlem, his political base, and told King to stay away.

But Powell could not return to his earlier position. For one thing, he wasn't young enough. For another, with the budding emphasis on blackness, Powell, who hardly looked black, was no longer physically suitable to be a Premier Negro Leader. Another factor against Powell was that, by now, black activists outside the corridors of power were far more popular among young blacks and their white allies than were blacks who had the ear of the white establishment. Members of Berkeley's Campus CORE made this clear in their 1964 newsletter, deriding politicians such as Powell with this observation: "Machine politicians . . . use Uncle Toms and opportunists like [Congressman William] Dawson and [Congressman Adam Clayton] Powell to identify their interests with those of the Negro—while they are his main enemy in the Northern ghetto." The zealous youthful Campus CORE members were wrong to call Powell an Uncle Tom. An opportunist, yes. But Powell wasn't an Uncle Tom. He was a political horsetrader par excellence.

As an organization SNCC had always been loath to develop one leader because it so hated the cult of personality it had long perceived surrounding Martin Luther King, but the increasing popularity of Stokely Carmichael was about to change that. Riding the crest of what he and his coworkers had accomplished in Lowndes County with the introduction of the word *black* in referring to Negroes, the introduction of the idea that blacks should seize power, and the representation of that new thrust through the symbol of the black panther, Carmichael defeated John Lewis at the Kingston Springs meeting and became chairman of SNCC.

In addition to being young and an activist rather than a politician like Powell, Carmichael was dark-skinned. He looked like a Nigerian prince. As well as introducing the replacement of the word *Negro* with *black*, Carmichael and his SNCC cohorts had begun wearing their naturally kinky hair unaltered and covering their entire scalps, rather than cutting it almost completely off and greasing down the little bit that remained, or processing (straightening) it, the two traditional styles among black men up to then. Carmichael also began to wear sunglasses even when the sun didn't shine brightly in his face. Increasingly, Stokely Carmichael, who was only twenty-five himself, seemed to be the man young blacks in particular were looking for to rival Martin Luther King. Carmichael's elevation to the forefront, along with elevation of the new ideas being presented by SNCC, would be completed in June 1966 during the last major southern march of the civil rights movement.

It all started with the iconoclastic James Meredith, who had become famous four years earlier for integrating the University of Mississippi. By the summer of 1966, Meredith, for a reason known only to him, decided that a march against fear was needed through the heart of Mississippi. It was as though he had been in a time warp, unaware that the nation was hardly fazed anymore by civil rights marches. Among black civil rights organizations, SNCC hated the idea of marches most of all, as it had demonstrated in its attitude toward the marches in Selma. It was as if Meredith had never heard of Mississippi Freedom Summer, when thousands of Mississippi blacks were encouraged to give up their fear and register to vote. Meredith was determined to stage his march, even without the support of a single civil rights group. He began his march on June 6 with just four supporters. On the second day, he was ambushed and wounded by an unemployed white hardware clerk waiting for him in the bushes along the highway. The photo of Meredith struggling in a pool of blood would be splashed across the nation, causing the entire civil rights apparatus to rally to his cause, most notably SNCC, of all groups. The organizations decided to complete Meredith's March Against Fear.

Because Meredith had been ambushed, Stokely Carmichael insisted that a group of black men who had armed themselves against the KKK in Bogalusa, Louisiana in 1964, giving themselves the name Deacons for Defense and Justice (similar to Robert Williams's North Carolina group), serve as security for the march. But groups like the Deacons for Defense and Justice were still anathema to civil rights leaders like the NAACP's Roy Wilkins. By 1966, Wilkins, who had always been more conservative than King, was so discredited among increasingly militant young blacks that they derisively referred to him as "Boy Wilkins." On hearing SNCC's demand, Wilkins and Whitney Young of the Urban League pulled their organizations out of the March Against Fear.

Now only CORE, SCLC, and SNCC remained as sponsors. Realizing that the media would be there in full force, SNCC had decided to take control of the march's tone and tenor for the purpose of introducing the entire nation to its new thrust. Carmichael called one of SNCC's most effective organizers, Willie Ricks, to Memphis, Tennessee—where the march would originate and then head into Mississippi—to help him with the plan. Ricks was at SNCC headquarters in Atlanta. Before leaving to join Carmichael, Ricks asked James Forman for his opinion on an idea. "Suppose when I get over to Mississippi and I'm speaking, I start hollering for Black Power?" In other words, why not shorten the idea of gaining power for black people into one neat slogan? Forman had been on board with his new trend since the beginning of the year. He told Ricks to go ahead.

When the march began, Carmichael, Floyd McKissick (the newly elected head of CORE), and Martin Luther King linked arms at the front of the line. Carmichael debuted for the national press part of the "uniform" that was to become standard issue for the black militant. It would feature his innovative hairstyle, which would later be named "the natural" (and, later still, be turned into the longer "Afro"), as well as the black sunglasses he was wearing, in contrast to the rest of the people toward the front of the line. Cameras clicked a photograph of the three linked leaders. King's facial expression ominously stated, "After this march, all appearances of unity in the movement shall cease." SNCC worker Cleveland Sellers had already sent Ricks and a scouting troop of twenty other SNCC workers ahead of the pack. Their mission was to go to the same old rickety wooden and tin-roofed plantation huts from which black and white SNCC volunteers had done their best to cajole black sharecroppers into registering to vote during Mississippi Freedom Summer. They were supposed to knock on those same doors and introduce those sharecroppers to Black Power. After completing their mission, and returning to the main body of the march, Ricks reported, "We ought to drop it now. The people are ready." SNCC's strongest base in Mississippi was Greenwood. So when the march reached Greenwood, SNCC would "drop it" at a rally there.

The Meredith march had attracted many blacks and whites from around the country. Most people were certain the sloganeering was to be the same as the normal sloganeering of any civil rights march, including repeated singing of "We Shall Overcome," and call-and-response shouts like "What do we want? Freedom. When do we want it? Now!" and so on. Thus, when Willie Ricks went to the microphone at the Greenwood rally with an angry rather than a conciliatory demeanor, the crowd was certain it was merely an expression of felt anger at the shooting of James Meredith and not the prelude to anything new. So when Ricks began and asked the standard "What do we want?" The crowd responded, "Freedom now!" "Uh uh," Ricks told them. The right response, the new one, was "Black Power!" "What do we want?" he asked again. Perplexed, most people answered once again, "Freedom now!" Willie stopped once more and told them what they wanted: "Black Power!" He asked again, "What do we want?" More people now responded as Willie wanted: "Black Power!" "Freedom now!" was being drowned out. Ricks repeated: "What do we want?" By now more and more of the crowd responded, "Black Power!" As Ricks kept at it again and again, the response came back stronger and stronger: "Black Power!" After the Greenwood rally, things were different. "Where a couple of days earlier we might stand around and listen [to] small groups of two or three younger black men . . . talking to each other," recalled white march participant David Dawley, a student at the University of Michigan, "now they told us to 'move out of the way honky!'"

That night at another rally in Greenwood, Stokely Carmichael repeated the new slogan. This time, after the priming by Ricks, the audience knew how to respond. Martin Luther King wasn't there. He had returned to Memphis to tape an edition of television's "Meet the Press." But when he got back to Greenwood, he attempted some damage control, begging Carmichael not to use the new incendiary slogan. It was no use. James Forman joined the march on its last day. John Lewis, who very shortly would leave SNCC for good, asked him to convince Ricks and the others from SNCC to stop chanting the new slogan because it made no sense. Instead of stopping them, Forman, and Ruby Doris Robinson, his new replacement as executive secretary (a post he no longer wanted), placed themselves in a strategic position close to the news cameras near the others who were chanting "Black Power," and joined in the chant. The cat was out of the bag—all three unfocused, energizing, alienating, undefined syllables.

The news media spread the new slogan to the entire country. After its introduction, certain media people, who earlier had felt comfortable around Stokely, now felt a palpable distance developing. Across the nation, angry, disenchanted, unfocused black youths took to the new slogan like schools of fishes to water. Fearful whites, with images of a burning Watts still dancing in their heads, locked the doors to both their homes and their minds. Many more well-meaning young whites either scratched their heads or pulled up the tents they had pitched in the camp of civil rights and headed to the welcoming arms of the anti–Vietnam War encampment.

And, according to King lieutenant Andrew Young, for all those who would call Martin Luther King an Uncle Tom because he opposed the new slogan there was this prophetic observation by King: "Jews have power, but if you ever accuse them of power, they deny it. Catholics have power, but they always deny it. If you go around claiming power, the whole society turns on you and crushes you. If you really have power you don't need a slogan."

5

Managing the Cat
Out of the Bag

THE INTRODUCTION OF THE NEW BLACK POWER SLOGAN could be compared to the hasty construction of a new airport. By 1966 the sky above the airport had been filled with planes of all kinds circling overhead, carrying impatient passengers and crew members searching for somewhere to land, particularly after the assassination of Malcolm X. SNCC not only constructed the new airport but manned the control tower, thinking it knew the nature of those aboard the planes about to land in its spanking new facility. Some of the planes landing were doing so at the express invitation of SNCC and would not otherwise be hovering in the sky above. One such plane was festooned with the label "Poor, Rural, Largely Illiterate Blacks of Mississippi"; another, "Poor, Rural, Largely Illiterate Blacks of Alabama." Other planes were hovering above of their own accord. They featured labels like "Angry Disenchanted Young Blacks of Watts"; "Angry Disenchanted Young Blacks of Chicago's Southside"; "Angry Disenchanted Young Blacks of Oakland," and so on.

SNCC simply ignored the fact that once all those planes landed, not everyone disembarking would proceed through its facility in an orderly fashion. Most of the passengers were either sincere rural blacks, sincere young black intellectuals, or sincere young blacks from the ghetto anxious for a chance to pursue a better life. However, mixed among all those passengers—particularly on the planes from the urban North and West—were street hustlers, burglars, winos, pimps, prostitutes, and gamblers who simply boarded the planes headed for the Black Power airport for the thrill of it. And no matter how much SNCC desired otherwise, such passengers would never proceed through the airport for any better reason than to engage in joyrides back and forth on the airplanes and to introduce their habits in the corridors of the terminal. The entire system—airport, planes, passengers, and crew members—could be called the products of human nature. Unfortunately, the blindness of American racism, and the resultant sensitivities of African Americans, rarely take human nature into account when pondering the behavior of African Americans.

Before the introduction of SNCC's Black Power slogan, Huey Newton and Bobby Seale—part of the Angry Disenchanted Young Blacks of Oakland searching for somewhere to land—routinely displayed behavior that others questioned. They had already broken with Warden's student association and the Oakland chapter of RAM, ostensibly because of those organizations' unwillingness to engage in real revolutionary activity. However, what Newton and his cohorts deemed "real revolutionary activity" could just as easily be interpreted as ill-advised boldness. They displayed such boldness not only with other young blacks but with the local police, often handing the police a reason to harass them. One such instance occurred when Newton, Seale, and some of their buddies were arrested on Telegraph Avenue in Berkeley. Allegedly, the trouble began when Bobby Seale started reciting an antiwhite poem. A police officer walked up and told him he was under arrest for blocking the sidewalk. Such an arrest would constitute uncalled-for police harassment. But then "one of the paddies [police officers] that had a hold of me, Huey knocked him in the head a couple of times, and a couple of other brothers stomped on the paddies," recalled Seale. This physical attack gave the police officers a reason to arrest Newton too. It also gave them a reason to watch out for him in the future.

Newton and his cohorts often engaged in other forms of behavior that students at Oakland City College found questionable. One of the black campus organizations that Newton and Seale belonged to was the Soul Students Advisory Council (SSAC). The organization's primary goal became getting a black studies program started at the school, but Newton and Seale suggested that the organization do something else—organize the "brothers off the block." Newton rationalized that organizing the "brothers off the block" was part of the revolutionary theory of Algerian writer Franz Fanon, author of the book *The Wretched of the Earth*. According to Fanon, such men constituted the lumpen proletariat. May 19 was Malcolm X's birthday; and that provided the opportunity to bring the issue to a head. (Malcolm had been assassinated that February.) To commemorate Malcolm's birthday, Newton and Seale wanted to strap guns on the "brothers off the block" and march them up and down the campus to show the college administration that SSAC meant business. Most SSAC members vetoed the idea as foolish and unnecessary. Newton accused them of being punks. So there was a standoff at an SSAC meeting. "I had a 9-mm pistol and Huey called up his boys—the pimps, thugs off the block—and he called up his nephew, who, like the brothers off the block, just liked to fight," recalled Bobby Seale. "They don't like to do much of anything but fight. . . . We stacked a whole [SSAC session with them]. That was the day Huey and I resigned from the SSAC. Huey said, 'Come on up here. These niggers think they're bad. We're going to show them if they're bad.'" Such behavior smacked of a gang mentality. But it was the type of behavior that would be swept under the rug as black consciousness rose among more and more young blacks, causing them to increasingly glamorize violence.

A person could see what was coming simply by examining the words Stokely Carmichael used when he attempted to explain what Black Power was all about. In a fall 1966 article in the *New York Review of Books*, Carmichael wrote that SNCC was expanding its organizing beyond Lowndes County into other rural areas of Alabama, running black candidates for sheriff, tax assessor, and membership on local school boards: "These men and women are up for

election in November. . . . Their ballot symbol is the black panther: a bold, beautiful animal, representing the strength and dignity
of the black demands today. A man needs a black panther on his
side when he and his family must endure loss of job, eviction,
starvation, and sometimes death, for political activity. He may also
need a gun, and SNCC reaffirms the right of black men everywhere to defend themselves if threatened or attacked."

Clearly, Carmichael was issuing one more repudiation of the
concept of nonviolence as it applied to southern activism. But he
also gave the impression that as the struggle headed north and west,
the need for a gun would be similar to what it had been in the
south. This would become par for the course among Black Power
advocates, in their efforts to find common ground between blacks
at the bottom in all sections of the country. Such blacks would be
granted a glow of righteousness, no matter where they lived or
what their predicament. Consequently, Carmichael blurred the
distinctions between blacks who hung out on the streets and low-
income blacks sincerely interested in self-improvement. He also
helped initiate the trend of demonizing blacks who achieved the
same upward mobility as other Americans, denouncing them for
seeking integration into the rest of society. "Integration today
means that the man who 'makes it' [leaves] his black brothers
behind in the ghetto as fast as his new sports car will take him. It
has no relevance to *the Harlem wino or to the cotton picker* [italics
added] making three dollars a day. As a lady I know in Alabama
once said, 'The food that Ralph Bunche eats [United Nations
diplomat who became the first black American to win the Nobel
Peace Prize] doesn't fill my stomach.'"

More often than not the blacks who "made it" escaped the
ghetto for middle-class black enclaves that became that way on
whites leaving at the first sign of a black face on their block. Such
blacks were merely engaging in an African American version of the
national trend to head to outlying areas rather than remain in the
central cities. Granted, a major reason for white flight to the
suburbs was the presence of blacks who had migrated to the cities.
But their flight was also promoted by postwar developers who
encouraged them to escape to "clean wide open suburban spaces."

That blacks would seek to imitate such behavior would hardly be surprising. But thanks to Carmichael and his imitators, they were henceforth to be labeled Uncle Toms. And Black Power militants would derive as much pleasure from haranguing them as they would from haranguing white racists. These were the wages of Carmichael's youthful hubris, combined with accumulated stress from having faced, within the Deep South, the most dangerous situations imaginable.

So Carmichael and the rest of SNCC named the destinies of all blacks at the bottom as identical, separated them from upwardly mobile blacks, and set out to popularize the Black Panther name and logo among them. And after breaking with the Soul Students Advisory Council, then creating their own organization in the fall of 1966, Huey Newton and Bobby Seale's Black Panther Party for Self-Defense became just one of many organizations across the country using the Black Panther name and logo. Their exclusive claim to being Black Panthers was still about two years away.

The blurring of the line between blacks at the bottom who had a street mentality and those sincerely interested in improving their lives began to set the stage for Newton's Black Panther Party to gain legitimacy. Although large numbers of whites who had enthusiastically joined in civil rights demonstrations and Mississippi Freedom Summer felt alienated by the rise in black militancy, some sought to understand it and find a way to continue aiding the racial struggle.

In the Bay Area, SDS helped such young whites who had aided blacks in the Deep South to transfer their hands-on experience to aiding blacks in East and West Oakland. One organization the students could aid through SDS was a public housing project tenants' association called the Peralta Improvement League (PIL). The goal was to help the tenants take control of a federal Job Corps beautification program that employed youths in improving the housing project. The Job Corps was part of President Lyndon Johnson's War on Poverty program, initiated in 1964. The idea of aiding PIL was in keeping with the old Freedom Summer philosophy of empowering people at the grassroots to take control of all aspects of their lives, a philosophy that facilitated the rise of assorted grassroots urban organizations to match the budding federal bureaucracy of the War on Poverty program. In Oakland it gave rise to black grassroots organizers like Mark Comfort, founder of the Oakland Direct Action Committee (ODAC). Comfort also started a club for young black males called the Amboy Dukes. He insisted on remaining a community organizer unconnected to the government because he realized that the federal bureaucracy being constructed to handle the War on Poverty was creating a situation where the continued existence of the ghetto was to that bureaucracy's benefit.

The journalist Peter Solomon and the Reverend Grover Washington, a black Oakland minister, witnessed one example of how a government antipoverty program could easily be taken advantage of, rendering the poor a permanent underclass. One day the two walked in on a Manpower Training Act divvy-up session. (The Manpower Training Act was one of many federal programs designed to provide employment opportunities to the poor.) It was a public meeting, but none of the bureaucratic or corporate principals really wanted the public to be present—and certainly not the media. The meeting was held to allocate the training act money in an unscrupulous manner. Solomon also suspected that the funds were not going to be used for creating the number of jobs for poor people they were designed to create. Present at the meeting were representatives of one of Oakland's major industrial employers, a local civil rights organization felt to be behind the times, two observers from the U.S. Department of Labor, the director of manpower development for the city of Oakland, and several other city officials. Washington and Solomon were the lone representatives of the public. They sat off in a corner for half an hour, waiting for everything to begin. Then one of the city officials asked if any members of the media were present. Solomon identified himself. At that point everyone started getting antsy. Suddenly the representative from the industrial company got up, stuffed his papers in his briefcase, and said, "I'm not going to put up with this anymore!"

"Stop!" Solomon told him. "Did I ever say anything in the newspaper [called *Flatlands*] that was untrue?"

"No," the company representative answered.

"Did I ever report anything in the newspaper that was inaccurate?"

"No."

"Then what's your problem?"

"We don't have to put up with this," the company representative repeated. At that point Solomon and the Reverend Washington left, and, not wanting to appear as colluders in anything shady, the observers from the Department of Labor left too.

Such apparently dishonest dealmaking indicated that the programs designed to aid the poor weren't always what they seemed to be. If you were upwardly mobile, you could depend on them only to a certain extent. At the same time, you had to ignore the street toughs who derided you. Most of Newton's "brothers off the block" looked down on anyone serious about graduating from college. They looked down on anyone serious about getting a job. "A man who lives on his wits, sleeping till ten in the morning, on the hustle in the streets or the poolrooms, he figures a guy working 8 hours a day for $80 per week just isn't smart," Julius Hobson, a CORE worker, would later observe.

White liberal and radical activists had no difficulty believing that some War on Poverty programs were being corrupted. But they did have difficulty acknowledging that not everyone in poor neighborhoods was just waiting for an opportunity to improve his or her life in a legitimate fashion. Although statements like Hobson's could apply to anyone who lived by their street sense, liberal and radical activists hesitated to embrace such notions if the hustlers were black, fearing that to do so would play into stereotypes of black laziness and criminality. Instead they followed the cues of activists such as Carmichael and the members of Berkeley's Campus CORE and SDS. They viewed all blacks at the bottom as noble. Nothing better demonstrated this attitude than a documentary, "Losing Just the Same," made by liberal whites from San Francisco public television station KQED.

The film followed a poor black family in West Oakland,

focusing on the teenage son. Its message was that money was tight for the family, food was rare, and dreams and hopes meant nothing because of inadequate schools, welfare restrictions, and police brutality, all of which certainly existed in Oakland. The film was a real tearjerker for whites. The teenage son was shown going about his life aimlessly, dreaming of real opportunity. And at the end, he was shown being arrested in the San Francisco riots of 1966, for throwing a Molotov cocktail as a defiant response to the hopelessness of his life. Being led to the prison bus, the boy turned to the camera to tell his mother, "Don't be mad!" Viewers saw the mother on camera lamenting that her son had no future. Little did they know that a certain amount of acting was going on among the family being portrayed. "I watched this film with a bunch of people from the community and they were laughing," recalls Peter Solomon. "They were rolling on the floor saying, 'Oh that's Mrs. Washington, she's doing her number again!'" Young white liberals couldn't help but be blind to such acting. But when some of them, like Peter Collier, did discover they were being hoodwinked, they overreacted.

In the summer of 1965, Collier, who had been a graduate student at UC Berkeley, decided to teach English at Miles College, a black school in Birmingham, Alabama. While there, he ran across a student named Hazel, who turned in some of the most brilliant essays he had ever read. "In my fantasies, Hazel became part of a parable of wasted potential—the one who, if she could be saved, would help redeem an evil situation. She became my project." Collier decided that such potential belonged in a good northern college. He began lobbying Hazel's mother and the faculty of Miles, trying to convince them to send her to a better school. Then one day a fellow teacher at Miles, to whom Collier had shown some of Hazel's essays, pulled out an anthology of literature from the Harlem Renaissance. He opened the book to a page marked for Collier, then left him to read it. Collier learned that Hazel's essays had been plagiarized from the book.

Hurt and embarrassed from having been taken in, Collier refused to see Hazel as an exception who demonstrated that blacks were neither more nor less fallible than other groups of people.

He left Alabama and the civil rights movement for good, and returned to Berkeley to join the antiwar movement (years later, Collier would be reviled by the white left for becoming a political conservative).

DESPITE THE EXPERIENCES OF PEOPLE LIKE COLLIER, most young liberal and radical whites continued to view blacks as noble. But they had a difficult time relating to the increasing anger of the Black Power movement, anger that seemed to be directed at all whites. That anger drove more and more young whites to the antiwar movement. Since both Black Power advocates and young white radicals opposed the Vietnam War, the lines of communication between the two remained open. Poor, rural, young black males, as well as the "brothers off the block," were among the first to be drafted into the war. SNCC continued to denounce this as part of its advocacy of Black Power.

Doing its best to keep one foot in budding antiwar activism and another in improving race relations, in October 1966 SDS sponsored a Black Power conference at UC Berkeley so that the one movement could better understand the other. The two-day conference featured panel discussions with titles such as "Black Power and American Politics"; "Historical and Cultural Roots of Black Power"; "Black Culture and Integration." Perhaps most revealing about the direction young blacks were taking was the panel "Black Power and Violence." It featured Austin Black, a man from an organization with the telling acronym "Watts BURN." At the conference, the door to the mentality of Newton and his "brothers off the block" was opened even wider on the second day of the conference, when SNCC's Ivanhoe Donaldson was asked about SNCC's position on violence. Donaldson replied, "We live in a violent country. If the establishment doesn't leave people any outs besides violence, we don't have any qualms about violence."

Stokely Carmichael was the conference keynote speaker. Before a predominantly white crowd of 12,000, he called Berkeley the "white intellectual ghetto of the West." He admonished white America to "move over, or we're gonna move over you." But it wasn't until he began denouncing the Vietnam War that the predominantly white students turned enthusiastic. "The war in Vietnam is an illegal and immoral war," he said to tumultuous applause. "There is a higher law than that of a racist named McNamara [Robert McNamara, secretary of defense], a fool named Rusk [Dean Rusk, secretary of state], and a buffoon named Johnson. . . ." And then, despite the attractiveness SNCC was attaching to violence as a solution to the problems of blacks, Carmichael made this observation with regard to using violence in Vietnam: "No one has the right to take a man's life for two years and train him to be a killer."

However, Carmichael and the other conference speakers failed to explain to the satisfaction of most white students what Black Power was about. Noted the *Daily Californian* of Carmichael's speech: "[It] showed that he, as the leader of a group supposedly *defining* black power, isn't necessarily able to define the concept after all, to the satisfaction of anyone who cares. . . ." The majority of young white activists settled for never really understanding the increasing militancy of their black counterparts. The two groups related to each other primarily through mutual pats on the back every time someone denounced the white establishment, their common enemy.

The white radicals redoubled their antiwar activities. Radical organizations such as UC Berkeley's Vietnam Day Committee (VDC) had already turned Berkeley into the place to be for opposers of the war. During the summer of 1965, approximately 300 Berkeley protesters blocked a troop train on its way to the Oakland Army Terminal. That fall, 7,000 protesters clashed with police at the Oakland-Berkeley border as they attempted to march through Oakland to the Army Terminal. Still later that fall, 10,000 mainly white student antiwar protesters held a rally in predominantly black West Oakland's DeFremery Park. The Berkeley radicals also pioneered the first serious electoral challenge to a U.S. congressman who refused to denounce the war. Jeffrey Cohelan was a favorite of President Johnson. He represented a district that straddled both Oakland and Berkeley—the district that would later be represented by C. L. Dellums's nephew, Ron Dellums.

The candidate the antiwar activists chose to challenge Co-helan was a man who personified the fragile bridge still being maintained between the increasingly militant black community and the radical whites of Berkeley. Bespectacled, goateed, twenty-nine-year-old white radical intellectual Bob Scheer had an interesting background. In 1960 he was an editor of a left-wing publication, *Root and Branch*, which had discovered Donald Warden. *Root and Branch* published an article by Warden, paving the way for his prominence as a local radio personality and founder of the Afro-American Association. Scheer had also been active in organizing protesters for the local Sheraton Palace and Auto Row civil rights demonstrations.

His antiwar credentials were among the most illustrious in the nation. After visiting South Vietnam, he wrote the book *How the United States Got Involved in Vietnam*, a seminal analysis of the war. *The Nation* magazine called it the most important analysis of the war up to that time. Scheer had also been a Ford Foundation fellow. After writing his book on Vietnam, he joined the staff of *Ramparts* magazine, which was about to become one of the nation's most influential radical journals. The research team he headed for that magazine would author the most impressive analysis of social and political conditions in the city of Oakland up to then.

No one in the Bay Area bridged the black community and the radical white community like Bob Scheer. In the course of his congressional campaign, Scheer sought the support of a variety of black leaders. He received endorsements from people like Mark Comfort, of the Oakland Direct Action Committee, and the prominent San Francisco physician and newspaper publisher Carlton B. Goodlett (who would run in the Democratic primary for governor). He also sought the support of the Soul Students Advisory Council at Oakland City College, then led by Newton and Seale. They turned him down, with the excuse that they didn't believe anyone could adequately voice their opinions. But they did hit Scheer up for a donation of $100, which they said they needed for their organizing efforts at Oakland City College. Scheer gave it to them.

Scheer ended up losing his congressional campaign in a close primary race that was alleged to have been followed by the White House (according to the Scheer campaign, presidential press secretary Bill Moyers monitored the race by placing a call to Cohelan's campaign office). Although he lost, Scheer carried every predominantly black precinct. And when he returned to the staff of *Ramparts*, Scheer became perhaps the key person to launch the career of Eldridge Cleaver, who would do more than anyone else to facilitate Huey Newton's Black Panther Party replacing SNCC as the national symbol of black disenchantment. Such replacement wouldn't begin until the fall of 1967, after Newton shot officer John Frey. The groundwork for that replacement would be laid by the ever-increasing calls for violent revolution among militant young blacks. It would be laid as well by what happened in November 1966 in Lowndes County.

As their organizing efforts progressed, SNCC/LCFO workers began to realize how difficult it would be to get the blacks in Lowndes County to vote for the ballot represented by the black panther, even if they were registered. There was the intimidation factor. There was the charge that forming an independent political party like LCFO amounted to separatism. But SNCC worked hard anyway. In addition to registering 2,600 black voters in Lowndes County, it held workshops teaching rural blacks the duties of the offices of sheriff, tax collector, tax assessor, county coroner, and school board member. SNCC had even prepared picture books to explain the duties to rural plantation workers who could not read.

On election day SNCC/LCFO headquarters received messages from various precincts: "Get over to Precinct 7, trouble there. Not letting our poll watchers observe everything. Whites going into booths with Negroes." "Check Precinct 2. Black people from plantations being given marked ballots before they go in." "Get up to Haynesville [county seat] right away. Intimidating our people outside." Some black workers from off of plantations were trucked in by their white employers. They outright refused to vote for the LCFO ticket because they were told that if they did, they would loose their meager jobs. On election night one LCFO worker who had spent the day driving voters to the polls was severely beaten by whites. And after putting in all that blood and sweat to educate and register black voters in a county that was 80 percent black, not a single LCFO candidate was elected to office as sheriff, county coroner, tax assessor, tax collector, or member of the board of education, although in some cases the vote was close.

The experience convinced SNCC that trying to get black people the ballot wasn't enough, whether the attempt was inside the Democratic party, as during Mississippi Freedom Summer, or outside of it, as in Lowndes County, Alabama. Out of SNCC's rural southern experiences, the belief grew that what was needed was further development of black pride and guns in the hands of black people. The Oakland Direct Action Committee head, Mark Comfort, had traveled to Lowndes County to help during the election, thinking that he could learn something from the southern organizing efforts to bring back to Oakland. After the Lowndes County vote, like the increasingly militant SNCC workers, Comfort continued to try to link the plight of rural black southerners with that of the increasingly violent ghetto youths in northern and West Coast cities.

At the same time, Premier Black Leader Martin Luther King had been busy trying to transfer his nonviolent style of activism to the problems of ghetto blacks in Chicago. But he was meeting with little success. The unique ward politics of that city, in which the Democratic machine easily bought the loyalties of black ministers and politicians who would otherwise be King allies, stifled him. The only thing King really succeeded in doing was dramatizing, through fair-housing demonstrations in suburbs like Cicero, the fact that northern whites could be every bit as racist as southern whites.

The struggle for black advancement was simply experiencing growing pains, but no one was willing to step back, reassess, examine. Progress had to be followed immediately by more progress. With King looking like a failure, Malcolm X dead, Watts having already exploded, and the call for Black Power generating increasing interest among young blacks, new black voices were being solicited by the media. If you were black and angry and could write, your time had arrived. Whites desiring to understand it all, like the readers of *Ramparts* magazine, were ready to hear from you.

While the civil rights revolution went on around him, Eldridge Cleaver had been educating himself in California's Soledad prison, where he was serving one to fourteen years for assault with intent to murder. Tall, handsome, dark-skinned, with a natural, and sporting a goatee, Cleaver wrote letters from prison to the radical Bay Area lawyer Beverly Axelrod, which were published in *Ramparts,* thanks to Bob Scheer.

In his first *Ramparts* piece, "Notes on a Native Son," which appeared in the magazine's June 1966 issue, Cleaver denounced the nation's leading African American writer of that era, James Baldwin. In the process he leveled a broadside against all black intellectuals, telling readers they were buckdancers who were worse than Uncle Toms: "Uncle Tom comes off much cleaner . . . because usually he is trying to survive, choosing to pretend to be something other than his true self in order to please the white man and thus receive favors. Whereas the intellectual sycophant does not pretend to be other than he actually is, but hates what he is and seeks to redefine himself in the image of his white idols. He becomes a white man in a black body. A self-willed, automated slave, he becomes the white man's most valuable tool in oppressing other blacks."

"True blacks," apparently, were more like Cleaver, who gave readers a real window into his mind in the following issue. "We are a very sick country—I perhaps am sicker than most," he wrote. "But I accept that. I told you in the beginning that I am extremist by nature—so it is only right that I should be extremely sick." Continuing to describe himself in the piece, Cleaver confirmed white America's worst notions about black men. "I became a rapist. To refine my technique and *modus operandi,* I started out practicing on black girls in the ghetto where dark and vicious deeds appear not as aberrations or deviations from the norm, but as part of the efficiency of the evil of the day—and when I considered myself smooth enough, I crossed the tracks and sought out white prey. . . . There are of course many young blacks out there right now who are slitting white throats and raping the white girl. . . ."

But Cleaver wasn't finished. His name couldn't have been

more appropriate. He was like a meat cleaver that could swing in any direction, including at white middle-class Americans. "A young white today cannot help but recoil against the base deeds of his people," he wrote in another essay. "There seems to be no end to the ghastly deeds of which his people are guilty. GUILTY. The slaughter of Jews by Germans, the dropping of atomic bombs on the Japanese people—these deeds weigh heavily on the prostrate souls and tumultuous consciences of the white youth. The white heroes, their hands dripping with blood, are dead."

Cleaver was capturing and tying together the entire rebellious phenomenon: the behavior of young whites filled with guilt, now angry about the Vietnam war, who had seen blacks as a beacon; and that of the frustrated young blacks who never had the same goals as a Martin Luther King or James Baldwin in the first place. And since white America in general had a difficult time imagining blacks as anything but a monolith, in the minds of left-leaning whites, the eloquent, deviant Cleaver could easily replace blacks like King as their image of "real" black people. Cleaver touched all their buttons. Heaping praise on him, Maxwell Geismar, a white associate editor at *Ramparts*, made this revealing and prophetic observation: "He rakes our favorite prejudices with the *savage claws* [italics added] of his prose until our wounds are bare, our psyche is exposed, and we must either fight back or laugh with him for the service he has done us."

From his springboard of essays, which would be turned into the best-selling book *Soul on Ice*, Cleaver's sponsors secured his release from prison on parole in December 1966. That same month, at an acrimonious staff meeting held at the upstate New York resort of blues musician Peg Leg Bates, SNCC officially resolved to broaden its goal from voter registration and the election of black officeholders to facilitating the development of comprehensive grassroots organizations in black communities across the country, with the black panther as their symbol. In essence, SNCC was admitting it was running out of gas, ready to pass the baton on to others.

Two months earlier, Huey Newton and Bobby Seale were

among those who, in effect, accepted the handoff. The actual idea for the organization they had been hoping to start among the "brothers off the block" was borrowed from the Community Alert Patrol (CAP), which began in Watts after the 1965 riots. CAP was funded largely by the federal government. Its function was to protect the black citizens of Watts from police harassment and brutality. Watts residents who observed police officers stopping someone black to investigate or interrogate that person were encouraged to call a central CAP headquarters and report where the police action was taking place. CAP would then dispatch one of its patrol cars to the scene to observe how the incident went down. They would also inform the person being interrogated of his or her legal rights. Newton and Seale decided on a similar model for their group, but with an added twist—loaded guns.

Newton got the idea to take the name of SNCC's symbol for the Lowndes County Freedom Organization, on coming across a pamphlet circulated by the Bay Area Friends of SNCC that explained what LCFO was about, just as the Lowndes County elections approached. The black panther symbol, originally designed for those from the most sincere and humble black southern backgrounds, was now to be used to organize the most delinquent elements in urban black America. "Whatever's good for the man can't be good for us," Seale would later write of the party's philosophy. "Huey wanted . . . brothers who had been out there robbing banks, brothers who had been pimping, brothers who had been peddling dope, brothers who ain't gonna take no shit, brothers who had been fighting the pigs. . . . Huey P. Newton knew that once you organize the brothers he ran with, he fought with, he fought against, who he fought harder than they fought him . . . you get revolutionaries who are too much."

Throughout the summer of 1966 and into the fall, Seale had been working at a government funded antipoverty agency called the North Oakland Neighborhood Anti-Poverty Center. He supervised approximately eighty youths ranging in age from sixteen to twenty-one, who were employed by the program to cut lawns, trim hedges, the sort of make-work assignments characteristic of such programs. Most of the youths hated school, engaged in shop-lifting, and were fond of petty gambling. Many could barely read.

At the same time, Newton, who also worked as a community organizer in an antipoverty program, was taking classes at Oakland City College and San Francisco Law School, and fraternizing with the "brothers off the block," including those engaged in criminal activity, talking up his idea of organizing them to openly carry arms and patrol the police. By late September, Newton and Seale were sitting in the library of the North Oakland Center researching a theoretical basis for their organization, which would derive its philosophy from the socialist and communist revolutionaries Newton was fond of. They also drew on the theories of Robert Williams of North Carolina's Deacons for Defense in his book *Negroes with Guns*. Newton had discovered a little-known California law allowing a person to carry a loaded rifle or shotgun as long as it was publicly displayed and pointed at no one. They came up with a ten-point platform and a uniform for their Black Panther Party for Self-Defense: blue shirts, black pants, black leather jackets, black berets, and openly displayed loaded shotguns. Huey's brother Melvin helped him to edit the platform. It read:

What We Want, What We Believe

1. We want freedom. We want power to determine the destiny of our Black Community.

We believe that black people will not be free until we are free to determine our own destiny.

2. We want full employment for our people.

We believe that the federal government is responsible and obligated to give every man employment or a guaranteed income. We believe that if the white American businessman will not give full employment, then the means of production should be taken away from the businessman and placed in the community so that the people of the community can organize and employ all of its people and give a high standard of living.

3. We want an end to the robbery by the capitalists of our black community.

We believe that this racist government has robbed us and now we are demanding the overdue debt of forty acres and two mules. Forty acres and two mules were promised 100 years ago as restitution for slave labor and mass murder of black people. We will accept the payment in currency which will be distributed to our many communities. The Germans are now aiding the Jews in Israel for the genocide of the Jewish people. The Germans murdered six million Jews. The American racist has taken part in the slaughter of over fifty million black people; therefore, we feel that this is a modest demand that we make.

4. We want decent housing fit for shelter of human beings.

We believe that if the white landlords will not give decent housing to our black community, then the housing and the land should be made into cooperatives so that our community, with government aid, can build and make decent housing for its people.

5. We want education for our people that exposes the true nature of this decadent American society. We want education that teaches us our true history and our role in the present-day society.

6. We want all black men to be exempt from military service.

We believe that black people should not be forced to fight in the military service to defend a racist government that does not protect us. We will not fight and kill other people of color in a world who, like black people, are victimized by the white racist government of America. We will protect ourselves from the force and violence of the racist police and the racist military, by whatever means necessary.

7. We want an immediate end to POLICE BRUTALITY and MURDER of black people.

We believe we can end police brutality in our black community by organizing black self-defense groups that are dedicated to defending our black community from racist police oppression and brutality. The Second Amendment to the Constitution of the United States gives a right to bear arms. We therefore believe that all black people should arm themselves for self-defense.

8. We want freedom for all black men held in federal, state, county and city prisons and jails.

We believe that all black people should be released from the many jails and prisons because they have not received a fair and impartial trial.

9. We want all black people when brought to court to be tried by a jury of their peer group from their black communities, as defined by the Constitution of the United States.

We believe that the courts should follow the United States Constitution so that black people will receive fair trials. The Fourteenth Amendment of the U.S. Constitution gives a man the right to be tried by his peer group. A peer is a person from a similar economic, social, religious, geographical, environmental, historical, and racial background. To do this the court will be forced to select a jury from the black community from which the black defendant came. We have been and are being tried by all-white juries that have no understanding of the "average reasoning man" of the black community.

10. We want land, bread, housing, education, clothing, justice, and peace. And as our major political objective, a United Nations–supervised plebiscite to be held throughout the black colony in which only black colonial subjects will be allowed to participate, for the purpose of determining the will of black people as to their national destiny.

The last point was followed by the words of the Declaration of Independence of the American Revolution.

Clearly, the party platform contained interesting, justifiable proposals (such as the call for forty acres and two mules). It made good points about historical realities for black people. But during the life of the party, most of the points in the platform would remain idealistic pronouncements rather than anything the Panthers actively pushed for. And the platform points about prison and the police clearly reflected a Newton obsession. He acted as though being brutalized by the police and unjustly imprisoned were principal problems most black people faced daily.

The Black Panther Party was officially launched on October 15, 1966. Bobby Seale took the title of party chairman, and Newton named himself minister of defense. Their first party recruit—sixteen-year-old Bobby Hutton, one of the youths Seale supervised in the antipoverty program—was typical of the earliest party members. Hutton would go to school, get kicked out, go back, and get kicked out again. He wasn't very articulate, and he often got in trouble with the police on petty charges. Newton and Seale obtained their first two guns from Richard Aoki, a Japanese American who saw himself as a revolutionary. Aoki gave them an M-1 rifle and a 9-mm pistol, free of charge, after they convinced him that this is what a "real revolutionary" would do.

But the other young blacks in Oakland, whom they considered "armchair revolutionaries," still had reservations about the open display of guns. One night Newton and Seale took out their guns, intending to patrol the police on the way to a party. They encountered no police patrol cars. But when they arrived at the house party, they decided to bring their loaded weapons inside. The others there grew nervous, which, given Newton's reputation for quick-trigger anger, was understandable. Newton told the partygoers that he and Seale had guns because they were starting a new revolutionary organization. They were asked to check their weapons anyway, which they did. But a few minutes later someone called the police. The host of the party simply didn't want loaded weapons in his apartment. Newton and Seale left, but not before Newton cursed out the host and his sister, calling them "bootlickin' bastards."

On January 1, 1967, Newton, Seale, and Bobby Hutton took their paychecks from the antipoverty program and opened up the first Black Panther office in a vacant building at 56th and Grove streets in North Oakland. They painted a large sign on the window in front that announced "Black Panther Party for Self-Defense." And young black men started coming by. They were told of the party's ten-point platform, and that if they joined there would be political education classes and training in use of weapons. Soon the party had more recruits: Reginald and Sherman Forte, John Sloan, Warren Tucker. They also obtained more weapons. Richard Aoki gave them a .357 magnum and two more pistols.

Then, remembering the radical nature of the UC Berkeley students he had seen brought in by the busloads to Santa Rita prison during the Free Speech Movement, Newton got the idea of selling Mao Tse-tung's "Little Red Book" (officially entitled *Quotations from Chairman Mao Tse-tung*), which he found at a bookstore in San Francisco's Chinatown, to UC Berkeley students. Newton, Seale, and Hutton stood in front of Sather Gate and hawked copies of the "Little Red Book" for a dollar apiece. The books sold like hotcakes, as Seale shouted, "All you free speechers up here who lost Mario Savio [by then Savio was a graduate student in Europe] must read the Red Book and do it like the Red Guards did it!" With the money they earned, they bought more guns and ammunition.

They accelerated their patrols of the police. In addition to loaded guns, they carried a law book, tape recorders, and cameras. While the Panthers stated that their aim was to prevent police from brutalizing black residents, the very act of their loading up in cars with openly displayed weapons was like a magnet that drew the police to them. An officer on patrol seeing a group of men in cars carrying weapons would understandably grow suspicious. Were they on their way to a robbery? Racism certainly entered into the equation since police were even more prone to stop such vehicles if the men carrying guns were black. And while Newton, Seale, and the rest of the Panthers were exercising their constitutional rights, it was also true that one of their main activities was fraternizing with black men who admittedly engaged in criminal activity.

On all the patrols, Newton was the point man. In one incident Newton, Seale, and the others were coming out of their Grove

Street office with their openly displayed weapons, when a police officer in a patrol car stopped and radioed in that he was seeing suspicious activity. As Newton, Seale, Hutton, and two other Panthers got in their car, the officer pulled up behind them. He got out of the patrol car, approached Newton at the driver's window, and asked for his license. "Is this your true name, Huey P. Newton?" the officer asked. Huey responded in the affirmative. "Is this your true address?" Huey again responded in the affirmative. Then the officer asked the key question. "What are you doing with the guns?" Huey responded as he would whenever officers asked him that question: "What are you doing with *your* gun?" This was to be the beginning of the battle royal between the Oakland police and the Black Panthers.

The officer returned to his patrol car to retrieve a writing pad. He went back to Newton's car and wrote down Newton's name and address. Then he asked Newton for his phone number. "Five," Newton responded. "Five what?" the officer asked. "The Fifth Amendment, you heard of it?" Newton asked. "Don't you know about the constitutional right of a person not to testify against himself? I don't have to give you anything but my identification, name and address. So therefore I don't even want to talk to you. . . . I don't even want to hear you."

Soon four more patrol cars pulled up. The officer from one of the cars approached and asked Newton what was going on. "The basic procedures that are supposed to go on!" Newton responded. One of the officers asked if he could see Bobby Seale's 9-mm pistol. "No you can't see it!" Newton answered. "No you can't see the pistol, nor this [his own rifle], and I don't want you to look at it." The officers grew beside themselves with anger. "Constitution my ass!" one of them said, perplexed by Newton's skill at turning the exact letter of the law around on the police department. "Who in the hell do you think you are?!?!"

All the Panthers in the car, except Huey, were nervous. They were ready to back down. Not Huey, who was now very angry. He opened the car door and asked, "Who in the hell do you think *you* are!?! . . . This police officer is supposed to be carrying out his duty, and here you come talking about our guns. We have a constitutional right to carry the guns anyway, and I don't want to *hear* it." Having carefully studied the law, which stated that you could carry a weapon in a vehicle as long as it wasn't loaded, Huey hopped out of the car and then dropped a round of ammo into his M-1.

By now a crowd of people had gathered, not believing what they saw before them—Huey Newton with a loaded M-1 rifle facing off with the police. Some of the officers tried to move the crowd along. But Huey told them to remain. They had a constitutional right to observe an officer carrying out his duty as long as they were at a reasonable distance. The officers threatened to arrest the people for disturbing the peace if they didn't move along. At that point, Newton took the keys to the Panther office, opened the office, and told the people to go inside and observe all they liked. They went in.

"What are you going to do with that gun?" one of the officers asked Newton. "What are you going to do with *your* gun?" Newton responded. "Because if you shoot me, or try to take this gun, I'm going to shoot back at you, swine. . . . If you draw that gun, I'll shoot back at you and blow your brains out!" The officers huddled together, befuddled. With so many witnesses to the confrontation, a major disturbance similar to what happened in Watts could be touched off, if they didn't keep their cool. Newton went back to the Panther office, opened the door, and allowed more people inside. "Now, what are you going to do?" he asked the officers.

One of them walked up to Huey and asked him if he was a Marxist. "Are you a fascist?" Huey responded. "Are you a Marxist?" the officer asked again. Huey asked him again if he was a fascist. This tit-for-tat went on for a few more minutes until the officer, unable to move against Newton, simply responded like a child, "I asked you first." "I asked you second," Huey answered. The spectators laughed. The officers seethed in their humiliation, certain to mark the Panthers, certain to begin their campaign to get them off the streets as soon as possible. Huey continued to insult them, calling them swine, sharecroppers, all sorts of names, daring them to go for their weapons. "If you shoot me, swine, I'll have to shoot you back!" The spectators with their faces pressed against the large window of the Panther office, cheered him on. "Tell it, *do* it brother."

Newton had provoked the Oakland police. But because the police were also racist, because they served a political and economic power structure in the city of Oakland that was racist, Huey Newton could do what he did and still receive the people's cheers. "These guys weren't like the Elijah Muhammad guys, who would sell you a two-week-old paper and laugh behind your back," recalls Peter Solomon. "They weren't like Don Warden, who was just on the radio and never did anything. Not like Martin Luther King or any of the others. These guys were *scary*. And the people who were locked out looked at them and said anything that scared the white establishment was good."

In 1966 the Oakland police force had just 19 black officers out of a total of over 600, which amounted to approximately 3 percent of the force in a city that was approximately one-quarter black. Most of the officers were contemptuous of blacks, particularly the black poor, even after the level of contempt the department displayed during the late 1940s was halted at the behest of the California legislature. There was the Oakland community newspaper that Solomon wrote for. *Flatlands* was published from the mid- to late 1960s. Its editor was an idealistic young white woman named Sandy Close, whose mission was to produce a newspaper as close to the grassroots as possible. *Flatlands* featured articles primarily by and about ordinary blacks in that area of Oakland. It also featured pieces about community organizers like Mark Comfort. It was distributed by neighborhood people and left at select spots, including right outside of the Oakland police station, so that the officers could learn something about blacks in the flatlands. But the officers hardly wanted to get to know such residents. Every time *Flatlands* was dropped off outside the police station, an officer was sent outside to throw all of the issues of the newspaper in the garbage can. So to Black Panther Huey P. Newton—the "Crazy Huey" so many community people had been afraid of all along, who was now provoking the cops, facing them down with an M-1 rifle, humiliating them—the community's message was "Tell it, *do* it brother!"

The people had experienced years of the Oakland power structure's practice of diluting black Oakland's political strength. Those who held office inherited their positions in a well-orchestrated practice of handing power over to others anointed by the Knowland family and other lesser power brokers. In 1966, those power brokers allowed Oakland to have just one black city councilman and one member of the school board. "The back scratching syndrome that keeps the Oakland political wheels grinding smoothly is like a connect-the-dots game," stated the *Ramparts* magazine report on the city. The key position in local patronage was district attorney. Earl Warren, chief justice of the U.S. Supreme Court, whose court was responsible for the favorable 1954 decision of *Brown* v. *Board of Education of Topeka*, which outlawed school segregation, came out of the Oakland district attorney's office. Warren became governor of California before going on to the Supreme Court. His career was launched with the backing of the Knowland family, when he began as an assistant district attorney appointed by District Attorney Ezra Dacoto. Dacoto later stepped down to make room for Warren's elevation to the district attorney's office. When Warren became governor, he appointed Dacato to the first vacancy on the Alameda County Superior Court bench. Then, as governor, Warren appointed Bill Knowland to fill an unexpired term in the U.S. Senate. Knowland, now retired from the Senate, was running the *Oakland Tribune*, a paper without a single black staff member.

The city's poorest section, West Oakland, was represented in the city council, where everyone was elected at large (that is, by all of the voters in the city rather than solely by the voters of each particular district), by a Chinese American named Ray Eng. Eng's elderly white predecessor, Howard Rilea, had followed tradition, stepping down to allow Mayor Houlihan to appoint Eng. Eng virtually never showed his face in West Oakland. When he did open his mouth at council meetings, saying, "I'd like to speak for all my constituents in West Oakland," there were huge guffaws. All of Oakland's blacks felt locked out. So to "Crazy Huey" giving the police officers of that same power structure fits, openly provoking them with an M-1 rifle at the corner of 56th and Grove streets, the answer from the ordinary locked-out black citizens was "Tell it, *do* it brother!"

But there was a flip side to this budding deal that the Black Panther Party for Self-Defense was making with the local black community: black criminality, for the most part, was to continue. From the beginning of the party, Newton was working out a deal with the black criminal elements of Oakland, couching the deal in revolutionary rhetoric—quid pro quo, the Panthers were saying. We'll undermine the police, making it easier for you to engage in your criminal activities, in exchange for a fee. Newton admitted as much, although you had to read between the lines. "Black consciousness had generally reached the point where a man felt guilty about exploiting the black community," he wrote of the party's beginnings. "However, if his daily activities for survival could be integrated with actions that undermined the established order, he felt good about it. In order to survive, they still had to sell their hot goods. *But at the same time they would pass some of their cash on to us* [italics added]. That way, ripping off became more than just an individual thing."

Rumors spread that the party had a small-scale protection racket going. At least one convenience-store owner professed to being happy to pay the party. He allegedly made a deal with the Panthers to stop some of the petty problems he was experiencing with local kids stealing entire racks of food. After he began paying off the Panthers, the kids stopped right away.

And just as the Black Panthers weren't saints, neither were the Oakland police. One evening a dramatic spectacle occurred on an Oakland freeway when a black police officer from San Francisco was chased by two white Oakland police officers. One of them pulled a gun and started firing at him. The reason? The two Oakland police officers thought the officer from San Francisco was trying to interfere with the prostitutes they were running (this was an activity the individual officers allegedly ran, not the Oakland police department itself).

While all of this was occurring, the Bay Area continued its role as a national pacesetter not only for radical white student activism but for Black Power activism too. Altogether approximately thirty black militant groups were competing for attention. Stokely Carmichael made the Bay Area one of his regular stops in appearances before militant groups in major cities across the country, as he pursued SNCC's policy of seeding new organizations to carry on the work SNCC had started.

Eldridge Cleaver, on release from prison, rented out a large Victorian house on Pine Street in San Francisco's predominantly black Filmore district. (His writings had provided him with national notoriety.) Using radical Bay Area lawyer Beverly Axelrod as a conduit, various San Francisco communist organizations allegedly picked up the tab. Axelrod was now Cleaver's mistress. The large Victorian house, named the Black House, became a cultural center where the various black organizations that Newton and Seale labeled "armchair revolutionaries" gathered every Friday to hold cultural events. The playwright LeRoi Jones (who later changed his name to Amiri Baraka) was teaching for a semester at San Francisco State. He also became a regular at the Black House.

Roy Ballard, who in 1963 as a member of San Francisco CORE helped found the Ad Hoc Committee to End Discrimination, became a regular at the Black House. Ballard later became active with SNCC and, inspired by Stokely Carmichael's call for a number of Black Panther organizations across the nation, helped start the only other Black Panther Party in the Bay Area. It was called the Black Panther Party of Northern California, the organization he was active in when the Black House was started.

In January 1967 all of the Bay Area black organizations and statewide black elected officials held an event called Conference 67, Survival of Black People. Paranoia was rampant among blacks across the country as the year began. Rumors abounded that because of the riots of the previous three years, concentration camps were being prepared to house blacks. Blacks throughout the country were also united in their anger about the mounting problems of earlier Premier Black Leader Adam Clayton Powell. Citing Powell's legal problems after a Harlem woman successfully sued him for slander and he refused to pay the judgment, as well as

Powell's excessive absentee record in Congress and padding of his payroll (a practice not uncommon among other members of congress), the entire U.S. House of Representatives was considering excluding him from their ranks. The Conference for Black Survival was designed both to find ways for blacks to counter the problems they saw developing in black America and to shore up support for Powell. The three-day event was held in San Francisco's Kezar stadium. Both Eldridge Cleaver and Stokely Carmichael were among the numerous featured speakers.

Roy Ballard and other members of the Black Panther Party of Northern California were having a dispute with the more moderate conference organizers. They were angry because no provisions had been made for grassroots blacks who couldn't afford to pay the admission fee and because the contributions of Malcolm X were excluded from the sessions at the conference. Looking to Stokely Carmichael for leadership, they asked him to use his speech to mention Malcolm X. Carmichael responded that his speech was already set. It was a position paper on the subject of alliances between black groups, and he had no intention of changing it. But he did agree that Malcolm was important and that the various budding black militant organizations throughout the country were riddled with too much divisiveness. Ballard thought the solution to both the exclusion of Malcolm X's teachings at the conference and the need for more unity among local militant black organizations was another conference on February 21, the anniversary of Malcolm X's assassination. Carmichael gave his blessing to the idea.

Newton and the Black Panther Party for Self-Defense still hadn't gained the respect of most of the black militant organizations in the Bay Area. Most members of the other groups were scared of Newton and his Black Panther Party. They considered them too street. But they felt Newton and the other members of the Black Panther Party for Self-Defense could be of strategic value to the upcoming First Annual Malcolm X Grass Roots Memorial, to be held in the Hunter's Point section of San Francisco. Allegedly, the various Bay Area communist organizations who were behind Cleaver and the Black House also picked up the tab for the

Malcolm X memorial, although most people participating at the time were unaware of it.

To kick it off, Ballard and the other planners invited Malcolm X's widow, Betty Shabazz, to be the opening-day speaker. They were paranoid about the possibility that Malcolm X's widow could be harmed, yet reluctant to handle security for her appearance by themselves. Despite their fear of Newton, for the purpose of protecting Betty Shabazz their thinking was: "Who do you call when you're nervous about protecting a very important woman? The most unsettling black men you can think of." So they asked the Black Panther Party for Self-Defense to add its presence to the security for Betty Shabazz. They invited them to a planning meeting for the event at the Black House.

Newton and Seale arrived, dressed in their official party regalia, complete with guns, bringing with them Bobby Hutton, Reginald and Sherman Forte, and Orleander Harrison. The whole room grew quiet when they walked in. Already there, sitting in a circle, were Ken Freeman, chairman of the Black Panther Party of Northern California; Eldridge Cleaver; Roy Ballard; Mark Comfort; and about twenty others. Newton, Seale, and Hutton sat down in chairs outside the circle, while the other members of their group stood at ease in a military manner. Cleaver seemed to be in charge of the discussion, which centered around who would speak at the three-day event on which subjects, and what the overall revolutionary philosophy of black people should be. According to Seale, both he and Newton remained quiet until Seale asked Ballard when the group was going to get around to a discussion of security for Shabazz. "He said, 'In a minute, brother. In a minute we're going to take care of that,' as an intellectual always does to a field nigger."

On the appointed day, dressed in black berets and leather jackets, guns in hand, eight members of Newton's Black Panther Party for Self-Defense, five members of the Black Panther Party of Northern California, and seven others headed to San Francisco International Airport in a five-car caravan to escort Betty Shabazz into San Francisco. When they arrived, they piled out of their cars to enter the bright beige terminal. But before they could get there, airport security chief George Nessel and his deputies confronted them. Newton told everyone to keep quiet, he would do the talking.

"What are you doing with these guns?" Nessel asked.

"Well you're a cop," Huey responded. "What are you doing with *your* gun?"

Then a black officer chimed in. "Is this gun loaded?"

"If I know it's loaded, that's good enough," Huey answered.

"Well, where are you going?"

"We're going to the airport to escort our sister Betty Shabazz. Why?"

According to Bobby Seale, at that point Roy Ballard cut in, believing he could negotiate better with the security officers. He told them that arguing was unnecessary. All they had to do was read *The Autobiography of Malcolm X*, and they would know why it was necessary to provide Betty Shabazz with an armed escort.

As if providing the official message that the "armchair revolutionaries" were about to take a backseat in the movement, Huey told Ballard to be quiet. "How do you explain to a racist, ignorant bastard cop, cops of the power structure who were behind the killing of Malcolm, who kill black people, and who are here to try to tell you you can't go anywhere. This is no time to stop and read the *Autobiography*."

Nessel told Newton that the terminal was private property. "Even if it is private property," Newton responded, "if it accommodates more than 200 people at a time, then any citizen has a right to exercise his rights on it. So get out of our way."

Nessel told him that three or four of the guard could go inside, but not the rest. Newton brushed him off. "We're going inside whether you like it or not, swine!"

"It was like a scene out of a western—you know this group of armed vigilantes," declared one bystander watching them enter the terminal. "Each one, like clockwork, set themselves up at various stations at the arrival gate and waited, rifles in hand." And when Betty Shabazz alighted from the plane, the Panthers escorted her into town.

The drama raised the ante in the Black Power community ever higher, as the caravan headed to the offices of *Ramparts* magazine at 301 Broadway Street in the North Beach section of San Francisco, where Eldridge Cleaver, now a staff writer for the magazine, was to interview Betty Shabazz. Cleaver had first met Newton in January at a local radio station where Cleaver was being interviewed. Newton made his way to the station to talk to Eldridge. What impressed Newton about Cleaver at least as equally as Cleaver's writing was that Cleaver had been in jail for nine years. Cleaver remained aloof from Newton. When he and Seale and the other members of their Black Panther Party appeared at the Black House planning meeting for the memorial event, he had been impressed by their presence and the unnerving effect it had on everyone in the room. But that was nothing compared to the way Newton would impress him after his meeting with Betty Shabazz at *Ramparts*.

The Panthers escorted Shabazz inside for her interview with Cleaver. Cleaver had revered Malcolm X, having, like Malcolm, converted to Elijah Muhammad's Nation of Islam while in prison. Like Malcolm he also broke with the group. He had dreams of using his own budding fame as a writer to follow in Malcolm's footsteps, perhaps even take up the challenge of rejuvenating Malcolm's Organization of African American Unity (OAAU). In fact, it was the stated aim of Cleaver's communist sponsors to promote him as the next Malcolm X. And Cleaver had originally hoped to use the Malcolm X memorial as the springboard for a new OAAU. The original idea behind the Black House was to facilitate this dream. But on this day, all of that was to change.

When the entourage arrived, Cleaver was sitting at his desk in the office when a white secretary burst in shouting, "We're being invaded! We're being invaded! There are about twenty men outside with guns!" Cleaver immediately knew to whom she was referring and replied, "Don't worry, they're friends." As he made his way to meet the party, he calmed down other frightened *Ramparts* staffers.

Outside, the entire street had stopped. San Francisco police squad cars raced to the scene, only to see Huey Newton, shotgun in hand, staring at them from a window. A police lieutenant went inside to investigate the situation. Bob Scheer, managing editor of *Ramparts*, and Warren Hinckle, the eye-patch–wearing editor in chief, assured him everything was fine. By now the entire local press had been alerted that a "frightening black army" had whisked the widow of Malcolm X from San Francisco's airport to the offices of *Ramparts*. The entire block around *Ramparts* was jammed with people curious about what was going on, as the local press, including television reporters and cameramen, tried squeezing their way into the *Ramparts* office.

One cameraman made it inside, whereupon two *Ramparts* staffers told him that he was trespassing on private property and threw him out. When the meeting between Shabazz and Cleaver was over, Newton took command to get her off the premises. He sent five men out ahead to clear a path through the throng of spectators. Then he had the rest of the Panthers surround Shabazz and her cousin Hakim Jamal as they left. Newton and Seale brought up the rear. Shabazz had said she wanted no photos taken. But as the party left, the television cameraman who had been thrown out thrust his camera at the party to film them. Huey took an envelope and thrust it at the camera to block the lens. The cameraman told Newton to get out of the way. When Huey didn't remove the envelope from in front of the lens, the cameraman reached out and knocked Huey's hand away with his fist. Huey grabbed the cameraman by the collar and slammed him against the wall. A police officer started to undo the strap holding his revolver in place. Realizing how hairy things could get, Bobby Seale stepped in and urged Huey to come on and go.

But Huey turned to the officers and said, "Alright. All you pigs, all you cops. That man assaulted me. Now why in the hell didn't you arrest him? Arrest that man."

"If we arrest anyone it will be you," an officer replied. Seale stepped in again and urged Newton to get going.

A few more officers started to undo the straps to their pistols. By this time Ken Freeman had whisked Betty Shabazz away. Only five Panthers were left at the scene. One of them had his back turned to police. Newton told him to turn around. "Don't turn your back on these backshooting motherfuckers!" Everyone turned to face the police, and Huey gave the signal to spread.

At that point an obese officer undid the strap holding his gun in place and walked up to Huey, shouting, "Don't point that gun at me! Stop pointing that gun at me!"

Everything stood still. Huey stared at the cop. Then he walked within a few feet of him and asked, "What's the matter? You got an itchy finger?" The officer didn't utter a word. He just stood there. The other officers told him to stay cool. "You want to draw your gun?" Huey asked him. They both stood there staring straight into each other's eyes. Newton pumped a round of ammunition into his shotgun. "Ok," he said. "You big fat racist pig, draw your gun! Draw it, you cowardly dog!" The officer didn't move. "I'm waiting," Huey said. He had his gun pointed at a forty-five-degree angle, facing downward.

All the other officers moved out of the line of fire. Eldridge Cleaver had been standing on the steps of the *Ramparts* office watching everything. He moved back too, thinking to himself, "Goddam, that nigger is c-r-a-z-y!"

Finally, the officer gave in. He let out a big sigh and hung his head. Huey practically laughed in his face. He and the other Panthers slowly backed away, heading for their cars across the street. Then they sped off. Eldridge Cleaver's idea to start a new organization to take the place of Malcolm's went up in smoke. He decided to become a member of Newton's Black Panther Party. Cleaver would take the title Minister of Information.

Shortly after the *Ramparts* incident, Newton discovered that the Black Panther Party of Northern California hadn't used loaded weapons during the Shabazz escort. A few weeks later, he and his Panther Party showed up at a fish fry in San Francisco sponsored by the Black Panther Party of Northern California and gave them an ultimatum: they could either change their name, merge with Newton's group, or be annihilated. When they said they would accept none of the alternatives, Newton and his men pounced on them. Moments later a shot was fired into the air. Everyone scattered. After this incident, the Black Panther Party of Northern California changed its name.

EVENTS WERE MOVING AT A DIZZYING PACE. BECAUSE OF the standoff at *Ramparts*, Newton's "crazy nigger" image grew. Yet at the same time he became more awe inspiring. Young blacks from different backgrounds talked more and more of armed confrontation. They became ever more strident. And now Newton had Cleaver, the man of growing fame and eloquence who had a sounding board in the white leftist media and the backing of extreme left-wing white radicals. Cleaver had already secured a bridge to the preeminent black militant leader—Stokely Carmichael. The eloquent Bigger Thomas had met with the increasingly restless civil rights veteran in Chicago. Cleaver traveled there to write a profile of Carmichael for *Ramparts*. Carmichael was in Chicago for the same reason he kept appearing in the San Francisco Bay Area— to continue drumming up grassroots activity among militant young blacks and to raise money for the increasingly faltering SNCC by accepting one more of the many speaking engagements he received from white colleges. This time it was to be the University of Chicago. He would also appear on a local television station along with a Chicago congressman who was a member of Congressman Adam Clayton Powell's House Education and Labor Committee. The House was still debating what to do about Powell.

On the day of the debate, Cleaver, Carmichael, and Cleveland Sellers made their way to the studio. Once in the building, they had to ride an elevator to get to their destination. On the way up, the elevator stopped on another floor. A white woman got on. She was reading a sheaf of papers when suddenly she looked up to see first the face of Sellers, then the face of Carmichael, who was wearing his ubiquitous sunglasses. Then she turned around and saw the face of Cleaver. She grew very rigid, and when the elevator stopped where she wanted to get off she rushed off, in Cleaver's words, "as though from some evil presence." As the elevator door closed, Sellers, Carmichael, and Cleaver had a big laugh.

On television the Chicago congressman stated that he was all in favor of stripping Adam Clayton Powell of his chairmanship of the House Education and Labor Committee. He hadn't an ounce of appreciation for what Powell meant to blacks despite Powell's many flaws. Not even the sentiments of newly elected black Detroit congressman John Conyers had reached him. Conyers had told the committee considering Powell's case, "When I was a little boy in Michigan, Adam Clayton Powell was the first and only black hero I ever heard of." When the camera turned to Carmichael, he hit the congressman with a question that, in essence, was the answer to why he and Sellers, at least, could take such joy in intimidating the white woman on the elevator: Why were the congressman and his fellow politicians so willing to strip Powell of his position, yet not willing to raise a finger to oust the many white congressmen from Alabama and Mississippi who held their seats by virtue of the fact that blacks had been murdered, intimidated, and kept from voting?

Later that day, Carmichael spoke with local militants at a social center that was Chicago's equivalent of San Francisco's Black House. They wanted to know why he was always meeting with white people. After all, one of them said, poet/playwright LeRoi Jones had declared it was no use talking to whites. Carmichael told them that his record spoke for itself. He told them he was going to the University of Chicago to speak because the school was paying him. He said that the problem with black people was that they always shouted for their own organizations, but they never came up with the money to support those organizations, and then instead of helping blacks like him who tried to raise that money, they sat back and took potshots. He told them that the answer to all their complaints was to get off their butts and organize.

All of this registered with Cleaver, the increasingly important facilitator, the man who would spread the word in his *Ramparts* article. And now that he was with Newton's Black Panthers, within one month of the article's appearance, Cleaver would join forces with Newton as the mastermind of a symbolic action that would electrify both Carmichael and the black militants at the Chicago social center—and further scare the hell out of whites like the woman on the elevator.

With the aid of Beverly Axelrod, Cleaver's first major move as a Black Panther was to help launch a Black Panther newspaper. The first edition appeared in April, its headline reading, "Why Did the Police Murder Denzil Dowell?" Dowell was a young black male with a criminal record who lived in the unincorporated, predominantly black area of North Richmond, on the other side of the bay from San Francisco. Many of the citizens of North Richmond, and the Panthers, alleged he was shot in the back by Contra Costa County police, unarmed, with his arms raised. The police insisted he was shot trying to escape after he was caught trying to break into a store. The Panthers went to North Richmond at the invitation of Mark Comfort of the Oakland Direct Action Committee, spoke with the Dowell family, and held two community rallies where they displayed their arms. In the second one they cordoned off the area, keeping the police away. They also circulated a petition to have North Richmond incorporated as a town so that it could have its own police force. Shortly after this, they were called to a junior high school in nearby San Pablo by black parents who accused schoolteachers of beating up two black pupils. They showed up there armed as well. Then, continuing with the Dowell matter, the armed Panthers traveled to nearby Martinez, the county seat, with the intention of going to the sheriff's office to demand prosecution of the police officer responsible for Dowell's death.

To the young northern and West Coast militants, defiant symbolism was everything. Just as Carmichael had said in Chicago, when it was time to pass the hat to collect money, when it was time to organize and actually address the problems they constantly complained about, such militants had difficulty replicating SNCC's activity in the Deep South. But when it was time to show *anger*, that was a different matter. Let some black youth, usually with a police record, get shot by the police, and mobilization in northern and West Coast ghettos was a breeze—mobilization to riot. The Black Panthers were the first group to organize such anger, put it in uniform, and give it a gun. In 1955, E. D. Nixon would never have organized the black citizens of Montgomery to protest a black youth with a police record of genuine criminal activity—possibly in the middle of such activity—getting shot in the back by the police. Things were different now, largely because of the Panthers, who very likely would have wanted Denzil Dowell to join their ranks *because* he had a police record.

The accumulation of incidents involving the armed Panthers grew to be too much for the white power structure of the Bay Area. First, it was the humiliation of the Oakland police, then the San Francisco airport scene, then the humiliation of the San Francisco police in front of *Ramparts*, then the humiliation of the Contra Costa County police at the Dowell rally. And then the confrontation at the sheriff's office in Martinez. The Panthers even had the audacity to walk around patrolling affluent white communities and suburbs. It was guerilla theater. Their message to the residents was, let's see how you like someone armed, in uniform, of a color different from you, walking around in *your* neighborhood.

One such community was Piedmont, a town totally surrounded by Oakland and represented by California Republican state legislator Donald Mulford. That April, as a response to all the Panther gun activity, Mulford introduced a bill that would prohibit the carrying of loaded firearms in public places. The bill was scheduled to go before the California State Assembly Committee on Criminal Procedure on May 2, 1967. Discovering this from the newspapers, Newton and Cleaver hatched the bold plan that would electrify militants across the country and frighten most of white America.

On the morning of May 2 an entourage of armed Panthers started from Oakland for the eighty-mile ride to Sacramento. On its way, one member of the group called a young journalist to find out how to ensure that their move would garner publicity. "What do you mean, how do you get publicity?" he replied. "Call the television stations and tell them we're the Black Panthers, we're coming from Oakland, we've got our leather jackets on, we've got our rifles, and we're going to walk into the legislature with guns. See what happens."

With the aid of the Watts, San Francisco, and Oakland riots, Ronald Reagan had been elected California's governor the previous fall. Stokely Carmichael helped as well with his UC Berkeley speech at the SDS-sponsored Black Power Conference. Commenting on Carmichael's attacks on white America at state-supported UC Berkeley, Reagan took a thinly veiled swipe at his gubernatorial opponent, Governor Edmund G. Brown, Sr., saying, "The time has come for the government to turn to the more responsible elements in the Negro community for leadership." Apparently, though, no such elements existed to Reagan's campaign operatives. During the campaign they also blanketed white neighborhoods with campaign literature known as "hit pieces," containing small photographs of his Democratic opponent shaking hands with black people.

On the afternoon of May 2, when Seale, eighteen of his armed protégés, and an unarmed Eldridge Cleaver showed up at the state capitol dressed in Black Panther regalia, Ronald Reagan was on the capitol lawn giving a speech before a youth group. Reagan was hustled inside. The Panther group made its way to the capitol building in search of the state assembly chamber. Seale, who carried a holstered pistol, made sure everyone was careful to keep their M-1 rifles and 12-gauge shotguns pointed either straight up in the air or straight down to the ground, since it was a felony to point a gun at anyone. Many of them also had cartridge belts around their waists. Not everyone in the group was a Panther, as would often be the case over the next few years when the party made public displays of its strength. Included among them as they headed for the domed building was Mark Comfort, and Denzil Dowell's brother, George. Huey Newton stayed in Oakland because the others feared he might be harmed.

When the group reached the steps of the capitol, the cameras were already there. Journalists, given their sensationalist bent, urged them inside. Once in the capitol, the Panthers didn't know where to go. They absorbed the shocked stares of government workers. News cameramen and photographers jumped back and forth in front of them, filming and clicking away. In his hand, Bobby Seale held a proclamation that the Panthers called an executive mandate, dictated by Newton and written up and perfected by Cleaver. Seale was to read the mandate.

The Panthers and an avalanche of photographers, cameramen, and reporters made their way to the second floor where the assembly met. When they reached the door of the chamber, a government worker simply opened the door and guided them onto the assembly floor. Everything stopped. The handful of black members of the assembly were embarrassed. Photos of the armed black men in black leather jackets and berets standing in the aisles would be seen around the world. A capitol hill police officer walked up to Bobby Hutton and took his gun. Hutton started to protest. Then Seale protested, asking if Hutton was under arrest. The officer answered that they weren't supposed to be on the assembly floor. Hutton told him to give him his gun back if he wasn't under arrest. The guns were taken from the other members of the entourage. The officers held on to the guns as the Panthers were led off the assembly floor.

Hutton began cursing out the officer who took his gun, demanding it back as the entourage moved to an elevator. An officer grabbed Seale by the arm as they walked, a gesture also caught on camera, destined to become a famous photo. Once inside the elevator, they returned to the first floor and were led to a small room where Bobby Seale read the executive mandate:

> The Black Panther Party for Self-Defense calls upon the American people in general and the black people in particular to take careful note of the racist California Legislature which is now considering legislation aimed at keeping the black people disarmed and powerless at the very same time that racist police agencies throughout the country are intensifying the terror, brutality, murder, and repression of black people.
>
> At the same time that the American government is waging a racist war of genocide in Vietnam, the concentration camps in which the Japanese Americans were interned during World War II are being renovated and expanded. Since Amer-

ica has historically reserved the most barbaric treatment for nonwhite people we are forced to conclude that the concentration camps are being prepared for black people who are determined to gain their freedom by any means necessary. The enslavement of black people from the very beginning of this country, the genocide practiced on the American Indians and the confining of the survivors on reservations, the savage lynching of thousands of black men and women, the dropping of atomic bombs on Hiroshima and Nagasaki, and now the cowardly massacre in Vietnam all testify to the fact that towards people of color, the racist power structure of America has but one policy: repression, genocide, terror, and the big stick.

Black people have begged, prayed, petitioned, demonstrated, and everything else to get the racist power structure of America to right the wrongs which have historically been perpetrated against black people. All of these efforts have been answered by more repression, deceit, and hypocrisy. As the aggression of the racist American government escalates in Vietnam, the police agencies of America escalate the repression of black people throughout the ghettoes of America. Vicious police dogs, cattle prods, and increased patrols have become familiar sights in black communities. City Hall turns a deaf ear to the pleas of black people for relief from this increasing terror.

The Black Panther Party for Self-Defense believes that the time has come for black people to arm themselves against this terror before it is too late. The pending Mulford Act brings the hour of doom one step nearer. A people who have suffered so much for so long at the hands of a racist society, must draw the line somewhere. We believe that the black communities of America must rise up as one man to halt the progression of a trend that leads inevitably to their total destruction.

When Seale finished reading the mandate, the Panthers' guns were returned to them. The media asked Seale to read the message twice more so they could get it right. He obliged them. Then the Panther entourage headed out of the state capitol. When Seale reached the bottom of the steps, he read the mandate once more. Then everyone left. On the way out of town, the Panthers stopped at a gas station. Suddenly, from all around, uniformed and plain-clothes officers converged and arrested the Panthers under the felony charge of conspiracy to disrupt a legislative session.

Two days after the Sacramento incident and the subsequent Panther arrests, a rally was held at San Francisco State to raise bail money for the arrested Panthers. The same black students at Bay Area campuses who only a year earlier had derided Newton and Seale as nuts now saw them as heroes. At the rally, to the applause of students, Barbara Arthur called the Panther action in Sacramento merely one of concerned citizens demonstrating their opposition to the proposed Mulford bill. Visiting faculty member LeRoi Jones advised the approximately 200 rally participants, "You better get yourself a gun if you want to survive the white man's wrath. . . . White policemen aren't here to protect you, they're here to kill you."

The playwright Ed Bullins, now director of the Black House in San Francisco, called black people a captive nation, telling the audience that blacks were going to take control of their own community. "We're going to refuse to recognize white laws. We're not going to have any whites coming into our community, even those of good faith."

The mainstream media called the Panthers' Sacramento gesture an "invasion." "What do you think this can do to some white people to see guns around them?" San Francisco police chief Thomas Cahill wondered out loud. The answer to his question came twelve days later when six armed, jack-booted members of the American Nazi party staged a weapons-waving demonstration in front of the Black Panthers' Grove Street headquarters in Oakland. There was no confrontation and they left peaceably.

Lyn Nofziger, Governor Reagan's communications director, who would later serve as press secretary when Reagan was president, stated that as a result of the Panther action, extra precautions had been taken to protect the governor. When asked what those precautions were, he refused to give details because "we don't want to tell people like that what we're doing." The symbolism of the cowboy in the white hat (from Reagan's days as a B-movie actor), who must do something to protect the townspeople from evil black desperadoes like the armed Panther "invaders" of the state capitol, began dancing in people's heads. "[Officials and employees talk of] what a great president Governor Reagan would make, and we have to deny it," Nofziger commented. Reagan would, in fact, make his first presidential bid the following year.

With the Sacramento publicity ploy, the Panthers were on their way to national notoriety as America's symbol of black extremism. Never mind that the executive mandate that Seale read at the state capitol clearly delineated the official Panther line of hating the white power structure and not all whites, which was the difference between the party's philosophy and that of other black militants. Or that Seale made a trip to UC Berkeley as soon as he was bailed out of jail to make clear to students that the party hated the power structure and not all whites. The ideological lines could be so easily blurred for two reasons: because of the symbolism of the gun, which black nationalists increasingly professed a belief in, and which the Panthers were specifically organized around from the start; and because of the obvious hysteria that seized most white Americans whenever anyone black carried a gun, for any reason.

Although the Panthers continued to have their local militant opponents, such opponents for the most part were drowned out by those who rallied to the Panther cause. At the end of May, another rally to raise more money for the Panthers—this time to cover the courtroom costs of defending Panthers against the Sacramento charges—was held in San Francisco at the Filmore Auditorium. It was sponsored by the San Francisco State Black Students Union (BSU), which at that time many referred to as the leading black student union of all college campuses across the nation. By now black nationalism had caused a marked turnaround in the styles of young blacks. They appeared at the rally in the attire of black African cultures. Many women wore their hair naturally kinky instead of straightened. The rally featured poetry, music, and a play as well as speeches. The ubiquitous Stokely Carmichael made an appearance, as did the equally ubiquitous LeRoi Jones, who emphasized increasing disdain for blacks in the middle class. "We're going to try to burn you black," Jones told them, "because if we don't burn you, nothing will but the actual fire, which we're trying to desperately bring about."

The blurring of the line between blacks with a street mentality and college-based black militants, both unifying around a romance with the gun, was completed by a one-act play staged by a black drama group at San Francisco State (whose membership included a young man who would one day become one of the most influential black actors in the country—Danny Glover). At the play's beginning, a member of the Black Panther Party for Self-Defense strode on stage with an M-1 rifle, pointed it at the ceiling, and swept it in a symbolic arc. The action of the play concerned two black guerilla fighters pinned down by the police in an unnamed American city. One was near death; the other recalled his mother, who he believed had emasculated him by wanting him to be white. The play ended with the murder of the mother, as the audience shouted, "Kill her! Kill her!" A major corner had been turned.

6

The Cat Slips Its Leash

A PERSON COULDN'T BE SURE THAT THE PANTHERS' MAY 2 state capitol gun display and executive mandate was the green light, but later that same month, in the South of all places, violent actions occurred among black Americans not expected to engage in such activities. The night and early-morning hours of May 16–17, after the arrest of a black youth, students at Houston's predominantly black Texas Southern University bombarded police cars with rocks and bottles. Then they started firing guns and hurling crude bombs (gasoline-filled bottles) at them. Snipers fired from dormitories, shooting three policemen, one fatally. Altogether, 488 students went to jail. Elsewhere, at Jackson State College in Jackson, Mississippi, two black patrolmen entered campus to arrest a speeding motorist, only to be confronted by approximately seventy-five angry students who told them the traffic violator wasn't going with them. By midnight a riot had developed, when hundreds of Jackson State students, joined by students from nearby Tougaloo College, threw rocks and bottles at police officers who were behind a barricade. Soon, shots were fired by either the police, the state patrolmen, or deputies from the sheriff's office serving as reinforcements.

When the smoke cleared, one young black man lay wounded and would later die.

The same night as the disturbance at Texas Southern, Stokely Carmichael made a speech in Washington, D.C., almost seeming to explain what would happen that night hundreds of miles to the south: "There is no need to go to Vietnam and shoot somebody who a honky says is your enemy [Carmichael would popularize the new derogatory term for white people—*honky*—among young blacks]. We're going to shoot the cops who are shooting our black brothers in the back in this country. That's where we're going."

In May, Carmichael was replaced as chairman of SNCC by twenty-three-year-old H. Rap Brown. Carmichael introduced the new chairman at a press conference, saying, "You'll be happy to have me back when you hear from him. He's a bad man." Perhaps Brown was a bad man privately. But at the time of his election as SNCC chairman, he had yet to effect the style by which the rest of the nation would soon know him. At the press conference he seemed shy and tentative. And at the end of the month, when Carmichael introduced him at the San Francisco State BSU–sponsored Filmore Auditorium benefit for the Panthers who were arrested in Sacramento, Brown didn't impress the crowd. Recalls Benny Stewart, who became president of the San Francisco State BSU that fall: "When the women saw him they were disappointed because he looked like a frat boy. He had on a blue blazer, and he wore glasses, and he was so much different than Stokely. He wasn't yet dynamic. He changed over the summer and came out and blew. He got it together and took it up another notch."

At the May 1967 press conference introducing him, Brown had meekly outlined SNCC's program for the coming year: a national antidraft campaign certain to keep lines open with the increasingly radical young whites of the antiwar movement, and a thrust for black economic and political control of the ghettos. But after he "got it together and blew," developing such programs wouldn't be H. Rap Brown's legacy.

Urban rioting that summer, 1967, was the worst of the 1960s. The first major flashpoint happened in Newark, New Jersey, home of the worst inner-city housing and crime rates in the nation. On

July 11, police officers arrested a black cab driver on traffic charges and began scuffling with him as a crowd from the housing project across the street from the precinct house watched. A rumor soon spread that the cabbie had been killed. A mob advanced on the precinct house, throwing bottles and bricks, and the police responded with billy clubs and tear gas. Soon looters began breaking into downtown Newark stores. Snipers fired at the police from rooftops. The disturbance lasted for five days and nights. When the smoke cleared, the damage was comparable to that in Watts two years earlier. There were 26 people dead, 1,004 injured, and 1,397 arrested. Among the arrested was LeRoi Jones, home from his teaching stint at San Francisco State. On July 23, Detroit erupted in a disturbance comparable to Newark's, touched off after police raided an after-hours drinking establishment. Forty-two people were killed, 386 were injured, and 5,557 were arrested. Lesser disturbances broke out in approximately sixty black communities across the nation.

On the heels of Newark and Detroit, H. Rap Brown spoke in Cambridge, Maryland, a town of 14,000 residents, one-fifth of whom were black. He had been invited because the black citizens were impatient about the lack of delivery by city fathers on pledges made after three years of unrest. Since his election to the leadership of SNCC, Brown had completely transformed himself. His natural was larger than Carmichael's, and he constantly wore sunglasses. He no longer sported fratboy-like clothing, choosing instead casual street clothes. And somehow, by the time he spoke in Cambridge, he was no longer a shy, tentative stump speaker. The H. Rap Brown that Cambridge saw "took it up another notch." "Detroit exploded, Newark exploded, Harlem exploded!" Brown told the crowd of about 300 people. "It is time for Cambridge to explode, baby. Black folks built America. If America don't come around, we're going to burn America down, brother. We're going to burn it if we can't get our share of it." Then Brown mentioned the run-down Pine Street elementary school nearby. "You should have burned it down a long time ago," he told the crowd. "Then you should have taken over the new elementary school on the other side of town."

A few hours after Brown's speech, a disturbance broke out.

During the melee, the Pine Street school was set ablaze and a police officer was wounded. Brown, who was at the scene, was grazed on the forehead by an officer's bullet. Angered because of Brown's inflammatory rhetoric, Cambridge's white volunteer fire fighters refused to respond to the blaze. And the town's white police chief refused to order the fire fighters into the neighborhood, telling black citizens, "You people stood by and let a bunch of goddam hoodlums come in and let my police get shot. Don't come to me with this." Not only the school but the entire heart of the black section of town was destroyed, leaving black businesses burned out and dozens of people homeless.

The following day Brown was arrested in Alexandria, Virginia, and charged with inciting a riot and arson. He was released on $10,000 bond, after which he promptly called a press conference at the Washington, D.C., office of SNCC, where he made further statements by which history would remember him. "I say you better get yourself a gun," he told the cheering crowd. "The honky don't respect nothing but guns." He accused President Johnson of starting all the riots, saying, "Johnson is a wild, mad dog—an outlaw from Texas." Then he uttered what would go down as one of the most famous lines from the 1960s: "Violence is necessary. It is as American as cherry pie." That night at a Washington church he told his audience that blacks should "do more shooting than looting when they riot. . . . If you are going to loot, loot yourself a gunstore. You got to arm yourself, brother."

Back in Sacramento, six of the members of Newton's Black Panther Party who went to the state capitol armed that first week in May were finally tried in court. Bobby Seale, Warren Tucker, Abbert Commo, Emory Douglas, Johnny Bethea, and Mikel Hall pleaded guilty to the misdemeanor charge of disrupting a legislative session. Felony charges of conspiracy were dismissed. Cases against all other participants were dismissed for lack of sufficient evidence to place them within the restricted area of the assembly chamber. After his arrest, Eldridge Cleaver had been released the following day because he wasn't carrying a gun and was formally covering the event for *Ramparts*. Seale and the others who pleaded guilty to the misdemeanor charges were sentenced to six months in prison. They began serving their sentences in August.

In the intervening time between the state capitol action and the trial, there had been no damper on Black Panther activity, although the party membership numbered no more than a dozen. The second issue of the Black Panther newspaper was produced at the San Francisco home of Beverly Axelrod. The headline read: "The Truth About Sacramento." During production, a photographer was called to take the picture of Newton for the newspaper that would become his most famous photograph; within a year it would be found on the walls of the residences of a large number of the nation's radicals and black militants. Eldridge Cleaver set up the photograph. He took a wicker chair and positioned it like a black African throne surrounded by appropriate decorations—two warrior's shields, and an animal pelt on the floor. Newton sat in the wicker chair in full Panther regalia, holding a spear in his left hand and a shotgun in his right. The warrior's shields were placed on either side of the chair. And history was made.

Meanwhile, with an eye toward civic-mindedness, the party became involved in a dispute about the lack of a traffic signal at a dangerous intersection at the corner of 55th and Market streets in black Oakland, where three children had been killed and seven injured. The city insisted that it couldn't install a traffic light at the spot until mid-1968 at the earliest. So the Panthers decided to establish their own patrol at the corner. Since the Mulford bill (which was passed in the state legislature, thanks largely to their gun display at the state capitol) had yet to be signed into law (Governor Reagan didn't sign it until the end of July), party members were able to display their guns as they stopped traffic and directed pedestrians across the intersection. Seeing this, the city immediately put up a traffic light at the corner.

The party also continued to hold rallies in Oakland, Berkeley, Richmond, and San Francisco, encouraging extreme animosity toward police officers, feeding efforts at an *organized* violent response to police presence in black communities. At a rally in San Francisco's Potrero Hill section, Bobby Seale stood on top of a garbage can and described how a couple of "bloods" could surprise police officers on their coffee break. All they had to do was march up on the cop and then "shoot him down—voom, voom—with a 12-gauge shotgun." Seale called such an action an example of righteous power. No more "bootlicking" or singing of "We Shall Overcome." At another rally, in North Richmond at the home of Denzil Dowell's brother George (now a member of the Panthers), a party member stood on the rooftop and demonstrated to the gathering below how to load a shotgun with a twenty-inch barrel, a gun that Bobby Seale said he highly recommended.

Although Carmichael became an SNCC field secretary after the elevation of H. Rap Brown, he remained in the limelight along with Brown, retaining enough of his notable militant aura that the Panthers sought to bring him into their party. At a San Francisco press conference at the end of June, Bobby Seale read an executive mandate issued by Newton, formally drafting Carmichael into the Black Panther Party, vesting him with the rank of field marshal, granting Carmichael the authority and responsibility for "establishing revolutionary law, order, and justice" east of the Continental Divide, while such authority was vested with the Black Panther Party itself to the west of the divide. The proclamation was more cosmetic than anything else. The Panthers and SNCC didn't hold serious discussions about a coalition until after Newton was arrested and charged with the shooting death of Officer John Frey. Besides Carmichael, the discussions would involve James Forman who, although increasingly at odds with Carmichael, was also growing more radical by the day (after the death of SNCC Executive Secretary Ruby Doris Robinson, he entered into intense studies of the works of Franz Fanon and other revolutionaries). Like Carmichael, Forman would be drawn into discussions with the Panthers out of knowledge that the more militant SNCC became, the more financial support it lost from liberal whites who admired SNCC's previous southern voter registration drives but not what they saw as its incitement of riots. The Panthers, however, were about to become the darlings of the white radical establishment, largely as a result of a major clash between white radicals and police a week and a half before the fateful early-morning hours of October 28, 1967.

That Huey Newton was capable of killing a police officer was predictable, given all his prior talk and actions. That the Oakland police were capable of inciting anyone to a desire to murder them was vividly realized by hundreds of black people in Oakland who had felt their brutality. But it became equally vivid to whites of all persuasions on the occasion of Stop the Draft Week.

With the election of the conservative Ronald Reagan as governor of California in November 1966, much enthusiasm had gone out of political movements among young white Californians. Although the antiwar movement continued, Berkeley retaining title as its principal epicenter, a new phenomenon was taking shape in the pacesetting Bay Area: the hippie movement. San Francisco, specifically the Haight-Ashbury district, fast became the center of the new movement, the culture of which was drug based, long-haired, and "natural." According to the writer Hunter S. Thompson, it believed in returning to the very basics of Adam and Eve. The same Filmore Auditorium used for a benefit concert to pay the court costs of Black Panthers was used to hold psychedelic acid-rock parties by revelers in the hippie movement, turned on to the theories of psychologist and drug guru Timothy Leary. Hundreds of young white refugees from the anti–Vietnam War activism of Berkeley and the earlier Bay Area civil rights demonstrations joined migrants from San Francisco's North Beach and others from across the country to make the Haight their home. The summer of 1967, known as the Summer of Love, was to be the zenith of the new hippie movement. That same summer, committed antiwar activists in organizations like SDS and other antiwar groups launched Vietnam Summer. This was their national effort modeled on SNCC's Mississippi Freedom Summer, designed to put thousands of volunteers to work educating hundreds of thousands of Americans against the war.

After witnessing the summer riots from afar and the boldness with which SNCC leaders like Brown and Carmichael as well as the Black Panthers encouraged open defiance of the authorities, antiwar organizers decided to get bold with their tactics too. The goal was to recapture lost fervor. By the fall of 1967, the number of concerned citizens with second thoughts about the war had grown to millions, thanks largely to Vietnam Summer, but also because of the steady increase in American troops being shipped to Vietnam. By the end of 1965, there were 184,000 troops; by the end of 1966, 385,000; by the end of 1967, 486,000. The majority of the 15,000 casualties of the war up to then would come in 1967 (60 percent). By that same year, leaders such as Dr. Martin Luther King and Dr. Benjamin Spock were speaking out against the war. And radical antiwar activists saw the chance to do as H. Rap Brown had done in the Black Power movement—take things up another notch.

The plan was to hold massive demonstrations at draft induction centers where thousands of young men would either burn or turn in their draft cards. A movement called The Resistance, founded at UC Berkeley and Stanford University, began catching on at campuses nationwide. And the decision was made that the week of October 16, 1967, Stop the Draft Week, would be the time for massive action at induction centers nationwide. Some Bay Area extremists had the idea that demonstrators not only should turn in or burn their draft cards at the downtown Oakland induction center, where inductees from all over northern California were bused in, but should block off and shut down the induction center completely. The final decision was that those who merely wished to sit in at the induction center and burn or turn in their draft cards would have the first day of protest, and the extremists who wanted to engage in more drastic measures would have the rest of the week.

As expected, that Monday the peaceful antiwar demonstrators gathered at the Oakland induction center. A total of 124 were arrested and sent to jail. The following day the antiwar extremists moved in. Approximately 4,000 demonstrators gathered at the induction center, closing it down for three hours. The media were there in full force. Across the street hundreds of police officers and members of the California Highway Patrol assembled at a three-story parking garage. When given the signal to move, they formed a flying wedge and waded into the demonstrators. Officers and troopers held a billy club in one hand and a can of Mace in the other, indiscriminately attacking anyone in their path, including newspeople. An ABC cameraman had his helmet torn from his head. Gordon Peters, a photographer for the *San Francisco Chronicle*, was shot in the face with Mace. A KRON-TV newscaster was squirted in both eyes "by a cop who knew damn well I wasn't a demonstrator." A UPI photographer was hit several times with a billy club. The news director at one television station reported that some members of the Oakland police force appeared to deliberately single out newspeople for the treatment.

The day would be known as Bloody Tuesday. In an official statement released after the carnage, Governor Ronald Reagan praised the perpetrators: "The work of the Oakland Police Department . . . was in the finest tradition of California's law enforcement agencies. The officers displayed exceptional ability and great professional skill. Their quick action is a tribute to the high caliber of the training they have received." After the behavior of the Oakland police force on Bloody Tuesday and Reagan's praise of it, the stage was set for Huey Newton to make an even greater impact on history than he otherwise would have made.

During the early-morning hours of October 28, near the corner of Seventh and Willow streets in West Oakland, Newton's car was pulled over by Oakland police officer John Frey. Newton and his friend Gene McKinney, also in the car, were out celebrating the end of Newton's probation after his release from jail for the knifing of Odell Lee. According to Newton, Officer Frey pulled him over for no apparent reason. Newton was driving his girlfriend's Volkswagen bug and carrying his pocket lawyer lawbook, which detailed a person's rights while being arrested, the search and seizure laws, and the rights of witnesses to an arrest. Frey, only twenty-three years old and a rookie cop, had, within his short time on the force, developed a reputation for being among the most brutal and racist of Oakland's police officers. (Allegedly, while on the police force visiting an English class at his high school alma mater, Frey repeatedly used the word *nigger* in reference to black people. It was also alleged that while on duty, Frey held down a

sixteen-year-old black youth while a white male client of a prostitute beat the youth for "incurring the man's displeasure.") On
realizing that he had stopped Black Panther leader Huey Newton,
he called for backup and was joined by twenty-four-year-old
Officer Herbert Heanes.

When Heanes arrived, Frey told Newton to get out of the car,
while Heanes said the same thing to McKinney. The details of the
sequence of events that led to the shooting remain shrouded in
confusing, contradictory testimony. According to Newton, while
Heanes stood with McKinney, Frey made Newton assume the
position so that he could be frisked for weapons. Heanes never
mentioned that such a search took place. Both Heanes and Newton
agree that Frey then led Newton toward the patrol cars. Newton
had his lawbook in his hand. Newton stated that while next to the
second patrol car, he began opening his lawbook as he told Frey,
"You have no reasonable cause to arrest me."

Frey's reply was, "You can take that book and shove it up your
ass, nigger."

During his trial for Frey's murder, Newton insisted that Frey,
after telling him what he could do with the lawbook, began to
physically abuse him. Then he pulled out his service revolver and
shot Newton in the stomach, after which Newton went into a daze.

Herbert Heanes's account of how the shooting began told a
different story. Heanes insisted that while standing at the back of
Frey's patrol car, Newton and Frey suddenly began to scuffle and
Frey was shot. He stated that Newton backed away from the dying
Frey and turned toward him. Although Heanes testified that he
didn't see a gun on Newton, Heanes shot Newton under the
assumption that Newton had shot Frey (years later Newton would
boast to close friends that he did, in fact, shoot John Frey). Heanes
was also wounded in the melee, although he could not identify the
source of the shot that wounded him. When the encounter was
over, Frey lay dead, Heanes lay wounded, and Huey Newton and
Gene McKinney had escaped the scene.

According to Dell Ross, a man driving in the vicinity, they
approached his car. One of them had a gun. They got in and
ordered him to drive them to 32nd and Chestnut streets. Ross

stated to the police and the grand jury investigating the case that the wounded Newton told him, "I just shot two dudes." Before they reached their stated destination, McKinney and Newton made Ross stop on Adeline Street. Then they got out and fled on foot.

Newton made it to the home of David Hilliard, who took him to Kaiser Hospital, where he was treated for his wound. While there he would be arrested and brutally handcuffed to an emergency room gurney. The photo of him lying there with a police officer standing in front of him was splashed across newspapers. Two weeks later an Alameda County grand jury returned a three-count indictment against Newton, charging him with first-degree murder, assault with a deadly weapon, and kidnapping (for forcing Dell Ross to drive him at gunpoint). With memories of Bloody Tuesday fresh in the heads of white radicals, and the black community long seething with animosity toward the police, Huey Newton became a national icon. And the Black Panther Party took over completely as the nation's premier symbol of black resistance to the entire American power structure.

IT WAS ELDRIDGE CLEAVER, WITH THE FINANCING OF HIS white backers, who made sure the transformation took place. With Seale in jail because of the Sacramento incident, Cleaver called the first of many meetings to be held regarding Huey's plight, at the apartment of an officer of the San Francisco State BSU. That a potential black martyr could galvanize young blacks of all persuasions, in a way that they couldn't be otherwise, was vividly demonstrated at that first meeting. According to Benny Stewart, "The guys who were there made a commitment that they would die or die trying so that Huey wouldn't go to the gas chamber. One brother said that if that's the case, then we're talking about going up into the jailhouse and getting him out, because ain't no court going to free no nigga who kills a cop." The most drastic action such emotions led to was the march of several Panthers and their supporters into the office of Oakland police chief Charles Gain to deliver a manifesto. It described the Oakland police as an occupying army in the black community, demanded that charges against

Newton be dropped, and said that if they weren't dropped and Newton wasn't released immediately, Chief Gain should resign.

At that first meeting, Cleaver introduced the real plan to set Huey free: hire the best lawyer that Newton's family, the party, and Eldridge's white radical supporters could agree on, and launch what was to become the infamous and far-reaching Free Huey publicity campaign. "Most people at that first meeting thought the campaign was stupid," remembers Stewart. "Because it just didn't seem that something like that would work." Bay Area black nationalists who wanted nothing to do with white people began denouncing the plan and the Black Panther Party for choosing a white lawyer, Charles Garry, rather than a black, to represent Newton. A few of those critics held protest demonstrations in front of the offices of *Ramparts*. But Cleaver was hardly the Mickey Mouse type who would take such dissent lightly. Black intellectual militants (or, as Newton and Seale called them, "armchair revolutionaries") who came to the Panthers' aid were in for a rude awakening. According to former Panther captain Earl Anthony, Cleaver had party members beat and pistol-whip some of the key leaders among other militant groups. Subsequently, many of those critics left town, and Cleaver's plans for the Free Huey movement prevailed.

While the movement was getting off the ground, a major turning point occurred in the Vietnam War. On January 31, 1968, North Vietnamese and Vietcong forces launched the Tet offensive, inflicting shocking casualties on U.S. and South Vietnamese forces. The offensive exposed as a lie President Johnson's insistence that America was winning the war. News of the offensive helped increase the militancy of white antiwar activists, adding one more reason for them to find common cause with young blacks who promoted radical measures for opposing the establishment. And the brutality of the police sent to quell antiwar demonstrations only ensured that more and more white radicals would readily join the Free Huey movement.

In San Francisco earlier that same month, 700 antiwar activists demonstrated on Nob Hill in front of the Fairmont Hotel, where Secretary of State Dean Rusk was addressing members of the Commonwealth Club. The result was Bloody Tuesday all over again, on a smaller scale. Police wielding billy clubs and Mace charged at them indiscriminately. "There was murder in those cops' eyes," observed one jailed UC Berkeley student. "They wanted to kill and would have if they could have gotten away with it. I *know* now that they were out to put Huey away, except Huey had the good sense to defend himself."

"For the first time, these whites can understand Huey when he says, 'The police must withdraw from our communities, cease their wanton murder and brutality and torture, or face the wrath of the people,'" wrote organizers for the Peace and Freedom Party (PFP), a predominantly white political organization that was just getting off the ground.

PFP was founded by an assorted collection of white leftists who decided that a third political party was needed if the nation was to ever really change its Vietnam War policy. The party's goal was to get on the ballot by the fall of 1968 in time for the presidential election. Among Peace and Freedom's supporters were Bob Scheer, Michael Lerner (who would later launch the influential Jewish bimonthly journal *Tikkun*), Tom Hayden, Jerry Rubin, and Huey Newton's old fellow student at Merritt, Joe Blum. The PFP attracted widespread support, particularly in California, and particularly in the Bay Area, where it held its official national founding convention in March 1968. By January of that year, PFP had obtained just over 100,000 signatures to put its candidates on the California ballot. But it needed more.

Although PFP functionaries had been working with Eldridge Cleaver on the Free Huey strategy since November 1967, the party officially approached Cleaver about an alliance with the Black Panthers the following February. Cleaver was ready with a deal of his own. PFP and the Black Panthers would have their coalition. But PFP had to accept most of the Panthers' ten-point platform, including calls for the exemption of blacks from the military; release of all blacks currently being held in prison; all future trials of blacks accused of committing crimes to take place before a jury of their peers. Besides calling for the release of Huey Newton, PFP nominated Newton as its congressional candidate in the Berkeley/Oakland district represented by Jeffrey Cohelan; Bobby

Seale was to be one of the party's state assembly candidates, as was
Kathleen Cleaver, a former SNCC worker, now Eldridge's wife,
whom he met while traveling with Stokely Carmichael to write the
Ramparts article on Carmichael. Eldridge himself was to become
the PFP presidential candidate, on a ticket with Jerry Rubin as his
running mate.

An alliance had effectively been made between the most radical white antiwar activists and the street blacks who dominated the
Black Panthers. Together they would stage the most extreme
events the nation had yet seen. Among them would be the Pre-
erection Day celebration, in which Cleaver called for pussy power,
and alliances with the Machine Gun Kellys (anyone who, like the
legendary gangster known by that name, was prepared to shoot it
out with any and all adversaries). He threatened to assassinate the
children of San Francisco mayor Joseph Allioto, and to beat Governor Reagan to death with a marshmallow. To many PFP supporters, accepting such outrageous behavior would be tantamount
to swallowing castor oil. But they did it to further what they saw
as their larger goals—supporting the defeat of American and South
Vietnamese forces in Vietnam, and fomenting the revolution in
America.

From the black side, although local militant critics had been
silenced, the staunchest, most organized criticism of the PFP/Black
Panther alliance come from national SNCC leaders, who, like PFP,
also made a serious attempt at an alliance with the Black Panthers
in February 1968. SNCC's lack of real programmatic success in
the North, the Free Huey movement, and the look the Black
Panthers presented of an organized, rising cadre of young revolutionary blacks from the streets, attracted Forman, Carmichael, and
H. Rap Brown (who was busy with his own legal problems). By
that time, the battle-weary and increasingly revolutionary Forman
was director of SNCC's New York office. Forman became seriously involved in discussions of an SNCC–Black Panther coalition
after making a speech in Los Angeles at the end of January, designed to help unify the various black militant organizations of that
city engaged in infighting. Forman met the Black Panther leader-

ship for the first time that following week, at a rally in Berkeley to which he was invited to speak.

The rally was held to support Dr. Benjamin Spock and five others in Boston who were indicted by the federal government for their antiwar activities. In his speech Forman made proposals that alienated the many white radicals who were present. He called for 50 percent black representation in any coalition between blacks and whites, since "we've suffered from racism, you have not." Forman's proposal may have driven the Peace and Freedom Party to later accept most of the Panther proposals, in an effort to compromise with black militants.

The Panthers simultaneously pursued affiliations with both SNCC and PFP. For their part, the Panthers were interested in a merger with SNCC, rather than a coalition. The Panthers thought that SNCC as a veteran organization could provide them with the structural apparatus they needed. The Panthers had been overwhelmed by the massive interest on the part of blacks from around the country who wanted to start Black Panther chapters. Forman was joined by Brown and Carmichael in California, and the three of them traveled back and forth between the Bay Area and Los Angeles to work out differences between the various West Coast militant groups. At that time the United Slaves (US), the Los Angeles chapter of SNCC, and the Black Panther Party, which had already launched a southern California chapter through Cleaver's old prisonmate, Alprentice "Bunchy" Carter, were the three most prominent groups.

Rallies, private meetings, and public meetings were held over a period of weeks. The veteran Forman introduced the Panthers to SNCC's 10-10-10 plan of organizing at the grassroots. The plan consisted of dividing a city into ten sections, subdividing those sections into ten more sections, and subdividing those ten sections into ten more sections. All sections were to have section leaders.

The activities culminated in two Free Huey birthday rallies, one in Oakland on February 17, Huey's actual birthday, and the other in Los Angeles the following day. During the rallies Eldridge Cleaver announced that James Forman had been drafted into the

Black Panther Party as minister of foreign affairs, H. Rap Brown as minister of justice, and Stokely Carmichael as prime minister of the party—augmenting Bobby Seale as party chairman (by now out of jail, Seale too spoke at the rally), Cleaver as minister of information, and Newton as minister of defense. Throughout, the Panthers kept speaking of the relationship with SNCC as a merger, while the SNCC leaders saw it as a coalition. SNCC leaders, in turn, would catch flak from the SNCC rank and file back east who were ambivalent about the entire relationship.

Despite the differences in outlook between the Black Panthers and SNCC regarding white involvement in the movement, during the two rallies, the SNCC leaders used their charismatic speaking ability to further project Huey Newton as a hero to all blacks—and help elevate him to mythical status. "Huey Newton is our only living revolutionary in this country today," declared H. Rap Brown to the crowd of 6,000 people gathered at Oakland Auditorium to celebrate Huey's birthday. "He has paid his dues. He has paid his dues. How many white folks did you kill today?" Carmichael told the crowd that if the authorities executed Huey, the final execution of the authorities rested in the people's hands.

But James Forman was the most electrifying and incendiary: "We must serve notice on our oppressors that we as a people are not going to be frightened by the attempted assassination of our leaders. For my assassination—and I'm a low man on the totem pole—I want 30 police stations blown up, one southern governor, two mayors, and 500 cops, dead. If they assassinate Brother Carmichael, Brother Brown . . . Brother Seale, this price is tripled. And if Huey Newton is not set free and dies, the sky is the limit!"

That such sentiments could be aroused in a veteran movement leader thirteen years older than Huey Newton, and one with far more experience, was amazing. But everyone was searching for something to sustain their various agendas, and Huey Newton was turned into the fertilizer for them all. Powder-blue flags with the elaborate black lettering reading "Free Huey," and a black panther coming at you, became standard issue at Free Huey rallies in Oakland, Berkeley, San Francisco, and other major cities across the

country. Free Huey buttons became as popular among white radicals as antiwar buttons with peace signs. Posters of Huey in the
wicker chair not only began gracing walls but were carried as
banners by Black Panthers, Black Panthers–for-a-day who were
given black leather jackets and black berets to augment real Panther numbers at rallies, and among outside black and white supporters. Whites for the Defense of Huey Newton (WDHN), as
well as Honkies for Huey, got together in the radical and liberal
apartments in the Bay Area and spread their message across the
nation. "Huey knows what is necessary to exterminate forever the
oppressive racism running rampant in this country," one WDHN
fundraising letter declared. "But the danger he poses is greater.
Huey not only expounds theoretically what must be done; he is
able to bring that message to the people. His love for people is so
strong that it is impossible not to feel it when in his presence."

From the mouths of Free Huey activists, Huey began to sound
like a messiah. Their enthusiasm to see Huey set free paralleled
the Christian enthusiasm for the second coming. "People kept
saying we're going to have a revolution when Huey gets out of
prison," recalls Mae Jackson, a member of SNCC. "And at twenty-
two, twenty-three, twenty-four, you think, oh yeah? But then a part
of you asks yourself, If he doesn't get out, does that mean we're
not going to have a revolution?" Young radicals and militants of all
persuasions began preparing for the rebellion they were sure Huey
would lead. "There was this notion that if you don't pick up the
gun you're holding the revolution back," remembers Peter Solomon. "And this was the attitude among black and white students.
There was a big program in Berkeley, many of the leading lights
of the feminist movement were taking lots of very heavy courses
in battlefield medicine. How to dress wounds, how to fire guns,
how to clean guns. People would learn to fire weapons at these sort
of half-secret schools with firing ranges."

A popular chant developed among Black Panthers decked out
in requisite Panther uniforms, who would line up for periodic
rallies in impressive military formation, holding large posters of
Huey Newton sitting in his wicker throne:

The revolution has co-ome!!!
Off the pig!!!
Time to pick up the gu-un!!!
Off the pig!!!

The revolutionaries were certain the future belonged to them and to the captive Huey. The assassination of Premier Black Leader Martin Luther King, Jr., on April 4, 1968, only confirmed this. Shocked and outraged by King's murder, although they had thoroughly discredited him during the last two years of his life, both blacks and whites engaged in the equally peculiar human phenomenon of elevating a new martyr-idol. Idol-making appeared to work in one of two ways—either the hated authorities captured the potential idol and threatened to execute him or never let him out of their clutches, or someone shot and killed the potential idol, after he had placed himself way out on a limb where no one else had the intestinal fortitude to go. King had achieved the status in the latter manner, and on his death, riots broke out in over one hundred cities. But not in Oakland. The Panthers helped keep a lid on things. And Eldridge Cleaver had a better idea than rioting anyway—a carefully targeted, symbolic show of violence to further stoke the image of Newton's Black Panther army as the future revolutionary vanguard. It happened on April 6, 1968, two nights after King's assassination.

According to four apprehended Panthers, whose police statements were corroborated several years later by Cleaver in an interview with journalist Kate Coleman, as well as by David Hilliard in his autobiography, *This Side of Glory*, Cleaver organized four carloads of Black Panthers to do "some shooting." The entourage included Bobby Hutton, Wendell Wade, Donell Lankford, Terry Cotton, Warren Wells, David Hilliard, and other Black Panthers. Their goal was to ambush a police officer while transporting a cache of the increasing number of weapons the Panthers possessed from Cleaver's house to one of their many stash spots at apartments throughout Oakland and Berkeley. On reaching their destination at 28th and Union streets in West Oakland, they encountered some police officers on routine patrol. Gunfire broke out. Some Panthers immediately either fled or dropped to the ground. Cleaver and Hutton fled into the basement of a nearby house occupied by people who had no Panther connection. Police officers from Oakland, Berkeley, and Emeryville were called in, and the area was sealed off.

Two officers had already been wounded, presumably by the Black Panthers, whom the police accused of shooting first. During a thirty-minute gun battle, the platoon of officers opened fire on the house Cleaver and Hutton were hiding in, and lobbed in tear gas. Cleaver was wounded in the foot by a ricocheting bullet, and hit in the chest by a tear-gas canister. A fire started in the basement of the house. Cleaver shouted that he and Hutton were surrendering. One of them threw out Hutton's rifle. Having no intention of giving the police a reason to shoot him, Cleaver emerged from the house stark naked with his arms high in the air. Bobby Hutton also emerged with his arms high in the air. But he was too modest to remove his clothes. The officers, angered by the fact that two among their ranks had been wounded in a gun battle with the very organization of the man they blamed for killing Officer John Frey, pounced on Cleaver and Hutton when both fell to the ground, spread-eagled.

There would be conflicting accounts of what happened next. White officers swore that Bobby Hutton got up off the ground and began to run. But Gwynne Peirson, a black officer who requested anonymity when he gave his account to the media, later stated that the officers simply got out of hand because they had been firing at the house for half an hour, not knowing what they were shooting at. They were "all worked up for various reasons, getting ready to do anything." As they directed Cleaver and Hutton up off the ground, both with their hands up, Hutton stumbled while walking to where the police told them to go, causing him to momentarily drop his arms. And the officers opened fire, killing him.

The fatal shooting of Bobby James Hutton created another martyr and more sympathy for the Black Panthers. At the time, Cleaver denied that the Panthers had set out to ambush police officers; he stated that they were out in their cars innocently preparing for a picnic to be held the following day, when a squad car abruptly pulled up and "suddenly a gun exploded right in my face." Of course, given the tenor of the times, liberal and radical whites, and most blacks, believed Cleaver's story.

Only days before the shootout, Marlon Brando had been in the Bay Area to show interest in Huey's case. He appeared at a hearing for Bobby Seale and his wife, who were being charged with felony gun possession, conspiracy to commit murder, possession of a sawed-off shotgun, and obliterating the serial numbers on a .45 automatic. The charges stemmed from a February police raid on their Berkeley home, where they and four other Black Panthers were arrested. When asked by reporters why he attended the hearing, Brando replied, "I'm listening to these black people and trying to do my best to understand." He called the Panthers "a group struggling to achieve a life of dignity and self-respect," saying there was a real need for them. Brando would also show up for Bobby Hutton's memorial service, and go out with the Panthers on a police patrol, allegedly as research for a movie he was to release a year later called *Burn!*

The killing of Hutton only accelerated the pace at which famed citizens like Brando jumped on the Black Panther bandwagon. A letter signed by James Baldwin, Ossie Davis, Elizabeth Hardwick, LeRoi Jones, Oscar Lewis, Norman Mailer, Floyd McKissick, and Susan Sontag read: "We find little fundamental difference between the assassin's bullet which killed Dr. King on April 4, and the police barrage which killed Bobby James Hutton two days later. Both were acts of racism against persons who had taken a militant stand on the right of black people to determine the conditions of their own lives. Both were attacks aimed at destroying this nation's black leadership." As tragic as the shooting death of a not-very-articulate high-school dropout like Bobby Hutton was, that he could now be called a leader and referred to in the same breath as Martin Luther King by some of America's most esteemed citizens was a testament to the tenor of the times, and the distance traveled since the 1955 Montgomery bus boycott.

San Jose State sociology professor Harry Edwards, who at the time was organizing a black boycott of the 1968 Olympics, declared his intention to join the Black Panther Party, although his affiliation would be short-lived. He urged blacks who had achieved social standing like doctors and lawyers to do the same in order to serve notice to society that "you can no longer ignore the Black Panthers. We have to go down to the grassroots to join [the Panthers] since they can't join us." Black people had an obligation to join the Panthers, Edwards said, even if they didn't agree with all their goals. "I personally encourage violence, until somebody shows me a better way. Nonviolence essentially has not worked."

The list of new Panther supporters went on and on, including seventy-five mostly white law students at UC Berkeley. Four white Bay Area college professors from San Francisco State, Stanford, and UC Berkeley attacked the "systematic harassment" of the Black Panthers and urged a U.S. civil rights investigation of the Oakland police department. A group of 400 mostly white Bay Area physicians and health care workers, called the Medical Committee for Human Rights, unveiled plans for a joint venture with the Black Panthers "designed to give an articulate and respectable voice to the black power movement." Their plan called for providing emergency medical attention to ghetto residents, including those who had been "worked over by cops"; having attorneys on hand to provide counsel for blacks who were arrested; and, once the number of volunteers among them grew, providing patrols in Bay Area ghettos, which they believed would discourage police from singling out Black Panthers and other blacks for attacks.

Oakland police chief Charles Gain angrily fought back. "An attempt is being made by the Panthers and others to deify one who tried to murder police officers [Bobby Hutton]. It is being conducted through false, lying statements charging the police with harassment, brutality and murder." Gain also attacked the Peace and Freedom Party, criticizing their alliance with the Panthers as an attempt to create chaos through "unlawful demonstrations, parades, and other activities."

But this hardly slowed the Panther juggernaut. In May, with Eldridge Cleaver in jail as a result of the Hutton shootout, Bobby Seale and Kathleen Cleaver journeyed to New York City to raise money and to help inaugurate the Panther chapters in the area. They appeared with LeRoi Jones at a rally at the Filmore East

attended by approximately 2,000 people. At least half of the atten-
dees were white, many of them middle-aged or older. With the
Hutton shooting and Martin Luther King's assassination fresh in
their memories, the crowd gave Jones a standing ovation when he
said, "We want to become masters of our own destiny . . . we want
to build a black nation to benefit black people." They applauded
too when Jones told them, "The white people who killed Bobby
Hutton are the same white people sitting here."

Despite the accelerated rate at which the juggernaut was moving, the SNCC members in New York City were beginning to
realize that irreconcilable differences existed between them and
most of the Black Panthers. According to Mae Jackson, "SNCC
people could go up against an entire town of Ku Klux Klanners,
but they didn't have that 'nigga I'm gonna kick yo ass' about them
the way the Panthers did. In the beginning I think SNCC thought:
we'll be the brain and they'll be the heart. And maybe the Panthers
thought we'll be the heart and they'll be the brain, except when
you deal with a lot of street people they always have another
agenda. It's like not only will I be the heart, but one day I'll *take
over* the brain."

The core of the Black Panther chapter organized in Brooklyn
would be composed of the young people essentially from off the
street who were part of SNCC's Brooklyn project but who weren't
SNCC members. "These folks were fascinated, because Bobby
[Seale] spoke their language," remembers Jackson of the rally at
the Filmore East. "He was their blood, so they left SNCC. And I
said that is *real* good, because it was a little too rough for me."

The New York area Black Panthers began by using SNCC's
offices as their principal headquarters. Eventually, there would be
Panther chapters in Harlem, Queens, Newark, Jersey City. Not
everyone in those chapters would be into gangism the way the
original Brooklyn group was. The number of chapters grew after
the relationship between SNCC and the Black Panthers had disintegrated. The difference between SNCC members and the first
Panther recruits was driven home to Jackson during an encounter
she had at the office with the head of the Brooklyn chapter of the
Black Panthers, Ron Penniwell: "One day I walked in and I didn't

salute him. And this man went off on me. He said, 'You black bitch, I'll throw you out of the window!' And I said, 'But we're on the eighth floor. I'll be dead if you throw me out of the window.' Then I called Rap Brown and told him what happened. Rap said he'd handle it."

The following day the same H. Rap Brown who almost a year earlier had been charged with promoting a riot in Cambridge, Maryland, confronted Ron Penniwell with a gun. "He told him, 'I don't want you fucking with Mae. Don't mess with her.' And after that nobody from the Panthers bothered me."

Incidents like that between Jackson and Penniwell, and Penniwell and H. Rap Brown, made it clear to SNCC that the Black Panthers had a thirst for violent confrontation that SNCC didn't share. The SNCC leaders began to realize that their coalition with the Black Panthers had been a mistake. But they were hardly going to admit it publicly. Black sensitivities were too great for that. White racists were too numerous, too ready to latch onto any and every reason to discredit blacks. Public admission that there were, in fact, blacks who fertilized stereotypes would have been too satisfying to white conservatives and racists who blamed SNCC for the phenomenon of the angry posturing black in the first place. So the story of the official break between SNCC and the Black Panthers had to be sanitized in assorted ways still being heard today, most recently in the autobiography of David Hilliard.

In telling the story of how the Black Panthers and SNCC developed their association and the way it fell apart, Hilliard first describes the series of February meetings with SNCC, culminating in the birthday rallies for Huey. He then mentions a trip the Panthers made to New York City to formalize a merger with SNCC, help James Forman organize Free Huey rallies there, and appear at a U.N. press conference. But he erroneously dates the trip as occurring just before Huey's trial began on July 15, 1968.

Hilliard states that both he and Huey's brother Melvin made the trip. He says they stayed at the home of James Forman, and that while they were there, Forman started to act peculiar. According to Hilliard, Forman accused the Black Panthers of trying to take over SNCC. Hilliard denied it, saying they wanted to be absorbed by SNCC. Forman continued to act strange. The following day he began to obsess about a watch Hilliard was wearing, telling him to leave the watch at Forman's house before they left to discuss the SNCC–Black Panther merger. Melvin Newton got involved in the argument, advising Hilliard to leave the watch behind, to keep the peace with Forman. Then later that day the discussion and the press conference ended in chaos. He concludes the description of the split as follows: "The SNCC people are split among themselves. . . . We must admit to ourselves that Huey's hope that they will provide us with some answers is ill-founded: we're leadership, no one else. For better and worse, we have no one to rely on but ourselves, and we return to Oakland for the start of Huey's trial."

But James Forman tells a different, far more believable story about the sequence of events leading to the break. After the February birthday rallies for Huey in Oakland and Los Angeles, Forman recounts, he traveled to Sweden for an international conference, where he represented both SNCC and the Black Panthers. Later, he formally introduced plans for an SNCC–Black Panther coalition at SNCC's annual meeting in June. Many SNCC members disagreed over much of the Panther ten-point platform, but consented to work out a plan for SNCC to assist the Black Panthers in their efforts to grow. This certainly was in keeping with SNCC's philosophy of seeding any black organization it saw as progressive.

Contrary to Hilliard's account, Forman dates the scheduled SNCC–Black Panther appearance before the United Nations, the New York City Free Huey rallies, and the split between SNCC and the Black Panthers as taking place *after* Huey's trial began. Forman in fact traveled to Oakland on July 13 to appear at local Free Huey rallies leading up to Huey's trial, attend the start of the trial two days later, and to discuss the SNCC–Black Panther coalition. That he was present when the trial began, and was still on good terms with the Panthers, is supported by an article in the *Oakland Post*, a local black-owned newspaper, describing Newton during the opening days of the trial as "frequently turning to look and smile at SNCC's James Forman, who sat in the first row behind him."

Forman states that two days later, along with Willie Ricks, John Wilson, and another SNCC member, he met with Cleaver, Seale, Hilliard, and two other Panther party members to discuss the decision of the SNCC rank and file on SNCC's relationship with the Black Panthers. (Cleaver had been released from prison on bail in June. Charges related to the Hutton shootout were still pending, but a Superior Court judge ruled that revocation of his December 1966 parole because of the shootout had been illegal.) During the meeting Cleaver kept referring to the relationship as a merger, while SNCC insisted it was a coalition. Cleaver attacked SNCC, accusing it of trying to co-opt the Black Panther Party. He asked Forman and the others if they were Black Panthers or SNCC.

Although he was insulted by Cleaver's hostility, Forman says that discussions continued the following day about joint SNCC–Black Panther rallies to be held in New York City on July 22–23, as well as a U.N. press conference that was also to be held on July 22. He states that on Friday, July 19, he, Hilliard, and Bill Brent flew to New York City to prepare for the events. He mentions no stayover at his house by Hilliard or Melvin Newton. On Monday, July 22, when the press conference was about to begin, the Black Panthers and Stokely Carmichael (who by now was at serious odds with Forman and Brown) briefly appeared at the United Nations before the press arrived, and then left. When the press did arrive, Forman could not find Carmichael or the Black Panthers. The press conference was called off, but the rallies were held under strained conditions between SNCC and the Black Panthers. Forman states that after this he avoided any further association with the Black Panthers.

But there is a third story of the split, buttressed by the accounts of federal authorities (presumably the FBI) in the *New York Times*, as well as by Panther captain Earl Anthony, who states that he was part of the Black Panther delegation that traveled to New York City for the U.N. press conference and Free Huey rallies.

According to Anthony, he flew with Cleaver and Seale to New York for the July 22–23 appearances. Presumably, Hilliard was already there, having flown out as described by Forman. Anthony alleges that he informed Cleaver and Seale during the flight that James Forman and H. Rap Brown were planning to back out of any further involvement with the Panthers because of the differences between the two organizations. That Forman and Brown were planning to back out was also reported in an FBI COINTEL-PRO memorandum, which described the following reason for their pullout: "James Forman and Rap Brown . . . have reportedly resigned their Black Panther Party membership because they find it difficult to go along with Black Panther Party violent schemes."

Anthony states that he told Cleaver and Seale that Forman and Brown were going to the Black Muslims to seek protection from the Black Panthers, to ensure their safe exit from any further involvement with the party. Anthony reports that when he, Cleaver, and Seale arrived in New York, they and Hilliard met with Stokely Carmichael, who confirmed Anthony's information about Forman and Brown. Later on, Anthony, Cleaver, Seale, and Hilliard held a meeting of their own, during which Cleaver raised the possibility of killing Forman, Brown, and Carmichael. Finally, they decided to leave Carmichael and Brown alone, reasoning that both were too famous to engage in any violent confrontation since it could lead to a war.

They decided instead to visit James Forman that night at his home, armed with pistols. Cleaver accused Forman of trying to precipitate a war between the Black Muslims and the Black Panthers. Forman laughed off the suggestion. Cleaver became very angry and ordered the unarmed Forman to play Russian roulette with two Black Panther bodyguards. Unbeknownst to Forman, the guns weren't loaded. He screamed for his life as Cleaver taunted him with insults.

A *New York Times* article also stated that the Black Panthers confronted Forman and tortured him with a pistol. But the *Times's* description of the incident differed from Earl Anthony's: "Members of the Black Panthers walked into James Forman's office at [SNCC] on Fifth Avenue in late July, according to Federal authorities. One of them produced a pistol and put it into Mr. Forman's mouth. He squeezed the trigger three times. The gun went click, click, click. It was unloaded."

Forman denies that the Black Panthers ever tortured him with a gun. The closest he comes to admitting any encounter with violence at their hands is in his explanation of why he refused any further association with the party: "Too much had happened in California and New York for me to trust certain forces in the Black Panther Party at the time. I had never worked in an organization where I felt my personal security and safety were threatened by internal elements and I did not intend to start doing it then."

However, Mae Jackson corroborates the story that Forman was tortured with a pistol. "And afterwards, Jim went berserk. He had a nervous breakdown. Jim had had a nervous breakdown before. So this was maybe his second one." As a result, James Forman, the civil rights veteran who marched with and argued with the now deceased Premier Black Leader Martin Luther King, who suffered savage blows in North Carolina while coming to the aid of Robert Williams, who developed ulcers and risked death dodging white racists in Mississippi, who agreed to the introduction of the Black Power slogan in Mississippi, checked into the psychiatric ward of a New York hospital.

STOKELY CARMICHAEL WAS EXPELLED FROM SNCC IN August 1968. A year later he decided that he too had had enough of the Black Panther Party. While affiliated with the party, Carmichael set up a few Panther chapters, the members of which, like him, would eventually become dissatisfied with the party's national leadership in Oakland. But their dissatisfaction wouldn't reach full bloom until a year after Carmichael's resignation. The departure of this other rebellious disciple of King, who had both learned from and argued with the assassinated Premier Black Leader, who had risked death toiling to register black voters from the sharecropping huts and farmhouses of Alabama and Mississippi, who was most responsible for popularizing the Black Power movement and giving the Black Panthers the idea for their name, signaled the complete severing of all the young rebellious civil rights leaders from their most notorious offspring.

Carmichael had met and married black South African singer Miriam Makeba and moved to the African nation of Ghana. Makeba journeyed to New York City in June 1969 for the express purpose of delivering Carmichael's resignation from the Black Panther Party, ensuring that a copy was mailed to the party's Central Committee in Oakland. Echoing the allegation that James Forman had been tortured by the Black Panther leadership, implying that such methods had been used on others, Carmichael wrote, "I cannot support the present tactics and methods which the party is using to coerce and force everyone to submit to its authority."

On Carmichael's dissociation, the rebellious young disciples of King who had been Black Power's architects, as well as H. Rap Brown, departed the national limelight (by then, Brown was underground because of recurring legal problems related to his speech in Cambridge, Maryland). SNCC faded into oblivion and, finally, had dissolved by the early 1970s. The Black Panthers were now firmly in the driver's seat of black militancy.

7

The Cat Prowls

THE BLACK PANTHERS WERE BLACK AMERICA'S HOTTEST
copy during the summer of 1968, absorbing members, opening up
chapter after chapter across the country, feeding off of the Free
Huey campaign that Eldridge Cleaver and his backers had successfully engineered. In April 1968 the FBI's counterintelligence program identified the party as one of the most dangerous threats
presented by black America (that fall, J. Edgar Hoover would deem
the party "the greatest threat to the internal security of the Country"). Soon after, the party was infiltrated with informants. Young
black Americans from all walks of life were attracted to the symbol
of defiant militancy presented by the party. But party leadership
continued to be made up largely of the "brothers off the block,"
and publicly stated party aims were sabotaged not only by informants but also by the party leadership. Corruption developed. By
the beginning of 1969, any party member who criticized the leadership for any reason was automatically deemed an informant, an
enemy of the people, or—in the party's own peculiar term, a
"jacanape"—and was successfully discredited. From the beginning
of 1968 on, controversy heated up intensely both within and outside the party.

Throughout the days and months leading to Huey's trial in July and August 1968, ordinary black people in the cities of the Bay Area viewed the party with a mixture of fear, embarrassment, and admiration. One young black man who had a well-paying job at Kaiser Hospital bought a gun at BBB, the cheapest place in the Bay Area to buy one. He considered himself to be preparing for the coming revolution. He was proud of the fact that his name appeared on the register at BBB next to the name of one of the Black Panther Party leaders. He would take his gun, practice firing it at one of the half-secret firing ranges in the Bay Area, dismantle it, place it in its case, and then go to his job at Kaiser Hospital. On his shirt he wore a Free Huey button, and when he rode the bus to work, the black bus driver, on seeing the button, would give him the clenched-fist gesture. The passengers, mostly black, would nod, wink, or mutter, "Right on."

Because of the controversy surrounding Huey, East Bay blacks stepped up their demands for changes in the Oakland police department. In June 1968 a group called the Blacks for Justice picketed downtown Oakland merchants. Their signs read, "By boycotting we can force the merchants to use their political power to make some basic changes in the power structure, specifically community control of police policy." Local ministers staged a monthlong vigil of the Oakland City Council and the mayor's office, protesting their lack of attention to demands for changes in the police department. The mayor finally responded by announcing plans to form a committee to consider some of the demands.

Most of the Bay Area's black bourgeoisie were ambivalent about the party. Like the black bourgeoisie across the rest of the country, they considered "the brothers off the block" to be wild, loud, unrefined. Although black lawyer Tom Berkley, publisher of the *Oakland Post*, did demand that Huey receive a fair trial, he also expressed irritation with whites' tendency to make their own designations of who was a "Negro leader": "The so-called militants whom the mayor designates the black leaders of Oakland were not the first and are not the only ones saying that there is something wrong with the police department of this city. This paper was the first to preach this." Others in the black middle and upper-middle class expressed their practical concern that blacks could never shoot it out with whites and hope to win.

A motley collection of interest groups throughout the Bay Area continued to be irritated, embarrassed, confused, fascinated, and inspired by the party. When Huey's trial finally began on July 15, the off-white Alameda County Courthouse, the top floors of which housed the prison in which Huey was kept, was deluged by a mob of close to 3,000 bearded, long-haired, sandal-wearing whites, as well as more conventionally attired whites, Asians, Latinos, and blacks, and a separate cadre of young Panthers wearing natural hairdos, berets, and black leather jackets. On the steps of the courthouse, nine to twelve Black Panthers lined up and stood stiffly at guard, alternating in two-hour shifts. Everyone wore the requisite Free Huey buttons, and many carried signs such as "The Nation Shall Be Reduced to Ashes, the Sky's the Limit if Anything Happens to Huey." The Oakland police department devised an unusual crowd-control method, placing a large net around the courthouse to prevent people from charging up the steps and rushing inside. When one demonstrator asked what the net was there for, an officer responded, "It's up there because we've been having trouble with blackbirds."

Shirley Lee, a white Oakland housewife in her thirties, marched in the Free Huey demonstration as part of a group of whites representing an organization called the Western Mobilization Against War. Hilda Cowan, an elderly white housewife, marched too. Lee told a reporter of her feelings of guilt for being white and previously oblivious to the plight of blacks. She expressed pride in having remedied her ignorance by visiting Huey Newton in jail the week before his trial, with two of her friends. "He's a very warm person," she insisted. "He has true beauty, strength and charisma. In fact, my friend compared him to Lenin and Christ."

Howard Jeeter, a black San Francisco high-school teacher, demonstrated. A few steps behind him were members of the Asian American Political Alliance, hoisting posters with "Free Huey" inscribed in Mandarin, Japanese, Tagalog, and English. A dozen young Latinos dressed in tan bush jackets and brown berets lined up in their own platoon and marched. Afro-Cuban rhythms were played on bongos to chants of "Free Huey." Bob Avakian, then a twenty-five-year-old radical activist and son of an Alameda County Superior Court judge, climbed a flagpole and cut down the American flag, while the crowd shouted, "Burn it!" Fifteen blue-uniformed, helmeted police officers promptly rushed out of Alameda County Courthouse, the inside of which had been sealed off as soon as the spectators' gallery had been filled, and arrested Avakian, causing the protesters to shout even louder, "Free Huey!" and "Off the Pigs!" The demonstrations died down after about a week, and the serious business of deciding Newton's fate progressed over a six-week trial.

After closing arguments, everyone in the Newton camp tensely awaited the verdict—except Huey, who was the calmest of all. Elsa Knight Thompson, from Berkeley radio station KPFA, described Newton as "the host of the tea party." His old college acquaintance Joe Blum, editor of the newspaper *The Movement*, which by then was more affiliated with SDS than with SNCC, interviewed him. During the interview they were interrupted by a national television news reporter who kept asking Huey if he hated white people, to which he replied no. "If I hated white people I wouldn't be talking to my friend Joe here."

On September 10 the jury found Huey Newton guilty of voluntary manslaughter in the death of Officer John Frey, and guilty of wounding Officer Herbert Heanes. Newton was sentenced to two to fifteen years in prison and shipped off to the Men's Colony in San Luis Obispo. The decision satisfied neither his supporters nor the Oakland police. Approximately 400 officers were placed on twelve-hour duty the night of the verdict, as were 75 California Highway Patrolmen. The Berkeley Socialist League announced that something would be done about the verdict within forty-eight hours. The white radical group planned an all-night vigil at Lake Merritt in front of the Alameda County Courthouse, followed by picketing the next morning. Huey's supporters provoked nothing violent, however, after he issued the order that they were to remain cool. But shortly after midnight on the day of the verdict, two officers showed up drunk in front of Black Panther

Party headquarters and fired twelve to thirty-eight rounds of ammunition into it. Their shots riddled not only the glass but a poster of Bobby Hutton, a large poster of Huey, and another of Eldridge Cleaver, who was busy continuing his own personal drama to the consternation and entertainment of millions of Californians.

Throughout the fall of 1968, Cleaver was the sort of black spokesperson Tom Berkley was raving against. Campuses nationwide were inviting him to spew his shocking and entertaining invective against the nation's power structure while he awaited trial on charges related to the April shootout that had left Bobby Hutton dead. UC Berkeley invited him to give a series of ten lectures in a class called Social Analysis 139X, prompting an outraged Governor Reagan to threaten to cut off funding for the school and take away the faculty's right to set course policy. Max Rafferty, state superintendent of instruction, expressed his outrage at the idea of Cleaver at UC Berkeley, observing, "A little bit of Eldridge Cleaver is like being a little bit pregnant."

In the process, Cleaver was masterfully at the center of one more storm involving the question of civil liberties as faculty members, students, and liberal commentators defended his right at least to speak at the university's discretion. Other schools such as the University of Santa Clara and Stanford invited Cleaver to speak. State assemblyman Willie Brown, whose seat was being challenged that fall on the Peace and Freedom ticket by Cleaver's wife, Kathleen, found it necessary to issue the statement, "Mr. Cleaver's credentials as an instructor are impressive." In a compromise, that October it was decided that Cleaver could teach some of the classes in the course at UC Berkeley as long as the course was deemed a noncredit one.

Even young lawyers in San Francisco's corporate corridors hungered for a taste of Cleaver, to fulfill the same craving to "try and understand these black people" identified by Marlon Brando when he showed up at the hearing for Bobby Seale and his wife, Artie. That September, Cleaver performed before a society of such lawyers in a downtown San Francisco dining room. Dressed in black, he told the barristers that they could best help the "black movement" by donating machine guns: "America is up against the wall. This whole apparatus—this capitalistic system and its institutions and police—all need to be assigned to the garbage can of history, and I don't give a fuck who doesn't like it, nobody's going to have it. . . ."

The lawyers politely sipped their drinks and ate their food.

"You're all chasing dollars," Cleaver told them, "but there are other people who are chasing dollars to buy guns to kill judges and police and corporation lawyers. We need lawyers who have a gun in one hand and a law book in the other, so if he goes to court and the shit doesn't come out right, he can pull out his gun and start shooting. . . ."

The lawyers politely sipped their drinks and ate their food.

"If I could get two machine guns out of this crowd, I wouldn't care if you applauded me or threw glasses at me, and then I'd get my black ass out of here," Cleaver continued. "I mean all my insults to those who don't choose my side, the right side. You people can take your wallets, credit cards, and cut your motherfucking necks. You people on the other side, I love you. I hope you'll take your guns and shoot some judges and police."

The lawyers gave Cleaver a polite ovation, after which one of them rose to ask, "What can we whites do to help the black man's cause?"

"Kill some white people!" Cleaver responded.

The lawyers politely filed out and turned on their analytical minds. One summarized his analysis of Cleaver to another this way: "His speech certainly reflects the growing polarization between the races, doesn't it?"

But the Eldridge Cleaver Show didn't have much longer to run. On September 27, once again Cleaver's parole was revoked after a judge decided he had indeed violated his December 1966 parole when he participated in the shootout that left Bobby Hutton dead. But Cleaver was granted a sixty-day stay before he had to give himself up. As the time approached, paranoia seized the Black Panthers as well as the Bay Area's radical community. They feared the police had plans to murder Cleaver. While armed Black Panthers guarded him inside his Pine Street home, an organization calling itself the Committee of People for Eldridge Cleaver staged a three-day, around-the-clock vigil outside, urging people to bring cameras, tape recorders, and blankets, to ensure Cleaver's safety. But Cleaver pulled a fast one on the authorities. Instead of giving himself up as scheduled, on November 24 Cleaver and his wife fled into exile, first to Cuba and then to Algeria.

8

Life in the Party

THE PARTY CONTINUED TO MAKE HEADLINES. AFTER Cleaver went into exile, Chief of Staff David Hilliard, took charge. Although Bobby Seale remained party chairman, his principal responsibility was speechmaking. With the quick growth in the party by the end of 1968, two tiers had developed—the leadership, composed of Hilliard, Seale, and their favored colleagues on the one hand, and ordinary rank-and-file members, on the other. The real work of the party was performed by the rank and file. Estimates placed the number of party members at the height of the Panthers at 2,000.

Landon Williams and Mary Kennedy were two Oakland rank-and-file members. Williams was an engineering major at San Francisco State University when he joined the party in the fall of 1967. An air force veteran, he became a weapons expert in the party. Mary Kennedy and her husband both joined the party in 1968 on hearing speeches by Bobby Seale and Eldridge Cleaver at predominantly black Saint Augustine Episcopal Church in Oakland. That any church would have gotten involved with the Black Panther Party, particularly in light of the language Cleaver normally used in his speeches, might seem incongruous. But the Reverend Earl

Neil, rector of Saint Augustine, not only allowed the party to use his church but became the party's religious adviser, although he remained an outsider. Neil felt a special commitment to the entire black community, especially after participating in Mississippi Freedom Summer, when the home he stayed at in McComb, Mississippi, was bombed. Six people had been killed that summer in McComb, in a total of twenty-eight bombings.

When Mary and her husband joined the party, Mary's husband, like Landon, become deeply involved in party affairs right away. By contrast, Mary at first had little to do with the party. She attended the rallies held in support of Huey, but the rest of the time she took care of her six children. The youngest, Louise, was only a baby. Mary was pregnant with their seventh child. One day Mary's husband came home and told her that he was going to quit his job and work full time for the party. Mary was adamantly opposed to that: "He had a good position. He was an apprentice welder, so I was plenty upset behind his decision. No income was coming in. I wasn't working. I had to get on welfare to support the family."

It reached the point where she saw her husband only once or twice per month. During the summer of 1968, at the height of Free Huey rallies, he and Landon were busy organizing security. Because he was always gone, Mary grew suspicious that her husband was cheating on her with other women in the party. She accused him of doing so, but he denied it. One day the Panthers held a rally at DeFremery Park, which they had renamed in honor of Bobby Hutton (a renaming that was never recognized by the city of Oakland). By this time Mary had gotten to know the wife of a top party leader. She too was despondent about her family life; her famous husband was always out and about on behalf of the party, meeting with journalists, Panther admirers, and hangers-on, and, she suspected, cheating on her too. Mary and the woman commiserated. While the rally was still in progress, they returned to Mary's home in East Oakland, got drunk, and then returned to the rally. Black Panther security caught both of them before they reached the park. There would be no embarrassing displays of the wives of men in the Black Panthers. Panther security whisked them home.

Landon began to move up in the Panther hierarchy, but he had to overcome the basic distrust most Panthers had for anyone who went to college. They were taking Marxist-Leninist and Maoist rhetoric and accusing college students of being petit bourgeois intellectuals. The degree of achievement of your family defined the extent to which you were an object of suspicion for being a petit bourgeois intellectual. Landon was close to acceptable because he was a college student from a working-class family. Had he come from a family of professionals, he would have been completely ostracized.

For college students in the Black Panthers to put up with the attitudes of the other Panthers, "the brothers off the block," took a certain discipline. For many of those from the streets, personal desires were inseparable from political rhetoric. One simply fit his political rhetoric to whatever his personal ends happened to be. When Landon joined the party, there weren't many programs. So the "brothers off the block" in the party had little real reason to change their behavior. Many of them would start drinking early in the morning; by noon they would be drunk. They had been in street-corner fights most of their lives. One of their principal interests remained being on the lookout for women. The street mentality had its own set of rules. One evening Landon and Mary's husband joined two other Panthers on an outing to a club. One Panther, named Jimmy, spotted a woman he liked. The woman was with her boyfriend, but that made no difference to Jimmy. He liked her and wanted to dance. She said no. He grabbed her, saying, "Come on. You're going to dance with me." The boyfriend and Jimmy fought, with the guy whipping Jimmy. And to Jimmy's surprise, his Panther colleagues wouldn't help him out. They didn't "have his back." To Jimmy, the Black Panther Party was little more than a gang.

The following day Jimmy brought Landon, Mary's husband, and the other party member up on charges before David Hilliard. Hilliard wanted to know how Landon and the others could call themselves Panthers when they let their fellow party member get his ass kicked at a dance club. Landon explained that as far as the others were concerned, what happened had nothing to do with party philosophy. Jimmy deserved to get beaten for disrespecting the woman in question. Hilliard backed down, refusing to press the issue. However, this wasn't the first encounter Landon would have with what would turn out to be a principal problem within the party—wanton disrespect for women by many male party members who just couldn't rid themselves of bad personal habits no matter how much they claimed allegiance to "the revolution."

Until the beginning of 1968, the party was rather small. Things didn't snowball until the large rally held for Huey at the Oakland Auditorium on February 17, where Stokely Carmichael, H. Rap Brown, and James Forman spoke. Panthers were brought in from all over California. And Landon gained more and more responsibility, largely because of his military experience.

By the spring of 1968, with membership rapidly growing, the party had acquired a better-defined structure. Aspiring members had to undergo a six-week training program, with three evenings every week devoted to Political Education class. They were given political instruction, most importantly from Mao's "Little Red Book," and they were instructed on the party's chain of command. At the top was Newton, minister of defense; then Seale, chairman of the party; then Cleaver, minister of information; then Hilliard, chief of staff. Positions with *minister* in the title continued in no particular order, with ministers of education, foreign affairs, justice, culture, and religion, and prime minister.

All of these officeholders sat on the Central Committee, which was augmented by the party field marshals (there were six by the end of 1968) and a communications secretary. Underneath them were the party captains and assistant captains who oversaw the various party chapters and offices. Then there were the party rank and file, who could serve in a position similar to that of a corporal where they were in charge of the duties performed by the other rank and file. That position was called Officer for the Day (OD). Theoretically, the Central Committee was an entity in which each member had a vote. Its responsibility was to set policy for the entire party (although it wouldn't always work out that way). Throughout the existence of the party, officeholders were added to or subtracted from the Central Committee. Membership remained fluid to reflect various changes in power (for instance, a prominent person newly added to the party might be given the title "deputy minister of defense" and added to the Central Committee to reflect his importance).

All party members learned how to strip and fire handguns and rifles at the firing ranges the party dug out six feet underneath Panther facilities. After six weeks a party recruit was examined by a party captain and was assigned a place in the party if he or she passed muster.

By the time David Hilliard began running the party, Landon had been promoted to the position of field marshal. As a field marshal he reported to Hilliard, usually by 10:30 A.M., at David's house. By now a separation was developing between the leadership cadre composed of people like David, Bobby Seale, June Hilliard (David's brother), John Seale (Bobby Seale's brother), and their personal friends, and ordinary rank-and-file members. More and more money had been rolling in from donations to the party, financial arrangements with the Peace and Freedom Party, and clandestine activities. As this happened the Panthers bought houses for rank-and-file members to live in. While David and other members of the leadership lived in relatively spacious homes, the rank and file lived two and three to a room in bunklike quarters, often with pallets on the floor. Landon Williams remained in his own apartment.

When Landon reported to David at David's house, David was usually still in bed. His wife, Pat, would be fixing breakfast while David was counting money (although Pat held the official title of party treasurer) or giving various instructions to Landon. After their morning meeting, Landon would return to the national headquarters on Shattuck Street in Berkeley, which the party had moved into after the previous one was shot up by the two officers angry about the Newton verdict. David wouldn't show up at the office until between two and four o'clock in the afternoon.

The Panthers felt the need to refine their ideology, make it more applicable to the black community. Their first minister of education was George Mason Murray, a graduate student at San Francisco State who, after joining the party, became mired in controversy at SF State because, as a member of the party, he had made very controversial statements (such as advising black students to bring guns to campus). He had also traveled to Cuba illegally and, while there, severely denounced the United States, threatening to kill politicians and judges (in a previous unsuccessful attempt to get to Cuba, Landon and David Hilliard had accompanied him, and all three were detained and turned around in Mexico). Then SF State hired him as a teaching assistant. The school later fired him, and his case became one of the issues in a five-month-long strike by the Black Students Union, during which it successfully demanded a Black Studies department. Murray became the victim of a series of arrests related to his speaking on campus after being fired, and various other charges, after which he resigned from the Black Panther Party.

He was replaced as minister of education by Masai Hewitt, out of the Los Angeles chapter. Hewitt had been part of a Marxist-Leninist group in LA. After Murray's departure and until Hewitt's arrival, the Panthers had been learning as they went along, doing their best to interpret how Mao's "Little Red Book" fit into the contemporary scene. Hewitt gave a more detailed analysis of the applications of communist theory to the Panthers. But Hewitt would soon experience the same problems that all intellectuals who joined the Panthers experienced—friction with the party members who were not of the same intellectual caliber as he. Such friction was ever present and known to COINTEL-PRO, which in one internal memorandum, dated September 9, 1968, noted of Kathleen Cleaver that she "lacks patience in dealing with the more lethargic elements in the black movement [because she possesses] more education and . . . a degree of 'class' when compared to the average Black Panther."

Once the Panthers opened their office on Shattuck Street, their plans became more grandiose. In November 1968, the party began its free breakfast program for children. There was a need to counter the grossly violent image the public had of them. The leaders spent a large amount of time at party headquarters, where they would meet with eager members of the press. Rarely did the leadership have contact with the rank-and-file members who were doing the actual work of selling the newspaper and, when the breakfast program was introduced, feeding breakfast to school children.

In a secret internal memo dated April 3, 1968, FBI headquarters told COINTELPRO agents in the Bay Area that "the two things foremost in the Black militant's mind are sex and money. The first is often promiscuous and frequently shared. White moral standards do not apply among this type of Negro." The memo neglected to note that "white moral standards" were also being abrogated in those days of free speech and chants for peace and love by plenty of white youths in the Bay Area. During the 1967 Summer of Love, it was not uncommon for a young white man to see a young white woman he didn't know on Haight Street; engage in a sexual romp with her in the back of a van, in the bushes in Golden Gate Park, or in a room in a nearby flat; and never lay eyes on her again. Sexual freedom, along with drugs, was par for the course.

By the end of 1968, free sexuality was flourishing within the Black Panther Party too, but with a twist. The flagrant disrespect for women on the part of many Panther men, which Landon first noticed when he joined the party, was becoming routine. According to both Landon Williams and Mary Kennedy, one party leader could never get dates with women. Soon he began to view his position not unlike a number of men view positions of authority when it comes to women. He began ordering women to go to bed with him. And because he was part of the leadership, his behavior went unchecked.

He and many other men in the party would lay guilt trips on the women they desired, coercing them to bed, applying Marxist-Leninist ideology to the situation if the woman refused their advances: "Here I am in the revolution putting my life on the line, and here you are denying me." The woman would be accused of harboring a petit bourgeois idealism that she needed to lose. Not every male in the party took advantage of women in this manner, but enough did that if a woman still refused to cooperate, she might be gang-raped.

COINTELPRO was pleased to learn of such behavior. They thought the Panthers would eventually turn against themselves. Thus if there were bona fide Panthers known to engage in sexual abuse, a male FBI informant was encouraged to engage in such activity too. With many members of the party leadership engaging in such abuse, the informant could melt in.

How far COINTELPRO agents and informants went to help destroy the party is difficult to gauge. Examination of key COIN-TELPRO memos available to the general public leads to the conclusion that COINTELPRO's campaign was primarily one of letter forging, wiretapping, and telephone voice impersonation. The memos provide strong evidence that whenever any planned counterintelligence activity was deemed dangerous to life, COIN-TELPRO backed away from it. However, COINTELPRO's Chicago office clearly ended up using an informant (William O'Neal) to collude with Chicago police in the shooting deaths of Chicago Panther leader Fred Hampton and Panther Mark Clark.

Other intelligence outfits also infiltrated the Black Panthers. It is similarly difficult to precisely apportion blame between their agents and informants, and genuine party members who incited divisions and violence within the party. Only a fraction of the existing documents from surveillance of the Black Panthers by COINTELPRO, the CIA, and other intelligence entities are available to the general public (hundreds of thousands of pages are yet to be processed). Documents from local police intelligence divisions aren't even available. And for the most clandestine work employed by non-COINTELPRO intelligence units, there is no paper trail.*

---

* According to agent/provocateur Louis Tackwood, the three most dangerous intelligence units used to damage the Black Panthers were operated by the Los Angeles police department. Operatives for those units were sent on missions nationwide. Tackwood—who passed all tests administered by investigative journalists to establish his credibility—says that the units engaged in efforts to destroy not only the Panthers but also other black and white radical groups "through any means necessary." Tackwood worked for two of those divisions, infiltrating both

COINTELPRO and local police intelligence divisions gained informants and agent-provocateurs in the Black Panther Party in one of three ways: they sent them directly into the party; they blackmailed existing party members; or party members readily agreed to inform on being approached about cooperating with law enforcement after becoming victims of outrageous behavior within the party.

The blackmail that COINTELPRO allegedly used to ensnare Panther captain Earl Anthony was a classic case. Because of his USC education, and because he had attended law school, Anthony was known inside the party as the bourgeois Panther. One day Robert O'Connor and Ron Kizenski, two COINTELPRO agents, knocked on the door of his San Francisco apartment. Once inside, the agents accused him of participating in the bombing of the Van Nuys, California, draft board building. Anthony replied that he knew nothing of such a bombing. But the agents made him an offer: they assured him that he would not be arrested and charged so long as he agreed to become an informant within the Black Panther Party. Anthony laughed at the impossibility of such a request, after which the two muscular Vietnam veterans allegedly administered a physical beating to him. Then they repeated their offer. This time Anthony agreed to become an informant, and, according to the agents, he became COINTELPRO's first recruit inside the party. Eventually, COINTELPRO would have sixty-four Black Panther informants nationwide.

That there were agents and informants soon became known within the party. The knowledge began to serve the purposes of those genuine party leaders and other members who were abusive, and who engaged in the misuse of party funds and in petty criminal activity of their own accord—that is, with no influence from government agents and informants. The existence of agents and informants served to inadvertently shield the party leadership from public criticism. A dissatisfied party member, for example, appalled

---

the Black Panthers and the LA militant group United Slaves. The intelligence divisions were so secret that not even rank-and-file Los Angeles police officers were aware of them.

at the difference between what he or she thought the party was all about and what he or she observed on the part of the party leadership, could risk speaking out. But if that person did so, the leadership called a press conference, or announced in the Panther newspaper that the person was an agent/provocateur and whatever he or she said about the party could not be true. The efforts to brand such Panthers as renegades, jacanapes, and informants whose activity the leadership in no way supported were almost always successful. Few people on the left or among the nation's liberals stopped to consider the circumstances under which a young former party member such as Jean Powell agreed to cooperate with Oakland law enforcement.

Jean Powell was the wife of Larry Clayton Powell. The Powells' involvement in the Black Panther Party began when Larry joined the Panther party's Los Angeles chapter in the spring of 1967. Larry, who had had many run-ins with the police, never saw his lawbreaking as anything but survival in the ghetto. And when he was arrested, he couldn't understand why the police didn't arrest him without inflicting physical harm since he gave himself up peaceably. Once, while arresting him, an officer hit him with the butt of his gun, leaving a gash in Larry's skull that would cause him occasional headaches for the rest of his life.

Two years before joining the Panthers, anger simmering about the unnecessary roughness of the police, Larry wanted badly to release steam, throw a few rocks and bottles, perhaps even fire off a few shots at the police during the Watts riots. But Jean convinced him otherwise. Larry remained angry, and wanted to channel his anger somewhere. Huey Newton and the Black Panther Party, replete with their black berets, black leather jackets, guns, and a law book, following the police around to ensure there was no more police brutality, seemed the answer to Larry's dilemma.

His first function within the LA chapter involved outreach to the community, explaining the party's ten-point program and trying to gain support for the party's call for community control of the police. Powell also tried to recruit new party members, presenting a party image that bordered on gangsterism. He warned prospective members to think it over carefully before joining the party because once they were in, there was no getting out. This was stretching the truth. He also told them that if they did join the party and turned out to be pigs or informants, the party would kill them.

At first, Powell took notes at meetings. But he quickly tired of that, believing it to be a woman's job. No women were active in the chapter at the time. His wife, Jean, had worked as a clerk for the county of Los Angeles, the federal government, the Veterans Administration, the registrar of voters, the Internal Revenue Service, and the county welfare department. Larry decided to recruit Jean into the party so she could take notes.

Jean took notes not only at Panther meetings but also at meetings between the Panthers and other groups. She took notes at meetings with the Black Congress, which was a consortium of black organizations including the Panthers, SNCC, CORE, and US, which maintained an office on 75th and Broadway. She took notes when the Panthers met with SNCC at SNCC's LA office on Jefferson Street. She took notes when they called press conferences. She took notes at the people's tribunal, a mock trial in which the people of the community served as judge and jury in cases involving brutal police officers. Eventually she also recruited more women into the party, becoming captain of the women. She also taught political-education classes.

Meanwhile, Larry became ensnared for the first time in an internal chapter dispute. Sermont Banks, who ran the Los Angeles chapter, had a rivalry going with Alprentice "Bunchy" Carter, Cleaver's old prisonmate, who had also been a notorious LA gang leader. On joining the party, Carter became deputy minister of defense. One day, a gun was sent from Oakland to Bunchy Carter's home in Los Angeles, for use by a Panther who was to serve on a security detail. Another Panther captain, Wilbert Terry, instructed Larry to pick it up. By now the LA police were monitoring the Panthers so closely that they knew the most opportune times to harass them. En route to his destination, Larry was stopped by the police and arrested for possession of a stolen gun.

Banks refused to bail Larry out with available party funds. This was Larry's first exposure to the party practice that eventually led to his decision to cooperate with the Oakland police department's intelligence division—the favoritism shown to a certain party elite who would be bailed out when arrested, while others would be left either to make bail on their own, or to sit and rot in jail only to be accused of being party renegades arrested in some foolish action not sanctioned by the party.

Powell made bail through a source secured by another party captain—the Committee for the Defense of the Bill of Rights, which also gave him a lawyer. He emerged from jail to get back to party business. Banks gave the excuse that he hadn't bailed Larry out because Larry had broken one of the first rules of guerilla warfare: Never go anywhere by yourself. Larry felt that was an empty excuse, because he often had traveled by himself on party business under party orders. Banks proceeded to suspend both Larry and Jean from the party.

Bunchy Carter immediately realized the pettiness of what Banks had done. So when Larry appealed Banks's decision to Carter, Bunchy immediately reinstated the couple. He also decided to remove Larry from Banks's responsibility. As deputy minister of defense, Carter was organizing an underground party unit in LA, trained in guerilla warfare tactics. Soon Larry would be making forays into the surrounding mountains to learn how to use weapons like the Panther Special, a 30-caliber semiautomatic rifle, and the 9-mm astro.

While in training, Larry had to appear in court on the gun charges. With conviction appearing imminent, Carter decided to place Larry underground. No one would know where he and Jean were for three months. But soon the LA Panthers would be called to Oakland to show Panther strength in numbers at the start of Huey's trial.

A place was reserved for Larry and Jean on a bus with Panthers headed to Oakland to demonstrate outside of the Alameda County Courthouse. Larry Powell was given a fictitious name. On arriving in Oakland, Bunchy Carter informed Bobby Seale that Larry was using a fictitious name because of the gun charges in Los Angeles. Larry and Jean found a place to live in Oakland, and, using his assumed name, Larry went to work in Oakland as a roofer. Jean was assigned to work as a secretary in the short-staffed Panther headquarters. One day Larry's boss went on vacation, so Larry accompanied Jean to the national office.

Funds for the party were rolling in from all over, thanks to the welter of sympathy generated during Huey's trial. Leaflets to inform people of Panther rallies were always in need of being run off on a special machine. On the day that Larry accompanied his wife to the office, no one was around to run the machine, but Larry knew how to run it. Realizing that Larry and Jean were quite valuable, the party somehow took care of the gun charges against Larry in Los Angeles, and Larry officially came out from underground. Fat in funds, by November 1968 the party had organized a permanent national staff and began to provide community service programs. Larry and Jean were ordered to join the national staff full time.

At first, Larry balked at quitting his job to work full time for the party. But everyone in the party was being ordered to work full time, and everyone was being told that their needs would be taken care of. Human greed then started to take over among the party leadership. According to Larry Powell, the leadership was collecting $50,000 to $100,000 every month, and the skimming began. After the Powells started to work for the party full time, they had a hard time getting paid. When their first month of rent was due, they had to practically beg to get the money. They received it from David Hilliard only after getting an eviction notice from their landlord. When Larry asked for money to pay the gas and electric bills, he was told that there was no money to pay for it. Larry knew that couldn't be true because he himself had handed over $1,000 from donations and various sources that very month. According to Larry and Jean, David Hilliard was embezzling the party's money.

The national staff was expected to work seven days per week, ten hours per day. The only spending money the Powells received was what they made from selling the one hundred issues of the Panther newspaper, which every rank-and-file Party member was required to sell each day. The Powells sold their copies after performing their duties at the national office.

Shortly after Larry began working in the national office, he was nominated to be a member of the Black Guard. Larry had proven himself worthy of this nomination by committing acts at the behest of the party such as stealing dynamite, stealing cars to commit robberies, and aiding in the performance of disciplinary action against party members who had violated the rules. An example of such a disciplinary action would be the pistol whipping of a party member who may have gotten drunk, taken a gun, and indiscriminately fired it outdoors, resulting in a visit by the police. A milder example of behavior requiring discipline would be a rank-and-file party member's failure to sell his or her share of the party newspapers or to collect enough party funds.

In all cases in which the rules were violated, the violator was written up. He or she then appeared before a representative of the party's Central Committee and a punishment was chosen. An infraction such as not selling enough newspapers could result in imprisonment by the party in one of its own holding cells for a few days.

A person could also be disciplined for confronting the leadership. According to Jean Powell, one party member, angry because David Hilliard refused to bail his brother out of jail after he was arrested performing party business at the behest of Hilliard, called Hilliard a "chicken shit son of a bitch." And he was beaten for doing so. But Hilliard wasn't so unreasonable when someone else was the object of scorn. Once another Panther in the leadership cadre argued with a member at the Shattuck headquarters and slapped him, whereupon the guy took his fist and knocked that leader almost clear across the room. The leader demanded that the guy be disciplined. David Hilliard refused, saying, "How can you expect him to call himself a Panther if he can't defend himself?"

According to Larry and Jean Powell, as well as other rank-and-file party members, certain party men were regularly organized into teams of two or three to commit robberies. They also engaged in extorting money from merchants. One-third of the robbery proceeds was supposed to go to the party.

On December 26, 1968, Larry was told to accompany Panther captain Wendell Wade on a robbery of the Aloha nightclub in East Oakland, allegedly set up by Hilliard himself. Armed with a 45-

caliber machine gun, Larry and Wendell Wade set out. Club owners called the police while the robbery was in process. The officers chased Larry and found him in the attic of a house. He tried to shoot the officers as they came through the square hole of the ceiling they had found him in. Both he and Wendell Wade were apprehended. Immediately the party called a press conference denouncing them, accusing them of being counterrevoluntionaries, of being "jive-time tavern robbers." It was the same thing Larry had experienced as a Panther in LA all over again—getting arrested and then seeing the party distance itself from you. Larry and Wendell were expelled from the party.

Although they had publicly denounced her husband and thrown him out of the party, according to Jean Powell she was ordered by David Hilliard and Bobby Seale to continue working at the party headquarters. She also became the object of sexual overtures by other men in the party. Understandably, Jean was more concerned about Larry. She was far more interested in getting him bailed out of prison and hiring a lawyer to defend him. Jean refused to work any longer within the party, and decided to establish a defense fund to bail out her husband and Wade. With the aid of other disenchanted former Panthers, Jean established the People's Defense Fund Committee, which was open to the public. Because the committee was composed almost entirely of disenchanted Panthers, the party hierarchy began to worry that the general public would find out about its clandestine activities. That March, the party announced, via the Black Panther newspaper, wholesale expulsions of all members known to be cooperating with the committee. Panthers in good standing were sent to committee meetings to spy on them and discover what was being said about the party. Allegedly, David Hilliard appeared at one of those meetings to denounce someone for criticizing the Black Panther Party in public. Although the committee originally had been formed to raise money to bail out Larry Powell and Wendell Wade, criticism of the party couldn't be avoided, thanks to the shabby treatment the arrested Panthers had received.

Jean Powell tried to reassure David that the express goal of the committee was to secure the freedom of her husband and

Wendell Wade. But according to Jean, the Panthers didn't buy it. They started a campaign of intimidation. They beat up ex-Panthers known to be cooperating with the defense committee, such as Oleander Harrison (an original party member who had gone to the state capitol during the party's gun display) and his brother Gregory. When Wendell Wade (also one of the first party members) was sentenced for his part in the Aloha nightclub robbery, he expressed to his probation officer fear that the party had marked him for death. Party members beat up ex-Panther Renee Rice after she appeared at the national office. Allegedly, Renee's boyfriend and six other ex-Panthers, including a man named Ron Black, confronted party leadership about the beating. Black had become so disenchanted with the party that on being expelled from it, he also disassociated himself from the proud black demeanor identified with the party by getting rid of his natural hairdo and returning to the greasy, straightened, processed hairstyle so popular among black men before SNCC and the Black Panthers came on the scene. Concluding that the beatings hadn't silenced those who were cooperating with the defense committee, the party allegedly decided that stronger measures were needed. On April 5, 1969, Ron Black was on his way to the barbershop next door to the national headquarters, when he was gunned down. According to Jean Powell, the Black Panthers performed the assassination. Later that same month, Ardell Butler, a Panther who had participated in the May 1967 state capitol gun display and who was purged from the party that January, was shot and critically wounded while walking near his Oakland home. After first telling police he had been shot by someone in a passing vehicle, Butler later changed his story, saying that he shot himself in a game of Russian roulette.

At a press conference a few days after the killing of Ron Black, ex-Panther captain Tommy Jones accused the party of the assassination and of other clandestine activities. The party then accused Jones in its newspaper of being an FBI agent. Allegedly, Jean Powell was also targeted for assassination, but the person assigned to kill her didn't go through with it. Jean then began to think about cooperating with the Oakland police department. After her husband's arrest she had been contacted by Sergeant Ray Gaul. She told Gaul about the troubling treatment she was receiving at the hands of the party. The Oakland police had been searching for someone with inside knowledge of the party to testify about its inner workings before U.S. Senator John McClellan's Permanent Subcommittee on Subversive Groups, part of the Senate Committee on Investigations. On hearing the complaints of Jean Powell, Gaul contacted Sergeant Stanley C. White and told him they might have a break. Their goal was to gain the cooperation of both Jean and her husband. This would require that White receive authorization to cut a deal with Larry. On discovering that White was proposing that a deal be made with Powell, his fellow police officers balked. The very idea of cutting a deal with any member of the hated Panthers was anathema. In the eyes of the police, Huey Newton had already escaped the gas chamber after murdering Frey. The police had been deliberately ambushed by the Panthers in the shootout resulting in the death of Bobby Hutton, and they were the constant objects of ridicule. Now here was White proposing a deal with an apprehended Panther?

White reasoned that no police officer had been killed or wounded in apprehending Powell, and the department was already under intense pressure to bring before the public admitted party members who could tell about the party's inner workings. White received the approval of the department to begin negotiating a deal with Powell.

Having already agreed to cooperate, Jean Powell and the couple's baby, Larry, Jr., were relocated to a motel on MacArthur Boulevard in Oakland. Jean was given the code name Owl. But Larry was in no mood to cooperate with the police. He still hated the police more than he began hating what had happened between himself and the Panthers. Neither did he want the label of "stooge." The prosecutor's office offered to plea-bargain his case and place him and his family in a witness protection program in exchange for the uncensored testimony of the Powells about their lives in the party. Larry refused. The police decided to take him out of jail and bring him to where his wife was being kept at the motel on MacArthur Boulevard. Jean told Larry that she had been expected to work within the party after the party had expelled him.

She told him about the sexual passes that were made. She told him that the only party member who had supported her and their baby was Tommy Jones. She told him about the beatings and about her belief that the Panthers had assassinated Ron Black. On hearing all of this, Larry agreed to cooperate and testify before the McClellan Subcommittee in June 1969. In exchange for his cooperation, Powell and his family were given protection, and for his part in the Aloha nightclub robbery, Powell was given an eight-month suspended prison sentence and three years' probation.

The Powells' testimony was identical to the charges made by Tommy Jones when he began to speak out against the party in April. Both Bobby Seale and David Hilliard denied all of the charges, calling the Powells liars. Just as they did to Tommy Jones, they accused the Powells of being agents-provocateurs. In April, Seale had responded to Jones's allegation that the party had assassinated Ron Black with the statement, "That sounds just like something FBI pig J. Edgar Hoover would say." But if the Powells and Jones were agents-provocateurs for the FBI, it was news to the FBI. Had they been agents-provocateurs, one would expect that COINTELPRO would be gloating in its internal memos over their success in sowing seeds of dissent, or lamenting the loss of informants once Seale kicked them out of the party. Instead COINTELPRO circulated an internal memo to all of its offices that clearly presented Jones, for instance, as someone it had no connection to. It treated the news of his break with the party as a new opportunity for COINTELPRO: "Seale denounced Jones as an FBI informant. . . . [At his press conference] Jones in return accused the Panthers of assassination and denied being an informant. . . . Unidentified women said that they left the Black Panther Party in disgust when they learned the Panthers did not respect Party doctrine concerning the protection of women. . . . The above situation presents a definite potential for counterintelligence which could result in the disruption of the Black Panther Party on both a national and local level. . . ."

The left-liberal community bought the party's explanation for the accusations of Tommy Jones and the Powells. The attitude of

San Francisco priest Eugene Boyle was typical of the attitude of Panther sympathizers. Commenting on the reliability of any Black Panther defector who publicly denounced the party or testified about its inner workings, Boyle stated it would be as unfair to believe what they had to say about the party as it would be to believe the word of defectors and dropouts from the Catholic church regarding its inner workings. The party successfully painted a picture that survives to this day, blaming its destruction on a well-coordinated conspiracy on the part of agents-provocateurs, rather than a combination of the behavior of such saboteurs and that of genuine party members who did not have to be induced by the agents to act as they did.

In his autobiography, David Hilliard denies that the party sanctioned any illegal activities, or the mistreatment of women while he was in it, stating that corrective measures were taken whenever such behavior was discovered. But other party veterans who neither testified before any government investigative bodies nor were identified as informants corroborate most of the accusations made by the Powells and Tommy Jones. Besides confirming the allegation that the mistreatment of women in the party went unchecked, Landon Williams agrees that Hilliard embezzled party funds: "People were criticizing David for all the excesses. He kicked those people criticizing him out of the party. If you look through the party newspaper you'll see how so-and-so was declared an enemy of the people for threatening David's life. Most of the time that was bull."

"It's true that the party underground engaged in robberies to help out the party," states a party veteran who requested anonymity.

"When David was running things, different situations were happening and problems weren't being resolved," agrees Benjamin Stewart, who at the time was a member of the Black Panther Party Advisory Committee (a separate body from the Central Committee, composed not of actual party members but of friends and key supporters of the party). "Some party members might not want to do something that involved the police, and that would create prob-

lems. Other brothers would do something on a 'get down basis'—
I'll just put it like that—and when they got busted, they were
labeled 'jacanapes.'"

After Tommy Jones and Jean Powell accused the party of
ordering Ron Black's assassination, the party member sought by
police as the suspect who carried out that order went into hiding.

The truth about the party was that it was made up of a cross
section of young African Americans, some who were law-abiding
and sincerely interested in being of value to the Black community,
others who had no qualms about breaking the law if it could be
rationalized as a revolutionary activity, and still others who were
just plain ruthless and criminal.

When a second purge of party members took place in March
1969, purged Panther member Tommy Wooten showed up at the
door of Mary Kennedy and her family. At the time Mary didn't
know that he had been kicked out of the party. Wooten went to
Mary's because he wanted one last connection with a party member
who, like him, had joined the party with a sincere interest in
changing conditions for the better. Mary was like a touchstone. She
invited him inside, but he declined. He just lingered at the door-
step, making small talk. Tommy asked how Mary and the kids were
doing. She said they were fine. He told her that he was on his way
to wash his clothes. Mary said he could wash his clothes in her
home, but he declined. After a few more minutes, he went on his
way. When her husband came home, Mary told him of Tommy's
behavior. Mary's husband, still a member in good standing, grew
nervous. "What the hell did he have to come over here for?!?!
What did you tell him?" Her husband feared that the party leadership would assume he too took the side of the disaffected Panthers who were angry about its treatment of Larry Powell and
Wendell Wade. "Didn't you read the party paper?" Mary's husband
asked. "Tommy was purged from the party."

In the spring of 1969, Mary Kennedy landed a temporary job
with the U.S. post office in Oakland and got off of welfare. But she
soon lost the job because of FBI intervention. The federal government was under intense pressure to investigate not only the Black
Panthers but the predominantly white SDS, as well as the Peace

and Freedom Party and other groups considered subversive. In addition to the McClellan Subcommittee in the Senate, there would soon be a House subcommittee engaging in similar investigations. And Mary and her family would not go unaffected by a secret federal grand jury convened in San Francisco in 1969 to investigate the party.

The FBI aided in the secret federal grand jury investigation, rounding up any and everyone known to be either a party member, a friend of the party, or a journalist covering the party. Journalist Earl Caldwell, then a West Coast reporter for the *New York Times*, refused to testify when he was subpoenaed to appear, leading to a protracted test case between the government and the *New York Times* to determine whether a newspaper reporter was obligated to divulge information on sources believed to be engaged in criminal activities (the *Times* eventually won).

Mary, being the wife of a key party member, became a target of the investigation as well. FBI agents visited her apartment on 79th Avenue in East Oakland while she wasn't home. A baby-sitter was watching Mary's children when the agents knocked on the door. Debra, Mary's second oldest daughter, opened the door only as far as the chain link on the door would allow. The agents identified themselves and said they were looking for Mary Kennedy. The baby-sitter told them that Mary wasn't home, so they couldn't come in. The agents insisted on entering, but Debra wouldn't release the chain latch. The agents grew angry and proceeded to pull Debra's arm through the door to prevent her from closing it. Horrified, the baby-sitter insisted that no one was home but she and the children. She begged the agents to leave. The agents left, promising to return later. When they did, they brought reinforcements and surrounded the entire building. This time Mary was home. The agents told her that they were going to subpoena her to appear before the federal grand jury being convened to investigate the Panthers. Mary said that she wasn't very active in the party. The agents replied that she would be subpoenaed anyway, and that if she ignored the subpoena she would be found in contempt of court. Not knowing what to do, Mary called Panther headquarters. Next time, June Hilliard instructed her, tell the agents to contact party lawyer Charles Garry. The secret grand jury investigation turned up nothing after most witnesses pleaded the Fifth Amendment to the questions asked of them.

Soon after, Mary's husband left again on party business. And that June, Landon Williams would find himself arrested—accused, along with Bobby Seale, Ericka Huggins, and other Panthers, of being part of a conspiracy to torture and murder New York Panther Alex Rackley, in New Haven, Connecticut (Seale would be arrested in August 1969). Landon would remain in jail first in Colorado then in Connecticut until May 1971, when the government dropped its case against him.*

In the meantime, Mary's involvement in the party deepened tremendously. She began living in Panther-owned housing. She moved into a Panther house on 73rd Avenue in East Oakland that had seven other Panthers in it, including a married couple and their baby who slept in a basement room. Only one member of the household had a room of his own. Everyone else shared rooms, while one household member slept in the living room. There were plenty of pallets and roll-up mattresses to accommodate people sleeping over because there were always people coming over from time to time, place to place.

On a typical day, a party member rose, washed up, put on clothes, and ate breakfast. Then it was time to sell newspapers, received from the Officer of the Day (OD). It was her or his responsibility to count out the newspapers, a set number of which

---

* The Rackley case became one of the most controversial Panther cases of all, a prime example of the question of which illegal activities could be blamed on genuine party leaders, and which on agents-provocateurs or just plain deviants in the party. Seale was accused of ordering Rackley's murder for being an alleged government agent, with the words, "Do away with him." Williams and others were accused of being present when Seale gave the command, George Sams accepting it, then he, Lonnie McLucas, and Warren Kimbro, the alleged triggermen, driving Rackley to a swamp to kill him. The case hinged largely on the questions of whether Seale actually did appear to give the command, and if so, how Seale's command could be interpreted. The Panthers would insist that party member George Sams, who had in fact spent plenty of time in a mental institution, ordered the murder of Rackley on his own.

were purchased for 12½ cents per copy from Central Headquarters. Each member, in turn, sold the papers for the printed price of 25 cents, receiving 5 cents for every copy sold. The remaining 7½-cent profit went to the person's local chapter, which took the other 12½ cents to pay for the next issue of the newspaper from Central Headquarters. In many cases the money made from selling newspapers was the only money that rank-and-file members ever got.

The OD gave each member the newspapers and a can for donations, and then suggested areas where the papers might sell. The papers were always sold in twos. Members each had to sell one hundred Panther newspapers per day, every so often calling in to the OD to say how it was going. If a person wasn't doing too well, the OD would suggest somewhere else the paper might sell more easily. If the OD could think of no such place, the conversation would go something like this:

OD: "How many papers did you sell?"

Rank-and-file member: "Fifty."

OD: "You were given one hundred."

Rank-and-file member: "I can't move any more of them!"

OD: "Stay out there and keep moving those papers! I don't care if it takes you till ten or eleven o'clock tonight!" [Click]

So where might the person go to sell them? To downtown Oakland, if someone hadn't gotten there first, since there were a lot of black people in downtown Oakland, which was being abandoned by whites. He or she might go to Telegraph Avenue, to Broadway, to the clubs, or to East 14th Street, or might go door to door in surrounding neighborhoods—but only in mixed or predominantly black neighborhoods. There were places a Panther absolutely wouldn't go, such as San Leandro, home to the Bay Area's Archie Bunker types, the ones who called the police at the first sighting of anyone black. If a Panther did end up in San Leandro, the only place he or she might stop at would be a large supermarket—leaving the papers there. Soliciting buyers would result in being completely ignored, being stared at with hostility, or having the police called.

The OD might tell a member who was moving papers swiftly to go to Central Headquarters and pick up a bunch that Central couldn't move because Central was too busy working on the next issue of the newspaper. By the end of 1969, as many as 140,000 copies of the party's weekly newspaper were being distributed nationally.

Certain people just had a knack for selling newspapers, such as a woman named Jackie who would easily come back to her Panther house with $100 in donations every day. The money earned from the sale of the newspapers by the chapter at large went to maintaining the Panther home—buying food, paying phone and utility bills, and so on. After that, any money left over would go to the personal needs of those living in the house. It was almost as if the member had adopted a new family. In many cases this actually was the case, because many of the younger rank-and-file members were kicked out of their parents' homes after joining the party.

Theoretically, it was all about introducing party members to a revolutionary collective lifestyle. But Mary began observing the human fallibility in the party, like the ease with which young girls were taken advantage of. The male party members had at their disposal impressionable teenaged girls, many of whom were off the streets. Mary discovered how easy it was for male Panthers, particularly in the leadership, to romp between the sheets with any impressionable young girl they desired. Many of the men in the party indulged in temptation with healthy doses of humor and misogyny.

On catching him in bed with a woman named Brenda Presley, David Hilliard's wife, Pat, pulled a gun on him. Hilliard talked her out of pulling the trigger. The wife of a San Francisco Panther leader had caught her husband cheating on her too, after which she slipped some LSD into the other woman's drink at a Panther function. Somehow the other woman avoided taking a sip, but she complained to headquarters and it was decided that the issue of cheating had grown serious enough to be dealt with officially. It was taken up in a political-education class one day, when Bay Area Panthers were called together to listen to a tape of what Huey had to say on the subject from jail. As the meeting started, Mary and the wife of the Panther leader she had befriended were busy consoling Pat Hilliard, telling her she should have shot both David and Brenda. But Huey's tape said something different. He told party members that it was all right for men in the party to have more than one woman, that the women should get over the old jealousies. Then he made an analogy. Using David Hilliard as an example, he called him a butterfly in a garden of roses. The women were the roses, and David, the butterfly, was going from rose to rose. He was getting his substance from all of the roses, but spreading the pollen. This was too much for one of the party women, who blurted out, "Well, what is David, a goddam bumblebee or a butterfly?"

On getting more involved in the party, Mary soon discovered that her husband was cheating on her too—that, in fact, another woman in the party was about to have his baby. Mary asked him for a divorce. He took the request lightly and decided to play with Mary's mind. He told her that since both of them were in the party, they didn't need to go the official route in getting a divorce. All they needed to do was repeat six times, "I divorce you, I divorce you, I divorce you," making 360-degree turns as they did so, and they would be divorced. So strongly did the party have a hold on many of its members that Mary was naive enough to believe this. She went to Central Headquarters and told June Hilliard, deputy chief of staff, that she had engaged in the proper procedure. June started laughing. He told Mary that her husband had been pulling her leg; then he explained to her the approved party procedure for getting a divorce. Mary was instructed to write up the complaint against her husband and bring it before the Central Committee.

This time Mary's husband didn't have a sense of humor. He saw Mary's effort to gain the party's blessing to divorce him as an effort to embarrass him. At the same time that Mary was seeking a divorce from her husband, the wife of the party leader whom Mary had befriended was seeking a divorce from her husband as well. The party's Central Committee heard both cases on the same day. The case of the wife of the leader came first. She alleged that her husband often hit her, and that rather than use his hand to strike her, he once used a bottle. She detailed other reasons for seeking the divorce, and then the Central Committee excused her. The leader in question had been sitting on the Central Committee listening to his wife's complaints, which the committee took with jocular humor and obvious contempt for the rights of party women. That attitude was dramatized as soon as the wife left the room when a principal committee member, a major leader himself, turned to the leader in question and said, "Evidently you didn't hit the bitch hard enough, because if you had she wouldn't even be in here." His wife's request was turned down. Then it was Mary's turn. After Mary told her story, the committee decided that since she was the only one of the two who wanted a divorce, the divorce would not receive party blessing. Mary continued in the party, and remained married for the time being. She chalked up such experiences as petty foolishness that shouldn't get in the way of her commitment to the people.

Soon Mary also became involved in the Panther free breakfast program for schoolchildren. The Panthers masterfully mixed the contradictions inherent in giving innocent youths free breakfasts with the implied violence out of the barrel of a gun. Some stores eagerly volunteered donations to the breakfast program; others required greater persuasion. Many took issue not with the idea of feeding free breakfasts to kids but with the idea of trusting the Panthers to feed free breakfasts to kids. And the manner of persuasion used by the party to convince those who were skeptical about the program came as no surprise to the skeptics. If convenience-store owners, supermarkets, dairy suppliers, and restaurants couldn't be embarrassed into donating to feed innocent children, the party decided, then they could be boycotted, firebombed, and beaten into doing so. To be sure, some sincere party members worked in the breakfast program out of a strong commitment to the community. But they were mixed in with party members who had the gang mentality.

The college students in the party ranks read up on price supports, discovering that dairy farmers dumped milk, butter, cheese and eggs, in order to guarantee a certain market price. They also knew that bakeries threw away unsold baked goods after a few days. The party would send out ten to twelve Black Panthers to convenience stores, supermarkets, dairy suppliers, and restaurants to ask for donations. A restaurant making french fries everyday would donate bags full of potato skins it would otherwise throw away, which became the basis for the hash browns fed in the free breakfast program. A convenience store, such as one in West Oakland, would donate a crate of eggs twice per month, while another would donate twenty pounds of bacon per month, and another, twenty cartons of milk.

In the beginning the supermarket chain Safeway refused to donate. But the Panthers were smart enough not to use extreme tactics with a supermarket chain like Safeway. Instead they leafleted the communities in an effort to get the community to boycott Safeway stores. The leaflet featured an adorable little black boy staring at the reader as he prepared to dig into his breakfast. "This avaricious greedy businessman who owns Safeway stores must come forth and donate to the breakfast program for school children," the leaflet read. "We the people shop there making the businessman fat and rich. . . . We the people must demand that each Safeway store donate in food items of $100 every week or cash. Not to feed hungry children is low and rotten. . . ." Eventually, Safeway donated food to the free breakfast program.

Smaller stores that didn't donate to the program became the victims of a different type of tactic. The owner of a convenience store on San Pablo Avenue in North Oakland had been asked to donate six dozen eggs to the program. Instead he donated only one dozen. So on May 10, 1969, Panther members Reginald Forte and John Sloan firebombed his store.

Mary Kennedy became involved in the East Oakland free breakfast program when she and her children moved again into a Panther-owned house on 99th Avenue. Party members prepared the breakfasts at a nearby Catholic church on Hyde Street. They also had a facility at the public housing project, Brookfield Village, where they fed children. Children in the project would get up at home, prepare for school, and then go down to the Panther free breakfast program to eat breakfast. Most of the children who were fed were in elementary school because most of the teenagers in Brookfield Village were too embarrassed to be seen going to get free breakfast from the Panthers. To the teenagers, getting food from the Panther free breakfast program amounted to saying your family was in need of charity. To the younger ones, though, it made no difference. And the program was a boon to families in which both the husband and the wife worked. Their children could get up, get ready for school, and go on down to the Panther breakfast program without their needing to worry.

The Panthers would prepare eggs, hash browns, bacon, sometimes french toast, sometimes pancakes, but *always* hot chocolate. The children at Brookfield Village loved the hot chocolate more than anything else. Many wanted nothing but the hot chocolate. They would leave the eggs, bacon, toast, and pancakes alone. The Panthers working the program would ask, "Don't you want something to eat?" They would respond no, they wanted only the hot chocolate. It reached the point where the workers were buying an inordinate number of Styrofoam cups to accommodate the requests for hot chocolate. And they kept a large pot of hot chocolate waiting at all times. Because the Panthers would have to eat the leftover food after the kids went off to school, or take it door to door up and down the neighborhood streets, giving it away, they switched to preparing the food as the children came in. But why, they wondered, were the children at Brookfield Village so in love with the hot chocolate? One day they discovered the answer to the mystery. In the late 1960s, Seconal was a popular street drug in poor black communities on the West Coast. Seconal came in little red capsules. The nickname for Seconal was "reds." Many of the kids in Brookfield Village who ate breakfast at the Panther free program were taking reds. They used the hot chocolate to pop the capsules the reds came in, which would release the drug and wash it down.

It wouldn't be the last the Panthers heard of reds. The free breakfast program brought them lots of positive, worldwide publicity, so much that a Swedish film crew decided one day to film the program for Swedish television. The Panthers viewed the filming as an excellent chance to sweeten their reputation. The film crew prepared to film one of the breakfast programs in West Oakland. To enhance the party's image, the Panthers decided not only to feed the children their usual bacon, eggs, toast, hash browns, and hot chocolate, but to supplement this routine breakfast with a one-a-day vitamin, which was the same color as reds. The kids sat down to their breakfast and the film crew began filming, when suddenly one little boy picked up his capsule and asked, "What's this?" "It's a vitamin pill," an embarrassed Panther answered. But the little boy was unconvinced. He took another look at the vitamin and blurted out, "Ooooh wee! They tryin to give us reds!" The little boy was snatched out of view of the camera.

IN THE SPRING OF 1970, MARY KENNEDY FOUND HERSELF face to face with another crisis involving her husband. It started with the arrest of four marijuana suspects at an intersection near Brookfield Village. A paddy wagon was called. When the wagon arrived, the two officers driving it were ambushed by three Black Panthers lying in wait in an open field, Mary's husband among them. At least ten shots hit the wagon, wounding the two officers inside. The four marijuana suspects were unharmed. Another officer was wounded as he stepped from his patrol car. Mary's husband and the other two Panthers fled in their own car. Backup units were called. Thirty patrol cars responded, and a five-mile high-speed chase ensued, during which Mary's husband and the other two Panthers threw small fragmentation bombs from their vehicle into the street, disabling three police cars. Two bystanders suffered minor gunshot wounds. Finally, the Panthers' car came to a halt near Lake Merritt. Mary's husband and the other Panthers fled on foot but were caught, arrested, and charged with assault with intent to murder.

At the time her husband was arrested, Mary was selling Black Panther newspapers. Because their marriage had deteriorated, Mary wasn't exactly sad about her husband's arrest, but "I knew I was supposed to cry, so I cried." Mary went to Central Headquarters to find out what she should do. David Hilliard decided that rather than have someone from the party take Mary to the jail, the next day she should take the city bus there. He instructed Mary not to answer any questions about the party once she arrived.

Mary went to the jail the next morning. She told the officers she had read in the newspaper that they had arrested her husband. A detective appeared and told her to have a seat. After ten or fifteen minutes, more detectives appeared. They took her to a room and began to ask her questions about the party. Mary refused to answer. The detectives told her that if she wasn't going to answer the questions, then she should leave. Mary caught the bus back to party headquarters.

The Panthers decided to call a lawyer named Peter Frank to return with her to the jail the following day. On arriving at the jail with Mary, Peter Frank identified himself as the lawyer for Mary's husband. The sergeant assigned to lead them to Mary's husband guided them down the corridors calmly, until they reached the visitors' room. He opened the metal door to let Peter Frank and Mary inside. Then, before having the guards bring in Mary's husband, he turned to address Peter and Mary.

"Let me tell you one motherfucking thing," he said, backing them both against a wall. "You better be goddamned glad I didn't go when they went to chase down that black motherfucker, because you wouldn't have a goddamned client, and you wouldn't have had a motherfucking husband! In fact, that bitch who birthed the motherfucker should have been killed for having him!" Then, to Peter Frank, the sergeant added, "And you, you're a disgrace to the white race!" Then he walked off.

The guards pushed Mary's husband into the visitors' room, where prisoners and visitors were separated by a glass partition. He had on coveralls, but he couldn't see. The officers and guards had given him such a vicious beating that his eyelids were swollen shut. His nose was messed up. Mary and Peter Frank talked him over to the chair in the room. "Come on, keep straight, reach out now. You can feel it." Finally, he sat down. One guard in the room told

Mary and Peter that they had just put the coveralls on him; before that, he was in the holding cell, naked. "Yeah," the other guard added, "we were hoping the motherfucker would catch pneumonia!" While Mary continued her life within the party, her husband was tried and convicted, destined to serve seven years in prison for assault with intent to murder.

9

Reactions to the Cat's Violence

AT THE TIME THAT MARY'S HUSBAND AND HIS ACCOM-
plices ambushed the Oakland police, Black Panther shootouts with
law enforcement were common, expected, and defended by most
of the nation's radicals. Hard-liners considered it an honor to be
arrested, and a real right of redress to injure a police officer. But
few had the daring to confront the police as the Panthers did
(except for the SDS offshoot, the Weathermen). To paraphrase
writer Julius Lester, the Left appeared to view the Panthers as
gladiators, cheering them on as they got themselves killed.

From 1968 to 1970, as antiwar and antiestablishment activities
became the rule across the country, most radicals advocated confrontations with police officers. There was the spring 1968 clash
between hundreds of predominantly white student strikers at Co-
lumbia University and police, resulting in excessive injuries and
arrests. In August 1968, predominantly white demonstrators and
police clashed in a virtual war at the Democratic National Convention in Chicago. (Bobby Seale made a speech there and a year
later, along with seven others, was arrested and charged with conspiracy to incite riots at the convention. During the trial Seale was
chained, gagged, and charged with and convicted of contempt of

court. But the charges were dropped in 1970.) In May 1969, Berkeley police stunned predominately white demonstrators at People's Park, raising the level of brutality they were willing to inflict to quell demonstrations ever higher, firing into fleeing demonstrators with buckshot, leaving several wounded and one killed. The list of confrontations went on and on.

But the Panthers "gladiated" with police in the most dramatic acts of all. From the fall of 1967 through the end of 1969, across the nation, nine police officers were killed and fifty-six wounded in confrontations with the Panthers, while ten Panthers were believed killed in such confrontations and an unknown number were wounded. In 1969 alone, 348 Panthers were arrested for a variety of crimes. A partial list of Panther–police clashes would include the following:

> JULY 28, 1968—Two members of the Black Panther Party in New York City throw a Molotov cocktail at an empty police car, completely destroying it.

> AUGUST 6, 1968—Police exchange gunfire at a service station with three members of the Los Angeles Black Panthers, resulting in the death of all three and the wounding of two police officers.

> AUGUST 31, 1968—Three members of the Los Angeles Panthers are arrested after an alleged unsuccessful attempt to ambush police officers.

> SEPTEMBER 24, 1968—Members of the Jersey City Black Panthers are arrested after allegedly attacking police officers who were in the process of arresting another Black Panther.

> NOVEMBER 18, 1968—Two Black Panthers in Berkeley allegedly open fire on police after their car is stopped for a traffic violation. Police return fire, wounding one of the Panthers.

> NOVEMBER 19, 1968—Bill Brent and seven Panthers are arrested in San Francisco after holding up a service station and exchanging gunfire with police, leaving two officers wounded.

NOVEMBER 29, 1968—A Black Panther in Jersey City is arrested for allegedly firing thirty-six rounds from a machine gun into the police department's Fifth Precinct station house.

DECEMBER 7, 1968—Forty-three Denver police raid the Panther office there. Panthers claim $9,000 in damage.

DECEMBER 12, 1968—Twelve Chicago Panthers are arrested on weapons charges.

DECEMBER 18, 1968—The Indianapolis Panther office is raided by the local police, looking for illegal weapons.

DECEMBER 21, 1968—The Denver Panther office is raided again by the local police.

DECEMBER 27, 1968—The San Francisco Panther office is raided by the local police.

JANUARY 11, 1969—A Black Panther Party member in Seattle is arrested for allegedly shooting at a police department patrol car.

JANUARY 17, 1969—Two Black Panthers allegedly open fire on two New York City patrolmen investigating their parked car along the expressway.

JANUARY 17, 1969—Los Angeles police exchange gunfire with four suspects from an armed robbery, one a member of the Black Panthers. Black Panthers Bunchy Carter and John Huggins are murdered on the campus of UCLA, allegedly by members of the rival militant group United Slaves. Police then raid the home of John Huggins and arrest all twelve people there, including Huggins's widow and infant child, charging them with assault with intent to commit murder.

APRIL 1969—The Los Angeles Panther office is attacked by the police and two Panthers are arrested.

APRIL 2, 1969—"New York 21" Panthers are arrested and charged with conspiracy to blow up department stores, police stations, and commuter railways (they will eventually be found innocent of the charges).

APRIL 26, 1969—The Des Moines Panther office is totally destroyed by a bomb. Two Panthers are injured. Several Panthers are arrested by state police after the blast.

MAY 1, 1969—The Los Angeles Panther office is raided again by local police, and in a two-week period the Los Angeles police arrest forty-two Black Panthers.

JUNE 4, 1969—The Detroit Panther office is raided in an attempt to find suspects in the Alex Rackley murder. The Chicago Panther office is raided for the same purpose, thirty Panthers are arrested in Chicago.

JUNE 7, 1969—The Indianapolis Panther office is raided again by the local police.

JUNE 15, 1969—The San Diego Panther office is raided by local police. The Sacramento Panther office is raided by local police.

JUNE 16, 1969—The Indianapolis Panther office is raided again by local police and sixteen Panthers are arrested.

JULY 31, 1969—The Chicago Panther office is raided by the local police, and three Black Panthers engage them in a forty-five-minute gun battle.

SEPTEMBER 8, 1969—The Black Panther free breakfast program in Watts is raided by armed police.

SEPTEMBER 23, 1969—The FBI and Philadelphia police raid the Philadelphia Panther office.

OCTOBER 18, 1969—The Los Angeles Panther office is raided again by local police.

DECEMBER 4, 1969—Chicago police raid the home of Chicago Panther leader Fred Hampton. The police allege that Panther Mark Clark fired a shot at them first. Others allege that Clark fired only after the police first fired. In any case, the police blasted the apartment with ninety-four shots, killing both Clark and Fred Hampton, and seriously wounding four other Panthers.

DECEMBER 8, 1969—Police again raid the Los Angeles Panther office, resulting in a four-hour gun battle in which three Panthers and three police officers are wounded.

Although the Panthers were certainly the boldest in engaging the police, their display of guns and their communal lifestyle were by no means unique to that era. By the close of the 1960s, collectives and communes that housed weapons and free sexuality were common among young leftist white radicals too, particularly in California. One of the more notorious communes, in Berkeley, was cofounded by Tom Hayden and called itself the Red Family. "A friend and I went over to visit Tom at the Red Family commune on a trip to the West Coast," remembers Mae Jackson. "We knew him from his days in Newark working with SNCC. The commune had guns all over the place; there was a girl sitting around with no underwear on. When you visited these places everyone had guns."

Tom Wolfe named it the era of radical chic, after liberal celebrities began to support the Black Panthers. But such support derived at least as much from the notorious brutality used by police in clamping down on the Panthers in the shooting death of Fred Hampton; the LA police raid on LA Panther headquarters four days later; and the rounding up of the "New York 21." Legal defense funds sprouted like weeds among the liberal wealthy. Celebrities such as Harry Belafonte, Dick Gregory, Donald and Shirley Sutherland, Otto Preminger, Angie Dickinson, Jane Fonda, and others contributed to the Black Panther cause, with perhaps the most famous fund-raising event—to raise money for the Panthers' "New York 21"—taking place at the Park Avenue duplex of conductor Leonard Bernstein. Panther field marshal Donald Cox came away with checks and pledges totaling approximately $10,000.

In the summer of 1970, at San Francisco's Glide Memorial Church, actress Jane Fonda declared, "Revolution is an act of love. We are the children of revolution, born to be rebels—it runs in our blood." She called the Black Panthers "our revolutionary vanguard. We must support them with love, money, propaganda, and risk."

"Even if there are only 2,000 or 1,000 or 500 Party members across the nation," wrote social activist–turned–journalist Nicholas Von Hoffman in his syndicated column, "The poorest, the semi-criminal of black men have made a useful social instrument of themselves."

Although many white liberals and leftists shared some variation of Von Hoffman's view, the same could not be said of his former boss. "I like the Panthers, I really do," commented social activist Saul Alinsky. "They're nuts of course, but they're really a fantasy of that senile political paranoid in Washington, J. Edgar Hoover. They haven't got the numbers and they know nothing about revolutionary tactics. What kind of revolutionary is it who shouts that all power comes out of the muzzle of a gun when he knows damn well the other side's got all the guns?"

Despite such rhetoric, the Panthers' stature in the eyes of the rest of black America was helped after the shooting deaths of Fred Hampton and Mark Clark, and the LA police raid on the party four days later. A nationwide Lou Harris poll taken in January 1970, one month after the incidents, found that 64 percent of blacks surveyed said the Panthers gave them a sense of pride. Yet many black Americans walked a fine line, not totally in support of the government cracking down on the Panthers but not seeing them as a progressive vanguard either. That same month, appearing on the television show "60 Minutes," NAACP leader Roy Wilkins cautiously commended the Panthers for boosting black confidence but called their philosophy behind the times, describing them as "articulate" and "alert" examples of "mouth power." Educated blacks like San Francisco–based U.S. attorney Cecil Poole (the same man whose office was invaded in 1964 by white CORE activists after the disappearance of Cheney, Goodman, and Schwerner) were also cautious, but less generous. Poole drew the assignment of helping to conduct the government's 1969–1970 secret grand jury investigation of the Black Panthers. He reluctantly carried it out, reasoning, "I find it difficult to believe that a group of men who succeed in getting all their men exiled, in prison, or killed, are any real danger in overthrowing this country. It is too easy to convince middle Americans—the great silent majority—that it is good that they [government officials] are after people who are ignorant, black, crude and violent."

Of course, not all Black Panthers fit Poole's description. Besides those such as Landon Williams, Kathleen Cleaver, and Masai Hewitt, there were the Frank Joneses who affiliated themselves with the party for brief stretches. In October 1970, Jones was subpoenaed to appear before the Committee on Internal Security of the House of Representatives. The owner of a Berkeley bookstore, he was asked by the Panthers to edit their newspaper, *The Black Panther*, which Mary Kennedy was selling on the day her husband shot it out with the Oakland police. It was filled with drawings of police officers as pigs, Black Panthers shooting pig police officers, lineups of blacks and whites considered to be "enemies of the people," and articles calling for violent retribution against anyone the party deemed a jacanape, or enemy of the people. Jones edited the paper for a brief period of time. "I think it is well that we have a witness who is a former Panther who can speak as well as you can," commented North Carolina congressman Richardson Preyer about Jones. "You obviously have more education and are more articulate than the other witnesses we have had here."

But Jones was of little use. He stated that he purposely got to know as little about the party as he could, just in case he was one day subpoenaed to appear before such a committee. He was evasive in his answers about the party in a way that irritated Congressman John Ashbrook, who congratulated himself for being far more racially conciliatory than the rabidly racist whites he knew. "In my office there are a lot of newspapers," he told Jones. "I get one from somebody in Virginia called *Statecraft* that is rabidly anti-Semitic and anti-Negro. I get a white citizen's paper out of Augusta, Georgia. The point that comes across to me all the time is that so many of my fellow white Americans look upon the White Citizens Council's *Statecraft*, and publications of that type, as just being a little more than nut publications. But there is a tendency of so many people in the black community to look upon *The Black Panther* not in that context, but as something you say is what people think in the community. Do you openly knock it? Do you think it's wrong to do this? I think *Statecraft* is about the nuttiest thing put together."

Jones replied, "I attribute to the black community the same amount of intelligence that you attribute to your white friends. That any man can interpret for himself."

"You won't knock the Black Panther publication?" pressed Ashbrook.

"I always make an attempt to do neither, but to understand."

Ashbrook had heard enough. "The hottest place in hell is reserved for those who, in time of moral crisis, maintain neutrality. I think you have to be one way or the other."

"That is only going to be a problem if you go to hell. If you go to heaven you don't sweat that," Jones answered.

Retorted Ashbrook, "I wish I was as sure as you are."

Responses like that of Jones were just the kind that many white Americans, horrified by the 1968–1970 Panther–police shootouts, used to further rationalize their racism. Frank Jones probably figured the next question from Ashbrook would be about alleged robberies, beatings, murders, shakedowns, the sexual abuse of women who entered the party all starry-eyed, anything and everything to confirm the notion that black people couldn't do anything right and were, at heart (particularly black men), criminal sex fiends. The Black Panthers were an organized, identifiable target. And law enforcement officials made a display of going after such targets. And the media filled newspapers and the evening news with pictures of captured, handcuffed Panthers as if America were exterminating so many black vermin. It all became the ingredients of middle-class black angst regarding the party.

But there was also the angst of disenchanted party members due to the belief that David Hilliard and his coterie had veered from Huey Newton's vision for the party. With Bobby Seale added to the list of jailed Black Panthers in August 1969, Hilliard *officially* rose to the top of the party hierarchy (having unofficially maintained the position from the time Cleaver went into exile). As such, he was called on to make speeches that Seale otherwise would have made. In November 1969, Hilliard ad-libbed an inflammatory speech in San Francisco's Golden Gate Park at a Vietnam Mobilization Day rally.

Perhaps he was trying to mimic Stokely Carmichael, James Forman, or, closer to home, Eldridge Cleaver, who pushed outrageous speech to its outer limits for that entire generation of young radicals. Vietnam Mobilization Day was a big event, attended not only by radical leftists of all colors but by thousands of people who were more a part of the American mainstream and who increasingly opposed the war, including San Francisco's mayor. The event was broadcast live. And when it was Hilliard's turn to speak, he cried out, "We say down with the American fascist society! Later for Richard Milhous Nixon, the motherfucker. . . ." But the crowd wasn't with him. Although it in no way included friends of Richard Nixon's, neither did it like Hilliard's use of foul language. It started booing him. But Hilliard continued to put his foot in his mouth, sounding increasingly pathetic: "Later for all the people out here who don't want to hear me curse because that's all that I know how to do. . . ." The crowd booed him even more. "Richard Nixon is an evil man. This is the motherfucker that unleashed the counterinsurgent teams upon the Black Panther Party. This is the man that's responsible for all the attacks on the Black Panther Party, nationally. This is the man that sends his vicious murderous dogs out into the black community and invades our Black Panther Party breakfast programs, destroys food that we have for hungry kids and expects us to accept shit like that idly."

Without question the law went after Black Panthers with far more gusto than it displayed when attacking whites it considered criminal. But among the many convenient truths about the Panthers that Hilliard left out at that point in his speech were details of a song about the police that children in some of the free breakfast programs were taught to sing. The stanzas? "I want a porkchop. Off the pig!"

Hilliard's tirade was the type that Saul Alinsky had in mind when he was interrupted by a member of the Black Panther Party during a speech he gave. Said Alinsky, "I told him I'd give him five minutes to speak on one condition: That he could speak for that length of time without using all that tired rhetoric about white, fascist, racist pigs."

Hilliard kept ridiculing Nixon: "Fuck that motherfucking man! We will kill Richard Nixon! We will kill any motherfucker who stands in the way of our freedom!" "Peace! Peace! Peace!" the crowd responded. Out of his element, Hilliard didn't know what to do. Two weeks later he was arrested for threatening the life of the president. And when he made bail, he promptly appeared on "Face the Nation" to speak for the party, which was freshly in the news after the black, liberal, and radical outcry over Fred Hampton's murder and the ferocity of the LA police in going after the Panthers four days later. On "Face the Nation," Hilliard was ground into mincemeat. The party was floundering, veering even farther away, so thought many party members, from the dictates of Huey P. Newton.

Jean Powell had never met Huey Newton, but she was certain of one thing when she testified about the inner workings of the party earlier that year. "When we came to Oakland," she told the McClellan Senate Subcommittee, "we saw how, for the first time, the party was getting away from *Huey's* aim. . . . At the end of Huey's trial . . . the interests of the people became unimportant. The interests of *Huey* became unimportant."

"With the label of infiltrator, spying for the FBI, CIA, or the local police department," testified Larry Powell, who hadn't met Newton either, "it gives [the party] the cause to turn the entire black community against you, thus preventing you from exposing the party and making black people aware of the exploitation, not only of its members, but of the entire black community by a handful of people who lead the party. The party that Huey Newton, who people are *really* dedicated to, started for the betterment of our people."

We're going to have a revolution when Huey gets out of jail, Mae Jackson was told.

Union organizing by the Brotherhood of Sleeping Car Porters was perhaps the key inspiration for the entire civil rights movement, which eventually led to greater radicalism among African Americans, leading to the birth of the Black Panther Party for Self-Defense. Pictured here is C. L. Dellums, a cofounder of the Brotherhood, standing in front of a train berthed in the Southern Pacific rail yard in West Oakland, circa 1970. Dellums was the uncle of current U.S. congressman Ronald Dellums (D-CA), chairman of the House Armed Services Committee. *(Photo courtesy of the Northern California Center for Afro-American History and Life)*

Sleeping car porters were initially among the most highly regarded members of the black community. They would later take a backseat to better-educated African Americans, while their union leaders remained prominent. Pictured in the first row are Brotherhood of Sleeping Car Porters national president A. Philip Randolph (first row, fourth from left); United Nations diplomat Ralph Bunche, who fervently preached education and integration into the larger society only to later be denounced by Black Power advocates (first row, sixth from left); and next to him C. L. Dellums (first row, seventh from left). They are at a function honoring Randolph, circa 1950. *(Photo courtesy of the Northern California Center for Afro-American History and Life)*

Oakland entrepreneur Slim Jenkins was considered by subsequent black entrepreneurs who had run-ins with the Black Panthers to be the dean among their ranks. Shown here is his restaurant and nightclub on West Oakland's once thriving Seventh Street, circa 1940. It attracted people of all races, including California governor and later Supreme Court chief justice Earl Warren. The place was only yards from where, twenty-seven years later, Huey Newton shot Oakland police officer John Frey, becoming an overnight cause célèbre, and only blocks from where, forty-nine years later, Newton was gunned down. *(Photo courtesy of the Northern California Center for Afro-American History and Life)*

Former Black Panther security chief Landon Williams (on right) was among the more educated Black Panthers, who didn't always get along with their less educated brethren. Williams nevertheless participated in and trained party members for many of the militaristic maneuvers of the party when he was convinced it was at open warfare with the larger society. In this 1969 photo, the twenty-five-year-old Williams and Panther Rory Hithe are being led away, as part of the arrest of Black Panthers suspected of torturing and murdering suspected police informer Alex Rackley. *(UPI/Bettmann)*

The Student Nonviolent Coordinating Committee (SNCC), originators of the Black Panther name and symbol later adopted by Huey Newton's California group, used the panther as part of a third-party voter registration effort. This resulted from SNCC's increased radicalization while conducting its dangerous work in Mississippi, Alabama, and elsewhere in the Deep South. Pictured here are a line of first-time black registrants entering a store called the Sugar Shack in rural Alabama, circa 1966. They were emboldened thanks to SNCC and passage of the 1965 Voter Registration Act. *(UPI/Bettmann)*

When their efforts turned from organizing voters to encouraging black empowerment by any means necessary, SNCC leaders such as Stokely Carmichael began taking their message throughout the country. Here Carmichael is shown in 1966, speaking to a crowd of 2,500 in Watts, one year after the riots, encouraging residents to bolt completely from the city of Los Angeles. *(UPI/Bettmann)*

By 1964, after experiencing the realities of the Deep South on helping SNCC and other civil rights organizations to register voters during Mississippi Freedom Summer, northern white college students returned to their campuses to encourage greater activism. UC Berkeley was a pacesetter. In December 1964, protesting the UC Berkeley administration's determination to discipline the leaders of the Free Speech movement, students occupied the administration building, inviting folk singer Joan Baez (shown here) to help motivate them. *(Photo courtesy of The Bancroft Library, UC Berkeley)*

By the summer of 1967, black anger because of racism had turned into violence across the country. Shown here is SNCC leader H. Rap Brown addressing a crowd in Cambridge, Maryland, that July. Following his incendiary speech, a riot started in which a local school was burned down. Brown, wounded in the melee, was accused of encouraging it, causing him legal problems from which he had a difficult time recovering. *(AP/Wide World Photos)*

The incident that started the UC Berkeley Free Speech protest: the October 1964 arrest of CORE activist Jack Weinberg, who was on the banned brick walkway outside of Sather Gate recruiting students for local and southern civil rights campaigns. Mario Savio mounted the squad car Weinberg had been placed in and marshaled thousands to help prevent his removal. *(Photo courtesy of The Bancroft Library, UC Berkeley)*

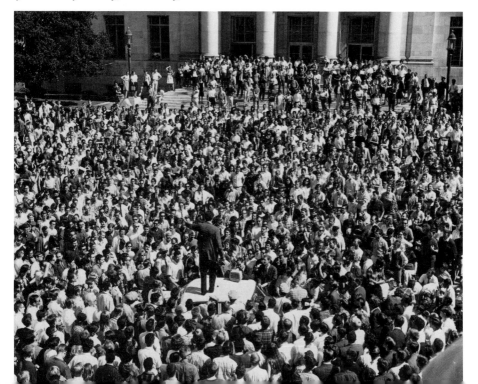

By the fall of 1967, Black Panther cofounder Huey Newton had shot and killed an Oakland police officer, becoming an overnight sensation in a year of rampant anger at the law enforcement in most major cities among youths of all colors, because of police suppression of riots and civil rights and anti-Vietnam war protests. Newton, who at the time pleaded his innocence, is shown here being interviewed from jail by a bevy of reporters. *(UPI/Bettmann Newsphotos)*

Newton and Seale *(below)* founded the Black Panther Party for Self-Defense in the fall of 1966. By the following winter they began gaining notoriety, posing for photos in front of their storefront headquarters in Oakland. *(AP/Wide World Photos)*

Bobby Seale (shown here speaking into the microphone), who cofounded the Black Panther Party for Self-Defense with Huey Newton, was a far better public speaker than Newton. He became the party's ambassador to the rest of the world, often joining forces with other student protest leaders such as Tom Hayden (shown on the right) of the Students for a Democratic Society (SDS). Seale is addressing reporters in Chicago after he, Hayden, and six others were charged with conspiring to incite riots at the 1968 Democratic National Convention. *(UPI/Bettmann Newsphotos)*

One of many vociferous Free Huey rallies held outside of the Alameda County Courthouse in the summer of 1968. *(Oakland Post/Cleveland Grover)*

Landon Williams in September 1993, sitting in his office where he heads an urban development program called the Marin City Project, Marin City, California. While being interviewed for this book he was an assistant city manager for the city of Berkeley. Of his Panther days Williams recalls an era of high expectations and many mistakes on all sides. But he doesn't regret having been a Black Panther. *(Photo by Nicola Kountoupes)*

By the fall of 1969, SNCC's Stokely Carmichael *(above)* was no longer a major American activist. Having become frustrated and disillusioned for a variety of reasons, he moved to West Africa along with his wife, singer Miriam Makeba. Carmichael, who changed his name to Kwame Touré, is shown here in 1970 addressing a Washington, D.C., gathering about his total transformation and new beliefs in Pan Africanism. *(UPI/Bettmann)*

By the summer of 1968, SNCC's James Forman had dropped out of the militance limelight in favor of a more low-key approach. Forman is shown here in 1969 educating students in Cincinnati on the structure of American capitalism. *(UPI/Bettmann)*

Released from prison in August 1970 after his conviction was overturned on a technicality, Newton emerges to a crushing crowd of admirers outside of the Alameda County Courthouse in Oakland. *(UPI/Bettmann)*

In the spring of 1967, the Black Panthers entered the California statehouse in Sacramento armed with guns, to protest passage of legislation preventing the open display of firearms. The legislation was passed as a direct response to the Panther practice of patrolling the police, armed. Their entry into the state capitol put them on the map, at the very forefront of the militant groups springing up throughout the country. *(Photo courtesy of the Sacramento Bee Collection, City of Sacramento, History and Science Division, Sacramento Archives and Museum Collection Center)*

Their icon out of prison only months before, radicals and militants of all colors discovered something they didn't know about Newton's public speaking talents. When he spoke at this conference in Philadelphia in the fall of 1970, said one participant, "He [had] this high voice and I [was] so disappointed." *(AP/Wide World Photos)*

(above) Huey Newton receiving a Ph.D. in the History of Consciousness from UC Santa Cruz in June 1980. *(Oakland Post/Donald Cunningham)*

(right) After returning from Cuba to stand trial on charges of having murdered a prostitute, Newton emerges from the courthouse with a leash. He told reporters that the charges against him had about as much substance as "Tom, my invisible dog." *(UPI/Bettmann)*

(*above*) Mourners flocked to the spot where Huey Newton was shot and killed in August 1989. A woman holds a photo of the old Huey Newton for a press photographer. (*San Francisco Examiner/Kim Komenich*)

(*left*) A little boy ponders the candlelit memorial to Huey Newton at the spot where he was killed. (*San Francisco Examiner/Kim Komenich*)

(*below*) Newton's funeral was held at Oakland's Allen Temple Baptist Church, to an overflow crowd. Ten thousand mourners filed past his casket. (*San Francisco Examiner/Gordon Stone*)

Newton's casket being loaded into a hearse after the Allen Temple service. *(San Francisco Examiner/Carolyn Cole)*

After Newton's death many former Black Panthers thought of either reorganizing the party or relaunching the party newspaper. Two different issues of the party newspaper ended up being launched in 1991. Looking over the first issue of one of those newspapers are party veterans Sheeba Haven, Zenobia Embry-Nimmer, and Landon Williams. *(Photo by Tom Erikson)*

Thanks to the legal work of Fay Stender, the liberal Jewish woman who went to Mississippi for Freedom Summer in 1964 and was now a lawyer, a member of Charles Garry's legal staff, Huey Newton's conviction for manslaughter in the shooting death of Officer John Frey was reversed. A new trial was ordered, and Newton posted the bail of $50,000 set for his release. On August 5, 1970, he emerged from prison to be greeted by 10,000 people of all colors, as if he were God.

10

When the Biggest Cat
Leaps Out of Prison

WHEN SHE WAS FIFTEEN YEARS OLD, GROWING UP IN A NEIGH-
borhood of yellow, white, and beige bungalows at the foot of the
Oakland hills, Sheeba Haven started a reading tutorial program at
her church. There were more businesses in East Oakland then than
there are now, and many business owners had complained that too
few of the neighborhood people knew how to fill out employment
applications or pass employment tests. Sheeba could also crochet.
When she was sixteen she was so good that she taught four women
to turn out designs to her specifications, and she was offered a
scholarship by the high-class department store I. Magnin's, which
wanted to send her to school for formal training to become one of
its designers. Her family vetoed the offer. When she was seventeen
she cochaired the Black Students Union at Castlemont High
School, where she led a student boycott, and from which she
graduated in 1970 at the top of her class. Haven earned a full
scholarship to UC Berkeley.

Because she led the student boycott at Castlemont, Sheeba
attracted the attention of the Black Panthers. A reporter for the
party newspaper wrote an article about her political activities, and
a party member approached her about becoming a Panther. Her

father, a truck driver, didn't want her to have anything to do with the Black Panthers. So when she decided to become a Panther community worker, he kicked her out of the house, which forced her to move to Panther-owned housing. On August 6, 1970, Sheeba Haven was a Panther community worker, and UC Berkeley subfreshman, selling copies of the party newspaper. Although at odds with her father, she continued to wear a large, heavy wool jacket he had given her, a jacket that had been his, a jacket that she viewed as her final connection to him although the jacket was too big. She wore it on that cool morning, typical of summer mornings in the Bay Area, as she sold the party newspaper in Sproul Plaza, the same place where, four years earlier, Huey Newton, Bobby Seale, and Bobby Hutton had hawked copies of Mao's *Little Red Book* to raise money so they could buy Panther guns.

While she sold the newspaper, a group of black M.B.A. students stood next to her, teasing her about her Black Panther affiliation. The sleeves of her father's jacket were very loose, and each time she turned away from the students, one of them tugged on a sleeve of the jacket and then rushed away. "The next time you do that," Haven assured him as he scurried away laughing, "I'm going to fire you up!" He and his friends feigned fear. They continued teasing her, jokingly reassuring her that since she was a notorious Black Panther, they would definitely obey her directive.

Moments later, her head once again turned in the opposite direction of the teasing business students, Haven felt a tug on the sleeve of her jacket. She had had enough of them. Apparently they thought she wasn't serious. She balled her fist and turned around to level her punch. Before she could do so, a long-haired white guy recognized the face of the man pulling on her sleeve. "Huey!" he cried out. Huey Newton turned his head in the direction of the voice. Haven stopped her fist in midair and glanced at the Panther newspaper (each issue of which carried a picture of Huey on the masthead) to make sure the man who had tugged on her sleeve was, in fact, Huey P. Newton. And as she recognized his face, he turned back around to hug her and greet her. "Sister. I'm so glad to see you. You're the first person I've seen selling the Black Panther paper since I got out of prison yesterday!"

While Newton continued talking to her, one arm around her shoulder, Haven, who had been taught a party hand signal to notify the party partner selling the newspaper with you of any trouble, signaled to her partner across the street. (Huey had eluded his bodyguards to be out among the UC Berkeley students; since it was considered too dangerous for him to engage in such mingling, and everyone in the party had been made aware of this as they prepared for Newton's prison release, Haven signaled trouble.) By now, students in the plaza were converging on her and Newton. A Panther lieutenant walked up. "Comrade, what are you doing here?" he asked Huey. Immediately, the lieutenant located David Hilliard and the bodyguards whom Newton had somehow broken away from. While Newton was still holding court, they walked up and whisked him away. Sheeba Haven had spoiled Huey's fun. So from that day forward he held a grudge against her.

It would be just one of those things, and a relatively minor one compared to the many "one of those things" between Newton and increasing numbers of party members in the years to come. Some would say that the seeds of his mounting paranoia were there from the beginning of the party, that his original coterie just glossed over the truth as Newton became more and more of an icon.

Others would swear, on a stack of Bibles if they could, that Newton's mounting paranoia was born in prison. Most law enforcement officers believed that Newton had purposely, deliberately killed John Frey. They could have done any number of things to him while he was in prison. And even if they hadn't, it certainly didn't help his mental state when he began to spend long periods of time in solitary confinement—as a result of his orneriness; his refusal to acquiesce to prison rules, like having to work in prison facilities for below minimum wage; his displaying his violent temper, such as when he smashed the Santa Rita prison mess hall attendant over the head with a steel tray for refusing him a bigger helping of food than usual.

Life in an ordinary ten- by seven-foot cell reserved for good prisoners was bad enough. But Newton had also spent time for his prison disobedience in the notorious dark, dank, slimy Soul

Breaker, also called the hole, because it had nothing but a hole to defecate and urinate in, and four black walls and a slit through which prison guards pushed to you the inedible mush served in prison, on trays washed in unsanitary water. Newton and everyone else who had survived the Soul Breaker told of being left to sit on a floor, made slimy because of their own waste, since the hole to urinate and defecate in was rarely cleaned out. He told of learning to master the rush of thoughts and images through his mind as he struggled to avoid insanity. He told of fasting and rushing to do push-ups as soon as he heard the footsteps of the prison guards, because he was determined not to give them the satisfaction of thinking the "hole" was conquering him rather than the other way around.

And then suddenly, due to the legal expertise of Fay Stender, on August 5, 1970 he was free. Stender had worked on the appeal for close to two years. In a 170-page brief, she outlined a number of grounds for appealing Newton's voluntary manslaughter conviction. Among them were the defense team's opinion that murder charges were brought against Newton by an illegally constituted grand jury that had "systematically excluded black, poor and other minority persons" and had denied Newton the constitutional right to pretrial confrontation of witnesses, or the opportunity to make the case for his innocence. (Newton did, of course, confront his accusers in his actual murder trial. That trial also set new standards for choosing juries. Numerous potential jurors were disqualified by Garry and his defense team because of their perceived racism. The final trial jury consisted of eleven whites and one black man, named David Harper, a Bank of America employee at the time, who resembled Newton enough to pass as a relative.) Stender's appellate brief also cited the extraordinary racial polarization in the East Bay as a result of the Frey shooting, stating that the heavy publicity surrounding the case made it impossible for Newton to receive a fair trial. It characterized West Oakland as a poor community with "a separate and distinct sub-culture, language, political behavior, and racial and socio-economic characteristics." The brief also stated that Newton's prior conviction in the stabbing of Odell Lee was unconstitutional because he had not been warned of the con-

sequences of representing himself in that trial. That conviction had
been cited by the prosecution in the Frey case as evidence of
Newton's violent nature. The defense team argued that citing the
conviction had unfairly prejudiced the jury in the Frey murder trial.

But the argument that would win reversal of Newton's conviction was based on the trial judge's failure to instruct the jury
that it could rule that Newton had committed either voluntary or
involuntary manslaughter in the shooting death of Officer Frey.
The rationale for a possible ruling of involuntary manslaughter,
the defense team theorized, was that if Newton actually shot Frey,
he did so only after he himself had been wounded (again, years
later Newton would boast to close friends that he willfully murdered John Frey). The theory held that Newton had suffered
neurogenic shock because of the amount of blood he lost from his
gunshot wound rendering him unable to make a clear, conscious
decision to shoot Frey—hence the possibility that Newton could
be found guilty of involuntary manslaughter. So Newton was freed,
pending retrial on the manslaughter conviction only (in other
words, the question of first- or second-degree murder was no
longer an issue).

While waiting for the court's decision, Newton's defense team
was divided in its opinion on how the Court of Appeal of the State
of California would rule. In May 1970, Stender sent word to
Newton that a decision would be issued shortly. Word was that the
court had issued a long decision. Stender was convinced that this
meant the appeal had been denied, because the court wished to
demonstrate it had carefully considered every argument in the case
of so public a figure as Huey P. Newton. Defense team member
Alex Hoffman, however, argued that a long opinion could mean a
reversal because the court wished to carefully lay out the grounds
for that decision, making it quite clear that it was based on a
technicality, leaving no room for those who would argue that the
court had caved in to the massive Free Huey publicity campaign.
The actual reversal was read on May 29, 1970, but because of
technical and paper work, the process of freeing Newton didn't
begin until August 3.

First he was brought up to Oakland from the Men's Colony

at San Luis Obispo, where he had been confined after his conviction. Once there, he remained in the Alameda County jail for two days. Describing the trip from San Luis Obispo, Newton later wrote: "[I had] the sensation of being bombarded with a variety of stimuli. Most people take those stimuli for granted, but after two years in a restricted and monotonous environment it is impossible to absorb what you see. We passed houses, fields, farm laborers, animals, and all sorts of sights grown dim in my memory. The mountains in the distance, the sky, the movements of life—I wanted them all at once, but I could not handle it. It disturbed me. . . . In my first few days outside of jail I had to make an attempt to remain calm, to keep the action and unpredictability from exciting my nervous system."

After being settled in at Alameda County prison, two days later Newton was released to multitudes who, thanks to the work of Eldridge Cleaver and his friends, viewed him as God, or, at the very least, Moses with his staff (he would later be presented a swagger stick by an admiring party officer), ready to part the Red Sea of hostility to and the bickering and infighting within the revolution that Mae Jackson and many others had been assured would finally commence now that he was out of jail. "On one level he was scared of the court reversal because he was scared of having to come out to what the Panthers became," recalls Alex Hoffman. "He always said he was not that poster on the wall, that that was Eldridge's notion of who he was, and he couldn't live up to it."

"I was there that day," remembers Peter Solomon of the 10,000 who greeted Newton outside of the Alameda County jail. "It was like one massive orgasm."

Since it was such a mob scene, instead of getting inside Alex Hoffman's Volkswagen, Newton, David Hilliard, and Elmer "Geronimo" Pratt, deputy minister of defense for the party, climbed on top of the car to speak to the crowd and clear a path. Newton took off his shirt and displayed his sculpted body to the crowd, a move that over the years would be interpreted by many as his effort to allow them to drink in their idol. But if Alex Hoffman is to be believed, he did it out of a sense of freedom and because he was on the verge of passing out.

From there it was on to Alex's apartment to get out of his prison clothes, and then to a press conference at the offices of Charles Garry, where, along with journalists principally from the alternative press, Benny Stewart stood front and center, waiting to greet him. "He had on all black and he looked good. He was muscular, he was built, we were so happy. And I remember when I shook his hand and said, 'Man, I sure am glad to see you. You don't know how many brothers just didn't live until this moment!'"

That same day, Mary Kennedy was based in Black Panther Party facilities in West Oakland. She was Officer for the Day and asked someone to relieve her so she could go to party headquarters (by then no longer on Shattuck Street in Berkeley but on Peralta Street, also in West Oakland) to get a glimpse of Huey. When she saw him he was at headquarters lifting weights. Then he walked throughout the neighborhood shaking hands with everyone. On that same day, Landon Williams sat languishing in prison in Colorado, where he had been arrested under suspicion of being an accessory to the Alex Rackley murder in Connecticut. Williams had been in Denver when he was arrested, in his capacity as a head of the party's internal security force, responsible for checking out chapters across the country. While in prison he was kept abreast of everything happening in the party, in the manner all jailed party members were kept abreast of developments. And he was eager to know what Huey Newton was really like.

Now that Huey was out of prison, as Benny Stewart said, "the brothers" were reborn, particularly those in the party from the eastern branches and in San Francisco and in Los Angeles who had joined the party since he had gone to jail—or *because* he had gone to jail. The first thing Newton did after freedom was to promise the National Liberation Front of Vietnam (the Vietcong) some Panther guerillas with which to continue fighting the Vietnam War. In reality, no guerillas would be forthcoming. But there was a matter for which Panther guerillas were really supposed to be dispatched, the plans having been made before Newton emerged from jail, and involving a seventeen-year-old named Jonathan Jackson.

Jonathan Jackson was the brother of noted incarcerated prison activist George Jackson. George was one of the three infamous Soledad Brothers, black men from Soledad prison who were charged with throwing a white prison guard over a balcony in retaliation for prison authorities refusing to press charges against a group of organized white racist prisoners who had killed a black Soledad prisoner in a fight. Jonathan had organized an elaborate plan to gain freedom for George and George's cohorts. Three teams of Panther guerillas were scheduled to support him, compliments of Eldridge Cleaver. One guerilla team was scheduled to hijack a jet at San Francisco International Airport; a second was to storm the Marin County Civic Center and seize as many hostages as possible; and the third was to assist Jonathan Jackson in taking over the Marin County courtroom of Judge Harold J. Haley, where the case of two allied inmates was being heard. Then the hostages seized at the Civic Center as well as Judge Haley and the others in his courtroom were to be used as barter for the release of George Jackson and other political prisoners from around the country. If immediate release wasn't forthcoming, the hostages were to be killed one by one. Once release of the prisoners was gained, all were to board a plane for Cuba, where presumably they would be granted political asylum.

Reportedly, Huey thought the plan was suicidal, so he called off Panther support. But on August 7, 1970, Jonathan Jackson went ahead with his end of the deal unassisted, taking Judge Haley, several jurors, and an assistant district attorney as hostages. Minutes later a shootout began. Jonathan, two escaping inmates, and Judge Haley were killed; three others were wounded. Many people in the revolutionary underground blamed Newton for the death of Jonathan Jackson—the first potentially lethal internal party flames after Newton's emergence from prison.

The second set of lethal flames would grow from continuing discord over the manner in which David Hilliard and his coterie had been running the party. Strong Panther chapters in places like Harlem, which contained dynamic leaders such as Michael Tabor and Dhuruba Moore, two of the "New York 21" defendants, wanted something done about the Hilliard faction's use of party funds for high living off the backs of rank-and-file party members and party chapters across the country, as well as their sexual abuse of party women. Some chapters outside Oakland, such as in New Haven, Connecticut, had developed a well-run free clinic, and breakfast programs where money *wasn't* being abused—an entirely different set of dynamics from the Panther chapters in the head-quarters city of Oakland. And those who were dedicated to party principles had chafed just as much under the leadership of David Hilliard and his coterie as had angry ex-party members such as Tommy Jones, Jean and Larry Powell, and the others thrown out of the Oakland chapters in January 1969. Many were just biding their time waiting for Newton's release, certain that he would clean up the party when he heard their complaints.

But Newton was unreceptive. Huey Newton, they immedi-ately discovered, brooked no criticisms. He stuck by David Hil-liard. Anyone with strong leadership potential quickly learned that Newton easily became jealous, easily became intimidated by Black Panthers with leadership skills such as Michael Tabor, Richard "Dhuruba" Moore, and Elmer "Geronimo" Pratt. Then, too, there were Newton's new distractions, creating a wild, meandering, thrilling, but destructive lifestyle for him.

FBI agents followed him everywhere he went, bugged his phones when they could and the places where he stayed. And then there were the "beautiful people," the radical chic from New York and Hollywood, ready to make him a star. They offered him drugs, alcohol, and women to fulfill his wildest dreams and heavy appe-tites. He began drinking tumblers of cognac, taking assorted pills, and, most of all, snorting cocaine. Large amounts of cocaine were delivered to him, snorted with him by the Hollywood beautiful people eager to get next to him, and the lovely starlets and female groupies of all colors, eager to bed him in one-on-ones, three-somes, or foursomes, whatever his choice, since he was so hand-some and famous. He had taken drugs, smoked marijuana for instance, even sold it to help finance the party in the very begin-ning. He had loved drinking too. Both habits were born prior to his imprisonment and were only exacerbated after getting out, most of all by the newly popular drug cocaine.

Amid this enormous amount of attention, tremendous expectations from a party he no longer recognized, and temptations he couldn't resist, Newton conducted party business. After deciding against getting rid of David Hilliard and his coterie, and aborting Panther plans to support Jonathan Jackson's jailbreak, the next order of party business was the Revolutionary People's Constitutional Convention, to be held at Temple University in Philadelphia. Like the plans for aiding Jonathan Jackson, the convention had been Eldridge's idea. Cleaver had been running an international wing from exile. He also had his own coterie of domestic supporters, which began to grow as party members who had been counting on Huey to do something about David Hilliard and his lieutenants—particularly the easterners—searched for someone to whom Huey might listen. Given his prior behavior and the kind he was said to still engage in in Algeria, Cleaver certainly wasn't a saint. Allegedly, he beat his wife, Kathleen; held certain Panthers exiled with him under house arrest (one rumor even had it that he had killed his wife's lover); and held drug guru Timothy Leary, who had escaped drug charges in America to be with Cleaver, under house arrest too. Cleaver was merely the person disenchanted Panthers approached by default. It all boiled down to two groups latching onto Cleaver simultaneously—those supportive of guerilla moves like Jonathan Jackson's, and those disgusted at the mismanagement of the party by the Hilliard faction. And to a large extent, both groups overlapped.

The Revolutionary People's Constitutional Convention was the first real opportunity for the East Coasters to get a look at Huey, find out if he really was God. Mae Jackson made the trip from New York City to Philadelphia to see for herself: "We get to the conference and Huey is going to speak. I have my Afro comb with me. And the Panthers search us. They take stuff from you. They put all the Afro combs in a box, and I say how am I supposed to find my Afro comb? That was minor. But to me it was really annoying. And then Huey speaks. He has this high voice and I'm just so disappointed. Soon all I became worried about was finding my Afro comb. It was that kind of show. It should have been quieter. It should have been more disciplined, more thought out.

THE SHADOW OF THE PANTHER 227

It was just too noisy. I had my doubts." Mae Jackson decided that Huey was not God.

Audiences discovered that Huey was a very poor public speaker who tended toward lecturing more than dynamic speech making. And the contrast was made all the sharper by the speech of New York Panther Michael Tabor, who preceded Newton. "Tabor's speech had mesmerized people," recalls Kiilu Nyasha, a Panther in the New Haven chapter. "Tabor had this deep voice like James Earl Jones. He was very impressive. And to tell you the truth, I think that threatened Huey."

Newton dug deeper into all the temptations spinning around him. Mary Kennedy watched as he sent emissaries to her Panther-owned home to pick out the most attractive women for him to sleep with, making him appear no different from so many other Panther men at national headquarters (over time, he would prove to be even worse in that regard). Rather than subside, the abuses that dedicated party members complained about escalated. Landon Williams began to receive letters in prison from people he trusted, telling him how bad things were getting: "Every time someone spoke up, they got identified in the party paper as an enemy of the people and were expelled from the party."

In the party newspaper, Huey's title kept changing. No longer Minister of Defense, he was now Supreme Commander, then Servant of the People, then Supreme Servant of the People. And the bodyguards drew a tighter and tighter circle around him.

In February 1971 he appeared in New Haven to attend the conspiracy trial of Bobby Seale and Ericka Huggins in the death of Alex Rackley, and to hold a series of seminars at Yale where he debated the eminent psychoanalyst Erik Erikson before a group of Yale students. (As it turned out, only George Sams, Warren Kimbo, Lonnie McLucas, Bobby Seale, and Ericka Huggins stood trial for the Rackley murder. Everyone else arrested, including Landon Williams, would eventually see charges dropped.)

Newton still relished intellectual challenges. In fact, he now sought to complete a degree. He had registered as an undergraduate student at the University of California at Santa Cruz, where he

chose to major in politics and education. And now he was visiting
Yale. The Yale community wasn't sure what to make of Newton
when he arrived for the pending seminars. It had been wreaked
with havoc the previous year when the entire student body voted
to strike as a show of support for the Panthers, as the first trials in
the Rackley affair began just a few hundred yards from the Yale
campus. The trials attracted nationwide attention, including support for the indicted Panthers by the entire white radical Left, with
leaders such as Abbie Hoffman, Jerry Rubin, and Tom Hayden
descending on New Haven and the Yale campus for massive rallies
on May Day weekend 1970. The privileged Yale students viewed
support for the Panthers as a matter of demonstrating solidarity
with black America, while the nervous Yale alumni canceled traditional events such as alumni weekend, which coincided with the
May Day protests, out of fear that as members of the wealthy
privileged, they would be harmed. Some conservative faculty members even sent loved ones out of town. But the bulk of the Yale
faculty voted to support the Yale student strike. And Yale's previously charmed, charismatic president, Kingman Brewster, issued
the statement, "I am skeptical of the ability of black revolutionaries
to achieve a fair trial anywhere in the United States."

Now that it was Bobby Seale's and Ericka Huggins's turn to
go on trial, only months after the Panther's biggest icon had been
released from prison, there was bitter debate on campus about the
pending seminars featuring Newton, the icon, and Erikson, the
eminent scholar visiting from Harvard. The night before the first
seminar, Newton appeared at Yale's Woolsey Hall. The Panthers'
management of the event rattled many Yale students. All but one
of the entrances to the hall were sealed. At the entrance that wasn't
sealed, all 1,400 students entering the hall were frisked. After they
waited for two hours, Huey Newton finally appeared, surrounded
by bodyguards. He walked to the podium, put on eyeglasses, and
proceeded to lecture the students about dialectical materialism and
the philosophies of Hegel, Kant, Peirce, and Marx, as well as the
psychological theories of Freud, Jung, James, and Erikson. Everyone left disappointed with Newton, just as Mae Jackson and the
rest of the crowd had been at Temple.

And then the seminars were held. While the students wanted to discuss the political activism of the Black Panthers, Newton continued down the path of abstract theory, doing his best to impress the Yale community with the quality of his intellect. He was clearly a complex man, capable of jousting with the scholarly Erikson. Yet unbeknownst to students, the same Newton sitting before them was sending out squads of Panthers, loyal to him, to brutalize disaffected party members critical of the Oakland leadership.

Concerned about the turn of events, Michael Tabor and Richard "Dhuruba" Moore—two of the New York 21 out on bail while their trial for conspiracy to blow up public facilities in New York City continued—showed up in New Haven to talk with Newton. The meeting didn't go well. Tabor had married Connie Matthews, who had been sent from Algeria by Eldridge Cleaver to work as Newton's secretary. Cleaver wanted her to obtain firsthand information about the way things were going at headquarters. Disenchanted with the meeting with Newton in New Haven, Tabor, Matthews, and Moore promptly resigned from the party. Tabor and Matthews later turned up in Algeria with Cleaver. In the party newspaper, Newton denounced all three of them as "enemies of the people."

Back in New York City, furious at Tabor and Moore for jumping bail, Judge John Murtaugh revoked bail for the other two members of the New York 21 who had been out free. Murtaugh's home was bombed; SDS splinter group the Weathermen took responsibility for the bombing. Members of the New York 21, who were every bit as dissatisfied with the Oakland leadership as Moore and Tabor had been, issued an open letter to the Weathermen praising them for the bombing, while openly criticizing Newton and the rest of the Oakland leadership. Since they felt that it would have been far too embarrassing for black people in general and a disservice to the party as a whole to directly address the issues of misuse of party funds, the sexual abuse of party women, and brutal gangism, the open letter used obliquely worded language, criticizing the Panther leadership for "tripping out, pseudo-machoism, arrogance, myrimidonism, dogmatism, regionalism, regimentation, and fear." Newton then expelled the New York 21 from the party.

From then on, tensions built rapidly. And they were further aggravated by the activities of COINTELPRO. Cleaver, as well as the rest of the Panther leadership, had been aware that they were being monitored by government intelligence. In fact, it was the principal reason that Cleaver had sent Connie Matthews to Oakland to investigate what was really happening at headquarters. With Matthews there, he wouldn't have to guess about the validity of information he was receiving over the telephone or by letter regarding problems in Oakland.

With the trusted Matthews back in Algeria, along with Tabor, Cleaver had solid information about the alleged abuses that so many disaffected party members hoped he would address. He continued to press Newton on the issue by telephone from Algeria. While this was going on, Newton moved into a $650-per-month penthouse apartment on Oakland's Lake Merritt, causing outcries from remaining Panthers as well as from many outside supporters. At the same time, the party made plans for the Intercommunal Day of Solidarity, an event to be held in Oakland on March 5 at the Oakland Auditorium. It was to be both a rally to demonstrate solidarity between the Panthers and white radical allies in support of Bobby Seale and Ericka Huggins, and a celebration of Newton's birthday. Kathleen Cleaver was scheduled as the keynote speaker. The Grateful Dead were to appear, as was the Panther's own musical group, called the Lumpen.

Although Cleaver and Newton continued to have their differences about party affairs, Newton was scheduled to appear on a local morning television program called "A.M. San Francisco," hosted by Jim Dunbar, to promote the March 5 event and to answer questions about why he had moved into a $650-per-month penthouse. Newton also got the idea that he and Cleaver could appear on the show together via telephone hookup to promote Intercommunal Day of Solidarity. When the call to Cleaver went through, Cleaver began by demanding that Newton reinstate the New York 21 as Panthers. Shocked by the direction in which Cleaver was taking the on-air discussion, Newton refused to reinstate them.

Cleaver next leveled an attack on David Hilliard and his coterie for mismanaging the party. He demanded that Newton and the rest of the Panther Central Committee kick Hilliard out of the party. Newton refused to discuss any more party business on the air. Then, once off the air, he returned to the telephone to discuss what Cleaver had said on television. Furious with Cleaver, Newton expelled him from the party. Cleaver in turn expelled Newton and the entire Oakland leadership, declaring that thereafter the party would be headquartered in New York City and Algeria.

The March 5 Intercommunal Day of Solidarity took place amid palpable tension, and without the participation of Kathleen Cleaver. Benny Stewart attended, along with 6,000 other people, mainly black and white. Newton, surrounded by a phalanx of bodyguards, gave a brief speech. "Huey came out with a swagger stick and said he'd kick Eldridge's ass," recalls Benny Stewart, who after that day ceased his involvement on the party's Advisory Committee. "The partners with me said, 'Let's get up and go.' And I sat there and said no. This can't be it. This can't be all that he's saying. And they told me, 'Come on, man, we better get up and get out of here before something goes down.'"

And plenty did go down. Immediately after the split was official, New York City Panthers as well as most of the East Coast Panther chapters declared their allegiance to Cleaver, as did San Francisco Panthers and a large share of those in Los Angeles. Fratricidal warfare ensued, with the first hit coming three days after the Oakland rally. Cleaverite Robert Webb was walking down 125th Street in Harlem. Webb had been on a local New York radio program only a week earlier, charging David Hilliard with squandering party funds on a "huge diamond ring," among other luxuries. Walking along 125th Street, he encountered three pro-Newton Panthers hawking the party newspaper. Apparently they were part of a team of Panthers from out of town, which local police expressed concern about, and pro-Cleaver Panthers would later describe as "seventy-five robots" sent by the Newton faction to wreak havoc in New York City. Webb began to argue with the pro-Newton Panthers; one of them opened fire, shooting him in the head and killing him.

About six weeks after Webb's death, the charred body of Samuel Napier, distribution manager for the party newspaper, who was on a visit with Panthers in Queens loyal to Newton, was discovered. He had been bound, gagged, shot six times, and left in a building that was set ablaze. His murder was blamed on Cleaver loyalists as retaliation for the murder of Webb.

Days after discovery of Napier's body, the pelvic bone of another Panther was discovered in California's Santa Cruz mountains just south of the Bay Area. Fred Bennett, head of the East Oakland chapter, had been shot in the head with a .357 magnum. His body was then doused with high-octane fuel and set ablaze. After his flesh burned, his bones were pulverized with a shovel and scattered in the woods outside two cabins where 149 sticks of dynamite had been discovered by police. His pelvic bone had been tossed in a streambed, apparently in the hope that it would wash away. The site of his murder was a known training ground for Panther underground guerillas. Some speculated that Bennett was murdered because he had turned pro-Cleaver. Others speculated that he had been exposed as an informant. A third rumor had it that Bennett was killed after getting the wife of a jailed Panther leader pregnant.

In any case, the murders, as well as testimony in the trials of those accused of killing Alex Rackley, had a conscience-rending effect on dedicated party members. In the Rackley case, many believed the claim of defense lawyer Charles Garry that a crazed George Sams had ordered the murder of Rackley on his own. On the other hand, there were those who were convinced by court-room testimony (including a tape recording the Panthers made of Rackley's torture, allegedly as a means of putting the fear of God in the rest of the New Haven chapter) that Seale did order Rackley's murder, believing that Rackley was an informant, and that the other Panthers present in the Kimbro home, where Rackley was tortured with scalding hot water, were simply caught up in the revolutionary mentality of the times.

Reasons Kiilu Nyasha who served as Charles Garry's secretary during the trials: "Given all the murders of black people through the years that the government ignored, suddenly they raided Panther offices across the country as if the Panthers had killed the Duchess of Windsor. They were *using* the case. For many party members, it had nothing to do with guilt or innocence. It had to do with overkill, people not wanting to see the party destroyed because of a possible mistake. You can't take Rackley's murder out of the context of the paranoia that prevailed then, because in war, things take on a different aspect than they do in everyday life."

Despite those sentiments, angst over the Rackley trial, coupled with factional fighting by supporters of Cleaver and Newton resulting in more frightening deaths, began to destroy the party in the eyes of dedicated members. They began to view the party the same way James Forman, H. Rap Brown, and Stokely Carmichael eventually did, convinced it was no longer leading a real revolution. Most such party members not expelled by Newton left on their own, channeling their idealism into local black community organizations, or their revolutionary zeal into the offshoot Black Liberation Army (BLA), begun by one group of Cleaver loyalists.

A few weeks after the murders began, days after the grisly remains of Bennett were found, Newton attempted to put the best face on everything by appearing on the David Frost television show. He blamed the murders of Sam Napier and Fred Bennett on the police. When Frost asked if he had bodyguards because he was under constant threat of assassination, Newton replied that he was under constant threat of assassination—but by the police, not by disenchanted Panthers. Appearing on the program just before Newton was Dr. David Mosell, an officer of the NAACP, who stated that the Panthers couldn't be compared to his organization, since the NAACP had put laws on the books and the Panthers had not. Mosell agreed with Panther demands for full employment and an end to police brutality and murder. But he couldn't agree with the demand that all black prisoners be freed; he stated that there were a great many who should be in jail.

Newton launched an intensive public relations campaign. A few weeks after his appearance on the Frost program, he spoke before a black audience at a Berkeley seminary and called for increased cooperation between the Panthers and established institutions in the black community. He stated that the party had been wrong in the manner that it attacked the police in its early days. He declared that black people simply weren't ready to make the revolutionary jump from point A to point Z. It was necessary to take them incrementally through revolution from point A, to point B, to point C, and so on.

He announced that no longer would the party be estranged from the black church, with which it had quite a few amends to make. Some speculated Newton's pang of conscience was the result of an appearance before a group of skeptical middle-aged blacks in early 1971, during which a woman stood up and declared that Newton and the Panthers had lost their souls and were going to hell. Newton, whose father had been an assistant minister, was said to have been shaken by the declaration. Perhaps the woman was aware of a shocking statement that party chief of staff David Hilliard allegedly had made before Newton got out of prison. Appearing before the National Committee of Black Churchmen, who were meeting in Berkeley, Hilliard allegedly had called black ministers a bunch of bootlicking pimps and motherfuckers. He threatened that if the preachers did not come around, the Panthers would "off" some of them. In his seminary speech, Newton denounced the statement as one more example of how the Panthers had been wrong.

Newton was a very complex man who wanted to function in a number of different places at once—among intellectuals like the professors and students at Yale, among the gangster elements of Oakland, among black churchgoers, and as somewhat of a godfather in the black community too (in fact, when the movie *The Godfather* premiered the following year, Huey Newton, high on coke, went to see it repeatedly and required party members to do the same).

The name for the new face he chose for the party was "revolutionary intercommunalism," the theory being that nations no longer had distinct borders but were instead economically interdependent on each other. Nations could either voluntarily link up an interdependent relationship (revolutionary intercommunalism) or be forced to react to others' attempts to control their destinies (reactionary intercommunalism). Newton viewed the black community as a captive nation within the United States. To demonstrate how revolutionary intercommunalism could work, he decided that Oakland's black community would become a proving ground.

In the next year, the party began what became known as survival programs—a free clinic in Berkeley, a free ambulance service, a free shoe factory, food giveaways, and a Panther elementary school. Newton closed most Panther chapters across the nation, calling all of his loyalists to Oakland in an effort to turn the city into a demonstration project of what could be accomplished when the entire black community cooperated with one another. He mapped plans to run Panthers as serious candidates for local office. He took a long hard look at the Port of Oakland, which at the time was the largest container port on the West Coast, theorizing that if blacks could seize political power in the city, then they could control the port and engage in international trade. His ideas showed that the same Newton who organized clandestine hit squads to engage in wanton murder was as capable of laying out legitimate strategies as some of the best political and economic organizers and consultants.

While one side of Newton mapped out Panther efforts to gain legitimacy aboveground, the other side mapped out a strategy for gaining control of the vices in Oakland. The centerpiece for control of the vices was to be a Panther-owned restaurant/club on Telegraph Avenue in Oakland, called the Lamp Post. The Lamp Post had been run by a Newton cousin named Jimmy Ward. Allegedly, Newton took over the club after Ward incurred debts to the Panthers that he couldn't repay. At the same time, Newton's cocaine addiction was growing, and he drastically changed the operating procedures of the party and its hierarchy to accommodate that addiction.

Some of the hierarchal shifts were related to the jury verdict in the Seale and Huggins trial. On May 24, 1971, the jury voted 10 to 2 in favor of acquittal for Huggins, and 11 to 1 in favor of acquittal for Seale. The next day the judge granted the motion of defense attorney Charles Garry for dismissal of all charges against both defendants. Seale returned to Oakland, keeping his title as party chairman, but for all intents and purposes it was still a glorified position. Huggins, who had opened up the party's New Haven chapter on moving back there after the 1969 murder of her husband, John, at UCLA in the Panther dispute with the militant group United Slaves, also came to Oakland and began running the party newspaper. Not long afterward, David Hilliard went on trial for his part in the April 6, 1968, shootout that had left Bobby Hutton dead. Hilliard was convicted of attempting to murder police officers and began to serve time in July 1971 (while in prison, Hilliard was kicked out of the party by a paranoid Newton, who was fearful that Hilliard was planning a coup). For all intents and purposes, his position was phased out. The party's new minister of information would be Elaine Brown, from the Los Angeles chapter.

Newton centralized all the money coming into the party. Whereas before each party chapter and entity (such as the Berkeley Free Clinic) had kept its own books, now all money was to go to Central Headquarters and Central would dispense what everyone needed. This proved to be a worse form of management than what chapters across the country had complained about under Hilliard. "When centralization was put into effect, no one could touch the paper money," remembers Mary Kennedy. "Before then you were allowed to take money from petty cash and if you missed breakfast you could go and get yourself something to eat while you were out in the field. People could get other things too on their own. But Huey squashed all that." The faith of remaining rank-and-file party members in what they were doing was tested more than ever before. "The beatings started, terrible beatings," recalls Kennedy. "People got to where they stopped selling newspapers. Then a lot of people would sell the newspapers, take the money, and get the hell out of there. They would take the papers and go on over to the airport. They had their parents send them plane tickets. People were deserting right and left."

Meanwhile, Sheeba Haven rose in the party. She had dropped out of UC Berkeley the same fall that she matriculated. Since chemistry had been one of her best subjects, the party assigned her to go over to the free clinic, which carpenters were preparing, and sort the medicine. They told her to secure other items too. At the tender age of eighteen, Haven opened the party's Berkeley free clinic.

She recruited people to train her in how to run the clinic. Dr. Tolbert Small was the clinic's physician, but Haven served as its first office manager. Party members were sent to the clinic as their work assignment. Haven developed a reputation for being somewhat of a staff sergeant. She demanded cleanliness, and sterile procedures. She also ran into the problems that party women typically encountered. Many male party members who were assigned to work in the clinic didn't like taking orders from her, a young woman. She would ask them to move boxes, help with cleaning, pull watch so she could sleep, and the like. But they would refuse. One day she brought in a pistol to back up her demands. This time when they refused, she told them they could deal with her, or they could deal with Mr. Smith and Mr. Wesson.

As a result of such confrontations, Newton decided to make Haven a party lieutenant, giving the male rank-and-file members no choice but to obey her. She continued to run the clinic, manage its staff, purchase supplies. When the order came down from Central Headquarters that she would no longer be purchasing supplies because all money in the party was to be centralized, Haven complained vociferously, breaking Newton's most important rule: Do not criticize him. He dismissed Haven from her responsibilities at the clinic and ordered her to move from Berkeley to the Panthers' East Oakland location. But Haven, aware of the severe beatings usually meted out to disobedient party members, feared that this fate awaited her. Dissatisfied with the new edict, in October 1971, just one year after she began working full time for the party, she left and moved underground to join up with dissatisfied Panthers who became part of the BLA.

More and more rank-and-file party members who were trying to hang on became convinced that the party was at its most frightening. Yet, at the same time, Newton was not without success in gaining positive publicity for the party in a local press that was fascinated, surprised, and pleased by Panther talk of putting down the gun and concentrating on intercommunalism and survival programs. That same press knew nothing of the party's clandestine activities.

Black Oakland realized what was really happening but for the most part kept its mouth shut, or made comments about the party that weren't for attribution, because most people were too scared and because many simply harbored mixed feelings. "There's nothing good that always remained that way," philosophizes Ralph Williams, former head of the West Oakland Planning Committee, looking back on that era. "We [blacks in Oakland] had the pious way of doing things, and the Panthers came along with the non-pious way. They got something for everyone. The tactics they used had never been used before. It was just like with some of the guys in the Mafia. If you were going to be a part of their movement, then you had to take the orders of the guys from the top down. You were part of the gang, you couldn't speak out."

That "black Mafia" intimidated one black Oakland dry cleaner into dry-cleaning the clothes of party members for free. But when the Panthers approached the California State Package Store and Tavern Owners Association (Cal-Pak), an organization of black convenience/liquor-store and club owners, demanding that it contribute $220 per week to the Panther survival programs, the relatively prosperous middle-class black business establishment in Oakland decided that, unlike party members and so many other blacks in Oakland, it would speak out loud and clear.

By the time Newton approached Cal-Pak, the black business establishment in the Bay Area had seen better days as a visible, centralized group. In Oakland its heyday had been the 1940s and 1950s, before the city had cleared more than 500 predominantly black West Oakland homes through the process of eminent domain to make room for a large postal distribution center and the Bay Area Rapid Transit (BART) train tracks, which for some strange reason had to go through Oakland's predominantly black commercial business districts aboveground, while the tracks coursed through the predominantly white commercial business districts of Berkeley and San Francisco belowground. Clearance had also been made for an urban renewal project called Acorn housing, as well as the Nimitz freeway, a stretch of which would collapse in the Bay Area earthquake of 1989. The area remained dormant for almost ten years before all the projects were finished.

During the heyday of black businesses in Oakland, the place to be was Seventh Street. In the 1940s the nearby port was bustling, as was the Southern Pacific Railroad Station at which C. L. Dellums had landed in the 1920s, and a large army base. Seventh Street was so crowded with people that it was difficult to walk down it. On weekends the clubs and restaurants raked in money. The marquis club was owned by Slim Jenkins at the corner of Seventh and Wood. Then there were the gambling establishments of a man named Charles Jones (nicknamed "Raincoat," because no matter what the weather he always wore his raincoat), who lived on mother wit. There was also Syl's Restaurant, which had the best soul food in town, and Earl's Barbecue, and a club called Harvey's (later Ester's Orbit Room), and another restaurant called The Barn. For looking good there was the Ford-O'Dell haberdashery near the corner of Seventh and Adeline streets, owned by Paul Ford and S. B. O'Dell, who went on to form his own real estate company and ultimately become a mortgage banker, cofounding Beneficial Savings and Loan.

"Raincoat" Jones might have wielded clout comparable to the white business titans had his biggest dream not gone up in smoke. He established a sawmill in Mendocino County, called Mendocino Timber, Inc. Then he leased 26,000 acres from a man named Simmons in Santa Ana, California, and began operations, opening up a lumber yard in West Oakland to handle the finished product. But the road to becoming a tycoon ended when something went wrong with his gambling operations on Seventh Street (presumably huge losses that had to be covered), forcing him to dissolve the entire lumber operation.

Slim Jenkins had been as respected as "Raincoat." His supper club and gambling establishment received the same wink from the powers-that-be that certain white businessmen regularly received, becoming so popular that the same Earl Warren who became chief justice of the U.S. Supreme Court occasionally dropped by Slim's while he was an Alameda County district attorney. Black businessmen in Oakland considered Slim a wizard, because he used tricks such as seating a black couple next to a white couple, ensuring that the black couple would spend as much as the white couple so as not to be embarrassed by being outspent. Slim gave every bartender $30 before going on shift, to use for "buying" drinks for regular customers, so that new customers would want to come back and become Slim's regulars.

Slim's featured national talent like Billie Holiday, Ray Charles, B. B. King, Sarah Vaughn, celebrities who usually trekked across the bay after playing at the clubs that catered to blacks in San Francisco's Filmore district. Places like Jack's on Sutter Street between Webster and Filmore, or Bop City on Post Street, or the Filmore Auditorium on Filmore Street itself, before its days as a center of late 1960s hard rock owned by impresario Bill Graham. Then there was the Texas Playhouse, owned by Wesley Johnson, a black man who wore a ten-gallon hat and kept money under the glass of his bar. And the celebrities might stay overnight at the Booker T. Washington Hotel or eat at the black-owned Plantation Club. But like Seventh Street in West Oakland, the black business presence in San Francisco's Filmore district was destroyed by the urban-renewal process. Slim's was never the same after moving to Oakland's predominantly white Jack London Square. "Raincoat" Jones died a pauper.

A legacy of that black business tradition was Cal-Pak, started in 1957 when a beer company in South San Francisco decided it would fire Tom Mosely, a black man who had been with the company for twenty-nine years, allegedly so that it wouldn't have to pay him retirement benefits. A group of nine black liquor-store and club owners met at Ester's Orbit Room on Seventh Street in West Oakland to do something about it. At that time 35 percent of all beer sold in the state of California was sold to blacks. With the help of black newspaper editors such as the *Oakland Post*'s Tom Nash, the store owners launched a campaign to have all black liquor stores and clubs in California keep the product of the beer company that had fired Mosely off their shelves. The company decided to negotiate, and Cal-Pak was formed. Eventually, virtually every black liquor-store and club owner in California became a member of Cal-Pak.

After the Mosely victory, Cal-Pak set its sights on gaining more clout over the beverage companies it did business with, demanding that each company whose beverages they sold hire black drivers to deliver the beverages. Cal-Pak members Bill Boyette and Bill Graves drove Charlie Hardy, a former member of the San Francisco 49ers, to the local Coca-Cola bottler and got him hired. Clarence Jacobs became a salesman-driver for Ham's Brewery. Eventually the black salesman-drivers formed their own organization, called the Hucksters. Cal-Pak and the Hucksters worked together to flex their muscle. By 1971, Cal-Pak was responsible for the creation of nearly 500 jobs for blacks in the beverage industry throughout California.

In May 1971, when Huey Newton came to flex Panther muscle with Cal-Pak, the organization wasn't about to flinch. At that time the president of Cal-Pak was big, burly Bill Boyette, who owned two convenience/liquor stores in North Oakland, one at 5350 Grove Street, the other at 2520 Grove Street (today Grove Street is known as Martin Luther King Jr. Way). In a civil suit filed in Alameda County Superior Court, Boyette stated that Newton approached him during the last week of May and requested that each of twenty-two local members of Cal-Pak pay the Black Panthers $5 per member per week. Later that same week, Newton visited Boyette again, raising the requested amount to $10 per member per week. Acting on behalf of the entire association, Boyette refused both requests.

On July 21, Bobby Seale attended a Cal-Pak meeting and repeated Newton's request. He told the members that if the payments were not made the Panthers would "close down the place of business of each of the members of the association." On July 29, Cal-Pak sent a letter to Newton offering a large donation of groceries to the Black Panther breakfast program for kids: 75 gallons of milk, 500 loaves of bread, 60 pounds of meat, 30 dozen eggs, and two cases of cereal to be used as the party saw fit. The following day Newton replied that the offer was insufficient, that his previous request for cash "donations" stood, and that if Boyette didn't make the "donations" then the Panthers would "immediately attempt to close down" Boyette's businesses, in an effort to make an example out of him.

On July 31, forty to fifty pickets showed up at Boyette's convenience/liquor store at 5350 Grove Street, carrying placards reading "He Must Contribute to People's Survival Programs." According to Boyette, the pickets not only blocked the entrance to his store but entered the store itself and blocked the parking lot, and that same day and for days afterward, Newton and other members of the Black Panthers acting as pickets threatened him, at one point chanting "Boyette Must Die!" A temporary restraining order was issued, preventing pickets from entering the store or blocking the parking lot but allowing them to continue picketing. Although he had been threatened with harm, Boyette expressed no fear for his own safety. But he did fear for the safety of his employees, who he said had received threatening phone calls.

Cal-Pak felt secure in rejecting Newton's request, because it had several worthwhile community projects such as a scholarship program. It also claimed to have secured 230 jobs for blacks in the previous six months. The issue simply boiled down to freedom of choice, and whether the Panthers were really requesting money for their survival programs or were engaging in a sophisticated form of extortion.

In an effort to seize the offensive, the Panthers declared in their newspaper that Cal-Pak's offer of food was turned down because it was a one-time offer. They also claimed that Cal-Pak had requested the Panthers' support in boycotting Mayfair's, a supermarket in North Oakland, because it wouldn't keep a certain beverage off its shelves, and that in exchange the Panthers had requested that Cal-Pak make small monetary donations to the Panther survival programs. Cal-Pak agreed that it had sanctioned the boycott of Mayfair's market. But it stated that the Panthers had provided assistance "without the invitation or request of the association."

The Panther boycott dragged on, virtually destroying

Boyette's business, because most people were too scared to cross the Panthers. Sales dropped off 98 percent. Only a handful of people, such as former senator Bill Knowland, publisher of the *Oakland Tribune*, were brave enough to cross the line. Knowland directed his chauffeur to drive him down to the 5350 Grove Street store to buy cases of liquor as a gesture of thumbing his nose at Newton, whom he detested. Cal-Pak member Bill Mabry and *Oakland Post* editor Tom Nash also crossed the line. After attending a ball game one day, they decided to go over to 5350 Grove Street. The pickets were out front. Mabry told them to get the hell out of his way. Nash followed. "Well, we know you, Mr. Mabry," the pickets replied. "And we know you too, Mr. Berkley." They had mistaken Tom Nash for Tom Berkley, the publisher of the *Oakland Post*, which was quite all right with Tom Nash, who answered, "You got that right!" The following day, Nash returned to the *Oakland Post* office and told Tom Berkley, "You know, the Panthers are down there bandying your name about." Tom Berkley immediately went to his law office upstairs, got his pistol, and put it in his pants.

Berkley had every reason for the precaution, but not nearly as much as another class of businessmen—the owners of the after hours clubs. The Panthers went after them for money too, places that stayed open from 2 A.M. to 6 A.M., played music, and served "setups" (drinks containing near-booze, such as a mixer like Tom Collins, and 7-Up). There were the legal after-hours clubs like the Lucky Seven and Jimbo's Bop City. But there were the illegal ones as well, which served booze in the hours they weren't supposed to, sold drugs, ran illegal card games. With the illegal clubs, Newton could use far rougher tactics in forcing them to contribute money, such as having his elite squad of enforcers firebomb or shoot up the establishments, even occasionally kill someone. And the same fate befell the pimps and drug dealers of the city. It was all easy to institute, given the party's huge arsenal of weapons located in Panther-owned housing throughout the Bay Area, an arsenal that reached into the thousands and included AR-18 rifles, .3030 Winchesters, .375 magnum rifles, M-15 and M-16 rifles, M-60 fully automatic machine guns, Thompson submachine guns, M-79 grenade launchers, Browning 9-mm pistols, .45 automatic pistols, .357 magnums, and many other types of guns, as well as boxes of ammunition, silencing devices, grenades, miscellaneous explosives, and so on.

Meanwhile, the boycott of Boyette as an example to legitimate black businesses dragged on. Bobby Seale would appear at the picket lines admonishing pickets to make people boycott Boyette "to death, till the brother realizes he's one of us. . . ." Panthers were pulled off of everything else to join the boycott. Mary Kennedy cooked for the line. "I could go to the Officer of the Day at Central Headquarters and tell the officer I was spending $45 for breakfast for the boycott line, or $50 or $60. I could get any amount of money for the boycott line, just as long as we kept it going. You could say, 'Huey, the Panther newspaper sales are dropping!' He'd say to hell with the newspaper. They have to be on that boycott line." After Mary began cooking for the boycott line, she was moved to the Lamp Post, where she became head cook.

Increasing numbers of the black business establishment, outraged at what was happening to Boyette, rallied to his support. Approximately 200 of them, owners of small retail establishments, real estate sales offices, law practices, beauty shops, funeral homes, and medical practices, formed the Ad Hoc Committee to Preserve Black Business in Oakland. Their name echoed that of a previous local organization formed not to break boycotts but to instigate them—the Ad Hoc Committee to End Discrimination. Matters had come full circle. The committee elected as cochairmen Albert McKee, a real estate broker, and Joseph Simmons, a local attorney. Then it set out "to break the boycott, and see to it that black people are given a choice of whether they want to contribute to any group or charity."

A meeting was held between the committee and the Panthers. Some angered committee members refused to attend when they learned they were to be frisked by Panthers. During the meeting, Boyette again made his offer to donate food rather than cash to the Panthers. "Newton slammed the desk three times and said that this was unacceptable, explaining that he wanted weekly cash contributions," recalled Albert McKee. "When Boyette refused, Newton said he would 'make [Boyette] a poor man.' I was angered and amazed because I had never heard anybody publicly threatened like this."

Newton also threatened McKee at the meeting: "I'd like to notify we plan to boycott my brother here next, because he went around and nagged against the Party and told many things that are not true. And I'd like to notify you you'll be under siege shortly." Then he expressed grudging respect for the black businessmen. "Really, I admire your show of unity. I didn't think you had it in you."

The Ad Hoc Committee continued to demonstrate fearlessness. "No black leader speaks for all black people just as no white leader speaks for the entire white community," Joseph Simmons declared during a press conference at Boyette's liquor store. McKee insisted that any cash contribution to the Panthers be subject to accountability: "If we contribute one dollar to the survival program we can't be sure that the money will be spent to buy breakfast cereal or medicine for children." Simmons criticized the Panther free food distribution program: "You just can't drive a truck [with food] into a neighborhood and open its doors. We want to make sure that the needy people receive the food and not the lazy ones who may turn around and sell it to their neighbors." An angry McKee objected to the assumption that black businessmen hadn't done anything for the black community, that the Panthers were the first benefactors: "Some of us were fighting against racial injustice when Newton was running around barefooted." Simmons accused the Panthers of hypocrisy, given the fact that for all their major legal cases they hired white lawyers, alleging that the Panthers paid Charles Garry "$500,000 over the years."

Other black leaders in the East Bay also spoke out. "Let us emphatically state that under no circumstances does Huey P. Newton, the Black Panther Party or the administrators of the present boycott have the support of these ministers or our congregations," stated the Reverend Charles Belcher, president of the Interdenominational Ministerial Alliance, representing black religious leaders in Oakland.

"Businessmen should be able to support any group they wish to without fear of anybody or any group," declared Frances Albrier, a member of the Berkeley NAACP.

The boycott dragged on until January 1972, when newly elected Congressman Ron Dellums, nephew of C. L. Dellums, stepped in to negotiate a settlement. The compromise agreement called for the formation of an umbrella organization of black businessmen called the United Black Fund of the Bay Area, which would donate food or money to a wide variety of black charitable causes at their own discretion. Among those programs were to be those of the Black Panthers. Donations to the Panthers were to be made through Saint Augustine's Episcopal, the church of the party's spiritual adviser, Father Earl Neil. In essence the compromise meant that the Panthers had lost their campaign to pressure aboveground black businesses to submit to their authority.

While many were angered and frightened by the entire Panther/black business confrontation, it ended up catalyzing a change beneficial to all of black Oakland. After the settlement was announced, Newton stated that the Panthers would next pressure white businesses to donate to the party's survival programs. This alarmed the white powers-that-be in Oakland, who feared that the Panthers would use the same violent tactics with whites that they used in the black community. Oakland's leading white businessmen went into action. Edgar Kaiser, Bill Knowland, and Safeway chairman Quentin Reynolds announced the formation of the New Oakland Committee. They formed three caucuses: one for business, one for labor, and one for minority relations.

According to Lionel Wilson, an Alameda County Superior Court judge at the time, they asked Don McCullum, Elijah Turner, Paul Cobb, and Daryl Galloway to represent black Oakland. All agreed to serve on the committee as long as they were exclusive representatives of the black community. The white powers-that-be balked. At the suggestion of the chief administrator of Kaiser Industries, they approached Wilson to form the caucus. Wilson agreed on one condition: that at every meeting of the New Oakland Committee either Kaiser, Knowland, Reynolds, and the other white economic leaders be present, or a second-level representative be there. The white business leaders gave Wilson their word that this would be the case. Wilson, in turn, formed the minority caucus. With the help of the Black Panthers, within five years Lionel Wilson would be elected Oakland's first black mayor. Confirms Wilson, the New Oakland Committee "was formed out of fear when the Panthers announced that they were going to move on the white business community."

By the beginning of 1972, the party was down to approximately 150 core members engaged in various pursuits, the most visible of which was the political organizing that would first be directed to Bobby Seale and Elaine Brown's political campaigns, and later to Lionel Wilson's. In preparation for their foray into politics, the Panthers held two grand-scale public events that year. The first, in March, was the three-day Black Community Survival Conference, which took place at the Oakland Auditorium and two local parks. Approximately 7,000 people attended. The second, the Anti-war, African Liberation Voter Registration Survival Conference, was a single-day event held in June at the Oakland Auditorium. Approximately 5,000 people attended. Both conferences featured speakers such as Bobby Seale and Ron Dellums, provided musical entertainment, registered voters, tested people for sickle cell anemia, and gave away bags of free groceries under the proverbial politician's cliché "a chicken in every pot!" The bill for both conferences was footed by the only white Panther at that time. He lived in Beverly Hills, produced films such as *Easy Rider*, dated actress Candice Bergen, paid for Huey's penthouse apartment, and wore one of the coveted gold rings Huey gave his inner circle. Bert Schneider footed the $300,000 bill, most observers believed, because he genuinely loved Huey P. Newton.

That August the party fielded a slate of candidates for nine of the eighteen seats on the governing board of the West Oakland Planning Committee, the official citizens' participation board of Oakland's Model Cities program, an urban-renewal project financed by the U.S. Department of Housing and Urban Development. Six Panthers won seats on the board, which was responsible for providing citizens' input on how the $4.9 million Model Cities budget was to be spent in providing social services and urban-renewal financing in a three-square-mile area of West Oakland. The Panthers entered the election as a trial run for the following year's Seale and Brown campaigns.

IN NOVEMBER 1971, LANDON WILLIAMS WAS RELEASED from prison. He returned to the Panthers, only to view the corruption in the party with dismay and disgust. Yet he remained nominally affiliated with the party until others he had joined the party with, such as his brother, emerged from serving prison sentences on various charges. His goal was to see if it would be possible to pull a coup, which was made all the more difficult when Newton escaped conviction that December, after the jury was unable to reach a verdict in the retrial of his case involving the shooting death of Officer John Frey. The charges were dropped after a second jury was also unable to reach a verdict. Landon Williams quickly discovered that life within the party was becoming more and more treacherous when the following year, Rory Hithe, a party member who had been in prison with him over the Alex Rackley case, was murdered during a Panther meeting in San Francisco. Landon occupied himself with returning to college. This time he enrolled at UC Berkeley and majored in economics.

Mary Kennedy was settled in as head cook at the Lamp Post, where she watched an increasingly coked-up, paranoid Huey Newton intimidate party members. Throughout the time the aboveground operations of the Panthers were having a positive effect, Newton's drug-crazed behavior was having its negative impact, frightening the people of Oakland as well as most members of the party. If you were integral to running very important party programs, or were part of Newton's exclusive squad responsible for enforcing the party's will on those who ran Oakland's vices, you could usually avoid his wrath. But if you were an ordinary rank-and-file member, it was far more difficult.

There were the dramatic moments involving some party higher-ups. One day at the Lamp Post, Mary was telling one of Huey's bodyguards about a problem she was having with an important party member named John. While she was telling the story,

Huey walked up, surrounded by his other bodyguards. Seeing Huey, Mary shut up. "No, don't stop telling the story!" said the bodyguard who had been listening to her. It was dangerous to suddenly become quiet when Newton approached, because he would think you had been talking about him. Mary kept telling her story, the upshot of which was that John told her he was going to kick her out of the party. "John told you he was going to kick you out of the party?" Newton asked. That night John was beaten.

There was no telling what a coked-up Huey Newton might do. One day one of his bodyguards was late in picking him up from court because he had to drive around the corner rather than wait out in front of the courthouse, a transgression that resulted in Newton's punching him, leaving him with a black eye. To make up for it, Newton gave him a cigar, because a cigar was "for a thinking man." Another night, a coked-up Newton received word that a rank-and-file party member who slept overnight at the home for party children had a little hobby. She told people their futures with tarot cards. Newton instructed one of his bodyguards to "take me over to where this bitch is reading futures!" When they arrived, the woman was in bed. Huey had her awakened. "I hear you've been telling people their futures," he said.

"It's just a little joke," she replied.

"Well, I want you to tell me mine. Get the cards."

The woman got the cards out, laid them across the table, and began to tell Newton his future. After a few minutes he asked her, "Did the cards tell you I'm going to whip your motherfucking ass?" At that point he had his bodyguard hold the woman while he beat her.

A coked-up Newton, surrounded by members of his squad, frequently prowled after-hours clubs not only for payoffs but also for women and drugs. Once he and his entourage arrived at their chosen spot, Newton instructed his bodyguards to watch the entrances and not let anyone out. At that point he would engage in a political tirade for hours, ending it with the repeated shout, "I am the Supreme Servant!!!" Or he would pick out a male at the club and engage him in a fistfight. Or he would choose a woman and engage in carnal pleasures with her. It didn't matter how she felt about it, or if she was with her boyfriend or her husband. If he wanted her, that was it. Should her companion object, Newton had one of his bodyguards pistol-whip him. If the police were called, once they arrived no one would admit to having seen anything. People were too scared.

The Black Panthers and the city of Oakland learned that the return of Huey Newton signaled both a steering of the party down a more pragmatic aboveground course of action, and the development of a black Mafia, so to speak, that was even more frightening and demanding than the "revolutionaries" who had engaged in small-time robberies and low-gain extortion while Newton was in jail from 1967 to 1970. (Under Hilliard, extortion demands were said to be limited to far lower dollar amounts and leveled at fewer storekeepers than under Newton.) The peculiar love/hate relationship between the party and the black citizens of Oakland still had almost a decade to run, and the increasingly tragic Newton had seventeen more years to continue charting his personal course of brilliance mixed with destruction.

11

Fellow Travelers in the Lair

WHILE HUEY NEWTON WAS ENGAGING THE BLACK PAN-thers in Oakland politics, community service, and gangland style strong-arming, the white leftists who only a short two years earlier had anointed the Panthers America's revolutionary vanguard, were splintering. Within a year of his release from prison, Newton was no longer a saint in their eyes. Much of that change of heart was due to the violence of the Newton/Cleaver split, which rattled and turned off most of the white Left in much the same manner it did young black activists. Many, like Newton's old college acquaintance Joe Blum, were further turned off when Newton moved into the Lake Merritt penthouse: "My image and what I put in my newspaper was that Huey was committed to being with the masses of people in Oakland who weren't doing very well. I could understand that there were people who were trying to kill him. But our notion was that part of being in the movement was risking the chance you would die."

Yet as the 1970s settled in, risking death for the movement became passé among white leftists too, largely because Richard Nixon began winding down American involvement in the Vietnam War (he would end the draft in January 1973). The SDS had dissolved, the only remnant being the same Weather Underground that took credit for bombing the home of the judge presiding over the New York 21's case. The Peace and Freedom Party saw its last days in this same time period. No longer having to worry about the possibility of ending up in Vietnam or seeing a boyfriend, brother, or husband sent there, young white activists branched off into various interest groups—the environmental movement, Ralph Nader–inspired consumer activism, the budding feminist movement. Others who received whiffs of tear gas or the sting of Mace at the 1968 Democratic National Convention in Chicago, at Berkeley's People's Park, and the countless other events that made the 1960s such a searing decade, headed off to graduate school, or law school, or medical school.

The Vietnam War was being left to the Vietnamese. And when white leftists looked for replacement activities, nowhere was the selection wider than in the Bay Area. Although at first shocked by the violence of the Newton/Cleaver split, many Bay Area white radicals were also attracted to Newton's announced plans for the party's survival programs. They recognized that "as whites" they would have to play an ancillary role, but a few found the programs as attractive an option as any. Among such whites was a coeditor at *Ramparts* magazine.

David Horowitz had been a lower-level editor at *Ramparts* during the heyday of Panther–police shootouts, taking orders from Bob Scheer. By 1971, after winning a power struggle in which Scheer and Warren Hinckle were booted out, Horowitz and Peter Collier were running the magazine. But the magazine had already seen its heyday and was barely able to make its payroll. In an effort to secure funds, Collier and Horowitz combed the Bay Area as well as the Los Angeles area for wealthy radical-chic benefactors. One such benefactor turned out to be Hollywood producer Bert Schneider, friend and benefactor of Huey Newton. In the fall of 1971, Schneider gave *Ramparts* a donation and suggested that if the *Ramparts* editors wanted to investigate a worthwhile story, they should see Huey Newton about the party's new survival programs.

Collier and Horowitz went to see Newton at his Lake Merritt penthouse. He had just returned from a two-week visit to China, and was back in Oakland orchestrating the Cal-Pak boycott and the other varied Panther activities. Although Newton was refining a new theory of revolutionary intercommunalism for the Black Panther Party, he viewed it as a means toward gradual progression to the same revolution that had taken place in Communist China. Having grown up a Red Diaper baby (the child of Communist party parents), Horowitz was tired of communist philosophies, particularly the Maoist variety. During the visit he engaged Newton in a debate about Maoism, then brought up the issue of the split with Eldridge, who was still on the *Ramparts* masthead (as international editor) although he wasn't writing for the magazine and was no friend of Horowitz's. Like everyone else outside the party, Horowitz thought the split had been strictly over whether to continue conducting a violent struggle or to engage in gradualism. He criticized the party for following Cleaver one day, then Newton the next.

To Horowitz's surprise, Newton responded positively to most of his criticisms. "The Black Panther Party is not a black students union. Most of the people in it are not intellectuals," Newton said. Then he asked Horowitz to help the party. Horowitz, eager to get up off his lofty intellectual perch and do something hands on, decided to get involved. He toured the party's free clinic, its newspaper, and its elementary school in the house on 29th Avenue in Oakland. He met party member Brenda Bay, who at that time was running the school. Horowitz was very impressed by what she was doing with it. He decided to get involved helping the school, while doing his best to steer clear of Panther politics.

He, and other outsiders like him who became involved with the party, saw the charming, intellectual side of Huey Newton. They saw the competent party people who were running programs, who had nothing to do with the Lamp Post or the terrorism of Newton's squad, people who were more sophisticated than most rank-and-file members and provided the party with a positive image at the same time that the other party images prevailed.

While Horowitz became involved in a positive aspect of the party, others saw a more troubling aspect. One such observer was Mae Jackson. Jackson was not under any illusions about Huey, after hearing his terrible fall 1970 speech in Philadelphia. Her activities with the prisoner's rights movement, however, led her into contact with Newton again. She increasingly saw one prisoner in particular, Johnny Spain, locked up in San Quentin. While in prison Spain became involved with the Black Panthers through his association with George Jackson (no relation to Mae).

On August 21, 1971, George Jackson, Johnny Spain, and others attempted to escape from San Quentin. The story of that attempt is one of the most bizarre, intricate, and confusing unsolved mysteries of that era. Jackson had just returned from a prison visit with his lawyer, Stephen Bingham, during which Jackson had worn an Afro wig and had been handed a tape recorder by Bingham. While Jackson was being skin-searched, as usual when prisoners returned from receiving visitors, a clip of bullets fell out from under his Afro wig. At that point Jackson mysteriously produced a 9-mm gun and forced the prison guards to open the cell blocks to free Jackson's prison friends. In the process, three prison guards and two white prisoners were killed. Soon the prison authorities had surrounded the cell block. But Johnny Spain stuck by Jackson. He and Jackson charged into the prison yard, with Jackson firing his gun, only to be killed in a hail of bullets.

The breakout had been planned differently. Hence, a multitude of theories developed about what went wrong, who was involved, and so on. Stephen Bingham became a fugitive, escaping to Europe for a number of years to avoid prosecution as an accessory to the event. As was the case when George Jackson's brother Jonathan planned to secure George's freedom from jail, other Panthers (this time those incarcerated at San Quentin with Jackson) allegedly were scheduled to do certain things during the breakout attempt which simply did not happen. One of the theories subscribed to by a number of people, including Jackson's comrades in the prison-based Black Guerilla Family, was that Huey Newton purposely called off Panther support for George's freedom because he didn't want a potential rival like Jackson to be freed. That theory gained all the more credence when it was learned that, days before the breakout attempt, George Jackson had made out a new will, signing over all royalties to his best-selling book, *Soledad Brother*, to the Black Panther Party. As a result of the failure of the Jackson breakout attempt and the suspicions, gangland style murders took place in and out of prison, in a war between Jackson loyalists and Newton loyalists.

Johnny Spain was considered a Jackson loyalist, since he had risked death with Jackson all the way to the end. He didn't subscribe to suspicions that the Panthers were involved in sabotaging the escape, however, so he kept his affiliation with the party. After the escape attempt, Spain became somewhat renowned in his own right. Poems he had written were being considered for publication, just as George Jackson's prison letters had been published as the book *Soledad Brother*. It was hoped that publication of the poems, which were considered quite good, would awaken public interest in Spain's plight. By 1972, Spain was in constant communication with Mae Jackson, who was based in New York. Spain had given his poems to the Black Panthers. On Mae's next trip to the Bay Area to see relatives in Oakland and to visit Johnny at San Quentin, he suggested that she meet with the Panthers and look at his poems. Mae agreed.

Since turning off of Huey Newton, Mae had had virtually no communication with the party. She heard stories about it—the split with Eldridge and the murders related to that split. She had also heard rumors about Huey's drug use from her Oakland relatives. She was aware too of the rumors that Huey had sabotaged George's escape attempt. Mae didn't know what to believe and was still quite frightened of the party. On the morning she was scheduled to meet with party members and read Johnny's poems, she was picked up by Panther minister of information Elaine Brown. After meeting with party members, they gave her the typed manuscript of Johnny's poems. Mae opened up the manuscript, only to see written notes clipped to it. Presumably they were left there by someone other than Johnny Spain, because they discussed Johnny. "The notes read 'Things to discuss with The Servant,'" recalls Jackson. "And the things listed were Johnny's book, and then the second or third line down, Johnny's will." The Servant, of course, was Huey Newton. George Jackson's mother told Mae that George had willed everything to the Panthers days before he died, including his book royalties. Now Mae was very nervous. She feared that the rumors of Panther complicity in the failure of George's escape attempt were true, and that the Panthers might be planning to have Johnny Spain killed, publish his poems, and collect the royalties.

On returning to New York, Mae wrote a letter to Elaine Wender, a young white radical attorney who was an assistant to Charles Garry, Spain's lawyer. Mae told Wender of her fear that the Panthers planned to kill Spain. By that time, Wender had the manuscript to Spain's poems at her San Francisco office. She placed the letter Mae sent her in a folder with the manuscript, and kept the poems in the office until she could figure out what to do.

Wender's newfound wariness increasingly irritated the Panthers. Panther minister of information Elaine Brown, who was in constant communication with Johnny Spain, grew more and more impatient by the day with Wender's stonewalling. Writing of the incident in her book *A Taste of Power*, Brown describes it as nothing more than a case of one more comfortable white woman infringing on the black movement and black men. Finally, Brown had had enough of it. She enlisted the aid of two other Panther women to storm into Wender's San Francisco office, demanding that she give up the poems on the spot; Wender and Anne Scheer, Bob Scheer's ex-wife, were there. Since Mae's warning letter was among the poems, to say nothing of the suspicion that Johnny's life would be endangered if the poems were published, Wender feigned misplacing the poems. Elaine Brown didn't believe her. She slapped Wender around, insisting that she give up the poems. Brown and the other Panther women swept things off Wender's desk and tore open her oak cabinets in search of them. Finally, Brown and her assistants stopped searching. They gave Wender twenty-four hours to produce the poems or else her office would be blown off the map. The following day Wender gave them the poems minus, of course, the warning from Mae.

According to Mae Jackson, Elaine Brown found out about her warning anyway, through another source. And the next time Jackson was in the Bay Area, Brown called her. "She told me, 'We've heard that you're saying things about The Servant. We will not tolerate you criticizing The Servant.' She didn't go into detail. But

I knew what she was talking about. I take the phone and hold it up so that Elaine Wender can hear. . . . We hang up and Elaine Wender says to me, 'That's a threat, and you better take it seriously.'" Mae Jackson steered clear of the Black Panthers; Johnny Spain lived, and was later released from prison, largely because of the sympathy generated by his writings and his tragic childhood.

MAE JACKSON'S AND ELAINE WENDER'S EXPERIENCES with the Panthers were to be additional controversies in the mixed legend of the party, accounts thrown in with the far more grisly stories, and the undeniable positives of its survival programs and political organizing. Those committed to doing something good through the party simply didn't open the Pandora's Box always on the table, or steal a look underneath the covers at the things that looked questionable. Eventually, David Horowitz also found himself living by that rule.

He labored to help Brenda Bay improve the Panther elementary school, going so far as to enlist alternative school expert Herbert Kohl, also white, to begin a teacher credentialing system. Kohl and Horowitz met with Huey at the penthouse. A few days later Kohl told Horowitz that Huey had all the signs of a cocaine addict. But Horowitz, who was unfamiliar with cocaine addiction, brushed off Kohl's observations, insisting that Huey had a cold when they visited. Horowitz kept up his commitment. He brought black friends such as Joel Clarke, another school expert, and Troy Duster, a sociologist, to see Huey. While acknowledging Huey's intelligence, both Clarke and Duster insisted on keeping their distance from him, which Horowitz at the time couldn't understand. He kept working with the Panthers because of competent party members such as Gwen Goodloe, Brenda Bay, Audrea Jones, and Donna Howell.

Huey continued to be a whirlwind of contradictions. Horowitz once sat down with him to discuss plans for the school, only to discover that Huey wanted to discuss things far more clandestine, not out of a desire for Horowitz's involvement but because he wanted Horowitz to know how truly complicated Huey Newton was. Insisting on changing the subject, Newton turned up the volume to his stereo to block out the bugs he knew the government had in his apartment. Then he leaned over and said, "David, I always promised myself that if I couldn't make it as a revolutionary, I'd make it as a bank robber." Pressing on, he told him, "There are things about me that you don't know."

Horowitz ignored the invitation to further inquiry, but after the meeting, he finally began to doubt. He became as riven with angst about the party as were the party members who were committed to doing something good. And whenever he contemplated abandoning it, he became wracked with guilt, knowing that as a white person he could return to his relatively comfortable white life, an option not open to other party members.

So he stayed, realizing that despite the troubling side of Huey becoming increasingly evident to him, Newton was also serious about improving the school; serious about involving the party in Oakland politics; serious about improving the party newspaper. On any given day, a wide variety of people paraded through Newton's penthouse residence, while he walked back and forth shirtless, coked up, stopping to peer through the telescope he constantly kept trained on his old Alameda County Courthouse prison cell. One day it might be Bert Schneider and Candice Bergen; another day it might be a prominent member of Oakland's black middle class, such as John George; another day it might be shady-looking characters in sunglasses packing pistols, who you knew had to be part of Oakland's underworld; another day it might be David Du Bois, stepson of W. E. B. Du Bois, who briefly ran the party newspaper. You might wait while Huey finished engaging in carnal pleasures with a prostitute he had had sent up to his bedroom.

"I went up there during Bobby's mayoral campaign," recalls Peter Solomon. "Huey was walking around with his shirt off, speeding off of something. And Bobby was there, and I said bluntly, because I had been in the community a fair amount of time and I sort of knew, I said, 'You're running a campaign you're going to lose.' I didn't say it quite that bluntly. But I said, 'Even so, this is a fantastic chance to get some information out. You take fifteen to twenty campaign workers, go to the unemployment lines and the other places poor people are, and get some information out, energize people.' And Huey said, 'When did you run a revolution last, brother?' 'I'm sorry,' I said. I shut up. I said one more thing. Then Bob [Heard] was called over. I was hugged, and asked very politely to leave."

Bobby Seale began to prepare for his mayoral run and Elaine Brown began to prepare for her run for the city council a full year before the April 17, 1973, election. Among the planks in their platform were calls for an International Trade Center, a program to safely escort senior citizens living in dangerous neighborhoods, and a preventative medicine screening program for the citizens of the city. Seale also called for two hours' paid leave from jobs so Oakland citizens could vote. The Panthers registered thousands of new voters during the bid; one estimate placed the number at 30,000. The party set up voter registration tables not only at its survival conferences but also outside of supermarkets, and went door-to-door registering voters. On election day, party workers took a fleet of station wagons and transported voters to the polls. Brown lost her city council bid by 4,000 votes. But Seale, who along with seven others (five of them black) challenged the incumbent Republican mayor John Reading, came in second and forced the mayor into a May 15 runoff. Seale lost the runoff by 50,000 votes. Tom Nash of the *Oakland Post* believes that Seale could have won the election in the overwhelmingly Democratic city if it hadn't been for one caveat: "The thing that kept Bobby from winning that election was his affiliation with the Black Panther Party."

What was one to make of the party, given the record of incidents during the year of campaigning? Fritz Pointer, a sociology instructor at Merritt College, was beaten right in front of students in his classroom, by "six or seven" Panther men who drew guns to prevent anyone from coming to his aid. Pointer allegedly had made comments about the party that they didn't like. Another jittery party worker, careening down an East Oakland street early one morning in a party station wagon, pulled out a gun apparently for no reason and shot and killed Anthony Costa, an East Oakland man who was innocently emptying his garbage. A couple of weeks before the mayoral runoff, three Panthers mysteriously exchanged gunfire with two other men at a North Oakland gas station.

These were just the incidents that made the newspapers. The troubling behavior of the party's clandestine elements escalated in frequency as Huey Newton's cocaine addiction increased, and his elite squad of enforcers took greater and greater liberties in their behavior.

Two months after the elections, questionable Panther behavior took place in front of thousands at an Ike and Tina Turner concert sponsored by the party at the Oakland Auditorium. According to the party, the trouble began when the musicians refused to accept a $540 check to cover the rest of its $7,500 advance, cutting their performance short as a result. According to the musicians, the trouble began when Ike Turner sent one of his guitar players offstage to investigate who had been entering their dressing room. After leaving the stage, he was beaten by a member of the party's security force. Seeing this, Turner announced to the audience that he would not continue to play under such conditions, and a larger melee broke out involving the entire group, Panther security, Huey Newton, Elaine Brown, and others.

While he loved a good fistfight, Newton could also hold his fire, finessing his way out of situations that might have turned violent. Such an occasion presented itself after the party reached an out-of-court settlement on a lawsuit it filed against the trucking firm Fruehauf. One of the settlement terms was that the firm's executives had to tour the party's survival programs. During the tour, the executives decided they liked Huey Newton, so they invited him to be their guest of honor at a pasta feast in Emeryville, at Fratalanza, an Italian lodge of which the company was a member. Huey agreed to appear at the dinner. He brought a bodyguard and his lawyer and friend Fred Hiestand, who had handled the suit for the party. As the guest of honor at the Fruehauf table, Newton was introduced to everyone there. It was a pure democracy. Some members booed, others applauded. And when Hiestand, Newton, and Huey's bodyguard took a break and went to the club's bar, three Fratalanza members walked up. "You're Huey Newton?" one of the three asked. As Huey replied in the affirmative, he stuck out his hand to shake with the man, who didn't respond. Instead he said, "Well, I just wanted to tell you I'm sorry John Frey didn't do the job on you." At that point, Huey's bodyguard reached into his jacket, and Hiestand looked around for a table to duck under. But Huey kept his cool. "Well, I don't believe you," he told the guy. "If you're prepared to die right now, then I believe you. But I don't think you're prepared to die now. So you're either a fool or a liar. And I don't think you're a fool. So I think you're a liar and you'd probably like to be my friend." Newton put his hand out again, the guy's two friends sort of fell back, and the guy reached out and shook Newton's hand. Afterward, Hiestand told Newton, "That was momentarily tense for me, and I was looking for cover. Did you just think of that on the spot?" "No," Newton replied. "When people were applauding and booing me, this guy was two tables from us, booing the loudest. So I already figured he was going to try and create a scene, and when he came up I was ready for him."

But Newton's more destructive behavior continued killing the party. Brenda Bay soon left. Other party workers such as Audrea Jones, Ericka Huggins, and outsiders involved in more positive Panther undertakings persevered. Huggins replaced Bay as director of the Panther elementary school. David Horowitz busied himself with raising money to buy a church in East Oakland that Huey wanted to turn into the new home for the Panther elementary school as well as a center for a variety of community-based activities. Horowitz raised about $100,000 dollars for the new facility, approaching a variety of different sources, including Bert Schneider and another Hollywood producer who jokingly told Horowitz it was going to be turned into a bayonet school. The producer opened up his checkbook and donated $10,000 so that "I won't have to give it to my kid's private school."

With the money raised, Horowitz approached the church's white congregation, which wanted assurances that the facility wasn't going to be turned over to violent blacks—that is, the Panthers. Horowitz assured them it would not be, which technically was the truth since he had created a 501(c)3 tax-exempt umbrella entity called the Educational Opportunities Corporation

(EOC), under which to protect the school and raise money for it, bypassing all the possible problems that association with the Panther name might have caused. The school became known as the Oakland Community Learning Center. Eventually, it enrolled approximately 150 children from kindergarten to the sixth grade, and became the most respected star in the Panther constellation. One of Mary Kennedy's daughters was the first graduate of the Oakland Community Learning Center.

By 1973, Mary, unlike her husband, decided she had enough of the party, given the atrocious incidents she kept witnessing. One day while she was cooking at the Lamp Post and Huey was there, a white man came in. Huey swore the white man was a police officer. The man insisted that he wasn't. But Huey insisted that he was, telling the staff, "You're serving pigs in here!" He ordered them to ignore the man. The man turned to one of the Lamp Post workers and asked her a question. She answered him. Huey walked up and slapped her. "When I tell you don't talk to anyone, you don't talk to them!" He had ordered all Lamp Post staffers, except Mary and one other cook, to turn their paychecks back in to the party. This practice was also routine with most other rank-and-file members working at the party school and elsewhere in party operations. They were meted out the bare minimum finances with which to live, while most of the wages they were supposed to keep were used to enrich Newton and his favored few.

David Horowitz occasionally heard complaints about other problems from people working at the school. He assumed for the most part that the problems were due to those in charge of certain operations, and not to Huey. "I'd say, 'Why don't you just tell Huey about it?' They'd tell me, 'David, you just don't know!'"

Mary Kennedy certainly knew: "After I left the party, people would come to my house, crying. At the Lamp Post there was a little of everything going on. I know there was prostitution. And they were selling drugs to anyone who wanted to buy them. They took the best-looking women from different sections and put them at the Lamp Post. It was more of a call-girl ring. If you wanted a good-looking woman and you had the money, you'd just pay Huey's ring and you'd get that woman."

By October 1973, when the spanking new Oakland Community Learning Center was opened on 63rd and East 14th streets in East Oakland to much fanfare, the party was also in its most troubling state. Newton began expelling or driving from the party what was left of its original leaders. He expelled David Hilliard while Hilliard served his sentence for his part in the Hutton shootout. Hilliard had been complaining about the abuses (without question far worse under Newton than they had ever been under him, making party members like Mary nostalgic for Hilliard's reign), and Newton entertained paranoid fantasies that Hilliard had been planning a coup from jail. Soon, Newton expelled David's brother June and David's wife, Pat. Masai Hewitt was beaten and expelled. Practically everyone who was in the original version of the party before Huey's release, except for a handful of people like Elaine Brown and Ericka Huggins, was gone or soon to be gone. Even Bobby Seale was tasting Huey's wrath. For Seale, everything went downhill after the mayoral election.

David Horowitz, still not privy to most of the negative aspects of the party, continued to hold out hope that things would right themselves. He had argued that the party should completely disband as a dogmatic socialist organization and become a community service entity, embracing the name Educational Opportunities Corporation. When the new East Oakland educational facility opened, with its thirty-five classrooms, the party took the 500-seat church sanctuary it was left with and created a nondenominational Sunday service called the Son of Man Temple. Horowitz was enthusiastic about Huey's stated ambition of turning the facility over to the community, although Huey had also asked architects to build a bulletproof, bombproof bunker at the center of it, to serve as his sanctuary from his growing list of enemies. He was persuaded against the idea.

Horowitz still clung to an optimism that things would proceed in the right direction. He brought in a jazz musician who taught classes at schools in Berkeley, to teach a class at the Oakland Community Learning Center. The musician took a popular song by Booker T. and the MG's and wrote an arrangement for each child in the class to play just one note on their instruments that would fit the song's melody. Horowitz brought his family to the Son of Man Temple services. By then he knew most faces in the party. And something began to trouble him. Practically everyone attending the Son of Man services was part of the party. The community wasn't there. On Malcolm X Day the following May, a celebration was held in the auditorium. Praise for Malcolm X was followed by the children reciting that the true continuation for Malcolm X was the Black Panther Party. Everyone, speaker after speaker, praised the Black Panther Party. Later, during a school planning-committee meeting attended by Newton, Horowitz voiced his anger about the focus of the Malcolm X celebration and the lack of the community's presence. Everyone but Newton, who feigned agreement with Horowitz's protest, remained silent. But nothing was done about Horowitz's complaints. He decided to make one more effort to get the Oakland Community Learning Center on the track he envisioned. He went to Huey's penthouse to press him further on the issue in private. But when he got there, Huey was in a cold sweat from heavy cocaine use.

The stage was set for Huey's most bizarre behavior of all. That summer, during a meeting of the Central Committee (which amounted to just a rubber stamp for Huey), Newton administered a most shocking exit to the party cofounder. According to sources who spoke with David Horowitz, after arguing with Bobby Seale about a proposed movie that Newton wanted Bert Schneider to produce, Newton dramatically beat Seale with a bullwhip and sodomized him so violently that his anus had to be surgically repaired by a physician who was a party supporter. Seale left town, went into hiding, and wasn't heard from for at least a year, when he turned up in Philadelphia, never to have anything again to do with the party. Days later, on July 30, in an incident at the Fox Lounge, Huey accused two plainclothes police officers of following him. He pointed a finger at one officer as though it were a gun, and ordered Bob Heard, his bodyguard, who was six feet eight inches tall and weighed about 400 pounds, to "shoot the pig-assed motherfucker!" Heard slipped his hand into a briefcase containing $1,000 and a .38 caliber pistol, and the officers drew their weapons.

Heard was arrested, and later that same night Newton and two other accomplices were also arrested.

On making bail, six days later Newton and his driver were careening down an Oakland street at night in a Continental Mark IV, when they passed a group of prostitutes hustling for customers. One of them yelled out, "Hey, baby!" It was the wrong thing to say to Huey; it reminded him too much of his hated childhood tease, "Baby Huey." Ten or fifteen minutes later, Newton had his driver return to the area. The driver parked among the prostitutes. Newton got out and asked, "Which one of you ladies called me?" Seventeen-year-old Kathleen Smith and a fellow prostitute, Crystal Gray, sensed trouble. Newton suddenly lunged at Kathleen and struck her. The other prostitutes on the block fled into the nearby Ebony Plaza Hotel. Just as Crystal Gray started to return to the scene to check on Kathleen, Newton pulled out a small caliber revolver from his breast pocket. He aimed it at Smith and shot her in the jaw, laughing as Kathleen fell. Then he hopped back in the car and sped off. The bullet struck Smith's spinal column and left her in a coma for three months. While being moved to another hospital, Smith finally died.

Immediately after shooting Smith, Newton ordered his driver to head for the San Rafael Bridge, where he tossed his pistol into the bay. Then he hid out in the Zen Center in Marin County, and after that headed south for a few days to the Beverly Hills home of supporter Bert Schneider, where allegedly he snorted cocaine and stated with some self-amazement that the Smith shooting was his first nonpolitical murder.

Days later, heading back to Oakland, Newton reestablished himself at the Lamp Post as if nothing had happened. He continued to charm customers and occasionally to terrorize staffers. Once, for an alleged indiscretion, he administered a pistol whipping to a staff member right in the Lamp Post's kitchen. The whipping was so severe that it knocked out her glass eye. She was a dedicated party member who hailed all the way from Connecticut when the party centralized its operations. A towel was wrapped around her head and she was taken to the hospital. After she was treated,

Newton threw her out of the party completely destitute, with no money for transportation back to Connecticut.

Not long after he returned from hiding in Beverly Hills, Huey's viciousness was administered to two Lamp Post customers. Two women entered a few minutes before 4 A.M, sat down, and ordered hamburgers. Then, according to a police statement made by one of the women, Helen Robinson, a Newton bodyguard approached. He "got smart" with her companion, Diane Washington, who got smart right back. The bodyguard then went back to Huey and told him. Newton approached the table and yanked Helen Robinson from her seat. He and the bodyguard pushed her back and forth, then knocked her to the floor. Then she was thrown outside. She got up and tried to retrieve her companion. Each time she tried to reenter the Lamp Post, she was pushed back outside. Meanwhile, Diane was stomped and punched by Newton and the bodyguard, and finally left with a bleeding lip, swollen jaw, and black eye.

Later that same day, Newton invited Preston Callins, a tailor he had met at the Lamp Post, to come up to the penthouse to measure him for a suit. Newton had begun dressing in a fedora, cape, and tailored suits after seeing the film *The Godfather*. He ordered his suits from a San Francisco men's store. Callins had informed Newton that the same men's store that took his suit orders farmed the job out to Callins. Newton agreed that they should eliminate the middle man. Callins arrived with his samples. Newton, who was drunk, greeted him and showed him around the sparsely furnished penthouse as he sipped cognac. Callins asked for a taste. Newton obliged, then told Callins he would give him a bottle to take home.

When they got down to the business of discussing suits, Newton complained to Callins about how much he had been ripped off in previous deals. Callins made him a better offer. "I can make you a suit for $180 with my material." But by now Newton was drunkenly fixated on the suit Callins was wearing. He told Callins how much he didn't like the suit. "Well, I didn't bring this suit over here for you to like," Callins replied. Then he tried to show Newton some samples. Newton went on and on about how much he had been ripped off in previous deals. Then Callins, who had a habit of calling friends and relatives "baby" made the mistake that Kathleen Smith had made; he answered Newton with "Oh, don't feel that way, baby!"

Suddenly, Newton's mood changed. "Nobody calls me no damn baby!" he told Callins. They were sitting in the dining area with another man who Callins thought was Newton's brother-in-law or uncle. Newton got up from the dining table and went into another room. Callins remained and continued talking to the other man. Newton returned to the room with a .357 magnum, walked up to where Callins was seated, and suddenly whacked him across the head with the pistol. Blood shot everywhere. Newton whacked Callins on the other side of his head. Then he told Callins he was going to shoot him.

"Aw, man!" Callins cried out. "Why you gonna invite me to your house and start some stuff for nothing!?!? What's wrong with you?"

"Uh, uh, man," Newton replied. "You called me a baby and I don't like you no way. You're a little bit yellower than I am. I don't like you." He hit Callins again. Then he hit him again, knocking him to the floor. Then he kicked Callins in the mouth. By then Callins had decided he had had enough. He got up and hit Newton in the mouth, knocking him against the wall.

Bleeding profusely, Callins managed to stumble out of the penthouse into the hallway. Newton followed him, this time with a new gun, because the grips of the first gun had broken on Callins's skull. Callins tried to hide from Newton in a small corner of the hallway, but Newton found him. Forcing Callins back into the penthouse, he told Callins he would kill him. Callins was bleeding so profusely that he fell on the floor. There was blood in the hallway, blood all over Newton's apartment. Callins begged the other man present to do something about the way Newton was treating him. The other man did his best to calm Newton. Newton called two bodyguards to come to the penthouse. Then he beat Callins again, brought out a tape recorder, and tried to force Callins to make a false statement to the effect that Callins had tried to molest him. Callins denied it, and with each denial Newton slapped him. Then the bodyguards brought the car from a garage. Callins was given his sample case and the bottle of cognac Newton promised him. The bodyguards put newspaper all over the seat where Callins was to sit, so that he wouldn't bleed all over the car, and drove him home. As Callins made it to his door, he fainted. His wife called an ambulance and the police. At the hospital, Callins was diagnosed as having four depressed skull fractures, requiring neurosurgery.

After his arrest for the pistol whipping of Callins, Newton posted $42,000 bail on August 17. He was immediately arrested again and charged with shooting Kathleen Smith. He was released on posting a second bail of $80,000. By then, Newton's family and friends decided there was only one alternative to his mounting troubles. He jumped bail and went to Cuba. His lawyers and closest Hollywood friends got together and had Newton and his principal companion, Gwen Fontaine (who became his wife), spirited through Mexico to the Caribbean coastline. From there, they boarded a yacht. When they reached the border of the international water limit and the waters of Cuba, Huey and Gwen were placed in a rowboat to row the remainder of the way. But the boat capsized just before they made it. Huey could not swim. Gwen saved his life. They made it to the shoreline. The two were granted asylum by the Cuban government under the condition that Newton would keep his nose clean while living in Cuba.

12

Keepers of the Lair

CHARLES GARRY HELD A PRESS CONFERENCE TO PUT THE BEST face on the disappearance of Huey Newton. He told the gathering that Newton had escaped Oakland in flight from pimps who had taken a $10,000 contract out on his life. Garry played a recording of Oakland police chief Charles Gain calling Newton to warn him of the contract (an interesting courtesy on Gain's part, given the contempt he had voiced for the Panthers in 1968). Through careful editing, Garry gave reporters the impression that the contract was taken out because Newton was trying to stamp out the pimps' activities. In reality, the call warning Newton of the contract had been made approximately one year earlier. And the pimps wanted to kill Newton not because he was trying to stamp out prostitution but because his extortion demands were squeezing their operations too much.

With Newton gone, leadership of the Black Panthers was turned over to the new party chairman, Elaine Brown. Brown was extremely smart and attractive—and, as both Mae Jackson and Elaine Wenders had discovered, quite vicious. In fact, as soon as Huey left and Elaine was named to head the party in his absence, everyone who worked with David Horowitz on the Planning Committee of the Oakland Community Learning Center, except Ericka Huggins, left the party. They described Elaine as a crazy woman.

Despite her reputation, on taking the helm Brown ushered in the greatest advances the party ever made among the Oakland establishment. She convinced Superior Court judge Lionel Wilson to serve on the board of the Educational Opportunities Corporation. She convinced the head of the Oakland Economic Development Council to serve as well. Brown upgraded the appearance of the school and began holding teen dances there too, for the community of East Oakland. Virtually all the concrete programs of the party, except the newspaper, were now run by party women. But the clandestine affairs of the party, the preserve of Huey's elite squad of enforcers, also continued. The truth was that Huey was really still running the party from Cuba. He kept in close contact with Brown, sometimes on a daily basis. Their conversations were monitored by the CIA. He was visited in Cuba by Brown, close friends, and his attorneys. Huey's elite squad obeyed Brown because Huey insisted on it. And Brown gave one member, Larry Henson, added incentive by becoming his lover and renting him an apartment near Oakland's Lake Merritt. Brown herself began tooling around the city smartly dressed and driving a red Mercedes.

Yet the defection of important party members who feared Elaine Brown continued. When party treasurer Gwen Goodloe left, many in the party went into an even greater panic. Shortly after, at the end of October, an incident occurred at the learning center during the second community dance. Four young Black Panthers were shot by members of a rival gang. Allegedly, the shooting was drug related.* One of the Panthers died. Elaine Brown held a press conference to explain the shooting. She called

---

*Panther veteran Flores Forbes, who was present at the dance, vehemently denies the allegation that drugs were involved in the incident, and states that it is ludicrous for anyone to believe the party would deal drugs in the same place it sent its children to school, no matter how sordid the party's underground activities were alleged to have been. He asserts that the incident was simply an argument between youths at the dance, with no Panther connection. Panther security was unarmed, choosing not to carry firearms around kids. The youths involved were obviously armed.

the incident an unfortunate case of the police or police agents conspiring to discredit the Black Panthers by setting up shooting incidents "to make the Party look like hookers and gangsters." The truth was, Brown's tenure as Panther leader would feature not only improved community and political relations, but a continuation of Panther clandestine activities and the violence that went along with it.

David Horowitz asked Betty Van Patter, an employee of his who did *Ramparts* bookkeeping, if she would like to replace Gwen Goodloe, keeping the Panther books. Van Patter was delighted at the opportunity to work with the Panthers, whom she admired. Horowitz warned her that she might discover activities that were questionable, and not to look too closely. However, Van Patter became scrupulously involved in her Panther bookkeeping. Doing a good job was a matter of pride for her. Like any good bookkeeper, she inquired about all aspects of the party finances she was charged with tracking. And that allegedly irritated Elaine Brown, although for some reason she still requested that Van Patter manage her next bid for the Oakland City Council that following spring.

Within months Betty had fallen out with Elaine. On a Friday night in early December, Van Patter was last seen alive at the Berkeley Square, a bar she frequented. Several witnesses saw a man approach her and hand her a note. She appeared to know him. And she abruptly got up and followed him out of the bar. Later people said that Van Patter enjoyed liaisons with questionable men. But her being handed a note and following someone out of a bar had all the markings of being summoned by an organization.

When Van Patter didn't show up at home the following Monday, her eighteen-year-old daughter, Tammy, called David Horowitz, who in turn called Elaine Brown, who immediately badmouthed Van Patter. She said Van Patter was stupid and wanted to know too much about the party's affairs. She stated that Van Patter had worked for a company with ties to the CIA. She asked Horowitz why he appeared more concerned with the fate of Van Patter, who was white, than with all the black men who were gunned down by police that no one cared about. When Van Patter was still missing a week later, Horowitz again called Brown.

According to Horowitz, Brown issued a thinly veiled threat to let him know he should stop probing: "If you were run over by a car or something, David, I would be very upset because people would say I did it." This was the final outrage for Horowitz, who from then on had nothing more to do with the party.

By that time, Berkeley police were convinced that the Panthers had taken Van Patter hostage and probably killed her. But they professed that their hands were tied. Five weeks later Van Patter's waterlogged body washed up on the western shore of San Francisco Bay. Her head had been caved in by a blunt instrument. It was estimated that she had been in the water for seventeen days. When questioned by police after the body was discovered, Elaine Brown told them she had fired Van Patter as a bookkeeper the week before her disappearance, although a Panther associate contradicted that claim. (In *A Taste of Power*, Brown states that Van Patter had a criminal record. There is no evidence that Van Patter ever had a criminal record.) Brown heard no further questions from the police, although some supporters nervously had second thoughts about her city council bid.

Yet she continued sewing up support for her campaign. A few members of the same black Oakland establishment that opposed the Panthers during the Cal-Pak boycott readily aided Brown during her city council race against the same Ray Eng who had been representing, among others, West Oaklanders who never saw him. Those particular individuals and groups may have been aware of the alleged negative activities of the Panthers, but they were integral Brown supporters. Otto Green, who had been a key participant in the Ad Hoc Committee to Preserve Black Business in Oakland during the Cal-Pak boycott, and was considered a moderate when he ran for mayor in 1973 against Seale and incumbent John Reading, served as Brown's campaign finance chairman. Her campaign manager was a woman named Beth Meader, who also sat on the executive advisory committee of Congressman Ron Dellums. Respected black attorney John George, who also headed a Democratic Club called the Mule Skinners, served as her campaign cochairman. She received the endorsement of Dellums as well as of an organization called the Black Women Organized for Action.

One very strategic member of the party (who requested anonymity) described the Panthers' relationship with a large share of Oakland's establishment during the Brown era as something out of a scene in *The Godfather:* "They knew all about our clandestine activities. We had politicians, judges, police, respected businessmen in our pockets. There were members of the police force who would call us up and tell us when someone in the department was going to move on us."

This might explain why so many of the violent activities in that same period of time believed to have been committed by Newton's elite squad went unsolved. According to Berkeley and Oakland police, the squad increased its extortion demands from pimps, drug dealers, and after-hours clubs. Just a week after Newton went into exile, a carload of men pulled up to the door of an after-hours club called the Brass Rail and opened fire, killing the nineteen-year-old doorman and wounding several customers. The club's owner had reportedly balked at squad extortion demands, which by that time had increased to as much as $500 per week, depending on what the squad determined to be your ability to pay. In January 1975, when a twenty-four-year-old heroin dealer named Willie Duke reportedly missed a payment because he had squandered his money gambling, the squad executed him. Duke was sitting with squad members inside the Brass Rail. A friend of Duke asked him to step outside, apparently to warn him that he was going to be killed. When Duke got up, witnesses said the three Panthers he had been sitting with opened fire. The friend was shot and killed as well. Months later, Wilfred La Tour, owner of the Brass Rail, was also murdered. His body was found stuffed in a sleeping bag in the trunk of his car, which had been left in the parking garage of the San Francisco International Airport. That same spring another drug dealer known as Preacherman was gunned down, allegedly because he had argued with squad members at the Lamp Post, when he refused to buy a party newspaper and commented, "The Panthers rip people off." But police investigators also believed that he was making extortion payments to the squad.

Meanwhile, Brown lost her council election bid, although she received 44 percent of the vote. And her clout in establishment

circles only increased. Brown took advantage of her connection to
Tony Kline, a Panther lawyer who had been a law school room-
mate of Governor Jerry Brown's and was now his legal affairs
secretary. She attended the 1976 Democratic National Convention
as a delegate for Jerry Brown, who was seeking the presidential
nomination. That November Elaine Brown marshaled Panthers to
help elect John George, an Alameda County supervisor from the
fifth supervisory district. The party provided sixty of his get-out-
the-vote workers. After George's election he placed Brown, as well
as party member Phyllis Jackson, on his executive committee. Party
member Joan Kelly was named to the Alameda County Juvenile
Delinquency Prevention Committee. Another Panther was placed
on George's health advisory committee. That same year Brown
used her clout with the governor to get him to complete an extension of the Grove-Shafer freeway, which the governor told Oakland's powerful white businessmen would occur only if Elaine
Brown was appointed to the powerful fifteen-member Oakland
Council for Economic Development (OCED), composed of the
city's key business leaders, and other powerful corporate concerns.
OCED was in the process of negotiating the development of City
Center, which was to have a major department store, hotel, and
skyscrapers, but would become a reality only if the proposed free-
way extension was built. Brown received appointment to the
OCED and negotiated for control of 10,000 city jobs.

Then in the spring of 1977 she marshaled all the Panther
forces to elect Superior Court judge Lionel Wilson the first black
mayor of Oakland. Brown and Wilson had been in alliance with
each other for quite some time before the mayoral election, with
Wilson providing some of the heaviest pressure to get her appointed to the OCED. The party registered thousands of new
voters. On election day it provided most of Wilson's get-out-the-
vote workers, literally pulling the poorest Oakland residents away
from whatever they were doing to vote him into office. The positive half of the double-edged Panther sword came through like it
never had before. Brown obtained an array of contributions and
grants for the Oakland Community Learning Center. Key party
members were placed on Wilson's staff, as well as municipal com-

missions. But the run of legitimate aboveground Panther power came to an abrupt end only months after Wilson's election. The cause was Huey Newton's return from exile in Cuba that July.

Newton had been impatient with life in Cuba. With the election of Lionel Wilson as Oakland's mayor, and the resultant unprecedented Panther clout, Newton felt sure he could beat charges of murdering Kathleen Smith and pistol-whipping Preston Callins. Before returning to the United States, he had to go through Canada and apply for reentry (Communist Cuba had no diplomatic relations with the United States). When he arrived at San Francisco International Airport on July 3, he alighted from the plane to a hero's welcome of hundreds of supporters and an adoring press.

Supervisor John George hailed the return of Newton as a positive development. "The Panthers . . . [have] taken responsible positions . . . and they have gone into what they were originally founded for, organizing the black community for survival." Playing to the public, Newton contended that the three charges he faced—the murder of Kathleen Smith, assault on police officers at the Fox Lounge, and the pistol-whipping of Preston Callins—were part of a government frame-up involving the FBI, CIA, and Oakland police. The party had already filed a $100 million lawsuit in December against the FBI, charging it with counterintelligence efforts to destroy the party, beginning in 1967 (the Panthers eventually lost the lawsuit). Newton was remaindered to jail until the Panthers could raise the $80,000 bail money required for his release. Part of the bail money came from the sale of bumper stickers reading "Justice for Huey."

On July 23 he emerged from prison to a lovely two-story, natural-wood home purchased for him by his wealthy benefactors (although it was deeded to the Educational Opportunities Corporation). The house was located in the Oakland hills, in the wealthy community of Montclair. Days later, the Oakland Community Learning Center received a commendation from California assemblymen Tom Bates and John Miller for its work with underprivileged children. But one condition for the learning center receiving the award at a ceremony at the state capitol was that Huey not show up. Newton was still far too controversial. The award proved how successfully the Panthers had made inroads while he was away. Newton showed up in Sacramento anyway, to the consternation and embarrassment of Assemblyman Tom Bates, the award's presenter.

While he began to prepare for his trial, Newton focused his attention on another ambition as well. He told Fred Hiestand that he wanted to go back to school for his Ph.D., explaining, "From the time you're young, black people will say you've got to get your education. Your degree is your ticket. If you've got your degree it can open all kinds of doors. I want to find out if that's true." He had already been awarded his bachelor's degree in politics and education from UC Santa Cruz in 1974. Now that he was back from Cuba, he decided to enroll again at UC Santa Cruz, in the Ph.D. program The History of Consciousness. The side of Newton that relished respectability was never more evident.

But the side that relished dominating the Oakland underworld prevailed again too. High on coke, hooking up with members of his elite squad, Newton began prowling the after-hours clubs again, intimidating owners and customers, taking their money and drugs, beating up men, taking their women. He also fielded the complaints of the squad about Elaine. The anger of squad members was due partly to the fact that a woman had been left in the leadership position. By that time Larry Henson and Elaine had fallen out. And tensions were building. Newton was torn between his desire to pursue his education, having nothing really to do with the operation of the party, and the temptation to take back control per the insistence of his squad members.

He was also dealing with his legal problems in the manner one would expect of someone who relished life in the underworld. Charges against him in the July 30, 1974, Fox Lounge incident and the beating of Diane Washington at the Lamp Post were reduced to a misdemeanor. At the preliminary hearing that fall on charges of pistol-whipping and beating Preston Callins, Callins suddenly stated that he couldn't remember who hit him. It turned out that Newton had threatened Callins, then paid him $6,000 to drop the charges. And as for the charges of killing Kathleen Smith, the party had a particularly frightening plan in mind for Crystal Gray, who was to be the star witness against Newton.

On October 9, 1977, Alameda County deputy district attorney Tom Orloff, who was prosecuting the Kathleen Smith case, was ordered by the municipal court to give Newton's attorney,* the Richmond, California, address of Crystal Gray, so that the defense could prepare for the October 24 preliminary hearing in the case. In the early-morning hours the day before the preliminary hearing, Mrs. Mary Matthews, Gray's landlord, was awake and sitting in her living room, because she couldn't sleep. Matthews lived in a house directly in front of the apartment she rented to Gray. Both her address and that of Gray were on the front of the house. Matthews heard someone knock on her front door. She asked who was there. There was no answer. Shortly after, she heard someone at the back door. It sounded as though they were tearing the door apart. The fifty-six-year-old Matthews ran into her bedroom and grabbed a .38 caliber handgun. Then she telephoned the Richmond police to report that someone was trying to break in. While still on the phone, she heard a loud blast. She dropped the phone, ran into the hallway, and fired two shots at the back door. The intruders returned fire. Mary Matthews ran back into her bedroom and hid behind a chair until she heard police sirens.

When the police arrived, they discovered a man lying on Matthews's front lawn, dead. He was later identified as Louis T. Johnson, a member of the Black Panther Party. He had suffered a neck wound that ricocheted and fatally damaged internal organs. He was wearing overalls, black leather gloves, and a ski mask pulled over his face. Blood smudges near his body leading from the alleyway next to the house suggested he had been dragged to the spot. In the alleyway, officers found an M-16 rifle, two additional pairs of gloves (one glove with a hole in it, and covered with blood), and two additional pairs of overalls, everything, of course, suggest-

---

*Sheldon Otis was the first attorney Newton hired to handle his case; he would later hire attorneys Michael Kennedy and Tony Serra to defend him.

ing that Johnson had accomplices who escaped the scene. Outside the rear door was a large pool of blood and a 12-gauge pump action shotgun, along with two expended shells and four expended rounds from an M-16 rifle. The door had a large hole in it caused by a shotgun blast. Johnson and his accomplices had panicked when Matthews fired her gun. Not only had they mistakenly gone to the home of Mary Matthews in their goal of killing Crystal Gray, but autopsy of Johnson's body revealed that the blast that killed him had come, accidentally, from the M-16 rifle fired by one of Johnson's accomplices.

The following day Panther party member Flores Forbes went to the emergency room of Provident Hospital, seeking treatment for a wound to his right hand consistent with the hole in the torn, bloody glove found next to the Matthews residence. He said the wound was sustained in an accident with a rivet gun. But the emergency room doctor knew a gunshot wound when he saw one. He told Forbes the wound would have to be reported to the police. Louis Johnson's accomplice in the botched murder attempt fled the hospital.

He and Nelson Malloy, a Panther paramedic who worked in the party's Berkeley free clinic (and who had wrapped the wounded hand in a music book for a splint), were taken to the airport the following day by another party member. They boarded a Western Airlines flight to Las Vegas. They were met there by another party member. Forbes was treated for his gunshot wound in a Las Vegas hospital under the assumed name James Johnson. Malloy checked into a Las Vegas motel. Several days later he was met at the motel by the same party member who drove him and Forbes to the airport in Oakland, as well as the one who met the two of them in Las Vegas. They told Malloy they had orders to drive him to Houston, Texas, so that he could avoid police questioning. They rented a van, and Malloy hopped in with them for the trip to Houston. About forty-five minutes outside Las Vegas they stopped for an alleged rest break. Malloy was standing next to the van when suddenly the two other party members pulled pistols and shot him in the back and the left arm. Malloy fell to the ground. The two other Panthers dragged him off from the side of the road and piled rocks on top of him, leaving him to die. Malloy was saved only because two tourists in the Nevada desert heard his groans and noticed his feet sticking out of a pile of rocks. They took a Polaroid shot of the spot and gave it to Nevada rangers, who rushed to the site and saved Malloy's life. Malloy was permanently paralyzed from the neck down.

Days earlier, Huey Newton had met with two reporters and denied official Panther involvement in the botched attempt on Crystal Gray's life. He insisted that the gunmen involved had quit the party before the attack and speculated that they attempted to kill Gray on their own, out of their own individual desires to protect him. And then Nelson Malloy was discovered. At first the frightened Malloy gave Nevada rangers a fake name. He did the same when Las Vegas police questioned him at the hospital. He insisted that he had been robbed and shot while hitchhiking. But days later he told the truth. The attempted murder of Malloy was an apparent "house cleaning" effort by the party, to prevent it from being connected with the botched attempt on Crystal Gray's life. Flores Forbes, who was treated earlier at a Las Vegas hospital, was assumed dead for the same reason Malloy was shot and left for dead. But three years later he would surface, stand trial, and be convicted for his part in the botched attempt on Gray's life, as well as the accidental murder of his accomplice Louis Johnson.* The third accomplice was never found.

After Malloy told his story, support for the Black Panther Party took a rapid nosedive. No longer could the party hide its clandestine activities from the general public, insisting that every-

---

*Forbes turned himself in after calling his brother and learning that their father had died of a heart attack. Flores's family assumed he was dead, and Flores himself felt that his Panther notoriety was largely the cause of his father's death. Upon emerging from Soledad prison in 1985, Forbes would make perhaps the most dramatic turnaround of any Panther veteran. He graduated from college and graduate school in urban planning, with honors. He then became a public policy analyst for a New York City think tank. Today, nearly seventeen years after the Richmond incident, he is a consultant to a New York City neighborhood housing project and a successful film producer.

thing sinister it was accused of was part of some government frame-up. Shortly before the botched attempt on Crystal Gray, Malloy had arrived in the Bay Area from North Carolina, where he was a member of the party's Winston-Salem chapter until it disbanded. Coverage of the paralyzed Malloy being returned from Las Vegas to his Winston-Salem hometown under heavy police protection further devastated the party's image in the public's eyes. Just a couple of weeks before the Malloy flight home, Elaine Brown announced that she had left the party for good.

Brown was said to be furious at the negative publicity that the botched attempt on Crystal Gray's life brought on the party. She was also said to be angered by Newton's attempt to redirect party funds from other sources to his legal defense efforts. In *A Taste of Power*, Brown gives other reasons for her departure. She writes that troubles between herself and Newton after his return from Cuba were due to a number of issues, one having to do with Panther males—like members of the squad—who were angry about her continued tenure running party affairs while Newton attended school and prepared for the Smith trial. Another had to do with Newton bodyguard Robert Heard being arrested one night after leaving the Lamp Post, drunk, unnecessarily armed, with a confiscated bottle of alcohol, and assaulting Oakland police officers assigned to surveillance of the Lamp Post. Brown writes that in her two and a half years at the party's helm, not one person was allowed to violate party rules as Heard had done. She writes that Newton insisted Heard be bailed out of jail, which she okayed reluctantly. The culminating issue, Brown writes, was the severe beating (with Newton's okay) of Ericka Huggins's assistant at the Panther school, Donna Howell, who had verbally reprimanded a male party member because he did not obey an order she gave. Howell was said to have added insult to injury by complaining that the women in the party did the work, while the men did nothing.

Declining to give an exact date, Brown writes that she left the party in the middle of the night, before a scheduled meeting of the puppet Central Committee the following day, where all the brewing disputes between Panther men and women were to be addressed.* But others familiar with party affairs insist she left after a dramatic confrontation with Newton in which she was severely beaten. Alleges Landon Williams, "Huey damn near beat her to death. . . . She denies it, but if you check up at Alta Bates Hospital you'll see how she had a fractured jaw, all kinds of contusions. . . ." Alta Bates Hospital doesn't keep records of one-time admissions to the hospital dating as far back as 1977 (as opposed to those admitted more than once in a given year). But similar allegations that Brown was severely beaten were reported to police. They were also reported in the press, and confirmed by a Panther physician.

Not long after the botched attempt on Crystal Gray's life, Landon Williams severed even the peripheral ties to the Black Panther party he had maintained since returning from prison in 1971. Williams's brother had been released from prison a week before the botched attempt on Gray's life. They both severed all ties with the party. Landon had received his bachelor's degree in economics from UC Berkeley in 1975, and would receive his master's in public policy from UC Berkeley in the spring of 1978.

The avalanche of negative party publicity caused the same public officials who had praised the Panthers, and who owed the advancement of their careers largely to the Elaine Brown era, to distance themselves from the party as well. Mayor Lionel Wilson resigned from the board of the Educational Opportunities Corporation, which ran the Panther's Oakland Community Learning Center. Investigations began into the use of federal, state, and municipal funds provided to the EOC. It was learned that members of Newton's elite squad, including Flores Forbes, Larry Henson, Robert Heard, and others, were on the payroll of a Youth Delinquency Prevention Program contracted to EOC that received a $110,000 federal grant. An audit revealed that EOC failed to comply with proper hiring and accounting procedures. Improper

---

*According to Flores Forbes, one of those brewing issues involved dating. The party had a policy that forbade party women from dating nonmembers, yet did not forbid party men from dating women outside the party. This was allegedly for security reasons, yet women in the party were fed up, and the issue came to a head at the Central Committee meeting.

procedures were also charged in the administration of two other grants to EOC, one of which was used to pay for apartments for Newton bodyguards Larry Henson and Bob Heard. After the improprieties were reported by *Oakland Tribune* reporters Pearl Stewart and Lance Williams, Stewart's car was "mysteriously" fire-bombed. (That Stewart was specifically targeted for the action was no surprise, because the previous November she had also written an article for the *Tribune* speculating that, given how the assassins dressed and the weapons they carried, the Panthers had tried to make their attempted murder of Crystal Gray look like an operation carried out by military hitmen sent by the government).

After the attempted murders, discovery of the improprieties, and departure of Elaine Brown, Panthers who had gained municipal and county appointments because of the party's aid in electing politicians like Lionel Wilson and John George lost their posts. EOC administrator Phyllis Jackson left town and resigned her appointment to the Oakland Civil Service Commission. After being sentenced to five days in jail for refusing to testify against Huey during his preliminary hearing in the Kathleen Smith murder case, party benefactor and Oakland Community Learning Center instructor Mary Ireland "Molly" Dougherty was removed from a county committee post she occupied. By the spring of 1978, only a handful of competent party members remained (such as Ericka Huggins, who continued running the Oakland Community Learning Center, and JoNina Abroun, who ran the party newspaper after the departure of Michael Fultz, who had replaced David Du Bois as editor). And the increasingly dim view of the party in the eyes of the public only accelerated when an investigative article titled "The Party's Over," written by journalist Kate Coleman with the assistance of Paul Avery, appeared in the July 10, 1978, issue of *New Times* magazine, detailing murders, extortions, and beatings by Newton and his elite squad of enforcers.

Newton attacked the Coleman-Avery piece, accusing the authors of relying too heavily on police accounts. (The article, in fact, did not rely as heavily on police accounts as it appeared. Many of Coleman's and Avery's other sources requested anonymity out of fear of reprisals by Newton, creating a situation where police sources were disproportionately attributed.) He stated his intention of suing *New Times*, Coleman, and Avery for $6.25 million, but the suit never materialized. As usual, Newton's explanation played into the standard party defense that almost all of its negative publicity was due to a well-orchestrated government-directed vendetta against the party.

When "The Party's Over" was published, no one was more disappointed than Huey's old college acquaintance Joe Blum, who had so admired Newton that on the birth of his son in 1969 he had named the boy Huey. After the Coleman piece was published, Blum's nine-year-old stopped using the name Huey, using instead his middle name, David.

As the party continued to constrict, Huey pursued his Ph.D. at UC Santa Cruz and continued preparing for the Kathleen Smith murder trial. He also kept up his coke bingeing, drinking, carousing ways, extending them to the town of Santa Cruz. In May 1978 he and bodyguard Bob Heard were arrested after a brawl in a Santa Cruz bar. Newton was charged with assault with intent to commit murder, assault with intent to commit bodily harm, and illegal gun possession. He was freed from prison on $50,000 bail, and his bail in the Kathleen Smith murder case was increased by an additional $75,000. Charges in Santa Cruz were later dropped. That September, with Preston Callins refusing to press charges in the pistol-whipping case, Newton was convicted only of illegal gun possession, stemming from a police search of his residence when Callins first pressed charges. But Newton didn't have to serve time immediately on that conviction. He was released on $50,000 bond, pending appeal. His trial for the murder of Kathleen Smith would begin the following year.

In between recurrent run-ins with the law, and his carousing, Newton displayed a complex character to his remaining circle of friends and acquaintances. One of his new friends was a Harvard-educated sociobiologist at UC Santa Cruz. Bob Trivors, who was white, had admired the Black Panthers from afar and long demonstrated an affinity for black people dating back to his childhood in suburban Maryland. His father worked for the State Department, and his family employed a black woman to look after Bob when he was very young. To the consternation of his family, Trivors dated only black women and married a woman from Jamaica, with whom he fathered two daughters. So strongly did he identify with black people that he reasoned they should hunt down and kill all the racist murderers of blacks in the South who had gotten off scot-free, in much the same manner that determined Jews (Trivors's father was Jewish), after World War II, hunted down the worst Nazis who had operated the concentration camps. Trivors and Newton became fast friends, with Trivors even joining the Black Panther Party in its last, limp years of operation.

Newton also spent time with Fred Hiestand and his live-in girlfriend. Friends of theirs who met Huey constantly remarked on how wound up he seemed. They observed that he couldn't sit still, that the imagery of the Panther suited him well because he always seemed ready to pounce. Newton not only drank heavily and snorted cocaine but chain-smoked cigarettes. He would light one up, smoke about half an inch of it, light up another one, smoke it down half an inch, and so on. When he sat, his leg usually shook; his eyes would dart around constantly, checking out his surroundings. But those same eyes could just as quickly hone in on an individual and virtually hypnotize her or him. He mesmerized people with his penetrating, long-winded verbiage, and motions that grabbed hold of their visual field. Recalls Bob Trivors, "A lot of people got high off of the energy he had."

It was easy to see why so many party members did whatever Huey demanded of them, including giving up their paychecks, living in cramped quarters, even killing out of a belief that they were fulfilling some greater duty to black America. As part of his studies for his Ph.D., Newton took two reading courses taught by Trivors. One was called Deceit and Self-Deception; the other, The Principals of Underlying Social Evolution. Recalls Trivors of the second course: "He read the stuff and he would point out subtleties in animal literature that had even escaped me. And I'm no slouch in animal literature. Huey was a brilliant guy. He was one of the four or five real geniuses I've met in my lifetime."

Occasionally, he could be quiet and withdrawn. That always

occurred when he was off drugs, drying out after one of his binges. He would fast for about two weeks, remaining in his home in the Oakland hills, eating only sperilina and drinking tea, while he sat up night after night, reading. Or he would go out with friends like Fred Hiestand and his girlfriend. But he couldn't dance. He would joke that unlike other blacks, he had no rhythm. His wife, Gwen, and Hiestand's girlfriend would dance, while Huey and Fred sat and talked. Or everyone else would talk and Huey would remain quiet, then suddenly speak up out of the blue: "You know, American blacks are the strongest, healthiest people in the United States today."

"Why do you say that, Huey?"

"Well, think about it. They came over here in boats as slaves, and the ones who were weak died. Only the strong ones could survive the boat ride. Then they became slaves and they lived in these places with no heat, or plumbing, nothing. They didn't get any medical care. There were rats and all kinds of diseases, and we're still alive."

But when he started doing lines of cocaine, his personality changed dramatically. He became very assertive, aggressive, angry, jumpy. He'd smoke a lot more cigarettes, then want to drink an alcoholic beverage, and the transformation was complete. At that point it was easy to imagine Newton committing the host of shocking atrocities he was accused of, ranting for hours on end at after-hours clubs, beating up men, taking their women. Recalls Hiestand's girlfriend, "I never saw anyone whose personality changed so completely when they were on drugs." During the Smith trials, he wouldn't let his friends go to sleep. He would talk on and on into dawn about the plight of black people, or relate his system of physics: space is dispersed matter and matter is dispersed space. And if someone dozed off, he was insulted: "That's a fine way to treat a friend who's on trial for murder. This could be my last night. . . ." The friend would feel bad, wake back up, and continue listening to him.

But Newton beat the rap for the murder of Kathleen Smith. During the trials one prostitute witness recanted her identification of Newton as the murderer. Crystal Gray admitted to being high on marijuana the night of the shooting, and having vision problems. Both trials resulted in hung juries voting 10 to 2 for acquittal the first time and 11 to 1 for acquittal the second. So Newton got off free. He continued fighting lesser charges against him, while finishing his Ph.D. requirements and experiencing days of brilliant coherence alternating with days in which he was drunk, or hyped up on cocaine.

The 1979–1980 academic term was an eventful one for the campus of UC Santa Cruz. Not all the faculty felt the same way about Huey as Bob Trivors, or another Newton friend on the faculty did. Some felt that the bachelor's degree he was awarded in 1974 was undeserved (although Newton was well read, his papers were written by others whom he dictated to), and that he certainly shouldn't have been admitted to a Ph.D. program, even one with an esoteric interdisciplinary title like The History of Consciousness. While Newton was serious about his desire to gain academic respectability, there were those who insisted that Newton was admitted to the program as a cynical joke.

Given the avant-garde bent of much of the UC Santa Cruz academic schedule, historian Page Smith, creator of the History of Consciousness program, was said to have admitted Newton out of disdain for graduate education—that he regarded admitting Newton as an opportunity to prove its irrelevance. Occasionally, classes were held expressly for Newton. One professor never forgot lecturing to Huey, while his wife, Gwen, filed her nails and his bodyguard Bob Heard dozed off to sleep. Another professor, evaluating Newton's performance, wrote that he was in class not to learn but to state his opinions. But the majority of professors expressed positive views about his academic performance. "He turned out to be a very good student," insisted anthropology professor Triloki Pandey, his Ph.D. adviser, who declared that his thesis was among the top 20 percent that passed muster.

But given the subject of Newton's thesis, the rigor of his

studies was doubtful. Submitting 175 pages titled "War Against the Panthers: A Study of Repression in America" hardly fit the definition of academic objectivity. The thesis relied heavily on FBI and CIA documents that Newton's lawyers were able to obtain in their suit against the federal government's surveillance of the Panthers, as well as on his personal recollections. Nowhere did the thesis mention the host of questionable dealings on the part of Newton and too many members of the party. Describing himself in one passage, Newton self-righteously noted: "These pages do not reflect the personal pain and anguish, the resulting physical and emotional disabilities, as well as the continual financial setbacks the writer has suffered. . . . The participant observer has been shot, ambushed, followed and verbally and physically threatened and abused. His wife and family are under constant surveillance and also have been attacked and threatened. . . . The participant-observer has spent a total of three years (1967–70) in prison, has been arrested numerous times, has spent the last thirteen years in court (an average of two trials per year), and from 1974 to 1977 was in involuntary exile as a protection from physical abuse and death."

Given Newton's notoriety after Kate Coleman's article appeared, and local news about Newton's often wild ways, Huey was a campus attraction. Students signed up for classes it was said he would be enrolled in, including a blind student who, not realizing he had often sat next to Newton during the quarter, blurted out one day in frustration, "When is Huey Newton coming? I enrolled in this class because Huey Newton is supposed to be here." Curiosity reached its zenith that academic year during Newton's oral exam. Orals were always open to the public, and were usually attended by a few close friends of the candidate. But when it was time for Newton's orals, a few thousand people showed up and the exam had to be moved to a campus auditorium. Some regarded Newton's presence on campus as an insult to the academic integrity of the school. So rather than remain silent, as they were supposed to throughout the test, some people shouted disapproving comments. The exam had to be rescheduled in private. Newton passed. And on a bright day in June, he was awarded his Ph.D. During a press conference just before the ceremony, he noted: "My foes have called me bum, hoodlum, criminal. Some have even called me nigger. I imagine now they'll at least have to call me Dr. Nigger."

DAVID HOROWITZ PLAYED A MAJOR ROLE IN KATE COLE-man's article exposing the most shocking secrets of the Black Panthers. Horowitz was one of the many sources Coleman and Avery talked to who requested anonymity out of fear of Newton's wrath. Wracked with guilt over his certainty that Betty Van Patter would still be alive if he hadn't recommended that she keep the Panther books, Horowitz had quietly investigated Panther secrets on his own by contacting the many old Panthers he knew of, uncovering the previously unknown existence of Newton's elite squad and quite a bit else.

By 1980, another tragic death had occurred among white radicals. Just weeks before Huey was awarded his Ph.D., Fay Stender, the woman responsible for unearthing the legal technicality that had secured his release from prison on the Frey conviction in 1970, committed suicide in Hong Kong. Stender was enacting the last chapter of her tangled involvement with the prisoners' rights movement. Convinced that she had something to do with the sabotaging of Jackson's August 1971 escape attempt, a pro-Jackson ex-convict had broken into her home the year before her suicide and shot her five times, paralyzing Stender from the waist down. Stender stayed alive just long enough to testify against her attacker. Her suicide provoked Horowitz and his colleague Peter Collier to write for *New West* magazine a devastating indictment of the entire leftist attachment to the prisoners' rights movement. In the piece Collier and Horowitz mentioned speculation that Huey may have had something to do with sabotaging Jackson's escape attempt. But they mentioned it only in passing. A book by author Jo Durden-Smith, *Who Killed George Jackson*, delved even more deeply into that speculation, noting that Newton benefactor Bert Schneider had been in constant contact with Newton during the escape attempt.

Schneider summoned Horowitz to his Beverly Hills home for

a severe dressing down, during which he told Horowitz that the *New West* article had endangered his life. "But Huey's not as angry as I am," he added. Horowitz decided that he wanted a meeting with Huey, whom he hadn't seen since 1974. Schneider set up the meeting, which took place in North Berkeley at a restaurant called Norman's.

Convinced by then that Huey would murder with no compunction, Horowitz nervously considered his circumstances and his family's as he made his way to the restaurant for his lunch appointment with Huey. Would Huey order his murder? How would his four kids fare if he was killed? During the course of getting to know Newton, Bob Trivors had come to realize "he definitely had aspects of his personality that resembled a Mafia don." Trivors once insulted Newton about his personal lifestyle. "He had a rule, three strikes and you were out," recalls Trivors. "So he warned me when I got the second strike. If you got the third strike and were out, out could mean you were killed, out could mean you were cut off, out could mean you would have to deal with the matter on a far more serious level."

When Horowitz arrived at the Normandy, Huey was already there, very drunk, too drunk to drive home after their luncheon meeting. So he asked Horowitz to drive him back to his Oakland Hills home. Although nervous about what that could mean, Horowitz drove him. When they reached the house, Huey invited him inside. Again Horowitz overcame his nervousness. He entered the nicely appointed two-story home, which contained a huge painting of a black Buddha samurai warrior in the living room, a result of Newton's fascination with Buddhism. As they sat down in the living room, Huey told David about a movie treatment he was working on—it was a contemporary version of the opera *Porgy and Bess*, set in Harlem, designed to star Mick Jagger and Stevie Wonder. Newton said that he had even prepared a treatment for Stevie Wonder in braille. But then he started to gnash his teeth, telling Horowitz that people around Stevie Wonder had turned the singer against him and killed the deal. As he said that, the expression on his face chilled Horowitz.

Then Newton suddenly fell silent. And out of the blue he

began to talk again. He looked at Horowitz and said, "You know, David, Elaine killed Betty." Then he added: "But if you print that, I'll deny it. I'm really sorry about what happened to Betty, but I was in Cuba and it was out of my hands." That Newton would claim such a thing in a display of disloyalty, even though Brown had been gone from the party by that time for nearly three years, surprised Horowitz. Up to that point, although he had no solid proof and Brown herself had denied it, Horowitz had been convinced that Elaine Brown ordered the murder of Betty Van Patter on her own. Now he suspected that Huey too must have had something to do with Betty's murder, and was trying to take the heat off himself by blaming Brown.

When he returned home, Horowitz flipped through his Rolodex and started calling old Panthers—the ones who had been so important to breaking the Kate Coleman story but who had insisted on anonymity. The Panther veterans told him that Huey had indeed remained in control of the party from Cuba. They told him that Betty had indeed been called away from the Berkeley Square bar by a note from an unidentified Black Panther. They alleged that Van Patter was held for a week, during which Huey was contacted and given all the reasons she should be killed. If this scenario was true, then in Huey's eyes, Betty Van Patter had three strikes: she was out, so in the end he gave the order to have her killed.

Increasingly, it became characteristic of Newton to reflect on the ghastly deeds he was responsible for. Coming off a coke binge one day, looking back on his life, he told Bob Trivors, "I feel so guilty!" Bob answered, "You must have a lot to feel guilty about." But he never came straight out and detailed his guilt in any murder. "Huey had a saying," recalls Trivors. "The statute of limitations never runs out on murder. And in the context of our discussion that meant that you can never expect to hear from me an honest account of a murder. And I never did."

There were plenty of generalized references to murder, however. Trivors was once visiting Huey at his Oakland Hills home, and a woman—one of the many groupies who hovered around Newton because he was so handsome and despite (or possibly because of) his notoriety—came by. (Such women habitually approached Newton and flirted with him in public in the most obvious and humiliating manner for his wife, Gwen, as happened one evening when Fred Hiestand, his girlfriend, Huey, and Gwen were having dinner at an upscale Oakland restaurant called the Dock of the Bay. An attractive woman pulled up a chair between Huey and Gwen and started rubbing Huey's leg with her foot while she talked to him. Then, turning to Gwen, she asked her, "Don't you want to go dance or something?") On the night that one more groupie appeared at Huey's Oakland Hills door, Huey simply told her to get out of his face and began slapping her—not hard, but with a back-and-forth action designed to drive her away. But Trivors intervened, forgetting that one simply did not contradict Huey. As they rode in the car afterward, Huey knew that Bob was trying to measure him as a person. In an effort to reassure, he told him, "Don't worry about what happened, Bob. I've killed more men than women."

Although Newton tended to be vague about his murders, he was unabashedly proud of one, although again he didn't go into details. "'The baddest nigger that ever walked' was the phrase he would use with me, because he had killed a white police officer and gotten away with it," remembers Trivors. Officer John Frey was known throughout West Oakland for his extreme brutality toward blacks. "The Panther Party had one of their warning posters with his face on it, ending with the standard FBI warning, 'This man is armed and should be considered extremely dangerous.' It wasn't coincidental that he was dead at the end of the shootout, and the other officer was not."

Describing his idea of revolutionary justice to another friend, Newton detailed the following scenario. A woman in the party, living in Panther-owned housing, once had problems with a man next door who kept taking carnal pleasures with her. The man would enter through a basement window and violate her sexually, at will. She told Newton about the problem, and he had her moved out of the house. But he made it appear that she was still living there, placing two members of his elite squad of enforcers in the house, instructing them to wait in the basement for the neighbor to come through the basement window again. Sure enough, the neighbor arrived. In Newton's eyes, by entering through the window he convicted himself much more effectively than had the Panthers instead knocked on his door and confronted him. Squad members then carried out the justice that Newton ordered: they killed the man.

How Huey Newton could have such a sense of moral outrage, such determination to exact chilling justice, and at the same time himself exhibit the cruelest behavior imaginable, was a mystery. The sexual behavior of the man he ordered killed was certainly not foreign to him. Besides having taken liberties with women in after-hours clubs with the backup of his squad, Newton once described how he had a squad member point a gun to the head of a man while he raped the man's wife. "There are two kinds of rape," Huey explained. "In one version, you simply take a woman's body. In the other, you not only take her body, you try to make her enjoy being raped."

At the dawn of the 1980s, Newton continued alternately to chill friends and acquaintances to the bone, to fascinate them with the quality of his intellect, or to elicit genuine feelings of pity. And he remained respected in some circles. At one point the Palestine Liberation Organization (PLO) was searching for people to visit the West Bank who weren't necessarily elected officials but who had influence over large groups of Americans. The goal was that the Palestinians be presented in a far more favorable light than usual. Someone recommended Huey Newton. Newton, who had a Jewish grandfather, refused to make the trip unless he could tour not only the West Bank but also Israel and Lebanon to see both sides of the Palestinian/Israeli conflict. The PLO agreed to finance the entire tour, which included Newton and an entourage of six others, including Hiestand's girlfriend and two instructors from the Panther school. It was to be one of Newton's last moments of feeling that he was an important leader in the eyes of people outside of black Oakland.

13

Cat in a Corner

As the 1980s settled in, the Black Panther Party started fading into history. Although Kate Coleman's article made a splash when it was published, it didn't completely destroy the legacy of the party among leftists and most black Americans. And although outside financial support for what little remained of the party rapidly fell away, the legacy of the Panthers remained favorable, perhaps out of nostalgia for the strident late 1960s now fading into history. The Black Panthers had been so much a part of that era, when black people, for the first time, told America they were proud of everything they were. The horrific truth of the party's downfall was an open secret among black Oaklanders and party veterans, but most of them insisted on silence (and still do to this day)—something akin to not discussing the state of a relative who has gone to pot, or, sensing that death might occur any day, preparing to recall only the best.

The era of black history spanning the mid-1960s to the early 1970s, characterized by the rise in black militancy, was being prepared for a museum of nostalgia in which the Black Panthers would receive prominent display. Bobby Seale, Eldridge Cleaver, and Huey Newton would be names featured in lights. The PLO hadn't realized when they invited Newton to the Middle East that outside of Oakland he was already being relegated to history and would hardly be the most effective sounding board for changing their image. Case in point was a speech Newton made in 1980 at a black southern college. During the question-and-answer period, a young woman raised her hand, stood up, and said, "I'm surprised you're here. I thought you were dead."

But none of the troika most identified with the party—Newton, Bobby Seale, and Eldridge Cleaver—was yet in his grave. Seale would be said to have simply retired from the party after losing his bid to become mayor of Oakland and heading to the East Coast, where he eventually turned up in Philadelphia working at Temple University and selling barbecue. Eldridge Cleaver had quietly returned to the Bay Area in 1975, not to challenge again for supremacy in the party but to face charges of attempted murder in the 1968 Panther–Oakland police shootout that had left Bobby Hutton dead. Cleaver would serve one year in prison, and then, in a complete about-face from his previous beliefs, explore the ideas of the Reverend Sun Yung Moon's Unification Church, then those of the Mormons.

The ultimate fate of the once-Cleaver-led Black Liberation Army (BLA) was all too predictable. Total disaster resulted from its efforts at violent revolution, efforts that continued throughout the 1970s and turned the lives of members such as Sheeba Haven upside down. The once promising honor graduate of Oakland's Castlemont High, sought-after clothing designer, first operator of the Panthers' George Jackson Free Clinic, was arrested while trying to rob a bank for the BLA on New Year's Day, 1973. She was convicted of attempted robbery and served one year in prison, during which she received formal training as a medical assistant. Since she already had informal training from her days running the Panther free clinic, Haven graduated at the top of her class. Yet on emerging from prison she obtained work as a legal secretary rather than as a medical assistant. She lost that job and next worked as a seamstress, first with a relative and then out of her own home. But that didn't sit too well with her parole officer, who pressured her into accepting a job sewing backpacks. Haven soon quit that job, professing she was being cheated out of her money. Unable to find work, she became so destitute that she was hospitalized for malnutrition. On emerging from the hospital, she started rebuilding her life. She enrolled in junior college, receiving her associate's degree in 1979. In 1980 she began working as a medical assistant in the office of Dr. Tolbert Small, the man who served as the principal physician in the Panther free clinic. (The free clinic was described by one doctor who worked there as the place in the Panther galaxy that "always came last." He stated that funds provided to the clinic by the city of Berkeley were siphoned off for other Panther projects. The Panther free clinic closed in 1980.)

While the process of rebuilding her life was bumpy for Sheeba Haven, it has been smoother for Mary Kennedy. After leaving the Black Panther Party in 1973, she dropped out of political activism altogether and divorced her husband. At first she went on welfare, but soon decided to get off of it. Mary attended the East Bay Skills Center, where in a twenty-eight-week program she learned the welding trade. Then she applied for work at a company in suburban Hayward, California, called Amouron Pipe, where she passed her welding test with an A+ and became the company's first woman welder. Mary eventually took her journeymanship test and became a journeyman pipe welder. Then she ran for a spot on the Grievance Committee of Teamsters Local 70, and won.

Landon Williams's upward trajectory continued to be among the most impressive of former Panthers. After receiving his master's in public policy in 1978 from UC Berkeley, Williams became a state solar-energy officer for a firm called Western Sun, a regional energy conduction center. In that capacity he helped educate organizations on the potential uses of solar energy. In 1982 he became executive assistant to the chairman of Stanford University's Institute of Energy Studies.

The Huey Newton story, however, continued its tragic trajectory. Some aspects of it resemble the tale of a fading beauty queen. Newton was shocked and saddened that the young southern college student thought he was dead, and proud to receive the invitation to tour the Middle East. But fame was the one addiction he both took to and increasingly had problems with. If it wasn't there, he became desperate for recognition; but when he received attention as a leader, he became desperate to be left alone. He need travel no farther than across the bay to San Francisco, where "people really weren't sure who he was," recalls Lianna.* "They remembered him as somebody and they'd see he was very attractive, but sometimes they couldn't place him." Once, while having dinner at the Fairmont Hotel, Newton and his friends were stopped by three people who asked Newton for his autograph. He obliged them. But as the people walked away, one was overheard saying to the others, "Huey Newton! Who's that? I thought he was Johnny Mathis, didn't you?" On another San Francisco outing, Newton appeared at a function where Andrew Young was speaking. As Newton and his entourage left, a janitor walked up to him and said, "Congratulations, Mr. Young, I really liked your talk."

But in Oakland he was still the legend. Accompanied to an after-hours club one night by Fred Hiestand, Newton entered into a debate with the bodyguard of a young member of Oakland's underworld, after which he lectured the young underworld figure: "You should never allow your bodyguard to be drawn into a debate, because then he's no longer useful to you as a bodyguard." Appreciative of the sage advice, the young man asked Huey, "When are you going to call us back together and lead us?" "I'm retired," Huey told him. "But I would be willing to consider a consulting position."

At other times he wondered what all the people who kept coming to him wanted. "He would feel, 'I don't have any more to give,'" recalls Lianna. "'I'm tapped out, guys. I have no more energy. I just want to get high.'" At such moments he wouldn't want to go out on the town at all. "I'm going to get there and people are going to ask, What are you doing, what are you up to?" he would complain. "And I don't have anything to say. And then I feel bad. I feel that I should be doing something. I feel that I should say I'm writing a book, or I'm starting this movement. The truth is, I can't do it anymore, but I feel this pressure from people."

---

*Lianna is the assumed name of a close personal friend of Newton's who requested anonymity.

The last leg propping up the image of Newton and the Black Panthers as a benefit to the black community came tumbling down in 1982. The unraveling began after Ericka Huggins, principal of the Oakland Community Learning Center, finally threw in the towel. Over the years the Black Panther Party had purchased a number of homes through shell organizations and the use of party members' names on deeds. The shell organizations included not only EOC but an entity called Stronghold Link (run by Huey's former right hand, Marty Kenner), which took in income from Huey's books *(To Die for the People, Revolutionary Suicide)* and other Panther enterprises. Many of the homes had been put up as bail for Panther leaders arrested on various charges—Huey in particular. And if bail was jumped, the party simply lost those houses. But in 1981 a number of homes were still owned by the party.

As legitimate funding sources for the party rapidly dried up in the late 1970s and early 1980s, the homes the party still owned, as well as stocks and bonds the Panthers had in a New York brokerage account set up by Newton's Hollywood friends, became the party's only assets other than the school. When extra money was needed, the party sold a house. Allegedly, not enough of the proceeds from those sales, or income from stocks and bonds, was going into the maintenance of the Oakland Community Learning Center. By 1981, Ericka Huggins simply became fed up with the situation. And after a falling-out with Huey over the issue, she resigned as principal of the school.

Huggins's departure left the Oakland Community Learning Center in a difficult situation. The school owed the California State Department of Education fiscal reports on the use of funds it had received from the Office of Child Development and the Office of Child Nutritional Services for the academic years 1980–1981 and 1981–1982. In that two-year period, the school had received a total of $620,000 from those sources. No one but Huggins knew how to properly file the fiscal reports, which required that the school provide enrollment figures accounting for each dollar of funds received. If enrollment fell short of what had been stated when the funds were applied for, the state required the extra funds to be reimbursed. It reached the point where the school was so late in filing the reports that something had to be done to prevent the state itself from coming in and auditing the school.

Bill Schuford, a Chicago teacher and activist who had great respect for the Black Panthers—the kind of image of the party typically held in the minds of progressive black Americans outside the Bay Area—came to Oakland and was introduced to Huey Newton. To Schuford, Newton was a genuine 1960s hero. With the threat of an audit breathing down the neck of the Oakland Community Learning Center, Newton told Schuford he could benefit the party greatly if he took over as school principal and straightened things out. Schuford was only too happy to do so.

On taking over as principal in February 1982, Schuford immediately noticed that several people on the payroll weren't actually working at the school. And when he tried to gather records to support the enrollment figures the school gave the state, he kept coming up short. In addition, money that the state said it had already paid the school was missing. To cover the payroll for the month of March, Schuford obtained a letter of credit from the State Department of Education, assuring the United Bank of California, where the school held its account, that State Department of Education funds were forthcoming to cover the overdraft that would result from meeting the payroll. Based on the letter of credit, the bank issued the funds, but Schuford never saw the check from the state. He kept contacting the state education department, asking about the check. The state kept insisting that it had been issued. Schuford traveled to Sacramento to straighten out the matter and discovered that the state was telling him the truth. So where had the check gone?

On returning to Oakland, Schuford called Newton and asked what had happened to the check. He also asked him about the discrepancy between the school's reported enrollment figures and its actual enrollment. There were discrepancies too between reported figures for indigent students attending the school and the actual numbers of students who were indigent, all resulting in extra money for the school from the state. The check that Schuford had been looking for had been cashed by Newton for personal use.

Newton admitted to Schuford that the school was using fraudulent enrollment figures. He told Schuford, "If you keep fooling around I'm going to end up in jail. So you had better get your black ass out of there before there's trouble between you and me."

Schuford was shocked. The Huey Newton he admired as an icon of the 1960s was misusing money and had threatened him. Right away he decided he would leave. Yet his conscience bothered him so much about what he had uncovered that he decided not only to leave but also to blow the whistle on Huey. He tried contacting state superintendent of schools Wilson Riles, Sr., about the misappropriations, but to no avail. He then contacted the FBI, who contacted the state, recommending that it investigate. The entire process catalyzed the closing of the Panther school and the eventual indictment of Huey Newton on several counts of embezzlement.

By the fall of 1982, most of the remaining Black Panther empire had come tumbling down. There was no more Lamp Post, no more newspaper, no more clinic, no more school. The last of the party members, including Newton's bodyguards and remaining squad members, left too. Then Newton's wife, Gwen, left him, turning up in Chicago, where she remarried. The sole remaining asset of the party was the EOC stock brokerage account with the New York City firm of Tucker, Anthony, and Day, which Newton continued to use illegally to pay his personal expenses. This practice too would come back to haunt him in three years, after the state of California built its embezzlement case against him and garnished the remaining assets of EOC to recover some of the embezzled money.

In the meantime, Newton's downward spiral worsened. He began to spend more and more time drinking and getting high, although he still had moments of intellectualizing. "We'd visit him at his Oakland Hills home, and then the next moment he'd ask us to drop him off on San Pablo Avenue [in Oakland], where he'd try to buy drugs," remembers Lianna of the final visits she had with him, which ended in 1983. "On one trip down there he came back to the car and said, 'Let's go. The guy wasn't home, so I kicked in his window.' You'd go through this really intellectual conversation with him, and then the next thing you know, you're down on San Pablo and he's kicking in windows."

Newton's desperation and recklessness became even more obvious when the state Justice Department began preparing its embezzlement case against him. Bill Schuford informed Justice Department investigator Ron Anderly that Newton conducted school-related business at his Oakland Hills home. So on April 15, 1985, Anderly showed up there with a search warrant. As he and his partner entered the foyer, they walked past a large rendition of the famous photo Newton was said to hate—the 1967 picture of him in beret, sitting in his wicker throne, gun in one hand, spear in the other. And as they searched the premises, they discovered much more than school-related documents. There was a loaded Colt .45 pistol in the bottom desk drawer of the master bedroom. They discovered a 12-gauge shotgun with four rounds of ammunition underneath the bed. They found the cylinder to a .357 magnum along with ammunition to the gun in the bottom dresser drawer of the bedroom. Parts to a 9-mm automatic as well as two 12-gauge shotgun barrels with ammunition to both guns were found in another dresser drawer. But most interesting of all, they found a leather embossed burglary tool kit containing "slim jim" lock picks, key blanks, and assorted tools and files in the basement. Why would Huey Newton need a burglary tool kit?

The answer was suggested the following year. At two o'clock one November morning, Oakland police were called to a home on the 1900 block of Linden Street. When the first officer arrived, he gave chase to a man in blue jeans and tennis shoes, but the man eluded him. When police combed the area, they found two portable radios, two cameras, seven cartons of cigarettes, a pry bar, and several more items on the sidewalk. About ten minutes later, Huey Newton was spotted walking a block away from the scene of the crime, wearing blue jeans and tennis shoes, and "heavily perspiring." Newton was questioned, and a witness fingered him as the burglary suspect. But the officers allowed Newton to leave the scene of the crime, and he was never charged. It was one more

example of Newton's apparent ability to avoid the full consequences of criminal activity.

By that time, animosity between Newton and the Oakland
police had decreased considerably. Many officers appeared to view
him as a piece of Oakland folklore, part of the city and the police
department's storied past. And Newton seemed to relish that role,
making for a relationship that contrasted starkly with what the two
enjoyed in the late 1960s. "When he'd be found in his car driving
on the sidewalk or something, the police would treat him as a
famous person," recalls Bob Trivors. "They'd say, 'Ahhh what do
we have here? The good Mr. Newton.' He showed me how he
would control himself to suck the aggression off of the police. His
body would be soft and yielding. He would try to relax them and
make the thing go smoothly."

One evening, while Huey sat in the Alexis Restaurant in San
Francisco's Fairmont Hotel with Fred Hiestand, drinks were
brought over to the two of them, compliments of two men sitting
at the bar. Huey nodded to the men in gratitude. They came to
the table and introduced themselves. One, who was black, said he
owned a janitorial service, while the other, who was white, said he
was a retiree who used to own a building maintenance company.
Both said they recognized Newton and just wanted to meet him.
The four men talked for about fifteen minutes. After a while Huey
said to the white fellow, "I keep getting a vision of gold when I
look at you. When you go home, is there something metallic in
your doorway?" The guy looked at Huey, reached into his breast
pocket, and pulled out a badge. He was a San Francisco police
detective. "I do think it was coincidental that he happened to be
there," recalls Hiestand. The detective was off duty and apparently
felt that Huey would react negatively if he told Newton his real
profession, thus blowing the opportunity for the two of them to
meet and talk.

Judges and juries kept granting him special dispensations, too.
In June 1986 he was acquitted of illegal gun possession, resulting
from Anderly's search of his home the previous year. His new wife,
Fredericka (whom he married in the fall of 1984), stated that the

two assembled guns that were found were there for her protection during a temporary separation between the two. And the trial judge ruled that the shotgun and the gun barrels also discovered were inadmissible as evidence. "The . . . guy's led a charmed life," commented state deputy attorney general Charles Kirk. "He keeps evading accountability. It's certainly disappointing."

Yet with all the charges he faced on various crimes, Newton did eventually have to serve prison time. In March 1987 he was ordered back to prison, after the appeals process on his 1978 conviction for illegal gun possession in the pistol whipping of Preston Callins finally ran its course. As usual, he claimed that conviction on the charge stemmed from continuing attempts by the government to "get him" for past radical activity: "Everything I represent they oppose, and everything I oppose they represent." But his stay was short. After serving a few months in jail, he was back on the streets, out on parole, continuing his life of desperation in Oakland's increasingly steamy underside.

After Lionel Wilson was elected Oakland's first black mayor in 1977 thanks to considerable Panther influence, things changed both for better and for worse among the city's black citizenry. By the mid-1980s not only was the mayor black, the city manager was black too, as was the city's director of economic development, the owner of the daily newspaper, and five of the nine members of the city council. The one municipal sector where things hadn't changed as much as hoped was the police department. Police chief Charles Gain, who had shown a willingness to do something about the police brutality in the department after being pressured by both the black community and Panther publicity, was replaced in 1973 by another white chief, George Hart, because of rebellion within the ranks. Although a majority of Oakland's citizens were nonwhite, the police force was still predominantly white (60 percent), with blacks making up 23 percent of the force (compared with 47 percent of the general population). Oakland's economy was still controlled by powerful white businessmen like the heads of Kaiser Industries, Clorox, and Safeway. But black political clout was forging a method for blacks to gain a legitimate piece of the economic pie with regard to contracts between the city and private industry.

By 1982 the commission controlling Oakland's impressive port had established a policy requiring partial minority ownership of any project developed at the port. And white businessmen began dealing with black businessmen who were in a position to take advantage of those new rules.

Among major American cities, Oakland enjoyed the distinction of being the most racially integrated. While blacks made up the largest single segment of the population, the city also harbored large Latino and Asian populations. And although the percentage of white citizens had declined over the years, whites weren't completely abandoning Oakland the way they were abandoning cities like Detroit, Gary, and Newark. Compared with most other U.S. cities with large black populations, something in Oakland seemed to work.

One aspect of life in Oakland was an eyesore, however. The poor were becoming worse off. In 1980, a full 20 percent of Oakland's population lived below the poverty line. And the new Reagan administration in Washington didn't help matters. Consequently, Oakland depended more and more on private industry to help solve its economic problems. In 1984 the city considered passing an ordinance requiring that businesses receiving generous discounts to develop city-owned property as well as tax breaks give priority to Oaklanders when hiring. The idea sparked tremendous debate. Every one of Oakland's most powerful heads of business and industry opposed it, as did a good many influential black Oaklanders. They reasoned that if Oakland were to pass such an ordinance, not only might Oakland be less attractive to businesses, but surrounding Bay Area cities and towns might pass similar ordinances, making it impossible for Oakland residents to obtain employment elsewhere in the Bay Area. A major factor in Oakland's success up to that point in attracting businesses to projects like City Center was its pro-business attitude, which was in stark contrast to the attitude prevailing in its far more glamorous cross-bay rival. Surrounding cities and suburbs in the Bay Area were eager to pick off frustrated businesses opting out of expensive, tax-heavy, left-leaning San Francisco. And because Oakland was seen as the Bay Area's black city, it had to lean over backward to make concessions to companies that otherwise would locate in heavily white suburbs. So the ordinance was defeated.

Consequently, companies could easily move into Oakland, deal only with the handful of black businesses in a position to take advantage of minority joint venture requirements (a small price to pay for cheap land and lower taxes), and hire only blacks who possessed the education to compete for skilled jobs. Poor blacks were left out in the cold. Unskilled manufacturing positions were being replaced by machines. Those that remained were being moved to countries where labor was cheaper. Longshoremen's jobs were being eliminated through automation, with remaining positions requiring greater and greater skills. Thus, greater black political clout in Oakland created an increasingly prosperous black middle class while an increasingly destitute black underclass emerged in the flatlands of the city where the Panthers once had recruited members. Only one economic activity grew rapidly in the poor areas of the city.

By the mid-1980s, the Oakland flatlands were the largest open drug market in the Bay Area. Sales proliferated in East and West Oakland. Suburbanites as well as residents of the flatlands became eager customers. No more than three blocks from the Oakland Coliseum, where the Oakland Athletics played baseball and the Oakland Raiders played football, a person could buy practically anything he or she wanted, twenty-four hours a day, without police interference. Drugs were openly dealt from as many as fifty flatlands street corners. The feeding frenzy encouraged by the lucrative trade eventually precipitated turf wars among the dealers. By the mid-1980s, drug-related murders had skyrocketed to an average of one every two weeks. The murder rate in Oakland placed it among the ten most violent cities in America. Four percent of Oakland's population was said to be drug addicted.

The drug-dealing gangs of the late 1980s were a legacy of the underworld apparatus that the Black Panthers had dominated at one point, an apparatus that by the end of the 1970s had developed some of the best-organized, richest, most powerful drug lords in America. In the days when Huey's legendary squad intimidated after-hours clubs and drug dealers into paying protection money, heroin was king. One dealer in particular made a name for himself; by the end of the 1970s, Felix Mitchell reigned supreme. He started selling marijuana and speed in San Antonio Village, the East Oakland housing project where he grew up on 69th Avenue. Then he made a Los Angeles connection for Mexican brown heroin, and his drug-dealing empire took off. He named his outfit the 69 Mob. By 1977 the 69 Mob was returning the gunfire and intimidation of Newton's squad. "Those are Huey's people," Mitchell said, on spotting Panther squad members just before a gun attack. "Get them!" Another encounter left an innocent man dead after the Mob opened fire, mistaking his van for one owned by the Panthers. On the decline of Newton and the Black Panthers, Mitchell's 69 Mob became the most feared outfit in the city. Its drug-dealing turf encompassed almost all of East and West Oakland.

The 69 Mob used black kids of the flatlands as lookouts and packed weapons as sophisticated as those carried by the Panthers in their heyday. Mob workers carried walkie-talkies, and took over entire housing projects from which to sell drugs in a sophisticated system: the addict would line up, face a wall, drop money into a hole, and see the drugs dropped at his or her feet. Like Newton's in his heyday, Mitchell's legend took on a dual aspect. On the one hand, he petrified subordinates and rivals with his willingness to order the grisly murder of anyone who threatened his hegemony. Yet, on the other hand, he enjoyed an admiration and respect from many people in the projects where he had grown up, where he hosted Easter egg hunts for children and distributed ice cream and sports equipment to them for free. He was deemed by many to be a true role model who took the only opportunity available to him to become an American success story and ran with it. Mitchell became a millionaire. He owned two homes, several cars (including a Rolls Royce), and three legitimate businesses. And the belief that his route to success was little different from that of other American tycoons was not without merit. Observed one East Oakland admirer, Mitchell's success could be compared to that of Joe Kennedy, who made part of his fortune selling bootlegged whiskey during Prohibition.

But Mitchell's dominance did not last. The 69 Mob inspired

a copycat outfit known as the Family, then another called Funk-town. In 1980 the rival organizations engaged in bloody warfare. But what really toppled Mitchell were 1983 federal charges of conspiracy, racketeering, and tax evasion. By 1985, when he was convicted and sentenced to life in prison without parole, the 69 Mob had virtually disbanded. The following year, Harvey Whis-enton, leader of Funktown, was sentenced to seventeen years in federal prison for selling cocaine and heroin. Four of his lieutenants were also imprisoned, all of which led to the demise of Funktown. Conspiracy charges and sustained federal raids led to the demise of the Family as well.

Before the demise of Funktown, Whisenton had made a con-nection with the prison-based Black Guerilla Family (BGF), hiring ex-convicts to serve as enforcers for Funktown. That connection paved the way for the first known BGF involvement with drug dealing in the Oakland flatlands. By 1984, heroin no longer was the most lucrative drug to deal on the streets, because the United States was flooded with high-quality Columbian cocaine.

The flood of cocaine precipitated a revolution in the drug trade that was responsible for transforming Huey Newton's drug habit in 1985, enabling him to continue his addiction no matter how bad his financial situation became. Roosevelt Taylor, a former Oakland drug dealer, told Lance Williams of the *San Francisco Examiner* that in 1977 he and fellow dealers were the first in the United States to experiment with processing powdered cocaine into a smokable substance so that customers who had developed "problems with their noses" from snorting cocaine could continue using it. "We used an ether base (to reprocess powdered cocaine) and it came back in a flaky form," explained Taylor. "But it was a hassle using the ether." So Taylor and his fellow dealers were taught a different process by someone who had learned it from a lab student at UC Berkeley. They took cake pans and mixed co-caine hydrochloride with baking soda and water, then applied heat to the concoction. When the brew became hot enough it would "rock up" into a hard, highly potent derivative, which became known as crack cocaine. "At first it was just a fad," said Taylor. "When we started introducing it to people from LA and Detroit

. . . they didn't know what we were doing." But after the United States was flooded with cocaine in 1984, what they were doing quickly caught on. It lowered the street price of cocaine, making it available to the masses. Dealers could turn one ounce of powdered cocaine hydrochloride, purchased from wholesalers for $1,500, into 168 rocks of crack cocaine sold for $25 each, allowing them to clear a profit of $2,700 per ounce. What's more, the crack derivative was even more highly addictive than regular powdered cocaine.

By the time Huey Newton emerged from serving his prison sentence in 1987 for illegal gun possession in the Callins case, crack-dealing gangs were operating all over East and West Oakland, and Newton was a ready crack customer. At one point he resurrected a scheme he was said to have first introduced in 1981, designed to establish what remained of the Panthers as major cocaine dealers in their own right, using a Cuban connection as the cocaine supplier. But once again, the scheme fell through. So Newton was reduced to watching others become rich off of crack. All he could do was ride his legendary reputation to secure free crack from dealers he would have further intimidated just a decade earlier.

According to the Oakland police, by that time Daryl Reed, Felix Mitchell's twenty-year-old nephew, had established what was said to be the largest crack-dealing empire in the city. The Black Guerilla Family was also said to be dealing in crack, with its own drug dealers in places such as West Oakland. Many BGF members still held grudges against Huey Newton, who showed up at one of their largest prison strongholds in July 1988. Newton was sentenced to six weeks in San Quentin for failing to report to his parole officer that he had been arrested for driving under the influence of alcohol, as well as for refusing to submit to a drug test after being arrested. Many BGF members serving time in San Quentin still blamed Newton for sabotaging George Jackson's failed San Quentin escape attempt in August 1971. Former party members who had been abandoned by Newton while they served long prison sentences for illegal activities on behalf of the party had also joined the BGF. And San Quentin was home to the former party member considered to be the most unjustly imprisoned Panther of them all, a party member who, along with David Hilliard, kept back the crowd in front of the Alameda County Courthouse on that jubilant August day in 1970, as it surged forward, eager to press flesh with the newly released Huey P. Newton. Photos of Elmer "Geronimo" Pratt in his cowboy hat, and David Hilliard, both flanking a bare-chested Newton on top of Alex Hoffman's Volkswagen bug, were among the most famous of the entire Panther era.

But a few months later, Pratt who at the time was deputy defense minister of the party and head of its southern California chapter, became one of many Panthers expelled from the party by Newton. In December of that year, Pratt was arrested and charged with the robbery and murder of a Santa Monica woman. Convincing evidence existed that Pratt was nowhere near the scene of that 1968 crime. But Newton-faction Panthers who could have testified that Pratt was in Oakland at the time of the murder never came forward. Pratt was seen as the victim of a frame-up, since the key witness placing him at the scene of the crime was an FBI informant. Pratt was sacrificed by Newton in Newton's war with the Cleaver faction.* And to top off his unjust imprisonment, Pratt also suffered the loss of his wife in the fratricidal violence that followed the Newton/Cleaver split. In November 1971, a pregnant Sandra Pratt was tortured, shot, and killed by Newton-faction Panthers.

Newton was entering a snake's pit of enemies when he arrived at San Quentin the summer of 1988. When Pratt saw Newton at San Quentin, however, he walked straight over to him and embraced him. He expressed no hard feelings, maintaining his extraordinarily magnanimous attitude about being unjustly imprisoned for so long. Pratt had shown the same attitude with Joe Blum when Blum interviewed him for an article around that same time. Pratt told Blum that the infamous 1968 interview Blum had held with Huey while Huey was awaiting the verdict in the Frey case—published in the newspaper *The Movement*—was responsible

---

*According to one party insider, Newton did in fact have something to do with Pratt being charged with the murder, since he had set up Pratt to be arrested: "He considered Geronimo to be expendable."

for his decision to join the Black Panthers. Given the fate of Pratt in the party, Blum apologized to Pratt for publishing the interview. But Pratt assured Blum he had no reason to feel guilty.

Newton also apologized to Pratt for the past, blaming CO-INTELPRO and other outside influences for pressuring him into his paranoid state of mind. "They offered me everything under the sun, money, drugs, women, everything I wanted when I got out in 1970," he explained. "I just couldn't resist it." Newton's sudden apology for his part in the injustice done to Pratt may have been genuine. Or it may have been a convenient effort to make amends, now that he was among so many enemies at San Quentin. In any case, on August 23, 1988, when it was time for his release on parole, Newton refused to leave San Quentin, in protest of eighteen years of unjust imprisonment of Pratt. His publicity move angered BGF members, who wondered out loud where Newton had been all those years. Newton was released from San Quentin four days later.

In the early 1970s the BGF, disaffected Panthers, and underworld figures, all seeking retribution for Newton-ordered expulsions, murders, or setups, had issued contracts on Newton's life. Obviously, none had been successfully carried out. Mae Jackson remembers encountering a team of men en route from New York City on their way to kill Newton. Fred Hiestand recalls people telling Newton that they had been offered money to kill him but couldn't go through with it. The walking wounded were everywhere. And on his release from San Quentin after his protest on behalf of Pratt, a broken, disheveled Newton continued to taunt some of those wounded. Among the crack dealers he had been pressuring to supply him with drugs free of charge were dealers connected to the BGF. Newton's rationale was that the dealers had to pay their dues to him, show their respect for the founder of the Black Panther Party. He continued to pick at old wounds and inflict new ones.

One BGF-connected drug dealer who had run-ins with Newton was a twenty-five-year-old named Tyrone Robinson, who spent time in prison on various charges of robbery in between dealing drugs. Robinson allegedly met Newton at the beginning of 1987, while dealing in East Oakland. According to Robinson, Newton occasionally purchased the drugs, but at other times robbed Robinson of drugs and money, intimidating him and other dealers with the pitch that they had better hand over some drugs or some money because "I'm Huey P. motherfuckin Newton!" Unlike the 69 Mob, or the Family, or Funktown, the crack-dealing gangs refrained from wearing identifying jackets that could easily lead to their facing charges of conspiracy and racketeering. But like those earlier gangs, they also operated out of housing projects. In addition, they purchased and rented homes in East and West Oakland where they dealt drugs and where crack addicts could smoke.

Bob Trivors accompanied Huey on many of his trips to crack houses in East and West Oakland. He witnessed an unarmed Huey demand drugs for free, certain that he could depend on his legendary reputation to protect him. Newton would have scary arguments with the armed dealers, arguments that would grow progressively louder. But Newton came away with the drugs because, more often than not, when they saw that Newton wasn't frightened by their guns, the dealers became frightened of Newton. None of Huey's friends and acquaintances expected that luck to last, however, and neither did Huey. One day in 1988 Bob Trivors told Huey how he would handle Huey's death, by way of telling him a story about Jamaica. Trivors was fond of Jamaica because it was much easier to bridge the racial gap there than in the United States. His wife was Jamaican, and he was friendly with the residents of a small Jamaican town. One of his Jamaican friends had been killed, and Trivors decided to make a trip to search for the murderer. He searched and searched in vain, until finally, out of frustration, he accused the entire town of conspiring to murder his friend. At the end of the story, he told Huey that when Huey was finally murdered in some crack den, Bob wouldn't bother to search for the killer. On hearing that, Huey's eyes misted up and he wiped away a tear. Those who knew Huey were certain that his death would come any day. And more than a few of his friends were convinced that it would be a blessing for him.

14

Death and Its Aftermath

In the early morning of Tuesday, August 22, 1989, Willie Payne, Jr., was too scared to return with Huey to the nearby crack house on 10th and Cypress streets in West Oakland. Earlier in the evening, someone had interrupted the crack-smoking party Newton had instigated in Willie's apartment with the words, "There are people looking for Huey." Huey had pressured a dealer into giving him an entire sandwich bag of free crack cocaine, and he was determined to get some more. The news that someone was looking for him could have meant simply that Newton was about to engage in one more of his many arguments with dealers. Or it could have meant the end.

When he told someone the previous evening that he had recently gotten out of prison and needed a dove of crack cocaine, Newton was referring to the three-and-a-half-month sentence he had finished serving that May. He had been returned to San Quentin in February 1989 after getting caught in a motel on MacArthur Boulevard with a prostitute, freebasing crack. Although he experienced intermittent periods of moderate comfort, Huey kept wanting to get high and forget about the life he was wasting. By the time he was returned to San Quentin, he was living in a modest, three-bedroom Berkeley home owned by his wife Fredericka, along with Fredericka's son, Kieron, whom he had adopted. They had lost their EOC-deeded Oakland Hills home in 1986 through the state's effort to recover misused EOC money. While Newton was serving time in San Quentin, the first case against him for embezzling EOC funds was winding its way through the court system.

Newton was charged with one count of embezzling $14,350. Many more counts of embezzlement were to come if he wished to make an issue of the charges. But this particular case had already cost the state Justice Department a lot of time, and the department knew it wouldn't be able to recover all the money. Neither was Newton in a position to continue dispensing money for legal fees, particularly in a huge case that he would clearly lose. The prosecutor's main goal was to expose Newton as an embezzler and ensure that he could never again get his hands on public money, or run for public office if he chose to down the road. From the time the case became public, Newton's position had been that the entire brouhaha was one more attempt by the state to harass him for past radical activity. Finally, he bargained. He pleaded no contest to the first count of embezzlement, in effect admitting that the state had a legitimate case against him. He was ordered to repay the $14,350, and the state wound down its case.

Two months later Newton was out of San Quentin, paroled on the crack cocaine charges. Although he faced no more legal hassles, he still seemed unable to pursue a productive life. Back at his wife's home on Francisco Street in Berkeley, a now bearded Newton remained clean for a few weeks. He lost a lot of money in one more illegal scheme gone sour. Then, once again, he began to disappear for days at a time, delving into the seedy drug underworld of the Oakland flatlands. On Monday evening, August 21, 1989, he hopped into his wife's burgundy Ford Escort and headed to Willie Payne's neighborhood. After the breakup of the small crack-smoking party he instigated in Willie's place, Newton sat smoking crack with Willie, reminiscing about the past, contemplating a death he had flirted with so often, yet had somehow, up to then, miraculously avoided. He told a *San Francisco Chronicle* reporter in November 1984 that he had tried to drink and drug himself to death, but it hadn't worked. In 1987, in the middle of a coke binge at his Hollywood friend Bert Schneider's estate, Newton said to one of Schneider's secretaries, "What I keep wondering is why someone hasn't put a bullet in my head yet." Newton had a continual fascination with death. He kept playing a cat-and-mouse game with it. And now, in the early-morning hours of Tuesday, August 22, maybe the game would be played again after a messenger at Willie Payne's apartment announced, "There are people looking for Huey."

West Oakland was considered poor, but demographically it was still somewhat of a mixed neighborhood. There were middle-class residents living in a few beautiful Victorian homes and bungalows. One of the residents was C. L. Dellums, who was among those sparks that lit the fire in the belly of black people, making them stand up and demand their rights—a spark that indirectly facilitated the migration of so many blacks to Oakland, a spark that eventually inspired the civil rights movement, which evolved into the Black Power movement that would catapult Huey to fame.

Things might have turned out differently for Huey P. Newton if the eighty-nine-year-old C. L. Dellums, fast asleep only blocks away, hadn't helped to found the Brotherhood of Sleeping Car Porters. If it hadn't been for all that both C. L. Dellums and A. Philip Randolph had inspired, Newton might have grown up in Monroe, Louisiana. He might have headed to New Orleans, where perhaps the conditions to form the Black Panther Party would never have existed. Maybe it had to be in Oakland, a city that, without a doubt, had been transformed both for better and for worse by Newton's Black Panthers.

A few blocks to the east of the crack house on 10th and Cypress streets where Newton headed after leaving Payne's apartment sits the once promising Acorn housing development. There had been much hope when those modern apartments went up in the late 1960s and early 1970s—hope that the Acorns would serve both racially and socioeconomically as an inspiration to good integrated living. The dream succeeded for only a little while. As unemployment increased, more and more Acorn tenants were poor and on welfare, or AFDC. The teenagers of the Acorns began introducing drugs into the housing development, just as drugs had been introduced in the far older Cypress Village next door. By August 1989, both housing developments were no different from many other Oakland flatlands housing projects that began serving as drug supermarkets in the mid-1970s. Newton had often purchased drugs in both developments. David Hilliard, former Panther chief of staff who also became a crack addict (Hilliard takes credit for having shown a disbelieving Huey the proper way to enjoy crack), purchased drugs there too, and lived briefly in the Acorns, withstanding the taunts of drug dealers who called him a "has-been." The new kids on the block, so young, many of them not even born yet when the Panthers were in their prime, treated the former Panthers who hadn't redirected their lives into productive activities like relics from the Stone Age. The only relic that still seemed to retain much of his bite was Huey.

Tyrone Robinson went by the nickname Double R. Two of his friends were Brian Walton (nicknamed B) and a guy nicknamed Shorty Red. Cypress Village, the Acorns, 10th Street, were locations they knew well because they had grown up in the area, and they were surviving as small-scale drug dealers there. They knew and dealt with Huey Newton, who had robbed them of drugs.

There were two locations on that block of 10th Street between Center and Cypress that dealt in crack cocaine. One was a house where Tyrone Robinson's cousin Peebles lived, near the corner of 10th and Center. A person could buy crack there, and at a house near the corner of 10th and Cypress he or she could smoke it. This was the "base house." After leaving Willie's apartment in the early-morning hours of Tuesday, August 22, unable to convince Willie to accompany him to get more crack, Huey Newton headed to the base house on 10th and Cypress streets. Once there, he demanded to be let in because he was Huey Newton. The dealers who ran the base house locked its doors, leaving Newton outside, still high on crack, to rant and rave about how he was the leader of the coming revolution.

Minutes later Double R and Brian Walton showed up at the base house from Peebles's place. They couldn't get inside because of Newton, however, so they turned around and headed for a convenience store at 7th and Center streets. The store was closed, so they headed back down Center Street toward Peebles's house, encountering Huey at the northwest corner of 9th and Center streets. Apparently, Newton was headed back to his car, which was parked on 9th Street. Now no one but Brian, Double R, and Huey was around. On seeing Brian and Double R, Newton asked if they had any crack cocaine. They told him yes, they did, but Newton would have to wait until they returned to the house at 10th and Center streets before they gave him any. Newton began to argue with them. Suddenly, Double R pulled out his .45 pistol and started pistol-whipping Huey. "Brian!" Huey cried out. "Why's Double R hitting me with his gun?" Brian started to walk away. But Double R's gun jammed. He ran up to Brian and said, "Gimme your gun! Gimme your gun!" Brian gave him his 9-mm automatic. All the while Huey just stood there, frozen. Double R walked back to Huey and pointed the gun at his left jaw. At that point Huey told him, "You can kill my body, but you can't kill my soul. My soul will live forever!" Double R fired the first shot. Huey fell to the ground. "I'll make rank! I'll make rank!" Double R cried out, referring to moving up in the BGF and becoming a "shot caller." Double R walked around to the right side of Newton's felled body. He pointed the gun at Huey's head and shot him two more times in the temple. Then he caught up with Brian and headed back to Peebles's place.

WHEN THE GIRLFRIEND OF WILLIE PAYNE'S DOWNSTAIRS neighbor called 911 because she, Willie, and her boyfriend saw someone lying on the sidewalk, they had no idea that that someone was Huey P. Newton. At approximately 5:30 A.M, the first responding police officer arrived, saw Newton lying there, and radioed for a code-three ambulance and fire truck. The officer felt Newton's body for a pulse. There was none, although he was still warm to the touch. Willie and his neighbors made their way to the corner, just as the Oakland fire department arrived. Willie recognized Huey lying there, while the fire department tried to administer

CPR. Minutes later an ambulance arrived. Willie tried to get a closer look. But the police made him stand back, along with the other gathering spectators.

Fire department rescuer Robert Morgan, who was also African American, couldn't believe his eyes when he reached the scene. "I thought it was going to be just another typical run. Then here I am on a cold dark street, and this is Huey Newton lying there . . . it just seemed so strange." The rescue squad administered CPR for approximately ten minutes, but to no avail. Then they loaded Huey's body into the ambulance and headed for Highland Hospital, where he was pronounced dead at 6:12 A.M. from three bullet wounds to the head.

Within hours, the spot where Newton died was swarming with police investigators, a crowd of spectators, the usual morning commuters who parked their cars nearby and headed for the BART train two blocks away, television news crews, and print reporters. The police officers who initially responded at the scene had already gone door to door up and down the block, waking everyone up, asking if they saw anything. No one said they had, although some said they had heard shots. Willie told the officers that he hadn't seen anything either but had talked to Huey earlier in the day. He wouldn't get off so easily, however: someone told the officers that Willie had been with Huey when he was shot. Later that morning, a swarm of police descended on the white frame house containing Willie's basement apartment. They even climbed the rooftop.

Because of the history of animosity between the Oakland police department and Huey, rumors were already spreading that the department had finally gotten him. After all those years, the rumor went, the police department had finally set Huey Newton up and killed him. So the department was pulling out all stops to clear its name. "We know you killed him," one interrogator told Willie, while another waited his turn to intimidate him into telling them what he knew. "You're just trying to make a name for yourself. We're going to make you famous. You're the guy who killed Huey Newton. We're going to put you in the papers. We're going to build you up. You did it for prestige. You want to be somebody."

Out of fear for his own life, Willie was hardly willing to

cooperate. He didn't want the police to know all the times Huey had been to his place that night, or all the stops that he knew Huey had made. Anybody could have killed Huey, and if word reached the streets that something Willie said led directly to the apprehension of a well-connected killer, Willie could end up dead too. Willie denied killing Huey, and he told the officers some of what he knew. Then they took him home.

That morning Landon Williams commuted to work in Berkeley. He had been named director of the Community Energy Service Corporation in 1986, and in 1988 became assistant to the city manager of Berkeley and project manager for the Economic Revitalization Project for South Berkeley. On hearing that Huey was dead, Landon wasn't particularly sad. Like many others who knew him, Landon expected Huey to die the way he did. Landon would be among those interviewed by the media, as they fanned out among former Panthers and friends of Newton to obtain comments. He told reporters from the *Oakland Tribune*, "If someone pulled a gun on you or me, we'd get real polite. But Huey would be the kind of guy to say 'OK, shoot me.' His ego would not allow him to back down. He would push the confrontation. Finding him dead on a street corner is consistent with his character."

"I'll be damned, Huey's dead," Mary Kennedy said after hearing the television news report that morning in her home in East Oakland. She had retired from her job at Amouron pipe after working there ten years, then sustaining a work-related injury to her knee. She telephoned another former party member, announcing, "Girl, guess what. Huey's dead." Mary was surprised in one sense, but not surprised in another. She was certain his death was drug related.

Sheeba Haven had the day off from her job as a medical assistant in Dr. Tolbert Small's office. The news of Huey's death didn't really surprise her or make her particularly sad. Haven was angry with Huey. Like many other former party members, she blamed him for destroying the Black Panther Party. And again, like many others, she had expected Huey to die violently.

Throughout the day and well into the night, the block where

Huey died remained the place to be for the media, curiosity seekers, social activists of all kinds, and worshipers of Huey Newton eager to turn him into a hero. A candlelight vigil was held. Candles, letters, and photographs were left at the spot where Huey was killed. Controversy swirled around what should be Huey's proper epitaph. At a news conference, Huey's widow, Fredericka, his brother Melvin, and other relatives, as well as former Panthers who remained his allies, expressed hope that his death would spark new activism to fight drugs, homelessness, poverty, and crime. They called him a hero. "Let Huey's death move us to some action," said David Hilliard, who appeared on television with Melvin Newton. "We're still up against the same problems the Panthers fought against."

But others were in no mood for blanket hero worship. Former Panthers who insisted on making Huey out to be a hero heard from Panthers who remembered how complicated the past really was, and how brutal the downfall of the party. Landon Williams and Sheeba Haven fell into the latter category. Predictably, the controversy surrounding Newton's proper epitaph became racial after Alameda County assistant district attorney Tom Orloff, who had prosecuted many of the legal cases against Newton, offered his opinion to the same *Oakland Tribune* reporters who had approached Landon. "The Newton I dealt with in the '70s was basically a gangster," said Orloff. "There was nothing political about him."

"A lot of black people are very angered by the fact that Huey Newton is being put in the box of a gangster," replied the Reverend Cecil Williams of San Francisco's Glide Memorial Church. Williams, who served as a spokesman for the Newton family and led a vigil to the spot where Newton was shot and killed, insisted that in the final analysis, society was responsible for Newton's negative behavior, which he called a "tension in Huey. . . ." "You've got to see that here was a man who went through a lot," he stated. "I'm sure that at times he did not please some folks. But Huey Newton was also a man who touched the ground with the poor. He could talk with the middle class and the upper class. But he never lost his common touch."

Oakland mayor Lionel Wilson spoke of how promising Newton's life had once been, and of what a pity it was he couldn't get it all together. Black state assemblyman Elihu Harris, who in 1991 would replace Wilson as the mayor of Oakland, recalled meeting Huey in the early 1960s when they were students at Merritt (Oakland City) College: "I remember him saying he liked Cuba because everybody had a gun. That's when I decided I didn't want to be part of that group. Newton was a larger-than-life figure, romanticized by some. Some people would argue that Huey's been dead a long time, and his body just caught up with the situation."

National NAACP head Benjamin Hooks called him an eloquent spokesman for "disillusioned and often bitter youths in the 1960s."

"America does not want [black people] to have heroes like Huey Newton," commented Biko Lumumba of Uhuru house, an ultramilitant Bay Area organization. "It wants us to have heroes like Bill Cosby and Eddie Murphy."

"What he did in the last decade is irrelevant," stated Charles Garry about the most famous client he ever had (other than People's Temple leader Jim Jones, who led his congregation into mass suicide in 1978). "Huey of the last ten years is not the Huey I knew. . . . He was founder of the renaissance of the black liberation movement."

Meanwhile, the investigation into who killed Huey continued. "There's no way in hell you don't know something," a police interrogator told Willie Payne after they picked him up again the following day for more questioning. They offered to place Willie in a witness protection program. They had pieced together enough to know that Huey had been doing drugs, and they already assumed that his death was related to a drug rip-off. Willie admitted that Huey had been to his house, but he insisted that he knew nothing about the killing itself. Once more they returned him to his apartment.

The media were still hovering around the neighborhood hoping for a scoop on the unsolved murder of Huey Newton. One of Willie's neighbors, with whom he had argued only days earlier, saw Willie sitting with his landlord on the landlord's porch. "You see there sitting on that porch?" he said to the reporters and camera-men. "That's the guy who was with Huey Newton when he got killed." They all rushed over to Willie. "That guy's crazy," Willie told them. "Put yourself in the shoes of the guy who killed Newton. Now if me and my landlord were sitting here, and you walked up and killed my landlord, don't you think you would shoot me too? Why would you leave me as an eyewitness? That wouldn't make any sense. It would only make sense to kill both of us and leave no witnesses." The media cut their cameras off and went back across the street.

The police weren't certain that they had picked up Newton's killer until Friday, August 25. They had apprehended him the same day he killed Huey, but had continued to squeeze Willie Payne for information to be certain they had the right man. Tyrone Robinson had been picked up on Tuesday evening, August 22, after a friend of a relative of Tyrone called police to relate that Tyrone had watched initial reports of Newton's murder on television and be-come very emotional. She stated that he said he was glad he killed Newton because Huey had "killed several of his brothers and that he had once shot at [Tyrone] and his pregnant girlfriend." Police were convinced they had a good lead when the woman described the weapon Newton was murdered with—information that hadn't been released to the public. On the way to police headquarters for questioning, the woman spotted Robinson and two colleagues get-ting out of Robinson's car. Police took the three men into custody after finding a gun in the car, allowing the officers to charge them with being convicted felons in possession of a handgun.

When police picked up the Robinson relative from whom the woman had obtained the information on Robinson, the relative said she had overheard Robinson and two other men "talking about getting rid of Huey Newton because he was causing problems for the BGF." She said that Robinson left her house that night and killed Newton, then returned to her house, picked up his girlfriend, and left. After several hours of interrogation that Friday morning, Robinson admitted to shooting Huey Newton. But he claimed he did so in self-defense. (Two years later a disbelieving jury convicted him of murdering Newton in the second degree.)

Groups of former Panthers held wakes for Huey. Mary Kennedy attended one of the wakes and found everyone else there in a mournful mood. "The son of a bitch should have died," Mary insisted. Everyone glared at her. Someone said everyone should forget about the bad and remember only the good because when a white man dies, no matter how bad he is, only the good things are remembered. Huey may have screwed up down the road, former party members at that particular wake insisted, but everyone should remember his good qualities. "That's fine if you didn't lose anything," argued Mary. "But look at all the party members who lost jobs, family ties, the ones in jail doing fifteen to twenty years because they made sacrifices for the party, and those who were killed because of Huey." She felt most embittered, she said, for all of them. They had joined the party in its heyday, the late 1960s, had made sacrifices in Huey's name, and were cut off and abandoned by Huey after he was released from prison. The ones who joined after Huey emerged from prison in 1970, who came to Oakland when Huey called all of his loyalists to the city, may have lost only a few years of time, months even. Getting a ticket out of somewhere like New Haven, Connecticut, to come to Oakland may have been their first chance to leave that city. It was the original party members who sacrificed the most. And it was for them that Mary felt Huey should have died.

Kiilu Nyasha, who was briefly a party member in New Haven and then a secretary to Charles Garry during the trials of the Black Panther New Haven Seven, was now a resident of San Francisco. On moving to the city in 1971, after Bobby Seale and Ericka Huggins were freed from prison that May, Nyasha became active in the George Jackson Defense Committee. She also began writing stories for the *San Francisco Sun-Reporter*. When she appeared at the Black Panther office in San Francisco at the request of George Jackson himself to check up on a Defense Committee matter, Panthers at the office called headquarters in Oakland. Headquarters told them that Huey Newton said she was banned from all party premises. Eighteen years later, when Nyasha heard of the death of Huey Newton, she remarked: "Even though I knew he was responsible for the loss of so many lives and knew he had threatened mine, I just kind of had a resigned feeling. The first thought that came to mind was what Malcolm had said when John Kennedy was assassinated—the chickens have come home to roost."

But then two nights later she woke up in the middle of the night, having dreamed about Huey. The following day she left her apartment in a public housing development in San Francisco's Chinatown and headed for her physical therapy sessions. (Kiilu sustained an injury in 1976 that left her largely wheelchair bound, although she can walk slowly with the aid of a walker.) While she was sitting outside the therapy center, someone who knew she had been active in the party mentioned Huey's death. "I started to talk, and all of a sudden tears started to come uncontrollably. I surprised myself, because I didn't know where the tears were coming from." Later on, she decided their source. For Kiilu, Huey's death provided the proverbial period on the entire radical era.

Bob Trivors was in Jamaica when Huey died. So certain was he that Huey's violent death would come any day that just a week earlier he had literally been contemplating what he would say if asked to give a eulogy at Huey's funeral. On Wednesday, August 23, he picked up a Jamaican newspaper and turned to page three, which had a picture of Huey. Trivors immediately guessed what it meant. Later that day he received a telegram from his wife, saying, "Huey shot dead." Melvin Newton had called down to Bob's home in Santa Cruz to ask that he give a eulogy. But Bob decided to remain in Jamaica; he figured Huey wasn't fond of funerals anyway.

The period of mourning caused a sensation among black Oaklanders and radicals of all persuasions that was hard to explain. What was one to make of middle-aged black ladies among the 6,000 who made their way to Palmer D. Whitted Mortuary on Foothill Boulevard in Oakland, just to stop in front of the body of Newton, as he lay in an elegant wooden casket, dressed in a conservative gray three-piece suit, white shirt, and red tie, his handsome face newly clean-shaven, looking as though he were having a peaceful sleep? They were there, as one such woman put it, simply to tell him, "Thank you, Huey." Thank you for showing us how to straighten out our backs and walk without a hump, even if some of us did so just briefly. Ordinary people were led away from his coffin in tears.

Stan Woods, a thirty-seven-year-old white bartender in line, commented on the controversy surrounding Huey, noting rumors that he was a criminal. "I don't know what's true or not about that stuff, but he made a huge contribution to the multi-racial left. I'm here to pay tribute to his legacy."

Some of those standing in line waiting for a glimpse of Huey's body were hostile toward the media. At one point a group of youths attacked a television news cameraman, hitting him in the face and kicking him. But Newton's family and Uhuru House soon took measures to prevent any more such occurrences. At Allen Temple Baptist Church later that evening, approximately 2,000 people gathered for prayers and hymns. Most of the mourners were black, but many whites and Latinos were present as well.

The funeral took place the following day. Neither Landon Williams, Sheeba Haven, nor Mary Kennedy was there. Instead Haven and Williams marked the occasion by meeting in a Berkeley bar with a group of former Panthers who had also fallen out with Huey. Thousands of others felt differently, however. Two thousand people jam-packed the sanctuary of Allen Temple Baptist Church in East Oakland, while thousands more spilled out into the streets and an adjacent hall, to listen to Huey's funeral service by loud-speaker. Members of the radical group Uhuru House set up a banner that read "Huey Lives!" White limousines pulled up at the church entrance, carrying former Panthers and 1960s radicals such as Elaine Brown, Angela Davis, Bobby Seale, Johnny Spain, and the former H. Rap Brown (who now goes by the name Jamal Abdulla Al-Amin as a result of his conversion to the Islamic faith, in which he serves as an Imam leading a mosque in Atlanta). Conspicuous among the missing were former militant luminaries such as Eldridge Cleaver and Stokely Carmichael.

As Bobby Seale mounted the podium, to the satisfaction of the crowd he pulled out a black beret. When he clenched his fists and raised them in the air, much of the audience cheered. "All power to the people," he said. "Like we used to say, right on." Then he began his eulogy, salvaging what could be salvaged from all the death, sweat, tears, pain, and suffering in the Black Panther Party. "Did anybody ever tell y'all that the Black Panther Party tested over 1h million black people for sickle cell anemia in the United States of America? That was more than was tested by all the government agencies and hospitals put together."

C. L. Dellums's nephew, Congressman Ron Dellums, who interceded during the 1971–1972 Cal-Pak boycott and had been friends with Newton as far back as the mid-1960s, stated of Huey, "The very same streets that he tried to make safe for the children are the streets that took his life." Dellums called for a revival of the civil rights movement, telling the crowd, "We ought to go to Washington in the tens of thousands, like the Chinese students went to Beijing."

Elaine Brown called Huey a "hero with not only a dream, but a plan, and his plan was the Black Panther Party."

Midway through the three-hour service, the electricity failed, prompting some to shout "Sabotage!" although the electric company attributed the outage to a truck hitting a pole on a nearby street. After several minutes, a bullhorn and small generator for a light were located, and the eulogies continued. Less than an hour later, electricity would be restored.

David Hilliard spoke about Huey's drug and alcohol addiction, as well as his own, stating, "The only thing that separated me from Huey that night [when he was shot] was that I was at an AA [Alcoholics Anonymous] fellowship."

The Reverend Cecil Williams spoke of Huey's recently expressing interest in becoming a minister. Holding up copies of Huey's three published books, the Reverend J. Alfred Smith said that Newton had joined Allen Temple several years ago. He criticized the media for not talking about Newton as an intellectual. Then Smith led the audience in chants of "Free Huey! Free Huey!" after which he declared, "He's free. He's free. He's free at last!"

When it was all over, Huey's wood, flower-draped casket was loaded into a hearse. At the urging of members of Uhuru House, much of the crowd began chanting, "Long Live Huey P., African people must be free!" and "Who killed Huey, don't tell no lie, the government, the government, the FBI!" An honor guard of about fifty Uhuru members in berets and T-shirts lined up alongside and behind the hearse, banging drums and carrying red, black, and green flags, as well as Panther posters. They trotted alongside the funeral procession as it slowly wound its way onto East Oakland's East 14th Street, past newly spray-painted silhouettes of Huey Newton in beret, toting a gun—silhouettes that were going up all over the Oakland flatlands. At his request, Huey's body was cremated and interred at Oakland's Evergreen Cemetery, with a plaque bearing his name. Now he was a legend.

Afterword

THREE WEEKS AFTER THE DEATH OF HUEY NEWTON, JOUR-
nalist Ken Kelly, who had once briefly performed public relations
work for the Black Panther Party, published a dramatic counter-
point to the glowing eulogies of Newton at his funeral. Kelly's
article, "Huey, I'll Never Forget . . . ," appeared in the Berkeley-
based *East Bay Express*, one of four Bay Area alternative weeklies.
Like Kate Coleman and Paul Avery, who had fired off the first
negative salvo about the fate of the Black Panther Party with their
New Times article "The Party's Over," Kelly was white. He had
been a part of the late 1960s–early 1970s radical scene, serving
briefly as minister of information for the White Panther Party, a
white radical group based in Ann Arbor, Michigan, whose members admired and supported the Black Panthers.

Kelly began the article with a description of an elderly black
woman he sat next to in an Oakland dentist's office. Reading about
Newton's funeral in the *San Francisco Chronicle*, she encountered
the quotation of a minister describing Newton as black America's
Moses. "If he's our Moses," she retorted, "then give me that old
Pharaoh Ramses any old day. . . . Huey Newton was just a plain
old thug. Period. All these fools are trying to make him into a saint,

but he was a real life sinner. Comparing him to Dr. King or Malcolm [X] is downright blasphemy."

Kelly described being dazzled by Newton's legend and eager to meet him when he emerged from prison in August 1970 ("'Free Huey' had, in the nomenclature of the times, become the leftist equivalent of 'Heil Hitler . . .'"). He recounted how Newton went on to puncture holes in his godlike image, proving that he not only was not the savior the Left painted him to be but was a man who eventually sank into madness. Kelly claimed that Newton confessed to him that he had indeed pistol-whipped Preston Callins and murdered Kathleen Smith; on another occasion, he confessed to ordering the murder of Betty Van Patter while he was in Cuba ("As I got to know him better, I found out that Huey was a real live Jekyll and Hyde case . . .").

Kelly's article was greeted with extreme outrage and scattered praise. "Thanks for the information, Ken Kelly, but we've heard most of that stuff before," Carl Miller responded in one of the many letters printed by the *Express*. "Sure the Huey Newton some riffraff shot was probably a murderer, thief, alcoholic, and drug addict. . . . But the man we remember was much more than just another thug. We remember the Huey Newton who stood up strong and black, who faced down the pigs and scared shit out of racists whose worst nightmare seemed about to come true. . . . We knew in our heart of hearts that [the Black Panthers] never really had a chance. And that the tactic of armed resistance was contradictory, at best counterproductive, and for sure downright dangerous. But oh what a rush Huey gave us. . . . The Huey we remember was a tonic that at the time our community sorely needed, so pardon us if we pay tribute to one of our own. . . ."

Plenty of other *Express* readers defended Newton against Kelly, but none more eloquently than Carl Miller, or an old instructor of Newton's at Merritt College, Ted Vincent. Vincent's letter dramatized just how complex Huey Newton really was. Mimicking the Kelly style of beginning each transition in his article with "I'll never forget . . . ," Vincent wrote: "'I'll never forget' my first college teaching experience at Merritt in 1963, when this young hotshot in the back row kept throwing at me these complex political interpretations of American history. 'What is that Newton guy going to think up next?' I would ask myself as I prepared my next lecture in a manner that tried to anticipate Huey Newton's brainstorms. . . ."

But Kelly had his defenders, too. Wrote Lawrence Schonbrun, "Were Ken Kelly's observations on Huey Newton any more 'one-sided and dishonest' than the remarks made by the celebrities at Newton's funeral, who chose to remember everything Newton did that was positive . . . and completely omitted the negative?" Referring to the Black Panthers' ten-point program as outlined by Art Goldberg in another *Express* letter defending Newton, Schonbrun asked: "Wouldn't it have been better if the party had stressed the responsibilities of parenthood than offering children free breakfasts? Shouldn't the emphasis have been on opening businesses and running them properly, rather than running for political office? Wouldn't a program geared to making robbery an unacceptable form of black behavior accomplish more than demands to free all black men held in federal, state, and county prisons and jails? Wouldn't a program geared to ending violence and brutality by black men against their fellow blacks . . . have been more productive than a demand to exempt all black men from military service?"

And there was Dugald Stermer's sobering tonic to all 1960s romantics, when he wrote, "In the wake of maudlin, nostalgic hypocrisy surrounding the '60s, [Kelly's] piece stands out for its courage, integrity, and even personal anguish. The truth may not . . . set us free, but we cannot be free without it."

In February 1990, journalist David Horowitz published a shocking profile of Newton for the nationally distributed *Smart* magazine, now defunct. However, Horowitz's profile was not a personal memoir. It was written in third person, complete with a description of Huey inviting a journalist sitting in his living room to ask questions about Newton's dark side. That journalist was, in fact, Horowitz himself. Horowitz's account generated a response from former party chairperson Elaine Brown, who acknowledged working with Horowitz on the Panther school. Brown accused Horowitz of being a racist who had once edited *Ramparts* magazine and wrested Eldridge Cleaver from prison. In fact, Horowitz had nothing to do with Cleaver's release from prison. He had not even joined the staff of *Ramparts* until a year after Cleaver's release. Brown also accused Horowitz of rationalizing Cleaver's confession of raping black women in his book *Soul on Ice*. Horowitz had never done anything of the sort and had minimal contact with Cleaver while Cleaver was associated with *Ramparts*.

One thing Brown did correctly criticize about the article was Horowitz's misuse of the "crazy nigger" imagery Newton wrote about in his autobiography, *Revolutionary Suicide*. Newton recounted an incident in which his father, Walter, had once refused to bow to traditional Jim Crow in Louisiana and as a result was called a "crazy nigger" by whites. This label was commonly applied to black men in the South who defied Jim Crow. It was a badge of honor to be so designated, although Negroes rarely risked the physical harm or economic ostracism that could result from it (Newton's father did leave Louisiana shortly after the incident). Such labeling is proudly recalled by many black families when it's time to tell stories of family members who earned small victories over racial humiliation during Jim Crow (including in the author's own family). But Horowitz took Newton's pride in his father being labeled a "crazy nigger" to mean that Newton aspired to being truly crazy in the typical manner of losing one's mental health. Clearly, as he engaged in conjecture about the gut-level motivations behind Newton's behavior, Horowitz demonstrated that he was out of touch with the nuances of African American culture. In all other respects, however, the factual basis of his article, which covered much of the same territory as Kelly's, was solid.

Veteran Panthers, too, felt the pull of nostalgia after Newton's death. But unlike Kelly and Horowitz, they declined the opportunity to write articles in the predominantly white press about Huey and the party. Key former leaders such as David Hilliard and Bobby Seale began to discuss the start of a new organization, People's Organized Response. And in line with the distrust of the mainstream that was a hallmark of their Panther years, other Panther veterans, including Landon Williams and Sheeba Haven, met to discuss resurrecting the Black Panther newspaper.

On December 9, 1989, Seale, Hilliard, former Panther attorney Stephen Bingham, and other Panther veterans announced the debut of People's Organized Response (POR). Mimicking the ten-point platform of the old Black Panther Party, POR mapped out a seven-point program, including demands for economic development, quality education, jobs and full employment, preventative health care, decent housing, and safe, drug-free communities. Much of the impetus for the organization came not only from the shooting death of Huey Newton but also from the earthquake of October 12, 1989, which devastated poor Bay Area residents more than anyone else. The organization was launched amid the activism of a string of other grassroots organizations that had been mobilized to respond to the earthquake. But amid the old unhealed wounds of past Black Panther divisiveness, it soon became evident that POR was not to be. Bobby Seale declined to return permanently to the Bay Area as he had announced he would. And David Hilliard and other organizers also backed out of POR.

More successful was the attempt to launch a new Black Panther newspaper, but that effort too was soon riddled by the old unhealed wounds of party factionalism. One group of Panther veterans, including David Hilliard and past official Panther newspaper artist Emory Douglas, wished to produce a newspaper largely devoted to paying homage to Huey Newton (with quotes of Newton and reprints of his articles); it also would provide its own take on current news events affecting poor and black communities. Another group of veterans who had fallen out with Newton, including Landon Williams and Sheeba Haven, preferred to produce a newspaper that not only interpreted current events but also explored past party mistakes and included contributions from party veterans across the country who had been expelled by Huey. Eventually, the two groups split. In the fall of 1990, those who wished to pay homage to Huey Newton launched a monthly newspaper called *The Commemorator*, because the other editorial group had already legally incorporated the Black Panther name. In February 1991, Landon Williams and his associates launched the quarterly newspaper *The Black Panther*. Both *The Commemorator* and *The Black Panther* print only a few thousand copies and show little indication of reaching the level of readership of the original Black Panther newspaper in its heyday.

Periodically, Panther veterans get together for anniversary celebrations of the founding of the party, to commemorate Huey's birthday, or to commemorate his death. Usually the events draw less than a hundred people. The exception was the Unity Rally held in August 1990 at the one-year anniversary of Huey's death. That event, which traveled from the spot where he was killed to DeFremery Park, drew a few hundred people. At many of these events a simmering tension can be felt, as old wounds aren't difficult to reopen. This was the case at the twenty-fifth anniversary celebration of the founding of the party, held in October 1991 in Oakland (other twenty-fifth anniversary celebrations were held in New York City and elsewhere). A party veteran living in Los Angeles brought a group of youths who were supposed to serve only as security for the all-day event, which featured workshops exploring various problems affecting black America. The youths interrupted the celebration's banquet that evening, chastising the participants for having a good time, and telling them that there was too much work to be done in black America to be celebrating anything. Old Newton squad gunmen who allegedly had been responsible for turning the guns on some party members, and, as a result, hadn't been invited to participate, were said to be behind the sabotage. Order was restored by party veteran John Seale. But the damage had been done, and the event was abruptly ended.

Many party veterans in addition to Landon Williams, Sheeba Haven, and Mary Kennedy are now leading productive lives. (For example, former newspaper editor Michael Fultz teaches at the School of Education at the University of Wisconsin; former Central Committee member Kathleen Cleaver, a Yale Law School graduate, teaches at Emory University Law School; and former deputy minister of defense Bobby Rush is now a member of the U.S. Congress.) But many former party members, as was initially the case with Sheeba Haven, didn't do very well on leaving the party. An illustration of such an outcome was provided by David Hilliard in his autobiography, *This Side of Glory*. Hilliard described a personal life that devolved into crack and alcohol abuse, and chronic unemployment. As indicated previously, he was only partially candid about the inner workings of the party.

Illustrating the fate of another leading party member was the autobiography of Elaine Brown, *A Taste of Power*. As indicated previously, Brown also was only partially candid about the party's inner workings. Commented Kathleen Cleaver when asked about the book, "There are whole truths, half-truths, half-lies and whole lies. . . ." Rarely are party veterans totally candid about life in the party. And most share a tendency to lay most of the blame for its failings on the counterintelligence campaign of the U.S. government. "To see a government totally, blatantly, flagrantly cancel out the constitutional rights of citizens who challenge its policies is what I'm offended by," observed Kathleen Cleaver about the party, in retrospect.

That the government had a host of other organizations, black, white, Latino, Asian, under surveillance as well, is often overlooked by party veterans. That the party at one point expressly encouraged the murder of police officers, providing an incentive for counterintelligence measures and the canceling out of constitutional rights in an effort to destroy the party, is also often overlooked by party veterans.

As mentioned earlier, among all of the Black Panther veterans perhaps the most amazing story of turning around a life is that of Flores Forbes. Forbes—who earned the nickname "Fly" as a member of Newton's elite squad of enforcers terrorizing Oakland and Berkeley through the late 1970s, and who was the principal man behind the attempt to murder Crystal Gray to prevent her testimony against Newton in the Kathleen Smith murder case—emerged from Soledad prison in 1985 with three years of college credits behind him in a joint program that the prison maintained with San Jose State College. The following year he received his bachelor's degree in the Interdisciplinary Study of Social Sciences from San Francisco State University, completing a highly lauded thesis, "A Marxist Analysis of the New York Stock Exchange's Dow Jones Industrial Average." Following this he attended New York University's Robert F. Wagner Graduate School of Public Service, where he was awarded a Patricial Roberts Harris Fellowship. On graduation in 1989, when he received his master's degree in urban planning, he also received the Dean's Award for Outstanding Student Leadership. Forbes went to work for a Queens, New York, community development corporation, and then became a public policy analyst for a New York City think tank. Today he is an independent consultant for a neighborhood development organization in New York City's East Village and an independent film producer in partnership with a group that recently completed a film starring veteran actor Martin Sheen and singer/composer Isaac Hayes.

Forbes, now in his early forties, looks back on his Panther days and sees a young man who regrettably engaged in shocking activities until he was twenty-five years old. He recounts being enthralled by Huey Newton, intent on murdering Crystal Gray on Newton's behalf because Gray "threatened my leader." To those who would insist he and others who carried out sordid assignments for the party had been brainwashed the same way cult leaders such as Jim Jones and Charles Manson brainwashed their followers, Forbes replies, "Yes, I was used, but I knew I was being used." He regrets many of the actions he engaged in, but states that in the final analysis he and his cohorts did what they did out of the belief that they were at war with the U.S. government (Forbes denies Panther involvement in the murder of Betty Van Patter, Wilfred La Tour, and many other deaths identified with the party by journalists like Kate Coleman, but he does admit extorting money from Oakland and Berkeley pimps and drug dealers as part of a dues-paying policy that the party maintained). They reasoned that the government engages in criminal acts, particularly outside of U.S. borders, to maintain the nation's international hegemony. So he and other members of the Black Panther squad of enforcers used similar reasoning while carrying out their activities, feeling that the Panthers were the undisputed vanguard of black America, justified in carrying out anything that furthered "the cause," even if it had to be carried out against fellow African Americans.

That no one had elected the Black Panthers as black America's vanguard didn't matter to Forbes and others in the party, because they saw themselves as more enlightened than the masses. Huey

Newton, in fact, instilled within Forbes and others he designated as the elite "chosen" among the Black Panthers (according to Forbes, his exact designation for them was the "Buddha Samurai") the sense that you couldn't wait for the masses to catch up. You did whatever it was you had to do on their behalf.

Despite how Forbes or anyone else feels about his Black Panther days, however, the principal value in Forbes's life story is his will to survive and transform his life—a will that was, in fact, characteristic of only a handful of the Black Panthers (and, ironically, in the final analysis was missing in Newton himself). Unlike so many other black men, since his Black Panther days Forbes has believed that nothing is beyond his reach. He credits Huey Newton with instilling this within him, agreeing that Newton had a mountain of faults, while maintaining—as Bob Trivors and so many others insist—that despite Newton's frightening character, he was a genius.

AFTER THE FINAL LEG OF NEWTON'S PANTHER EMPIRE (The Oakland Community Learning Center) closed down, the facility was bought by the Black Muslims, who transformed it into a mosque. Then in 1987 it was purchased by Bay Area radio evangelist Bob Jackson and turned into Acts Full Gospel Church, becoming one of the most successful institutions in America at turning young African Americans away from the drug that ultimately consumed Huey Newton—crack cocaine. Today Acts has a congregation of just over 3,000 members and is one of the fastest-growing churches in the Bay Area. It uses specialized teams in its free residential treatment program, supervised by associate minister Roosevelt Taylor, the former drug dealer who takes responsibility for being one of the pioneers of crack cocaine. In the opinion of Mildred Hornbeck, a successful businesswoman whose son was once hopelessly lost to crack and then freed from its grip by Acts, the church can do a much better job than any secular institution "because of its theatrical atmosphere during services. It plays on the emotions of the addicted in a way the secular world cannot reach them."

Despite the resurgence of religious institutions as the vanguard of self-help in the black community, the Black Panthers still hold legendary appeal to many young blacks who were either infants or toddlers in the party's heyday, or not even born yet. Popular rap performers such as Oscar Jackson, Jr., who goes by the stage name Paris, and Tupac Shakur (whose mother, Assata Shakur, was a member of the Black Panther New York 21 who were expelled from the party by Huey Newton) promote the party as black American heroes. And the party's defiant, uniformed imagery holds potency for many other young blacks who are searching for images on which to base their self-esteem (the filmmaker John Singleton, in a 1993 publicity photo with the poet Maya Angelou, was shown donning a baseball cap with the words *Black Panthers* sewn on the front of it). How else to explain the fact that the Black Panthers are far more indelibly stamped in their imaginations than are, for example, the images of SNCC members such as John Lewis, Bob Moses, and their cohorts?

Even former Panthers see the danger in this idolatry. "A lot of young people look back on the Black Panther Party and they see icons," Elaine Brown observed in a radio interview while on tour promoting her autobiography. "But icons are a very dangerous thing to create. Icons make mistakes." But black America finds it difficult to review its mistakes while white America is watching, since African American mistakes are often used to rationalize racism.

However, increasingly, the eventual emphasis on defiant symbolism over concrete achievements that characterized the era of civil rights and Black Power is being interpreted as a mistake. Respected veterans of the era, such as SNCC's Bob Moses, who dropped out of SNCC not only because of its turn toward defiant symbolism but to leave the country and escape the draft, are retooling for challenges they feel must be met if African Americans are to prosper in the future. Moses, along with Mississippi CORE veteran David Dennis, has returned to Mississippi to lead the Algebra Project, a program designed to improve the math skills of the children and grandchildren of the very people for whom Moses and Dennis risked their lives to help empower at the ballot box.

SNCC veteran John Lewis, who also dropped out of SNCC after its turn toward defiant symbolism, now sits in the U.S. Congress with Panther veteran Bobby Rush.

As for the veteran leaders of SNCC who actively promoted Black Power, their lives too have been redirected into constructive pursuits. As mentioned earlier, H. Rap Brown is currently an Islamic Imam in Atlanta who goes by the name Jamal Al-Amin. Al-Amin leads a small congregation that worships out of a converted clapboard house on Atlanta's west side. He also quietly runs a small convenience store around the corner from the mosque. (On a visit to his store in the summer of 1992, the author observed Al-Amin playfully chastise two small boys as he retrieved his basketball for them to borrow. Three small girls were there, purchasing candy. All seemed to know him very well and love him. Al-Amin appeared quiet, reflective, and determined to lead his congregation modestly, minus the glare of the media.) James Forman, the man who didn't give up his direct involvement in furthering the concept of Black Power until he allegedly was confronted by Eldridge Cleaver and other Black Panthers with a gun, currently resides in Washington, D.C., where he is president of the Unemployment and Poverty Action Committee.

Stokely Carmichael, who did so much to promote the Black Power slogan and inspire offspring of the slogan such as the Black Panther Party (which he joined briefly before denouncing the party's violent tactics against its own members), now goes by the name Kwame Touré. He remains in the African nation of Guinea-Bissau, where he serves as political adviser to the Democratic party of that nation. Touré, who became a fervent believer in Pan Africanism as a result of his frustration with American electoral politics while working in SNCC, still believes in Pan Africanism, despite the depressing political realities throughout black Africa. And he feels the sting of bitterness that electoral politics hasn't generated major change in the lives of so many African Americans. "[African Americans] have more elected officials in the Democratic party than any other ethnic group in this country," he told Gary Byrd of New York City radio station WLIB in January 1993. "Yet we have no power at all in the Democratic party. That's why racism continues to run rampant and will continue to run rampant until we get power to stop it."

There must be some meaning buried in the fact that all five principal leaders of SNCC—Lewis, Moses, Forman, Carmichael, and Brown—redirected their postactivist lives into constructive, noncriminal behavior, while not one of the top three leaders of the Black Panther Party—Newton, Seale, and Cleaver—had much success in doing the same. Eldridge Cleaver's life has spiraled down a course that in some ways is similar to the direction Huey's life took before he was murdered. Although he became involved in conservative causes like the Mormon Church and with the Reverend Sun Yung Moon's Unification Church, in 1987, Cleaver, still a Bay Area resident, was arrested for possession of crack cocaine. In 1988 he was jailed for violating his probation after testing positive for cocaine. That same year he was placed on probation after being convicted of burglarizing a house under renovation. In the summer of 1990 he entered a drug rehabilitation center to recover from what he said was an addiction to crack cocaine. And in June 1992 he was again arrested for possession of crack cocaine after allegedly being seen coming out of a crack house on Adeline Street in West Oakland. Only Bobby Seale, with his Temple University affiliation, has had anything approaching success in redirecting his life. But Seale, a recovering alcoholic, also had a post-Panther era brush with the law. In November 1989 he pleaded guilty to four misdemeanor counts of passing bad checks totaling in value more than $10,700, at a National Barbecue Rib Cook-Off in Cleveland. Seale was sentenced to one year of probation, fined $1,000, and ordered to perform one hundred hours of community service.

The comparative outcome of the lives of top SNCC leaders versus top Panther leaders should lead us all to wonder if the media intentionally placed so much emphasis in the late 1960s and early 1970s on African American leaders with criminal mind-sets, encouraging the notion that "true blacks" are those most alienated from American society. Granted, Stokely Carmichael, James Forman, H. Rap Brown, and the others in SNCC who birthed the concept of Black Power must share much of the blame for the turn of events. However, although SNCC originated the symbol of the

Black Panther, SNCC's leaders did not promote the Black Panther Party for Self-Defense until they saw that their organization was losing steam while the Panthers were gaining steam. And once they realized the mistake they had made, the SNCC leaders backed away, while the radical Left and the left-liberal media continued to play a major role in elevating the rudest, most outlaw element of black America as the true keepers of the flame in all it means to be black. We see how intact this idea remains via the popularity of the musical genre "gangsta rap." And it has again shown up in the literary world. The year 1993 saw the debut of a memoir by an African American male who was promoted in a way frighteningly similar to the way Eldridge Cleaver was introduced to the public in the late 1960s.

Former LA gang member Cody Scott, who earned the moniker Monster Cody from LA police after he brutally beat a man to death, describes in his memoir, *Monster: The Autobiography of an LA Gang Member*, the senseless murders of other blacks which he also engaged in as a member of LA's Eight Tray Crips. White journalist William Broyles, who facilitated the publication of Scott's book, is analogous to journalist Bob Scheer, who in 1966 was a facilitator of Eldridge Cleaver's career. Atlantic Monthly Press, publisher of Scott's book, is analogous to Ramparts Books, publisher of Cleaver's *Soul on Ice*. Just as Cleaver's book was touted by Maxwell Geismar of *Ramparts* as "a document of prime importance for an understanding of the outcast black American soul today," Morgan Entrekin of the Atlantic Monthly Press has said that Scott, as a result of his memoir, is a "primary voice of the black experience."

Scott was also written about by Leon Bing, a white former fashion model who in 1991 wrote a book about black gangs called *Do or Die*. Bing, a woman, could be analogous to that other facilitator of Cleaver's career, Beverly Axelrod.

"The whole of Bing's book rests subliminally on a 'threat of rape' foundation," wrote African American critic Leonce Gaither, a Harvard graduate who was outraged that Scott's former life was being enthusiastically examined by the predominantly white press. Of course, rape fantasies were given direct voice in Cleaver's *Soul on Ice*. And although Scott is now reformed and professes a belief in Afrocentricity (as do many others who have led a life like his, including Cleaver, he states he underwent his conversion in prison), the cover of his memoir is an approximation of the old Monster—shirtless, with pumped-up muscles and gang tattoos, he holds a semiautomatic weapon, providing the subliminal message that black men are the embodiment of raw, sexually charged societal rapists.

Might the gun-toting Black Panther images of the late 1960s and early 1970s (including Huey Newton in the wicker chair, gun in one hand, spear in the other) have delivered the same ultimate message as Scott's book cover? Indeed, the line may be blurred between the proud black imagery that Huey Newton provided, when black America needed such imagery, and his role in providing, along with the rest of the Black Panthers, an image that could have been not a racist's worst nightmare but a racist's ultimate dream.

The shadow of the Panther casts images that are good and bad, but principally they are images of defiant posturing over substance. We will continue to see the predominance of posturing over substance among African Americans as long as so many promote themselves and are promoted by the media as pathological outsiders to the American mainstream. And the Black Panther Party will remain a historical phenomenon that was the quintessential intersection of all the confusion inherent in what it has meant to be African American for the past thirty years.

Acknowledgments

I ORIGINALLY BEGAN THIS BOOK WITH THE GENUINE CURI-
osity of an African American who came of age during the era of
black militancy. When Stokely Carmichael called for Black Power
in the summer of 1966, I was eight years old going on nine, and
about to enter the fourth grade in the predominantly white elementary school I attended on the outskirts of Fort Wayne, Indiana.
My father was a physician, originally from Georgia, brought up
in the old-school black bourgeoisie way of thinking. Both my
mother's and father's sides of the family had been solidly middle
class virtually since the end of slavery, residing primarily in Georgia
(my mother, father, and year-old sister moved to Fort Wayne just
before I was born). During the days of Jim Crow, my maternal
grandmother's oldest brother, Dr. Joseph Howard Griffin, built
and operated the largest and best-equipped hospital for blacks in
all of Georgia.

Like many other middle-class blacks in the 1960s, I felt the
sting of rejection by other blacks because my family was successful.
As a precocious eight-year-old who liked to read, I was searching
for my identity, so I enthusiastically read about the Black Power
movement. And as a result of such reading, I and two other black

boys in my elementary school class decided to stop doing our schoolwork because, we concluded, to do the work would mean that we were becoming like white people, and not being genuinely black.

But my elementary school years were also characterized by something else—the sting of rejection I felt because my birth name was Huey. I had been named after my father. Like Huey Newton, I was ridiculed because of that name. But when I reached the seventh grade, I discovered the book *Free Huey*. It was the first time I had seen the handsome face of Huey Newton. I read the book and became quite elated that someone named Huey could be such a hero to so many people. I also began reading about the Black Panther Party and easily accepted the left-liberal notions of that day, which painted the party as principally an altruistic group of young black people who were being hounded by a racist establishment.

In junior high school and, most important, in high school, I finally became convinced that it was possible, even necessary, to get good grades in every subject and still be black. I kept reading about the Black Panthers, including Huey Newton's books *To Die for the People* and *Revolutionary Suicide*. But I also read a book around that time called *The Best and the Brightest*, by David Halberstam, which was filled with Vietnam War advisers who attended Ivy League schools. For some reason I was more fascinated by the minds of advisers such as McGeorge Bundy than repulsed by the manner in which the United States became involved in that tragic war. One peculiar side effect of the book was that I became convinced that I too needed an Ivy League education. I hit the books, and by the time I graduated from my predominantly white high school, I was among the best students in the school and had earned admission to Brown University.

At Brown I suffered from the same confused notions of elitism mixed with a determination to "remain black" that characterize the behavior of black students at prestigious predominantly white universities today. I never quite figured out what I really wanted to do. After a short stint in medical school, followed by graduate school in Urban Planning, an internship with urban developer James Rouse, then a brief stint working as a project manager for the Harlem Urban Development Corporation, I decided to return to writing, in which I had made my mark as a high school and college student.

In the spring of 1988, I saw my first professional writing piece published in *New York Newsday*. It was an opinion editorial. More *Newsday* opinion editorials followed, and eventually came an assignment from *The Village Voice*. While I was completing that assignment, during the summer of 1989, Huey Newton was shot and killed, rekindling my interest in the Black Panthers. In fact, one of the editors at *The Village Voice* asked me if I would like to write *The Voice*'s tribute to Newton. Wisely, *The Voice* decided on someone else who had a far greater understanding of the Black Panther era at that time—Kathleen Cleaver.

Along with my renewed interest in the Black Panthers came the idea for a book about the survivors of the party. As a way into the research, I suggested an article to the *San Francisco Weekly* about the proposed People's Organized Response. The *Weekly* bought the idea, and in February 1990 I met with David Hilliard in an office on Telegraph Avenue in Oakland to discuss the proposed organization. Still green about the party, I had no reason to be suspicious of anything Hilliard told me about the proposed organization or the history of the Black Panthers. I also interviewed former Panther attorney Stephen Bingham and former party lawyer Charles Garry. Ultimately, I wrote a story that implied the Black Panthers were about to make a comeback. It took the typical leftist line about the old party—that it had been railroaded out of existence by the American establishment, that the party itself was not to blame for its fate.

Pursuing the book idea, I decided that the best way to say the positive things I wanted to say about Newton and the party was to write parallel biographies of Huey Newton and selected Panther veterans who had successfully redirected their lives into positive pursuits. I was particularly interested in writing about Panther men, since I was convinced that the public had read enough about the negative behavior of black men and I had no interest in writing solely about the downward spiral of Huey Newton. The goal was to provide snapshots of the complexity of black life, rather than the simplistic cliché of a black man who sank into brutal madness.

Pursuant to the idea, someone recommended that I talk to Panther veteran Landon Williams, who was doing very positive work for the city of Berkeley. I called Williams, sat down with him in October 1991, and told him my idea. He was very enthusiastic about it. He also gave me my first window into how brutal the downfall of the party really had been. The more people I talked to, the more I became convinced that there was far more to the Panther story and the downward spiral of Huey Newton's life than the Left was willing to admit.

I also attended the trial of Tyrone Robinson, the accused triggerman in the murder of Huey Newton. While at the trial, I approached Willie Payne, who gave his testimony about what had happened on the night of Newton's murder. Payne agreed to grant me an interview after the trial was over and a verdict had been reached. In the meantime, my idea of getting three male Panther veterans who had positively redirected their lives to be part of the book wasn't going as well as I had wished. Landon Williams was the only one on board. I had also come across a woman who had been in the party, Sheeba Haven. At that point I altered my idea to include both a female Panther veteran and a male Panther veteran, whose lives would be contrasted with Newton's.

I discovered that it was virtually impossible to walk a fine line between all the Black Panther factions. When many of the party veterans who felt protective of Huey's image discovered that I was talking with those who didn't feel the same way—veterans such as Landon Williams and Sheeba Haven—they refused to cooperate. Ironically, it was easiest to gain the cooperation of nonblacks who had been affiliated with Newton and the party. People like Fred Hiestand, Alex Hoffman, Bob Trivors, "Lianna," all friends of Huey—most of them until the day he died—were quite helpful. Hiestand was completely repulsed by writers like Ken Kelly, Kate Coleman, and David Horowitz, who had written negative accounts of Newton's life. Yet he was willing to cooperate with me in the goal of writing a nonpartisan account of Huey's life. He even tried to put me in contact with Bert Schneider, although Schneider never responded to my overtures.

More problematic were the many former Panthers who refused to cooperate unless there was money involved, and those who were just plain miffed that someone who hadn't been in the party would have the audacity to write about it. My response to all requests for money was "No."

Huey's brother Melvin was among those I hoped would be cooperative. I spoke with him, along with one of Huey's most trusted friends, at Melvin Newton's home in the Oakland Hills in the summer of 1992. Both men agreed to be interviewed for an objective portrayal of Huey. But when I returned to Melvin Newton's home in August 1992 for another interview, I discovered how painful it was for him to talk about his brother. As David Hilliard made clear in his autobiography, although Melvin Newton loved his brother, the constant trouble Huey got into with the law had caused Melvin tremendous headaches during most of their lives together.

Getting Melvin to talk about Huey during the August interview was like trying to squeeze blood out of a stone. He suggested that I talk to David Hilliard. But Hilliard refused to cooperate because he was working on his own book. I still had the agreement of Huey's close friend whom I had met at Melvin's house some weeks prior to August 1992. But when I traveled to where he lived to meet with him, he responded the same way that many others had responded: he wanted my publisher to cut him in on the contract for a share of royalties or he wouldn't cooperate. So, essentially, for the life inside the party from the point of view of party veterans I was left with those who would never forgive Huey for what he did to the party. But in November 1993, Panther veteran Flores Forbes, an integral member of the party in its later years, as the text makes clear—whom I had contacted one year earlier and who at the time expressed reservations about cooperating—had a change of heart. Just before this book went to press, Forbes gave me valuable insight into party philosophy from the years 1974 to 1977, as well as into the thinking of Huey Newton—

insight that became indispensable to my final assessment of Newton. Ultimately, Landon Williams and Mary Kennedy, whom I
added to the book in August 1992 as a result of her very candid
and shocking revelations about life in the party, were the most
illuminating interviewees. I also secured major amounts of information from congressional investigations, old newspaper clips, old
courthouse documents from the testimony of witnesses in Panther-
related criminal cases, and the other sources listed in the source
notes.

I interviewed David Horowitz at his home in October 1992.
The entire account of his involvement with the party is based on
that interview and not on the article he wrote for his magazine
Heterodoxy in March 1993, about his encounter with the Panthers,
an account that was also reprinted in the *San Francisco Examiner* in
May 1993. Horowitz wrote the article out of understandable anger
over the falsehoods contained in Elaine Brown's autobiography. I
see no reason to question the validity of his account of his experiences in the party. The lack of response by Elaine Brown to the
specific charges Horowitz makes—a response sought by the *Examiner* before reprinting the *Heterodoxy* article—speaks for itself.*

This book was not intended as a comprehensive history of the
Black Panther Party. Such a project would take many years to
complete and would require the navigation of political minefields
I have no interest in traversing. One of the things that struck me
as I wrote was how disappointed, even angry, I often became at our

---

*Like Horowitz, Tamara Van Patter Baltar, Betty Van Patter's daughter, also
believes that the Black Panther Party murdered her mother, although she doesn't
share Horowitz's conservative political views. "It wasn't until Elaine Brown's book
came out that I became willing to talk to journalists about what happened to my
mother [due to that book's false criminal accusations about Betty Van Patter],"
says Baltar. "Me and my family did hire a private investigator in 1984 to look into
the murder." The investigator agreed that the Black Panthers had murdered Van
Patter, but advised her family that they risked their personal safety if they investigated any further. His only departure from the Horowitz scenario of how the
murder might have occurred was in theorizing that Van Patter may have been
murdered after driving to the Lamp Post and confronting the Panthers about
illegal activities, only to be murdered on the spot in a fit of Panther anger (and
her body later dumped in San Francisco Bay), buttressing Huey Newton's insistence to Horowitz that Van Patter's murder "was out of my hands."

society and myself, for paying so much attention to an organization that, arguably, in so many ways amounted to little more than a temporary media phenomenon. I was also disappointed that I had to write about so much negative behavior after believing, initially, that most of what I heard about the party—the beauty of its breakfast programs, its communal theories, and so on—far outweighed the negative. However, I could not conceal the truth. Most painful for me was writing about the stereotypical behavior of so many Panther men. I have prided myself in being a writer who focuses on black men who call the lie to the notion that all of us are brutal, and I have pursued that goal with a passion. To turn around, then, and write a book that fuels racist notions was not something I intended. I hope that the historical accounts of black men in the pre-Panther era, as well as accounts of the outcome of Landon Williams's life and the behavior of men like former Panther school principal William Schuford, counter much of the negativity in the book.

As for Huey Newton himself, enough has been written on previous pages. But let me add this: I am convinced that his enigmatic behavior had something to do with his carrying the name Huey. His reaction was the polar opposite to mine while I was growing up with that name. Rather than shrink from potential tormentors, as I did, Newton terrorized them with preemptive assaults. I wish I had met him.

I want to acknowledge those who helped make this book possible. Candice Fuhrman, my agent, has been a tremendous help along the way. Elizabeth Perle McKenna, Vice President and Publisher of Addison-Wesley, is the one whose initial faith and foresight gave me the confidence—and a contract—to write this book. Thanks also to Don Fehr, my editor at Addison-Wesley; art director Jean Seal, for the outstanding book cover she helped create; production supervisor Pat Jalbert, for walking me through the production schedule; Nancy Bell Scott, for copyediting the manuscript; and editorial assistant Wendy Hickok Robinson, for handling the small details that must be taken care of when an author corresponds with his publisher.

Special thanks to Sandy Close, executive editor at Pacific

News Service, who has helped me as a writer in ways it is impossible to repay, and to author and Pacific News Service editor Richard Rodriguez for being the exacting taskmaster he has been over the last four years while critiquing my writing at Pacific News Service, forcing me to hone my skills in ways I otherwise would not have done. I am also indebted to Franz Schurrman, another invaluable member of the Pacific News Service family, and the first two editors I ever worked with professionally: Jim Sleeper, formerly of *New York Newsday*, now an urban affairs columnist for the *Daily News;* and Ben Gerson, Sunday opinion page editor at *Newsday*.

Finally, I want to thank the many people who agreed to be interviewed for this book, cited in the source notes—especially Mae Jackson, who was a constant source of inspiration during my most frustrated moments, and Kiilu Nyasha, who served much the same role. I would also like to thank Richard Geiger, Director of Libraries at the *San Francisco Chronicle*, for allowing me access to everything the *Chronicle* had on the Black Panthers; the staff of the Bancroft Library at UC Berkeley for patiently fulfilling my many document requests; the personnel of the archives reading room at the FBI headquarters in Washington, D.C., for doing the same; and the personnel at public libraries in San Francisco and Oakland, as well as the Library of Congress in Washington, D.C. Thank you all.

Hugh Pearson
New York City
December 1993

Notes

CHAPTER 1

1 Profile of Willie Payne and details of his encounter with Huey on Newton's last day: Interview with Willie Payne, Oakland, July 28, 1992.

2 Panthers first meeting on Peralta Street in West Oakland: "Huey Newton Shot Dead on West Oakland Street," by Lori Olazewski and Rick DelVecchio, *San Francisco Chronicle*, August 23, 1989.

3 Details of Newton/Frey encounter: "The Persecution and Assassination of the Black Panthers as Performed by the Oakland Police under the Direction of Chief Charles R. Gain, Mayor Reading, et al," by Gene Marine, *Ramparts*, July 13, 1968; *Revolutionary Suicide*, by Huey Newton (Harcourt Brace Jovanovich, 1973), pp. 171–176; *A Panther Is a Black Cat*, by Reginald Major (William Morrow, 1971), pp. 179–182, 221, 234–235.

3 Newton admitting to killing Frey: Interview with Robert Trivors, Santa Cruz, October 2, 1992; interview with Willie Payne, Oakland, July 28, 1992.

4 Bios of Landon Williams, Mary Kennedy, Sheeba Haven: Interview with Landon Williams, Berkeley, October 1991; interview with Mary

Kennedy, Oakland, August 29, 1992; interview with Sheeba Haven, San Francisco, October 1991.

4 Rise of drug-dealing empires like the 69 Mob, and relations with Huey Newton: "A Small War in Oakland," by Carla Marinucci and Lance Williams (four-part series), *San Francisco Examiner*, November 25, 26, 27, 28, 1984; "Conspiracy Trial in Big Heroin Case," by Lance Williams, *San Francisco Examiner*, January 20, 1985.

5 Allegations of Huey planning to use Cuban cocaine connection to establish cocaine empire: *Spitting in the Wind*, by Earl Anthony (Roundtable, 1990), p. 189.

5 Charges against Newton in killing of the prostitute and his beating the charges: Newton chronology accompanying series of stories "The Death of Huey Newton," *Oakland Tribune*, August 23, 1989.

5 Start of embezzlement investigation of Oakland Community Learning Center: From transcripts of "People of the State of California vs. Huey P. Newton," Superior Court of the State of California, County of Alameda, June 23, 1987.

5 Fate of Felix Mitchell and rise of relative, Daryl Reed, as drug dealer: "Mitchell Kin Inherited Drug Empire, Police Say," by Lance Williams, *San Francisco Examiner*, December 11, 1988.

6 Rumors connecting BGF to murder of Newton: "Huey Newton Gunned Down in West Oakland, The Final Chapter: Police Suspect Drugs Involved," by Harry Harris, *Oakland Tribune*, August 23, 1989; "Confessions in Slaying of Newton," by Lonn Johnston and Clarence Johnson, *San Francisco Chronicle*, August 26, 1989.

6 BGF alleged to have approximately twenty dealers in Oakland: "Newton Slaying Suspect Arrested," by Harry Harris and Paul Grabowicz, *Oakland Tribune*, August 26, 1989.

7 Willie Payne's last moments with Huey Newton: Interview with Willie Payne, Oakland, July 28, 1992.

CHAPTER 2

12 Description of the situation at Southern Pacific Railroad helping lead to the creation of the Brotherhood of Sleeping Car Porters: Oral history of C. L. Dellums, Bancroft Collection, Bancroft Library, UC Berkeley.

13 360,000 black men in World War I: "Black Power and Coalition Politics," by Bayard Rustin, *Commentary*, September 1966.

14 Marcus Garvey's "Buy Black" campaigns: Ibid.

16 Negro participation in WPA projects: Ibid.

16 Randolph's role in Roosevelt's issuance of executive order 8802: Oral history of C. L. Dellums, Bancroft Collection, Bancroft Library, UC Berkeley.

17 E. D. Nixon as admirer of A. Philip Randolph and head of Alabama Brotherhood of Sleeping Car Porters: *Parting the Waters*, by Taylor Branch (Simon and Schuster, 1988), p. 121.

18 Powell running for congressional seat it was hoped A. Philip Randolph would run for: *Adam Clayton Powell, Jr.*, by Charles V. Hamilton (Atheneum, 1991), p. 146.

18 E. D. Nixon as the man Negroes would go to for civil rights complaints in Montgomery: *Parting the Waters*, by Taylor Branch (Simon and Schuster, 1988), p. 121.

19 Rosa Parks's arrest on Montgomery bus, E. D. Nixon's involvement in instigating court case, and Montgomery Negro women involved in suggesting boycott: Ibid., pp. 129–130.

20 E. D. Nixon telling others at first Montgomery boycott meeting it was time to be "mens," and Martin Luther King responding: Ibid., pp. 136–137.

21 Bob Moses's initial impressions of civil rights movement and his background: Ibid., pp. 300–301, 325.

22 James Forman's background and initial impressions of civil rights movement: *The Making of Black Revolutionaries*, by James Forman (Macmillan, 1972; Open Hand, 1990), p. 85.

23 Mike Wallace's description of criminal records of Malcolm X and Elijah Muhammad in "The Hate That Hate Produced" *Malcolm X, the FBI File*, ed. by Clayborne Carson (Carroll and Graf, 1991), p. 162.

23 Only the finest upstanding Negroes picked by organizer E. D. Nixon: *Parting the Waters*, by Taylor Branch (Simon and Schuster, 1988), p. 123.

23 Mike Wallace showing Hulan Jack and Roy Wilkins meeting with

Malcolm X in "The Hate That Hate Produced": *Malcolm X, the FBI File*, ed. by Clayborne Carson (Carroll and Graf, 1991), p. 161.

24 Cooperation from local authorities helping whites to oppress Negroes while the North looked the other way: *Dark Journey, Black Mississippians in the Age of Jim Crow*, by Neil R. McMillen (Univ. of Illinois Press, 1989), pp. 228–233.

24 Gruesome torture and murder of black couple described in Vicksburg, MS, newspaper: Ibid., p. 234.

25 Racist incidents experienced by Dr. Albert Perry and Robert Williams in Monroe, NC: *The Making of Black Revolutionaries*, by James Forman (Macmillan, 1972; Open Hand, 1990), pp. 165–166.

26 Robert Williams: "What are you fellows doing here?" Ibid., p. 167.

26 Abortion accusation against Dr. Albert Perry: Ibid., p. 167.

27 "Kissing case": Ibid., pp. 172–174.

27 Monroe area rape cases: Ibid., p. 175.

28 Robert Williams quoted saying, "We cannot rely on the law" and falling-out with NAACP: Ibid., p. 176.

29 John Lewis's background and initial civil rights training: *Parting the Waters*, by Taylor Branch (Simon and Schuster, 1988), pp. 261–263.

29 Initial lunch counter sit-ins in Greensboro, NC: Ibid., p. 271.

29 John Lewis leading Nashville sit-ins: Ibid., p. 279.

31 Ella Baker, Martin Luther King, and Wyatt T. Walker's involvement in the formation of SNCC over Easter weekend, 1960: *The Making of Black Revolutionaries*, by James Forman (Macmillan, 1972; Open Hand, 1990), pp. 216–217.

31 History of CORE and Freedom Rides: *Parting the Waters*, by Taylor Branch (Simon and Schuster, 1988), pp. 389–390, 417–477; *The Making of Black Revolutionaries*, by James Forman (Macmillan, 1972; Open Hand, 1990), pp. 150–157.

35 James Forman's first involvement in southern activism: *The Making of Black Revolutionaries*, by James Forman (Macmillan, 1972; Open Hand, 1990), pp. 137–138.

35 James Forman being informed about Robert Williams by Paul Brooks: Ibid., p. 158.

35 Robert Williams's letter to Cuban ambassador: Ibid., p. 177.

36 Ramming incidents to Williams's car: Ibid., pp. 179–180.

36 List of demands to city of Monroe: Ibid., p. 187.

36 Quote of exchange among Forman, Brooks, and Pullman porter on the way to Monroe, NC: Ibid., p. 162.

37 Marshaling of Freedom Riders to go to Monroe: Ibid., p. 187.

37 Statistics on black disenfranchisement in Mississippi: *Dark Journey,* by Neil R. McMillen (Univ. of Illinois Press, 1989), pp. 35–71.

37 Justice Department's urging of voter registration and debate within SNCC between direct action and voter registration advocates: *Parting the Waters,* by Taylor Branch (Simon and Schuster, 1988), pp. 404–405; *The Making of Black Revolutionaries,* by James Forman (Macmillan, 1972; Open Hand, 1990), p. 187.

38 Taunts by Monroe whites, including "Your mama's at home sleeping with a nigger": *The Making of Black Revolutionaries,* by James Forman (Macmillan, 1972; Open Hand, 1990), pp. 188–189.

38 Forman describing black prisoners as being in prison for other unjust causes, conviction of Forman and others: Ibid., pp. 200, 209–210.

38 Account of black crowd gathering in Newtown and the alleged kidnapping of white couple by Robert Williams: Ibid., pp. 207–208; "The Monroe Kidnapping," by Julian Mayfield, *West Indian Gazette and Afro-Asian Caribbean News,* November 1961, contained in Bancroft Collection on Social Protest Movements, Bancroft Library, UC Berkeley.

40 Invitation to Bob Moses to begin voter registration work in McComb, MS: *Parting the Waters,* by Taylor Branch (Simon and Schuster, 1988), pp. 492–494.

40 Moses's arrest, then bailout by reluctant NAACP: Ibid., p. 495.

40 Involvement of Hollis Watkins in voter registration, direct action, and arrest by Mississippi police: *The Making of Black Revolutionaries,* by James Forman (Macmillan, 1972; Open Hand, 1990), pp. 227–228.

41 Encounter between E. H. Hurst and Herbert Lee, and Lee's widow and Bob Moses: *Parting the Waters,* by Taylor Branch (Simon and Schuster, 1988), pp. 510–511.

CHAPTER 3

43 Background of Joe Blum, atmosphere at Oakland City College (Merritt College), and recollections of Huey Newton as a student there: Interview with Joe Blum, San Francisco, September 9, 1992.

45 Newton as part of Donald Warden's Afro-American Association: *Revolutionary Suicide*, by Huey Newton (Harcourt Brace Jovanovich, 1973), p. 63.

45 Newton's family background and youth: *Revolutionary Suicide*, by Huey Newton (Harcourt Brace Jovanovich, 1973).

46 Quote of Newton regarding his father's work habits: *Revolutionary Suicide*, by Huey Newton (Harcourt Brace Jovanovich, 1973), p. 12.

46 Melvin Newton's denial that Huey graduated from high school without knowing how to read: Interview with Melvin Newton, Oakland, August 3, 1992. *Note:* Because Melvin Newton demonstrated such reluctance to talk about his brother and the Black Panthers, I decided not to contact him anymore after the first interview. Thus, later in the book when controversial matters involving Melvin Newton (such as the breakup of the alliance between the Black Panthers and SNCC) are mentioned, Melvin was not contacted for his take on the controversy. When I asked his advice on how best to secure further information about the party, he told me to talk to David Hilliard. David Hilliard refused all requests for interviews.

48 Negro migration to the East Bay and employment and union statistics: "On the Sidewalk," by Tom Berkley, *Oakland Post*, October 9, 1968; *A Fine Old Conflict*, by Jessica Mitford (Knopf, 1977), pp. 106–107; "Metropoly: The Story of Oakland California," by Warren Hinckle, *Ramparts*, February 1966.

49 Quote of Jessica Mitford on police brutality in Oakland: *A Fine Old Conflict*, by Jessica Mitford (Knopf, 1977), p. 108.

49 Police brutality in Oakland, composition of the Oakland power structure, employment statistics, and public school conditions: "Metropoly: The Story of Oakland, California," by Warren Hinckle, *Ramparts*, February 1966.

50 House Un-American Activities Committee and UC Berkeley: *Destructive Generation*, by Peter Collier and David Horowitz (Summit, 1989), chapter "Slouching Towards Berkeley."

51 Initial picketing style of Campus CORE: "Recent Trends in the

Local Civil Rights Movement," by Jack Weinberg *Berkeley Campus CORE Newsletter*, June 1964, contained in Bancroft Collection on Social Protest Movements, Bancroft Library, UC Berkeley.

51 Campus CORE action against Montgomery Ward: Ibid.

52 James Baldwin quote, "I'm not going to go into the details . . .": "Overflow Crowd Hears Baldwin on Race Issues," *Daily Californian*, May 8, 1963.

52 Statistics on number of demonstrations and arrests after Birmingham campaign: *Parting the Waters*, by Taylor Branch (Simon and Schuster, 1988), p. 825.

52 Description of Mel's Drive-In restaurant picketing: "Recent Trends in the Local Civil Rights Movement," by Jack Weinberg *Berkeley Campus CORE Newsletter*, June 1964, contained in Bancroft Collection on Social Protest Movements, Bancroft Library, UC Berkeley; "Picketers Want Negroes Hired in Top Positions Now," *Daily Californian*, November 8, 1963; "Pickets Claim Hiring Victory," Ibid., November 11, 1963.

53 John Lewis's description of SNCC to UC Berkeley students and criticism of other civil rights organizations: "SNCC Chairman Here; Says Negroes May March," by Diane Gifford, *Daily Californian*, December 9, 1963.

54 Voter Education Project meetings and opposition to and support of the project: *The Making of Black Revolutionaries*, by James Forman (Macmillan, 1972; Open Hand, 1990), pp. 266, 288; *Parting the Waters*, by Taylor Branch (Simon and Schuster, 1988), p. 578.

54 Freedom Vote in Mississippi: "Freedom Man 'Wins'," by Dave Allen, *Daily Californian*, November 11, 1963.

55 Recruitment of Yale and Stanford students by Allard Lowenstein: *The Making of Black Revolutionaries*, by James Forman (Macmillan, 1972; Open Hand, 1990), pp. 356–357.

55 Full-page ad by twenty-six UC Berkeley faculty: "In Support of SNCC," *Daily Californian*, December 12, 1963.

56 Origin of the Ad Hoc Committee to End Discrimination: "Ad Hoc Demonstrations Defended," by Aune Van Dyke, *Daily Californian*, March 16, 1964.

56 Campus CORE Lucky store demonstrations: *Daily Californian*, issues dated February 19, 21, 25, 27, 1964; "Recent Trends in the Local

Civil Rights Movement," by Jack Weinberg, *Berkeley Campus CORE Newsletter*, June 1964, contained in Bancroft Collection on Social Protest Movements, Bancroft Library, UC Berkeley; and Campus CORE fund-raising flyer from summer 1964, contained in Bancroft Collection on Social Protest Movements, Bancroft Library, UC Berkeley.

57 Sheraton Palace demonstration: "Demonstrators—1, Sheraton—0," by Nancy Tolbert, "A Weekend of Songs, Sit-ins and Sleep-ins," by Jim Willwerth, *Daily Californian*, March 9, 1964.

59 Cadillac demonstrations on San Francisco's Auto Row: "Cadillac 'Pickets' Arrested," *Daily Californian*, March 16, 1964.

60 Quote of Dick Gregory regarding reason for success of San Francisco demonstrations: Newsletter *Justice in Civil Rights Trials*, produced by Committee for Justice in Civil Rights Cases, Berkeley, fall 1964, contained in Bancroft Collection on Social Protest Movements, Bancroft Library, UC Berkeley.

60 Moratorium on demonstrations and negotiation committee set up by San Francisco mayor: "Shelley Announces Rights Truce; Proposes 'Peace Committee'," *Daily Californian*, March 16, 1964.

61 Quote of James Forman on purpose of Mississippi Freedom Summer: *The Making of Black Revolutionaries*, by James Forman (Macmillan, 1972; Open Hand, 1990), p. 372.

62 Quote of Bob Zellner on racial tensions of Mississippi Freedom Summer: *The Promised Land*, by Nicholas Lemann (Knopf, 1991), p. 161.

63 Reaction of Berkeley Campus CORE students to the news that Cheney, Goodman, and Schwerner were missing: "Sit-in at Cecil Poole's Office," by Michael Anker and David Friedman, *Berkeley Campus CORE Newsletter*, June 1964, contained in Bancroft Collection on Social Protest Movements, Bancroft Library, UC Berkeley.

64 Condition of Cheney's body worse than others: *Voices of Freedom, an Oral History of the Civil Rights Movement*, ed. by Henry Hampton and Steve Fayer (Bantam, 1990), p. 195.

64 Quote of David Dennis's at James Cheney's funeral: Ibid., p. 195.

65 Compromise pushed by Humphrey at Democratic National Convention: *The Promised Land*, by Nicholas Lemann (Knopf, 1991), p. 162.

66 Quotes of Bayard Rustin, Mendy Samstein, and Martin Luther King in MFDP caucus at convention: *The Making of Black Revolutionaries*, by James Forman (Macmillan, 1972; Open Hand, 1990), p. 392.

67 Quote of Fannie Lou Hammer after compromise: Ibid., p. 395.

67 Quote of Charles Leinenweber on future of civil rights movement and new Uncle Toms: "Prospects for Civil Rights," by Charles Leinenweber; Quote of Jack Weinberg on definition of an Uncle Tom: "We Will Not Stop Demonstrating!" both in *Campus CORE Newsletter*, June 1964, contained in Bancroft Collection on Social Protest Movements, Bancroft Library, UC Berkeley.

68 Newton's knifing of Odell Lee and quotation of him explaining how a fair judicial outcome could have been achieved: *Revolutionary Suicide*, by Huey Newton (Harcourt Brace Jovanovich, 1973), p. 88.

69 Newton smashing inmate over head with steel tray and calling him for protecting the oppressor's interests: Ibid., p. 103.

69 First organizational meeting of SDS: Transcript of testimony by Sgt. Stanley C. White, Oakland Police Intelligence Division, before U.S. Senate Permanent Subcommittee on Investigations, chaired by Sen. John McClellan, Washington, DC, June 18, 1969.

69 Organizing of UC Berkeley students to solicit against bill blocking fair-housing legislation: "Berkeley Peace Plan Backed by Students," by Wallace Turner, *New York Times*, December 9, 1964.

70 Campus CORE gathering of statistics on nonwhite employees in upfront restaurant positions: Campus CORE flyer distributed in fall 1964, contained in Bancroft Collection on Social Protest Movements, Bancroft Library, UC Berkeley.

70 Organizing of students to demonstrate against *Oakland Tribune*: "Berkeley Peace Plan Backed by Students," by Wallace Turner, *New York Times*, December 9, 1964.

70 Trial outcome of Cadillac Row demonstrators and quotes of James Farmer and Art Hoppe: Newsletter *Justice in Civil Rights Trials*, produced by Committee for Justice in Civil Rights Cases, Berkeley, fall 1964, contained in Bancroft Collection on Social Protest Movements, Bancroft Library, UC Berkeley.

70 Bill Knowland pressuring UC Berkeley to prevent recruiting of demonstrators against *Oakland Tribune*: *A Panther Is a Black Cat*, by Reginald Major (William Morrow, 1971), p. 14.

71 University action to prevent recruiting of demonstrators outside Sather Gate: "Berkeley Peace Plan Backed by Students," by Wallace Turner, *New York Times*, December 9, 1964.

71 Jack Weinberg arrested while soliciting on banned walkway, and attributed as source of quote, "Don't trust anyone over thirty!": *Uncovering the Sixties: The Life and Times of the Underground Press*, by Abe Peck (Pantheon, 1985), p. 28.

71 Savio's explanation of what drove him to lead the Free Speech Movement: "A Rebel on Campus: Mario Savio," "Man in the News" sidebar, *New York Times*, December 9, 1964.

72 Explanation of what drove the university to discipline FSM organizers even after rescinding the ban, thus reigniting student indignation and protest: Paper "Two Fronts in the Same War: The Free Speech Movement and Civil Rights," by Jack Weinberg, contained in Bancroft Collection on Social Protest Movements, Bancroft Library, UC Berkeley; "Battle of Sproul Hall," *Newsweek*, December 14, 1964.

72 Description of student occupation of Sproul Hall and subsequent mass arrests: "Battle of Sproul Hall," *Newsweek*, December 14, 1964.

73 Description of Huey Newton watching FSM protesters being brought to Santa Rita Prison and quote of what he said: Interview with Joe Blum, San Francisco, September 1992.

CHAPTER 4

76 Antiwar teach-ins at UC Berkeley: *Uncovering the Sixties: The Life and Times of the Underground Press*, by Abe Peck (Pantheon, 1985), p. 29.

76 Revolutionary Action Movement (RAM) establishing a chapter in Oakland and Bobby Seale joining: *Revolutionary Suicide*, by Huey Newton (Harcourt Brace Jovanovich, 1973), p. 106.

76 Background of RAM and quotes from Robert Williams's newsletter *The Crusader*: "Kill Baby Kill: The Robert F. Williams Story," by Henry P. Durkin, *Combat*, October 15, 1969, contained in Bancroft Collection on Social Protest Movements, Bancroft Library, UC Berkeley.

77 RAM members in Oakland not being truly revolutionary, and Huey Newton and Bobby Seale not fitting in: *Revolutionary Suicide*, by

Huey Newton (Harcourt Brace Jovanovich, 1973), p. 106; *Seize the Time*, by Bobby Seale (Random House, 1970; Black Classic Press, 1991), pp. 30–31.

78 SNCC members making effort to incorporate Malcolm X's teachings into their philosophy and bringing Mississippi young people to hear him in New York City: *Voices of Freedom, an Oral History of the Civil Rights Movement*, ed. by Henry Hampton and Steve Fayer (Bantam, 1990), pp. 206–207.

78 SNCC invitation to Malcolm X to speak in Selma: Ibid., p. 220.

78 SCLC involvement in Selma voter registration after citizen frustration with SNCC, confrontations between Sheriff Jim Clark and Selma voter registration aspirants, and Clark's attack of Rev. C. T. Vivian: Ibid., pp. 213–222.

78 SNCC's decision not to participate in Selma to Montgomery march, John Lewis's participation as individual, and quote of Lewis after march melee: Ibid., pp. 227–228.

79 Second march from Selma, SNCC's ridicule of the second march as Turn Around Tuesday: Ibid., pp. 232–233; *The Making of Black Revolutionaries*, by James Forman (Macmillan, 1972; Open Hand, 1990), p. 441.

79 Jimmy Lee Jackson as first martyr in Selma campaign: *Voices of Freedom, an Oral History of the Civil Rights Movement*, ed. by Henry Hampton and Steve Fayer (Bantam, 1990), pp. 224–226, 233.

80 Death of Jim Reeb and Stokely Carmichael's anger at difference between reaction to Reeb's death and reaction to Jackson's: Ibid., pp. 232–234.

81 Carmichael recording names and addresses of Negroes in Lowndes County as Selma to Montgomery march came through county, and conditions in the county: Ibid., pp. 238, 267.

81 Ninety percent of Lowndes County land owned by eighty-six white families: *Black Power*, by Stokely Carmichael and Charles V. Hamilton (Vintage, 1967), p. 103.

82 No blacks were registered to vote in Lowndes County until John Hulett registered: *Voices of Freedom, an Oral History of the Civil Rights Movement*, ed. by Henry Hampton and Steve Fayer (Bantam, 1990) p. 270.

82 SNCC's helping John Hulett organize, and officially organizing

Lowndes County Freedom Organization after discovering little-known Alabama law: *Black Power*, by Stokely Carmichael and Charles V. Hamilton (Vintage, 1967), p. 106.

83 Courtland Cox demonstrating on blackboard at SNCC staff meeting, SNCC's aim to "Get power for black people" in Lowndes County: *The Making of Black Revolutionaries*, by James Forman (Macmillan, 1972; Open Hand, 1990), p. 444.

83 Description of murder of Sammy Younge, Jr., and quote of James Forman on end of patience with nonviolence afterward: Ibid., pp. 445–446.

84 Bob Moses's change of name to Bob Parris: Ibid., p. 439.

85 Reason for choice of black panther to symbolize the Lowndes County Freedom Organization: "The 'Black Panther' Party, Negro Third Party Forming in Alabama," *The Movement*, January 1966.

85 Struggle within SNCC at Kingston Springs meeting: *The Making of Black Revolutionaries*, by James Forman (Macmillan, 1972; Open Hand, 1990), p. 450.

86 Description of Watts upheaval: "Los Angeles: The Fire This Time," *Newsweek*, August 23, 1965.

87 Booing of King on visit to Watts, and Powell drawing line around Harlem: *Voices of Freedom, an Oral History of the Civil Rights Movement*, ed. by Henry Hampton and Steve Fayer (Bantam, 1990), p. 298.

87 Quote of Campus CORE newsletter on Adam Clayton Powell and William Dawson: "Prospects for Civil Rights," by Charles Leinenweber, *Campus CORE Newsletter*, June 1964, p. 27, contained in Bancroft Collection on Social Protest Movements, Bancroft Library, UC Berkeley.

88 Circumstances surrounding James Meredith March: *Voices of Freedom, an Oral History of the Civil Rights Movement*, ed. by Henry Hampton and Steve Fayer (Bantam, 1990), pp. 284–294; *The Making of Black Revolutionaries*, by James Forman (Macmillan, 1972; Open Hand, 1990), pp. 456–457.

89 Quote of Willie Ricks asking James Forman about coining phrase Black Power during the march: *The Making of Black Revolutionaries*, by James Forman (Macmillan, 1972; Open Hand, 1990), p. 456.

90 Quote of Ricks on "dropping it": *Voices of Freedom, an Oral History of the Civil Rights Movement*, ed. by Henry Hampton and Steve Fayer (Bantam, 1990), p. 289.

90 Quotes of Ricks urging people to say "Black Power": Ibid., p. 290.

91 Quote of David Dawley on change in march atmosphere: Ibid., p. 294.

92 Quote of Andrew Young on Martin Luther King's attitude toward new slogan: Ibid., p. 294.

CHAPTER 5

94 Bobby Seale and Huey Newton fighting with police on Telegraph Ave.: *Seize the Time*, by Bobby Seale (Random House, 1970; Black Classic Press, 1991), p. 28.

95 Idea of Newton and Seale to organize the "brothers off the block" for Malcolm's birthday: *Seize the Time*, by Bobby Seale (Random House, 1970; Black Classic Press, 1991), pp. 30–31; *Revolutionary Suicide*, by Huey Newton (Harcourt Brace Jovanovich, 1973), pp. 108–109.

95 Quote of Seale regarding standoff at SSAC meeting: *Seize the Time*, by Bobby Seale (Random House, 1970; Black Classic Press, 1991), p. 32.

95 Stokely Carmichael's explanation of Black Power and quote regarding meaning of black panther: "SNCC Chairman Talks About Black Power," by Stokely Carmichael, *New York Review of Books*, September 22, 1966.

96 Carmichael's definition of integration: Ibid.

97 SDS aiding Peralta Improvement League: "West Oakland Residents Fight Destruction," *The Movement*, January 1966.

98 Mark Comfort as organizer of the Oakland Direct Action Committee and the Amboy Dukes, and activities of the two organizations: "Oakland Is a Powder Keg," and "Gang Member Speaks: 'Negroes Should Stop Fighting,'" *The Movement*, October 1966.

98 Peter Solomon and minister walking in on "divvy-up" session: Interview with Peter Solomon, Berkeley, July 24, 1992.

99 Quote of CORE activist Julius Hobson on street mentality: "A

Conversation with Catfish," by Stewart Alsop, *Saturday Evening Post*, February 24, 1968.

99 Description of film *Losing Just the Same:* "An Hour of Liberal Racism," by Dave Wellman, *The Movement*, December 1966.

100 Neighborhood reaction to the film: Interview with Peter Solomon, Berkeley, July 24, 1992.

100 Peter Collier's account of being hoodwinked by student at Miles College: *Destructive Generation*, by Peter Collier and David Horowitz (Summit, 1990), pp. 282–284.

101 Description of Black Power conference at UC Berkeley: From flyer describing conference schedule, distributed by Campus SDS, contained in Bancroft Collection on Social Protest Movements, Bancroft Library, UC Berkeley.

101 Quote of Ivanhoe Donaldson on appropriateness of violence: "Black Power Meet: Old Stands Rejected," by Gary Plotkin, *Daily Californian*, October 31, 1966.

101 Carmichael's address at Berkeley Black Power conference: "'Power' Aftermath: Brown Lashes Stokely," by Rich Weinhold, *Daily Californian*, October 31, 1966.

102 *Daily Californian* editorial on conference: "What's Black Power?" November 1, 1966.

102 Berkeley protesters block troop train: "Vietnam Critics Board Troop Train," by John Rogers, *Daily Californian*, August 13, 1965.

102 Seven thousand clash with Oakland police: "7,000 March Down Telegraph," *Daily Californian*, October 18, 1965.

102 Protest rally in DeFremery Park: "Next Time—the Army Terminal: 10,000 Protest at Oakland," *Daily Californian*, November 22, 1965.

102 Campaign begins against Cohelan: "Vietnam Day Group Declares War on Cohelan," *Daily Californian*, August 26, 1965.

103 Background of Robert Scheer: Interview with Peter Solomon, Berkeley, July 24, 1992; biographies of Scheer in "Scheer for Congress" campaign literature from winter and spring of 1966, contained in Bancroft Collection on Social Protest Movements, Bancroft Library, UC Berkeley.

103 Endorsements of Scheer from Mark Comfort and Dr. Carlton B. Goodlett: Listed on "Scheer for Congress" stationery dated January

29, 1966, contained in Bancroft Collection on Social Protest Movements, Bancroft Library, UC Berkeley.

103 Scheer's approach to Newton and Seale: *Seize the Time*, by Bobby Seale (Random House, 1970; Black Classic Press, 1991), p. 30.

104 White House monitoring of Cohelan-Scheer congressional race and precinct outcomes: Noted in letter typed on "Scheer for Congress" stationery sent to Scheer supporters after the June 7, 1966, primary, and signed by Robert Scheer, contained in Bancroft Collection on Social Protest Movements, Bancroft Library, UC Berkeley.

104 Scheer as perhaps the integral person to launch Eldridge Cleaver's career as a writer: Conclusion based on Scheer's presence as managing editor of *Ramparts* when Cleaver's writing began appearing in the magazine, as well as the introductory editorial comments to Cleaver's first *Ramparts* piece in the June 1966 issue; also based on comments to that effect in interview with David Horowitz, a former *Ramparts* staffer, October 6, 1992, Los Angeles. *Note:* efforts to contact Robert Scheer for interview were unsuccessful.

104 SNCC holding workshops for Lowndes County, Alabama, Negroes: "The 'Black Panther' Party, Negro Third Party Forming in Alabama," *The Movement*, January 1966.

104 LCFO problems at voting booths: *Black Power*, by Stokely Carmichael and Charles V. Hamilton (Vintage, 1967), p. 116.

105 Mark Comfort traveling to Lowndes County, Alabama, to aid election effort: "Lowndes County: Candidates Lose, But Black Panther Strong," by Terrence Cannon, *The Movement*, December 1966.

105 King stifled in Chicago: *The Promised Land*, by Nicholas Lemann (Knopf, 1991), pp. 234–240.

106 Background of Eldridge Cleaver: "Notes on a Native Son," by Eldridge Cleaver, *Ramparts*, June 1966.

106 Cleaver's denunciation of Baldwin: Ibid.

106 Cleaver's window into his own mind: "Letters from Prison," by Eldridge Cleaver, *Ramparts*, July 1966.

107 Cleaver on young white people: *Soul on Ice*, by Eldridge Cleaver (Ramparts Books, 1968), p. 83.

107 Maxwell Geismar's praise of Cleaver: Introduction to *Soul on Ice*, by Eldridge Cleaver (Ramparts Books, 1968).

107 SNCC resolution at Peg Leg Bates conference: *The Making of Black Revolutionaries*, by James Forman (Macmillan, 1972; Open Hand, 1990), p. 477.

108 The Black Panther Party borrowing ideas from Watts Community Alert Patrol and SNCC symbol of the black panthers: "A Night with the Watts Community Alert Patrol," by Terrence Cannon, *The Movement*, August 1966; *Revolutionary Suicide*, by Huey Newton (Harcourt Brace Jovanovich, 1973), p. 113; interview with Joe Blum, San Francisco, September 1992.

108 Quotes of Bobby Seale stating what's good for whites isn't good for blacks, and who Huey wanted in the Panthers: *Seize the Time*, by Bobby Seale (Random House, 1970; Black Classic Press, 1991), pp. 71, 64, respectively.

108 Seale and Newton's employment situations when they began the Party: *Seize the Time*, by Bobby Seale (Random House, 1970; Black Classic Press, 1991), pp. 35–56; *Revolutionary Suicide*, by Huey Newton (Harcourt Brace Jovanovich, 1973), pp. 112–115.

109 Panther ten-point platform: *Revolutionary Suicide*, by Huey Newton (Harcourt Brace Jovanovich, 1973), pp. 116–118.

112 Bobby Hutton's background: *Seize the Time*, by Bobby Seale (Random House, 1970; Black Classic Press, 1991), pp. 43, 81.

112 Obtaining first two guns from Richard Aoki: Ibid., pp. 72–73, 79.

112 Confrontation at private party: Ibid., pp. 73–74.

112 Opening up first Panther office and obtaining more guns from Richard Aoki: Ibid., pp. 77–79.

113 Selling *Red Books* for guns at UC Berkeley: Ibid., pp. 79–81.

113 Patrolling the police with a law book, camera, tape recorders: Ibid., p. 85.

113 First major Panther confrontation with police: Ibid., pp. 85–92.

116 Peter Solomon's assessment of initial reactions to the Panthers: Interview with Peter Solomon, Berkeley, July 24, 1992.

116 Oakland police force personnel statistics for 1966 and the approximation of black percentage in Oakland's total population: "Metropoly: The Story of Oakland," by Warren Hinckle, *Ramparts*, February 1966.

116 Practice of Oakland police throwing away issues of *Flatlands:* Interview with Peter Solomon, Berkeley, July 24, 1992.

117 Oakland power structure's back-scratching syndrome, causing launch of career of Earl Warren: "Metropoly: The Story of Oakland," by Warren Hinckle, *Ramparts*, February 1966.

117 Eng's predecessor stepping down to make room for Eng, then Eng rarely if ever showing his face in West Oakland: "Ten Years of Oakland City Politics," *Oakland Post* editorial, August 14, 1968, and *Oakland Post* article on "Model Cities," January 24, 1968.

118 Huge guffaws greeting Eng when he said he was speaking for West Oakland: Interview with Peter Solomon, Berkeley, July 24, 1992.

118 Newton describing how Black Panthers made deal with criminal elements of Oakland from the very beginning of party: *Revolutionary Suicide*, by Huey Newton (Harcourt Brace Jovanovich, 1973), p. 127.

118 Small-scale protection racket rumored to have been started by Panthers, and account of satisfied store owner: Interview with Peter Solomon, Berkeley, July 24, 1992.

118 Dispute between San Francisco police officer and Oakland police involved in Oakland prostitution: Interview with Peter Solomon, Berkeley, July 24, 1992.

119 Eldridge Cleaver setting up Black House: "A Letter from Jail," by Eldridge Cleaver, *Ramparts*, June 15, 1968.

119 Various Bay Area white radicals allegedly picking up the tab for Black House and Beverly Axelrod serving as Cleaver's mistress *Spitting in the Wind*, by Earl Anthony (Roundtable, 1990), p. 15.

119 LeRoi Jones as Black House regular: *Revolutionary Suicide*, by Huey Newton (Harcourt Brace Jovanovich, 1973), p. 130.

119 Roy Ballard as member of the Black Panther Party of Northern California and Black House regular: *Seize the Time*, by Bobby Seale (Random House, 1970; Black Classic Press, 1991), pp. 113–114; *Spitting in the Wind*, by Earl Anthony (Roundtable, 1990), p. 17.

119 Planners of Conference 67, Survival of Black People, concerned about concentration camps and possible ousting of Adam Clayton Powell, Jr., from U.S. Congress: *A Panther Is a Black Cat*, by Reginald Major (William Morrow, 1971), p. 70.

119 Problems of Adam Clayton Powell with U.S. Congress.: *Adam Clay-*

ton Powell, Jr., by Charles V. Hamilton (Atheneum, 1991), pp. 455–487.

120 Speakers at Conference 67, Survival of Black People, and concern of Roy Ballard and others about lack of inclusion of Malcolm X: From accounts of the event provided in *Spitting in the Wind*, by Earl Anthony (Roundtable, 1990), p. 17; *A Panther Is a Black Cat*, by Reginald Major (William Morrow, 1971), pp. 70–71.

120 Planners of Malcolm X commemoration fearing Newton and the Black Panther Party for Self-Defense and considering them to be too street: Based on description of the relationship in *Seize the Time*, by Bobby Seale (Random House, 1970; Black Classic Press, 1991), pp. 115–117.

120 Malcolm X commemoration allegedly financed by Bay Area communist groups: *Spitting in the Wind*, by Earl Anthony (Roundtable, 1990), p. 20.

121 Newton and other Panthers walking in on Malcolm X planning meeting: Based on three accounts: *Spitting in the Wind*, by Earl Anthony (Roundtable, 1990), pp. 20–21; *Seize the Time*, by Bobby Seale (Random House, 1970; Black Classic Press, 1991), pp. 115–116; "A Letter from Jail," by Eldridge Cleaver, *Ramparts*, June 15, 1968.

121 Quote of Ballard to Bobby Seale at Malcolm X memorial planning meeting: *Seize the Time*, by Bobby Seale (Random House, 1970; Black Classic Press, 1991), p. 116.

121 San Francisco International Airport confrontation between Panther escorts for Shabazz and airport security, including quotes: Combined from accounts in *Seize the Time*, by Bobby Seale (Random House, 1970; Black Classic Press, 1991), pp. 120–121; "Frightening Army at San Francisco Airport," *San Francisco Chronicle*, February 22, 1967.

123 Newton's first impression of and encounter with Eldridge Cleaver: *Seize the Time*, by Bobby Seale (Random House, 1970; Black Classic Press, 1991), p. 132; *Revolutionary Suicide*, by Huey Newton (Harcourt Brace Jovanovich, 1973), p. 128.

123 Cleaver's first impressions of Newton: "A Letter from Jail," by Eldridge Cleaver, *Ramparts*, June 15, 1968.

123 Entire incident at *Ramparts* headquarters, including quotes: Combined from accounts in *Revolutionary Suicide*, by Huey Newton (Harcourt Brace Jovanovich, 1973), pp. 131–132; *Seize the Time*, by Bobby Seale (Random House, 1970; Black Classic Press, 1991), pp. 125–130; *Spitting in the Wind*, by Earl Anthony (Roundtable, 1990), p. 23; "A Letter from Jail," by Eldridge Cleaver, *Ramparts*, June 15, 1968.

125 Incident at San Francisco fish fry: *Revolutionary Suicide*, by Huey Newton (Harcourt Brace Jovanovich, 1973), p. 132.

126 Cleaver's experiences with Stokely Carmichael and Cleveland Sellers in Chicago for *Ramparts* article: "My Father and Stokely Carmichael," by Eldridge Cleaver, *Ramparts*, April 1967.

127 Quote of John Conyers regarding Adam Clayton Powell: *Adam Clayton Powell, Jr.*, by Charles V. Hamilton (Atheneum, 1991), p. 461.

128 Cleaver's first major Panther action involving production of Panther newspaper: *Seize the Time*, by Bobby Seale (Random House, 1970; Black Classic Press, 1991), p. 147.

128 Panther involvement in the case of Denzil Dowell, and alleged circumstances surrounding the killing of Denzil Dowell: *Spitting in the Wind*, by Earl Anthony (Roundtable, 1990), p. 28; "Oakland Black Panthers Wear Guns, Talk Revolution," by Jerry Belcher, *San Francisco Examiner*, April 30, 1967.

128 Panther San Pablo school incident and confrontation in Martinez: "Oakland Black Panthers Wear Guns, Talk Revolution," by Jerry Belcher, *San Francisco Examiner*, April 30, 1967.

129 Panthers patrolling affluent white suburbs: Interview with Peter Solomon, Berkeley, July 24, 1992.

129 Introduction of Mulford bill to curb activities of Black Panthers, and Panther reaction: "Oakland Black Panthers Wear Guns, Talk Revolution" by Jerry Belcher, *San Francisco Examiner*, April 30, 1967; *Revolutionary Suicide*, by Huey Newton (Harcourt Brace Jovanovich, 1973), pp. 146–147.

129 Panthers calling up journalist and asking how to get publicity for state capitol gun display: Interviewee requested anonymity.

130 Quote of Reagan taking swipe at Edmund G. Brown after Carmichael speech: "'Power' Aftermath: Brown Lashes Stokely," by Rich Weinhold, *Daily Californian*, October 31, 1966.

130 Campaign "hit pieces" appearing in white neighborhoods showing

Brown shaking hands with black people: Interview with Peter Solomon, Berkeley, July 24, 1992.

130 Panther state capitol gun display: *Seize the Time*, by Bobby Seale (Random House, 1970; Black Classic Press, 1991), pp. 153–165; "The Call of the Black Panthers," by Sol Stern, *New York Times Magazine*, August 6, 1967.

133 San Francisco State rally praising Panther action, including quotes: "Ugly Words at S.F. State—A Pro-Panther Rally," by Maitland Zane, *San Francisco Chronicle*, May 5, 1967.

133 Quote of San Francisco police chief after Panther action: "Police Chief Alarmed by Panthers," *San Francisco Chronicle*, May 8, 1967.

133 Nazi weapons waving demonstration: "Six Nazis Wave Guns at Panthers," *San Francisco Chronicle*, May 14, 1967.

133 Nofziger on Panther action with regard to Reagan and extra precautions: "Police Chief Alarmed by Panthers," *San Francisco Chronicle*, May 8, 1967.

134 Seale appealing to Berkeley students after state capitol incident: "Black Panthers at Rally, Friendly, Unarmed," *San Francisco Chronicle*, May 11, 1967.

134 Filmore Auditorium benefit: "An Angry Benefit for Black Panthers," *San Francisco Chronicle*, May 26, 1967.

CHAPTER 6

137 Unrest at Texas Southern: "Black Power Explodes Again—Policeman Slain," *U.S. News and World Report*, May 29, 1967.

137 Unrest at Jackson State: "Mississippi: Hot Spring," *Newsweek*, May 27, 1967.

138 Quote of Stokely Carmichael in Washington, DC: "We're Going to Shoot the Cops," *U.S. News and World Report*, May 29, 1967.

138 Carmichael on H. Rap Brown: "The Fire This Time," *Time*, August 4, 1967.

138 Quote of Benjamin Stewart on H. Rap Brown: Interview with Benjamin Stewart, Marin City, CA, October 8, 1992.

138 Brown at first press conference: "The Man from SNCC," *Newsweek*, May 22, 1967.

138 Description of Newark unrest: "Newark Boils Over," *Newsweek*, July 24, 1992.

139 Injury statistics on Newark and Detroit unrest and number of cities experiencing unrest that summer: "The Cities: What Next?" *Time*, August 11, 1967.

139 Origin of Detroit riot: "Toll of Detroit Riots Worst in U.S. History," *U.S. News and World Report*, August 7, 1967.

139 H. Rap Brown "explosion" quote: "The Fire This Time," *Time*, August 4, 1967.

139 H. Rap Brown quoted advising the burning down of elementary school: "The Firebrand," *Newsweek*, August 7, 1967.

140 Cambridge, MD, police chief quote: Ibid.

140 H. Rap Brown arrested and released on bond: "The Fire This Time," *Time*, August 4, 1967.

140 Quotes of H. Rap Brown advising getting gun, stating violence is American, and advising looting gun store: "If You Have Any Doubts About H. Rap Brown Inciting Riots," *U.S. News and World Report*, August 7, 1967.

140 Seale et al. pleading guilty to assembly intrusion: "Guilty Plea in Assembly Intrusion," *San Francisco Chronicle*, July 21, 1967.

141 Second issue of Panther paper produced and set up of Newton photo in wicker chair: *Seize the Time*, by Bobby Seale (Random House, 1970; Black Classic Press, 1991), pp. 181–182.

141 Traffic light incident: Interview with Robert Trivors, Santa Cruz, October 2, 1992.

142 Quote of Bobby Seale in Protrero Hill, and Panther demonstrating how to load gun in North Richmond: "The Call of the Black Panthers," by Sol Stern, *New York Times Magazine*, August 6, 1967.

142 Bobby Seale drafting Carmichael into Panthers: "Carmichael 'Drafted' by Panthers," *San Francisco Chronicle*, June 30, 1967.

142 James Forman's increasing radicalism: *The Making of Black Revolutionaries*, by James Forman (Macmillan, 1972; Open Hand, 1990), pp. 480–481.

142 SNCC's increasing problems with white donors: *A Panther Is a Black Cat*, by Reginald Major (William Morrow, 1971), pp. 88–89.

143 Rise of hippie movement in San Francisco: "The Hashbury Is the Capital of the Hippies," by Hunter S. Thompson, *New York Times Magazine*, May 14, 1967.

144 Launching of Vietnam Summer and Vietnam War troop and death statistics: *The Sixties: Years of Hope, Days of Rage*, by Tod Gitlin (Bantam, 1989), pp. 242–249.

144 Rationale behind Stop the Draft Week: "Tactics of Disruption," by Michael Miles, *New Republic*, November 4, 1967.

144 Split among planners of Bay Area Stop the Draft activities: *The Sixties: Years of Hope, Days of Rage*, by Tod Gitlin (Bantam, 1989), pp. 248–249.

144 "Bloody Tuesday": "Tactics of Disruption," by Michael Miles, *New Republic*, November 4, 1967; "Reagan on Police Brutality," *The Nation*, November 6, 1967.

145 Quotes of newscaster and Reagan on "Bloody Tuesday": "Reagan on Police Brutality," *The Nation*, November 6, 1967.

145 Encounter between Huey and Officers Frey and Heanes, and indictment: "The Persecution and Assassination of the Black Panthers as Performed by the Oakland Police under the Direction of Chief Charles R. Gain, Mayor Reading, et al," by Gene Marine, *Ramparts*, July 13, 1968; *A Panther Is a Black Cat*, by Reginald Major (William Morrow, 1971), pp. 179–182, 221, 234–235; *Revolutionary Suicide*, by Huey Newton (Harcourt Brace Jovanovich, 1973), pp. 171–176.

145 Alleged previous racism of John Frey: *In the Court of Appeal of the State of California: People of the State of California vs. Huey P. Newton, Appellant's Opening Brief*, submitted by Fay Stender, August 1969, pp. 20–21.

147 Hilliard taking Newton to hospital after Frey incident: *This Side of Glory*, by David Hillard and Lewis Cole (Little, Brown, 1993), p. 131.

147 Cleaver taking charge of Free Huey effort with aid of white backers, and calling first Free Huey meeting: *Spitting in the Wind*, by Earl Anthony (Roundtable, 1990), pp. 41–42; interview with Benjamin Stewart, Marin City, CA, October 8, 1992.

147 Panther confrontation in Chief Gain's office: "A Black Panther Call On Police," *San Francisco Chronicle*, November 10, 1967.

148 Quotes of Benjamin Stewart on first Free Huey meeting: Interview with Benjamin Stewart, Marin City, CA, October 8, 1992.

148 Cleaver silencing critics of Free Huey plan: *Spitting in the Wind*, by Earl Anthony (Roundtable, 1990), pp. 43–44.

148 Clash between antiwar demonstrators and San Francisco police, and quotes of arrested demonstrators: From flier distributed by organizers for the Peace and Freedom Party, January 1968, contained in Bancroft Collection on Social Protest Movements, Bancroft Library, UC Berkeley.

149 Supporters of Peace and Freedom Party (PFP) and details of its organizing efforts: From PFP documents contained in Bancroft Collection on Social Protest Movements, Bancroft Library, UC Berkeley.

149 Cleaver/PFP deal for Panther/PFP alliance and PFP nominees for office: From PFP documents and "Eldridge Cleaver for President" file contained in Bancroft Collection on Social Protest Movements, Bancroft Library, UC Berkeley.

150 Characteristics of Pre-erection Day celebration and Cleaver-Rubin presidential campaign: *Destructive Generation*, by Peter Collier and David Horowitz (Summit, 1989), p. 152; interview with Joe Blum, San Francisco, September 9, 1992; interview with David Horowitz, Los Angeles, October 6, 1992.

150 Origins of SNCC–Black Panther relationship: *The Making of Black Revolutionaries*, by James Forman (Macmillan, 1972; Open Hand, 1990), pp. 524–527.

151 Panther aims in seeking out SNCC: *Seize the Time*, by Bobby Seale (Random House, 1970; Black Classic Press, 1991), p. 221; *This Side of Glory*, by David Hillard and Lewis Cole (Little, Brown, 1993), p. 171; *The Making of Black Revolutionaries*, by James Forman (Macmillan, 1972; Open Hand, 1990), p. 531.

151 Activities surrounding development of SNCC-Panther relationship: *Seize the Time*, by Bobby Seale (Random House, 1970; Black Classic Press, 1991), pp. 220–222; *The Making of Black Revolutionaries*, by James Forman (Macmillan, 1972; Open Hand, 1990), pp. 528–531; *This Side of Glory*, by David Hillard and Lewis Cole (Little, Brown, 1993), pp. 171–174.

152 SNCC leaders having trouble with SNCC rank and file over Black

Panther relationship: Interview with Mae Jackson, Brooklyn, NY, December 25, 1992; *The Making of Black Revolutionaries,* by James Forman (Macmillan, 1972; Open Hand, 1990), pp. 531–532.

152 Announcements by Cleaver and quotes of H. Rap Brown, Stokely Carmichael, and James Forman at Free Huey rallies: *The Making of Black Revolutionaries,* by James Forman (Macmillan, 1972; Open Hand, 1990), p. 526; transcript of Committee Exhibit No. 373, presented to U.S. Senate Permanent Subcommittee on Investigations, chaired by Sen. John McClellan, Washington, DC, June 18, 1969.

153 Whites for the Defense of Huey Newton (WDHN) statement about Huey: Fund-raising letter of Whites for the Defense of Huey Newton, April 1968, signed by Cecele Levinson, contained in Bancroft Collection on Social Protest Movements, Bancroft Library, UC Berkeley.

153 Quote of Mae Jackson on Free Huey movement: Interview with Mae Jackson, Brooklyn, NY, December 25, 1992.

153 Quote of Peter Solomon on radical atmosphere at time of Free Huey movement: Interview with Peter Solomon, Berkeley, July 24, 1992.

154 April 6 Panther–police shootout: "The Persecution and Assassination of the Black Panthers as Performed by the Oakland Police under the Direction of Chief Charles R. Gain, Mayor Reading, et al," by Gene Marine, *Ramparts,* July 13, 1968; "Grand Jury Version of Oakland Gun Battle," by Charles Raudenbaugh, *San Francisco Chronicle,* April 26, 1968; "Exclusive Talk with Eldridge Cleaver," by Charles Howe, *San Francisco Chronicle,* April 26, 1968; "New Version of Hutton Slaying," by Dexter Waugh, *San Francisco Sunday Examiner and Chronicle,* April 18, 1971; *This Side of Glory,* by David Hillard and Lewis Cole (Little, Brown, 1993), p. 183.

156 Quote of Cleaver on shootout: "Exclusive Talk with Eldridge Cleaver," by Charles Howe, *San Francisco Chronicle,* April 26, 1968.

156 Quote of Marlon Brando on Panthers: "Brando Turns Up at Seale Hearing," *San Francisco Chronicle,* April 3, 1968.

156 Brando's presence at Hutton memorial and to patrol with Panthers, allegedly for film research: *This Side of Glory,* by David Hillard and Lewis Cole (Little, Brown, 1993), p. 197.

156 Letter signed by various celebrities protesting Hutton killing: "Letter from New York," by James Baldwin, Ossie Davis, Elizabeth Harwick, LeRoi Jones, Oscar Lewis, Norman Mailer, Floyd McKissick, Susan Sontag, *San Francisco Chronicle*, May 17, 1968.

157 Quote of Harry Edwards supporting Panthers, and four Bay Area college professors supporting them too: "San Jose Professor Joins Black Panthers," by Dick Halgren, *San Francisco Chronicle*, April 12, 1968.

157 Law students supporting Panthers: "Law Students Side with Panthers," *San Francisco Chronicle*, April 27, 1968.

157 Bay Area physicians' organization supporting Panthers: "Bay Doctors Will Help the Panthers," by Charles Howe, *San Francisco Chronicle*, April 17, 1968.

157 Quote of Charles Gain fighting back: "Oakland Chief Attacks the Panthers," by Scott Thurber, *San Francisco Chronicle*, April 26, 1968.

158 Quote of LeRoi Jones speaking of the Panthers at the Filmore East: "Big New York Rally for Oakland Panthers," (AP), *San Francisco Chronicle*, May 21, 1968.

158 Quote of Mae Jackson on difference between SNCC and Panthers: Interview with Mae Jackson, Brooklyn, NY, December 25, 1992.

158 Quote of Jackson on confrontation between herself and Ron Penniwell, and H. Rap Brown's response: Ibid.

159 David Hilliard's account of the split between SNCC and the Black Panthers: *This Side of Glory*, by David Hillard and Lewis Cole (Little, Brown, 1993), pp. 202–204.

160 James Forman's account of the split between SNCC and the Black Panthers: *The Making of Black Revolutionaries*, by James Forman (Macmillan, 1972; Open Hand, 1990), pp. 533–538.

160 *Oakland Post* account of Forman's presence at start of Newton's trial: "Huey Newton Takes Stand, Says He's Destitute, Says Can't Pay Lawyer," by Alamena Lomax and Tom Nash, *Oakland Post*, July 17, 1968.

161 Cleaver's parole revocation reversed: "Eldridge Cleaver, 'Recalled to Life,' Plans Huey March," *Oakland Post*, July 10, 1968.

161 Earl Anthony's account of the split between SNCC and the Black Panthers: *Spitting in the Wind*, by Earl Anthony (Roundtable, 1990), pp. 48–49.

162 FBI COINTELPRO memo on reason for split between SNCC and the Black Panthers: Memo dated August 8, 1968, from New York City FBI office to the director of the FBI, contained in COINTEL-PRO files on Black Panthers, General Public Reading Room, FBI Headquarters, Washington, DC.

162 *New York Times* article on confrontation between Forman and Black Panthers at SNCC offices: "SNCC in Decline After 8 Years in Lead, Pace-Setter in Civil Rights Displaced by Black Panthers," by C. Gerald Fraser, *New York Times*, October 7, 1968.

163 Forman's denial of being tortured by Black Panthers: *The Making of Black Revolutionaries*, by James Forman (Macmillan, 1972; Open Hand, 1990), p. 539.

163 Quote of Mae Jackson corroborating story of Forman's torture: Interview with Mae Jackson, Brooklyn, NY, December 25, 1992.

163 Forman checking into psychiatric ward of New York hospital: Interview with Mae Jackson, Brooklyn, NY, December 25, 1992; memo dated August 7, 1968, from New York City FBI office to the director of the FBI, contained in COINTELPRO files on Black Panthers, General Public Reading Room, FBI Headquarters, Washington, DC.

163 Carmichael's ouster from SNCC: Contained in "Carmichael Quits the Panthers—Vicious" (reprint from *New York Times*), *San Francisco Chronicle*, July 4, 1969. In that article it is reported that Carmichael was ousted from SNCC "last year." In *The Making of Black Revolutionaries*, by James Forman (Macmillan, 1972; Open Hand, 1990), p. 521, Forman also reports Carmichael's expulsion but dates it as occurring in August 1969. The author believes that, given the circumstances surrounding the turn of events, James Forman has the month of Carmichael's ouster right but the year wrong, probably due to a typographical error.

164 Carmichael's resignation from the Black Panthers and quoted reason for resigning: "Carmichael Quits the Panthers—Vicious" (reprint from *New York Times*), *San Francisco Chronicle*, July 4, 1969.

CHAPTER 7

165 Identification of the Panthers as one of the most dangerous threats presented by black America: Memo dated April 3, 1968, from San Francisco FBI office to FBI headquarters, contained in COINTEL-

PRO files on Black Panthers, General Public Reading Room, FBI Headquarters, Washington, DC.

165 Quote of J. Edgar Hoover identifying the party as the greatest threat to nation's internal security: *Racial Matters: The FBI's Secret File on Black America*, by Kenneth O'Reilly (Free Press, 1989), p. 290.

165 Automatic labeling of any party member who criticized the leadership as "enemy of the people" and informant: Interview with Landon Williams, Berkeley, October 1991; interview with Benjamin Stewart, Marin City, October 8, 1992; transcript of testimony by Jean and Larry Powell before U.S. Senate Permanent Subcommittee on Investigations, chaired by Sen. John McClellan, Washington, DC, June 18, 1969.

166 Black male Kaiser Hospital employee purchasing gun to prepare for revolution: Interview with Peter Solomon, Berkeley, July 24, 1992.

166 Picketing of downtown Oakland merchants and Oakland ministers staging vigil before city council: "Never a Dull Moment in Oakland," *Oakland Post*, June 26, 1968.

166 *Oakland Post* publisher Tom Berkley on Newton and Panthers: "Oakland's Cry Baby Mayor," *Oakland Post* editorial, July 31, 1968.

166 Comments of middle-class blacks in Bay Area on use of violence as means to ends: "Prominent S.F. Negroes View the Militants," by George Draper, *San Francisco Chronicle*, March 27, 1968.

167 Activities of Free Huey demonstrators at start of trial: "'Free Huey, Free Huey'—An Awesome Outburst," *San Francisco Chronicle*, July 16, 1968; "The Leather Jacket Drill," by Tim Findley, *San Francisco Chronicle*, July 22, 1968.

167 Demonstrator being told by police about trouble with blackbirds: Interview with Mary Kennedy, Oakland, September 11, 1992.

167 Quote of Shirley Lee on visit with Huey: "The Leather Jacket Drill," by Tim Findley, *San Francisco Chronicle*, July 22, 1968.

167 All other Free Huey demonstration descriptions: "'Why I'm Marching to Free Huey," by Dale Champion, *San Francisco Chronicle*, July 16, 1968; "'Free Huey, Free Huey'—An Awesome Outburst," *San Francisco Chronicle*, July 16, 1968.

168 Elsa Knight Thompson's description of Huey: Interview with Alex Hoffman, Oakland, October 1991.

168 Huey's words to reporter asking if he hated white people: Interview with Joe Blum, San Francisco, September 9, 1992.

168 Sentencing of Newton and reaction of police officers and Berkeley Socialist League: "Two Cops Jump Gun in Alleged Panther Headquarters Shootup," *Oakland Post*, September 11, 1968.

169 Eldridge Cleaver as course instructor at UC Berkeley and other schools, and reactions, including quotes of Rafferty, and Willie Brown on his presence: "Cleaver Now Political Issue Like Those Grapes," *Oakland Post*, September 25, 1968.

169 Cleaver's appearance before San Francisco lawyers: "Cleaver Tells It Like It Is," by George Putnam, aired on Los Angeles TV news station KTLA, September 11, 1968; transcript sent from FBI office in Los Angeles to FBI director, September 25, 1968, contained in COINTELPRO files on Black Panthers, General Public Reading Room, FBI Headquarters, Washington, DC.

170 Parole revocation of Cleaver and three-day, round-the-clock vigil: "Cleaver to Go Quietly to Pokey, But in High Style," *Oakland Post*, November 20, 1968.

CHAPTER 8

173 Party principally run by Hilliard after Cleaver's exile, and real work being among rank and file: Transcript of testimony by Jean and Larry Powell before U.S. Senate Permanent Subcommittee on Investigations, chaired by Sen. John McClellan, Washington, DC, June 18, 1969; interview with Mary Kennedy, Oakland, August 29, 1992; interview with Landon Williams, Berkeley, October 1991; information from Committee Exhibit No. 8, at hearings before the Committee on Internal Security, House of Representatives, chaired by Cong. Richard Ichord, Washington, DC, October 6, 1970.

173 All material on Mary Kennedy and Landon Williams and their experiences in the party: Interviews with Mary Kennedy, Oakland, August 29, 1992, and September 11, 1992; interviews with Landon Williams, Berkeley, October 1991, and March 2, 1992.

173 Background of Father Earl Neil: "Oakland Minister Befriends Newton and Black Panthers," by Rush Greenlee, *San Francisco Examiner*, November 24, 1968.

176 Party chain of command and training procedures: Transcript of

Committee Exhibit No. 372, presented to U.S. Senate Permanent Subcommittee on Investigations, chaired by Sen. John McClellan, Washington, DC, June 18, 1969; information from Committee Exhibit No. 8, at hearings before the Committee on Internal Security, House of Representatives, chaired by Cong. Richard Ichord, Washington, DC, October 6, 1970; interviews with Landon Williams, Berkeley, October 1991, and March 2, 1992; interview with former party member requesting anonymity, Oakland, September 28, 1992.

177 Money rolling in from clandestine activities: Transcript of testimony by Jean and Larry Powell before U.S. Senate Permanent Subcommittee on Investigations, chaired by Sen. John McClellan, Washington, DC, June 18, 1969; information from Committee Exhibit No. 8, at hearings before the Committee on Internal Security, House of Representatives, chaired by Cong. Richard Ichord, Washington, DC, October 6, 1970; interview with Benjamin Stewart, Marin City, CA, October 8, 1992; interview with former party member requesting anonymity, Oakland, September 28, 1992.

177 Lifestyle of leadership relative to rank and file: Interviews with Mary Kennedy, Oakland, August 29, 1992, and September 11, 1992; interviews with Landon Williams, Berkeley, October 1991, and March 2, 1992; transcript of testimony by Jean and Larry Powell before U.S. Senate Permanent Subcommittee on Investigations, chaired by Sen. John McClellan, Washington, DC, June 18, 1969; information from Committee Exhibit No. 8, at hearings before the Committee on Internal Security, House of Representatives, chaired by Cong. Richard Ichord, Washington, DC, October 6, 1970; interview with former party member requesting anonymity, Oakland, September 28, 1992.

178 George Mason Murray in the party and at S.F. State: "S.F. State Puts Admirer of Mao On Teaching Staff," by Ed Montgomery, *San Francisco Examiner*, September 15, 1968; *A Panther Is a Black Cat*, by Reginald Major (William Morrow, 1971), pp. 83–84.

178 Murray, Hilliard, and Williams being turned around in Mexico after trying to go to Cuba: *A Panther Is a Black Cat*, by Reginald Major (William Morrow, 1971), pp. 83–84; memo from San Francisco office of FBI to FBI director, September 5, 1968, contained in COINTELPRO files on Black Panthers, General Public Reading Room, FBI Headquarters, Washington, DC.

178 Masai Hewitt in the Black Panther Party: Interview with Landon

Williams, Berkeley, March 2, 1992; interview with former party member requesting anonymity, Oakland, September 28, 1992.

178 Kathleen Cleaver lacking patience with most rank and file: Memo from San Francisco office of FBI to FBI director, September 5, 1968, contained in COINTELPRO files on Black Panthers, General Public Reading Room, FBI Headquarters, Washington, DC.

178 Free breakfast program designed in part to counter violent party image: Information from Committee Exhibit No. 8, at hearings before the Committee on Internal Security, House of Representatives, chaired by Cong. Richard Ichord, Washington, DC, October 6, 1970.

179 Leadership, for most part, staying at headquarters: Interviews with Landon Williams, Berkeley, October 1991, and March 2, 1992; transcript of testimony by Jean and Larry Powell before U.S. Senate Permanent Subcommittee on Investigations, chaired by Sen. John McClellan, Washington, DC, June 18, 1969; interview with former party member requesting anonymity, Oakland, September 28, 1992.

179 FBI memo on promiscuity: Memo from San Francisco office to director of FBI, April 3, 1968, contained in COINTELPRO files on Black Panthers, General Public Reading Room, FBI Headquarters, Washington, DC.

180 Involvement of William O'Neal in death of Fred Hampton: *Racial Matters: The FBI's Secret File on Black America*, by Kenneth O'Reilly, (Free Press, 1989), pp. 310–315.

180 Louis Tackwood's account of level of clandestine activities by government organizations: *Who Killed George Jackson?* by Jo Durden-Smith (Knopf, 1976), pp. 127–131.

181 COINTELPRO blackmail of Earl Anthony: *Spitting in the Wind*, by Earl Anthony (Roundtable, 1990), p. 38.

181 Labeling critics of party leadership renegades and jacanapes: Interview with Landon Williams, Berkeley, October 1991; interview with Benjamin Stewart, Marin City, CA, October 8, 1992; information from Committee Exhibit No. 8, at hearings before the Committee on Internal Security, House of Representatives, chaired by Cong. Richard Ichord, Washington, DC, October 6, 1970; transcript of testimony by Jean and Larry Powell before U.S. Senate Permanent Subcommittee on Investigations, chaired by Sen. John McClellan, Washington, DC, June 18, 1969.

182 Jean and Larry Powell's experiences in the party: Transcript of testimony by Jean and Larry Powell before U.S. Senate Permanent Subcommittee on Investigations, chaired by Sen. John McClellan, Washington, DC, June 18, 1969.

187 Arrest of Larry Powell and Wendell Wade in Aloha nightclub hold-up: "Charges Filed Against Six Panthers Following Holdup," *Oakland Tribune*, January 3, 1969; transcript of testimony by Jean and Larry Powell before U.S. Senate Permanent Subcommittee on Investigations, chaired by Sen. John McClellan, Washington, DC, June 18, 1969.

187 Denunciation of Wade and Powell by party after robbery: "Panthers Denounce 'Agents and Fools,'" *Oakland Tribune*, January 3, 1969.

188 Wendell Wade expressing fear of being marked for death by Panthers: "Fearful Ex-Panther Sentenced," *San Francisco Chronicle*, May 3, 1969.

188 Party members beating Renee Rice and allegedly killing Ron Black: Transcript of testimony by Jean and Larry Powell before U.S. Senate Permanent Subcommittee on Investigations, chaired by Sen. John McClellan, Washington, DC, June 18, 1969.

188 Ardell Butler story: "Strange Shooting of Oakland Man," *San Francisco Chronicle*, April 26, 1969.

188 Tommy Jones's accusations against the party and the party's denial: "Chairman Bobby's Press Statement at Alvert Linthcome's Funeral," *The Black Panther*, April 20, 1969.

188 Circumstances surrounding Jean and Larry Powell's cooperation with the Oakland police: Telephone interview with former Oakland Police Sergeant Ray Gaul, October 1992.

190 Denials by Bobby Seale and David Hilliard of charges by the Powells: "Angry Denial of Ex-Panther's Story," *San Francisco Chronicle*, June 19, 1969.

190 Quote of Bobby Seale on Jones charges: "Chairman Bobby's Press Statement at Alvert Linthcome's Funeral," *The Black Panther*, April 20, 1969.

190 FBI COINTELPRO memo seeking to take advantage of dissent among Panthers: Memo from San Francisco office to FBI director, April 23, 1969, contained in COINTELPRO files on Black Panthers, General Public Reading Room, FBI Headquarters, Washington, DC.

191 Comments by Father Eugene Boyle on Panther defectors: "S.F. Warned on 'Climate of Hate,'" by Maitland Zane, *San Francisco Chronicle*, May 1, 1969.

191 Quote of Landon Williams on Hilliard's excesses: Interview with Landon Williams, Berkeley, October 1991.

191 Quote of anonymous party veteran on party-sanctioned robberies: Interview with former party member requesting anonymity, Oakland, September 28, 1992.

191 Quote of Benjamin Stewart on Hilliard and excesses: Interview with Benjamin Stewart, Marin City, CA, October 8, 1992.

193 Journalist Earl Caldwell's refusal to testify before Special Grand Jury: "U.S. Subpoena: N.Y. Times Acts to Protect a Reporter Here," by William Cooney, *San Francisco Chronicle*, February 4, 1970.

194 The Alex Rackley case: "Witness Says Seale Gave Death Order," *San Francisco Chronicle*, April 2, 1970; *Agony in New Haven: The Trial of Bobby Seale, Ericka Huggins and The Black Panther Party*, by Donald Freed (Simon and Schuster, 1973).

196 Black Panther newspaper distribution figures: Information from Committee Exhibit No. 6, at hearings before the Committee on Internal Security, House of Representatives, chaired by Cong. Richard Ichord, Washington, DC, October 6, 1970.

196 David Hilliard's wife pulling a gun on him: Interview with Mary Kennedy, Oakland, August 29, 1992; *This Side of Glory*, by David Hilliard and Lewis Cole (Little, Brown, 1993), pp. 251–252.

196 Wife of another leader catching him in infidelity and subsequent meeting being called to discuss the subject of infidelity: Interview with Mary Kennedy, Oakland, August 29, 1992.

199 Panther Party boycott of Safeway stores: Committee Exhibit No. 379, presented before U.S. Senate Permanent Subcommittee on Investigations, chaired by Sen. John McClellan, Washington, DC, June 18, 1969.

199 Firebombing of convenience store by Black Panthers: "Black Panther Says He Made Fire Bomb," *San Francisco Chronicle*, June 25, 1970.

201 Account of the incident involving the arrest of Mary Kennedy's husband: The source is both Alameda County Courthouse documents and newspaper accounts of the incident. The names and dates of the documents and newspapers have been left out to protect the identity of Mary's husband (Kennedy is Mary's maiden name), since he refused to cooperate in the writing of this book.

CHAPTER 9

205 Bobby Seale chained, bound, and gagged: *The Black Panther Speaks*, ed. by Phillip S. Foner (Lippincott, 1970), p. 183.

206 People's Park confrontation: *The Sixties: Years of Hope, Days of Rage*, by Tod Gitlin (Bantam, 1989), pp. 354–361.

206 Statistics on the number of killed and wounded police in Panther–police confrontations: Information from Committee Exhibit No. 3, at hearings before the Committee on Internal Security, House of Representatives, chaired by Cong. Richard Ichord, Washington, DC, October 6, 1970.

206 Statistics on number of Panthers killed and arrested in confrontations with the police: *Racial Matters: The FBI's Secret File on Black America*, by Kenneth O'Reilly (Free Press, 1989), p. 297.

206 Partial listing of Panther–police confrontations from 1968 to 1969: From statistics contained in COINTELPRO files on Black Panthers, General Public Reading Room, FBI Headquarters, Washington, DC; and *A Panther Is a Black Cat*, by Reginald Major (William Morrow, 1971), appendix E.

209 Tom Hayden and the Red Family: *The Sixties: Years of Hope, Days of Rage*, by Tod Gitlin (Bantam, 1989), p. 353; interview with Mae Jackson, Brooklyn, NY, December 25, 1992.

209 Bernstein benefit for the Panther Party: "Upper East Side Story," *Time*, January 26, 1970; "Concern Grows on Private Armies," by Frank Murray (AP story), *San Francisco Sunday Examiner and Chronicle*, March 8, 1970.

209 Jane Fonda at Glide Memorial on the Black Panthers: "Jane Fonda Takes Pulpit—Her Revolutionary Credo," by Jim Brewer, *San Francisco Chronicle*, July 8, 1970.

210 Nicholas Von Hoffman on the Black Panthers: "Our Lively World:

The Black Panthers," by Nicholas Von Hoffman, *San Francisco Chronicle*, June 11, 1970.

210 Saul Alinsky on the Black Panthers: "Killing Will Go On Until Blacks Clamp Down: Alinsky," by Tom Fitzpatrick (reprint from *Chicago Sun-Times*), *San Francisco Sunday Examiner and Chronicle*, September 13, 1970.

210 Roy Wilkins on the Black Panthers: *San Francisco Chronicle*, January 8, 1970.

210 Cecil Poole on the Black Panthers: "Party Paper: Grand Jury Here Calls 3 Panthers," *San Francisco Chronicle*, January 14, 1970.

211 Comments of Richardson Preyer and exchange between Frank Jones and John Ashbrook at committee hearing: Testimony of Frank Jones at hearings before the Committee on Internal Security, House of Representatives, chaired by Cong. Richard Ichord, Washington, DC, October 6, 1970.

213 David Hilliard's November 1969 speech at Golden Gate Park and subsequent interview on "Face the Nation": "U.S. Agents Hold Hilliard—'Threat to the President,'" *San Francisco Chronicle*, December 4, 1969; *The Black Panther Speaks*, ed. by Phillip S. Foner (Lippincott, 1970), pp. 128–136.

213 Children in the free breakfast program singing song about offing the pig: "Black Panther Revolutionary Wedding," *The Black Panther*, May 11, 1969.

214 Saul Alinsky on confrontation with a Black Panther: "Killing Will Go On Until Blacks Clamp Down: Alinsky," by Tom Fitzpatrick (reprint from *Chicago Sun-Times*), *San Francisco Sunday Examiner and Chronicle*, September 13, 1970.

214 Hilliard arrested for threatening life of the President: "U.S. Agents Hold Hilliard—'Threat to the President,'" *San Francisco Chronicle*, December 4, 1969.

214 Jean and Larry Powell on Huey Newton: Transcript of testimony by Jean and Larry Powell before U.S. Senate Permanent Subcommittee on Investigations, chaired by Sen. John McClellan, Washington, DC, June 18, 1969.

215 Fay Stender discovering legal technicality that freed Huey Newton: *Destructive Generation*, by Peter Collier and David Horowitz (Summit, 1989), p. 31.

215 Newton gaining freedom after posting bail of $50,000: *Revolutionary Suicide*, by Huey Newton (Harcourt Brace Jovanovich, 1973), p. 287.

CHAPTER 10

217 Sheeba Haven's backgound and her encounter with Huey Newton: Interview with Sheeba Haven, San Francisco, October 1991.

219 Newton's recollections of his prison experiences: *Revolutionary Suicide*, by Huey Newton (Harcourt Brace Jovanovich, 1973), pp. 247–270.

220 Rationales for appealing Newton's conviction, and Newton defense team opinions on which way decision would go: *In the Court of Appeal of the State of California: People of the State of California vs. Huey P. Newton, Appellant's Opening Brief*, submitted by Fay Stender, August 1969; *Revolutionary Suicide*, by Huey Newton (Harcourt Brace Jovanovich, 1973), pp. 265–267; Interview with Alex Hoffman, Oakland, September 1993.

222 Quote of Newton riding to Oakland after his prison release: Ibid., p. 276.

222 Quote of Alex Hoffman on Huey's state of mind regarding pending prison release: Interview with Alex Hoffman, Oakland, October 1991.

222 Quote of Peter Solomon on atmosphere at Alameda County Courthouse on day of Newton's release: Interview with Peter Solomon, Berkeley, July 24, 1992.

222 Newton, Hilliard, and Pratt on top of Alex Hoffman's car in front of crowd at release: Interview with Alex Hoffman, Oakland, October 1991; "Huey Freed," *Newsweek*, August 17, 1970.

223 Quote of Benjamin Stewart regarding Newton's first press conference after release: Interview with Benjamin Stewart, Marin City, CA, October 8, 1992.

223 Mary Kennedy's whereabouts on day of Newton's release: Interview with Mary Kennedy, Oakland, September 11, 1992.

223 Landon Williams in prison, being kept abreast of party developments: Interview with Landon Williams, Berkeley, October 1991.

223 Newton's promise to the Vietcong of Panther guerrillas: "Huey Freed," *Newsweek*, August 17, 1970.

223 Original plan for Jonathan Jackson breakout involving the Black Panthers: "Clues in Secret Document," by Paul Avery, Jim Brewer, and Rick Carroll, *San Francisco Chronicle*, June 23, 1975.

224 Eldridge Cleaver being in on providing Jonathan Jackson with assistance: *Destructive Generation*, by Peter Collier and David Horowitz (Summit, 1990), p. 150.

224 Huey reportedly calling off Panther support for Jonathan Jackson's Marin escape plan: *Who Killed George Jackson?* by Jo Durden-Smith, (Knopf, 1976), p. 144.

224 Chapters outside of Oakland desiring that something be done about various abuses of Hilliard and other leaders: Interview with Landon Williams, Berkeley, October 1991; interview with Mae Jackson, Brooklyn, NY, December 25, 1992; interview with Benjamin Stewart, Marin City, CA, October 8, 1992; "The Panthers: Their Decline—and Fall?" *Newsweek*, March 22, 1971.

225 Newton sensitivity to criticism: Interview with Landon Williams, Berkeley, October 1991; interview with Kiilu Nyasha, San Francisco, April, 1992; COINTELPRO memo from FBI Director to FBI offices in Boston, Los Angeles, New York, and San Francisco, contained in COINTELPRO files on Black Panthers, General Public Reading Room, FBI Headquarters, Washington, DC.

225 Newton turned on to women and drugs by "beautiful people": Interview with Landon Williams, Berkeley, October 1991; interview with Sheeba Haven, San Francisco, October 1991; interview with Kiilu Nyasha, San Francisco, April 1992; *Destructive Generation*, by Peter Collier and David Horowitz (Summit, 1990), p. 154.

225 Newton engaging in drinking and drugs before going to prison for Frey shooting: Interview with Willie Payne, Oakland, July 28, 1992; *Spitting in the Wind*, by Earl Anthony (Roundtable, 1990), p. 32; *This Side of Glory*, by David Hilliard and Lewis Cole (Little, Brown, 1993), p. 123.

226 Revolutionary People's Constitutional Convention as Eldridge Cleaver's idea: *Revolutionary Suicide*, by Huey Newton (Harcourt Brace Jovanovich, 1973), p. 294.

226 Cleaver approached by party members outside of Oakland as person to rectify party problems: Interview with Landon Williams, Berkeley, October 1991; interview with Benjamin Stewart, Marin City, CA,

October 8, 1992; interview with Kiilu Nyasha, San Francisco, April 1992; "The Panthers: Their Decline—and Fall?" *Newsweek*, March 22, 1971; "Whatever Happened to . . . the 'United' Black Panthers," *U.S. News and World Report*, May 3, 1971; "Cleaver Tells of Power Struggle," *San Francisco Chronicle*, March 5, 1971.

226 Cleaver as alleged wife beater and holding Timothy Leary under "house arrest": "The Panthers: Their Decline—and Fall?" *Newsweek*, March 22, 1971; "Whatever Happened to . . . the 'United' Black Panthers," *U.S. News and World Report*, May 3, 1971.

226 Mae Jackson's impression of Huey at the Revolutionary People's Constitutional Convention: Interview with Mae Jackson, Brooklyn, NY, December 25, 1992.

227 Kiilu Nyasha on Huey at the Philadelphia convention: Interview with Kiilu Nyasha, San Francisco, April 1992.

227 Huey sending emissaries to Panther housing to get women: Interview with Mary Kennedy, Oakland, August 29, 1992.

227 Quote of Landon Williams on party members being identified as enemies of the people: Interview with Landon Williams, Berkeley, October 1991.

228 May Day Panther support rally at Yale and quote of Kingman Brewster: "Panther and Bulldog," *Newsweek*, May 4, 1970.

228 Newton at Yale in February 1971: *In Search of Common Ground, Conversations with Erik H. Erikson and Huey Newton* (Norton, 1973), pp. 15–17.

229 Newton sending out squads to brutalize critics inside the party: Interviews with Landon Williams, Berkeley, October 1991, and March 2, 1992.

229 Connie Matthews sent to Oakland by Cleaver to serve as Newton's secretary: *Revolutionary Suicide*, by Huey Newton (Harcourt Brace Jovanovich, 1973), pp. 299–300.

229 Matthews sent as emissary by Cleaver to avoid government intelligence: *A Taste of Power*, by Elaine Brown (Pantheon, 1993), p. 294. *Note:* Brown specifically notes that Matthews was sent to avoid the telephone monitoring of the police. It is my interpretation that this can be summed up as an effort to avoid "government intelligence," since at that time the Panthers were receiving letters back and forth (authored by COINTELPRO), the authenticity of which they were questioning.

229 Meeting of Newton, Tabor, Moore, and Matthews in New Haven: Interview with Kiilu Nyasha, San Francisco, April 1992; *Huey Newton and the Black Panther Party*, by Michael Newton (Holloway House, 1980, 1991), p. 204.

229 Matthews and Tabor providing solid information on abuses that disaffected party members were hoping Cleaver would rectify: "Destroying the Panther Myth," *Time*, March 22, 1971; *Huey Newton and the Black Panther Party*, by Michael Newton (Holloway House, 1980, 1991), p. 205.

230 Newton appearing on Jim Dunbar Show to explain why he had moved into penthouse: Airtel dated February 25, 1971, from San Francisco FBI office to FBI director, contained in COINTELPRO files on Black Panthers, General Public Reading Room, FBI Headquarters, Washington, DC.

230 Newton appearing on the Dunbar show to promote Intercommunal Day of Solidarity: *Revolutionary Suicide*, by Huey Newton (Harcourt Brace Jovanovich, 1973), p. 301.

230 Cleaver demanding reinstatement of New York 21 and the ouster of Hilliard for mismanaging the party: *Huey Newton and the Black Panther Party*, by Michael Newton (Holloway House, 1980, 1991), p. 206.

230 Grateful Dead at Intercommunal Day of Solidarity: "Newton Attacks 'Sexual Fascism," *San Francisco Chronicle*, March 6, 1971.

231 Quote of Benjamin Stewart on Intercommunal Day of Solidarity: Interview with Benjamin Stewart, Marin City, CA, October 8, 1992.

231 Murder of Robert Webb: "New York Slaying Tied to Panther Split," (AP) *San Francisco Chronicle*, March 10, 1971; "The Panthers: Their Decline—and Fall?" *Newsweek*, March 22, 1971.

232 Murder of Sam Napier: "Whatever Happened to . . . the 'United' Black Panthers," *U.S. News and World Report*, May 3, 1971.

232 Murder of Fred Bennett: "Shattered Body of Panther Found," *San Francisco Chronicle*, April 21, 1971.

232 Effect of the murder of Alex Rackley on other Panthers: Interview with Kiilu Nyasha, San Francisco, March 1993.

233 Newton putting best face on the Panther murders, and NAACP official on the Panthers: "Newton Says Police Slew Panthers," by Alamena Lomax, *San Francisco Examiner*, May 1, 1971.

233 Newton appearing at seminary in Berkeley to announce return to church: *To Die for the People*, by Huey Newton (Random House, 1972), pp. 60–75.

234 Middle-aged black woman telling Newton the Panthers had lost their souls: "The Black Panthers' New Approach to 'Survival,'" by Ross Baker (Washington Post Service), *San Francisco Sunday Examiner and Chronicle*, February 27, 1972.

234 Hilliard's statement about "offing" black preachers: *To Die for the People*, by Huey Newton, pp. 73–74.

234 Newton seeing *The Godfather* and requiring party members to do the same: Interview with Landon Williams, Berkeley, March 2, 1992.

235 Verdicts in Huggins and Seale cases: *Agony in New Haven: The Trial of Bobby Seale, Ericka Huggins and The Black Panther Party*, by Donald Freed (Simon and Schuster, 1973), pp. 318–320.

236 Hilliard conviction: From court records, State of California vs. David Hilliard, Alameda County Courthouse, Oakland.

236 Newton kicking Hilliard out of the party because of alleged coup plan: "The Party's Over," by Kate Coleman with Paul Avery, *New Times*, July 10, 1978.

236 Quote of Mary Kennedy regarding Newton centralizing money: Interview with Mary Kennedy, Oakland, August 29, 1992.

236 Haven as opener of the party's free clinic and leaving party to join BLA: Interview with Sheeba Haven, San Francisco, October 1991.

238 Quote of Ralph Williams regarding the Panthers, and the intimidation of black dry cleaner: Interview with Ralph Williams, Oakland, August 8, 1992.

238 Newton requesting $220 per week from Cal-Pak: "Merchants' Group Accuses Panthers," *San Francisco Chronicle*, August 11, 1971.

238 History of black Oakland: Interview with Tom Nash, Oakland, July 29, 1992; Interview with Ralph Williams, Oakland, August 8, 1992; "On the Sidewalk," column by Tom Berkley, *Oakland Post*, March 13, 1968, and October 9, 1968.

240 History of black San Francisco: Interview with Benjamin Stewart, Marin City, CA, October 8, 1992.

240 History of Cal-Pak: Interview with Tom Nash, Oakland, July 29, 1992.

241 Cal-Pak securing nearly 500 jobs for blacks in beverage industry: "Black Backlash Hits Panther Liquor Store Boycott," by Don Martinez, *San Francisco Sunday Examiner and Chronicle*, September 26, 1971.

241 Actions of Bill Boyette on behalf of Cal-Pak and quote of Bobby Seale regarding Cal-Pak: "Merchants' Group Accuses Panthers," *San Francisco Chronicle*, August 11, 1971.

241 Details of Panthers boycott of Cal-Pak: "Merchants' Group Accuses Panthers," *San Francisco Chronicle*, August 11, 1971; "Merchant Fights Panther Boycott," *San Francisco Chronicle*, August 11, 1971; "Oakland Group: Blacks to Fight Panther Boycott," *San Francisco Chronicle* September 18, 1971; "Black Backlash Hits Panther Liquor Store Boycott," by Don Martinez, *San Francisco Sunday Examiner and Chronicle*, September 26, 1971; "Panthers Boycott—Can Blacks Resist?" *Oakland Tribune*, September 23, 1971.

243 Bill Mabry and Tom Nash walking through the picket line and Tom Berkley getting his gun: Interview with Tom Nash, Oakland, July 29, 1992.

243 Panthers approaching after-hours clubs for donations: Interview with Landon Williams, Berkeley, March 2, 1992.

243 Characteristics of after-hours clubs: Interview with Peter Solomon, Berkeley, July 24, 1992.

243 Panther weapons arsenal: *A Taste of Power*, by Elaine Brown (Pantheon, 1993), p. 19.

244 Quote of Bobby Seale admonishing pickets of Boyette's store: "Merchant Fights Panther Boycott," *San Francisco Examiner*, August 11, 1971.

244 Quote of Mary Kennedy on Cal-Pak boycott: Interview with Mary Kennedy, Oakland, August 29, 1992.

244 Quote of Albert McKee regarding Newton's behavior at meeting between Ad Hoc Committee and Panthers: "Black Backlash Hits

Panther Liquor Store Boycott," by Don Martinez, *San Francisco Sunday Examiner and Chronicle*, September 26, 1971.

245 Quote of Newton at the Ad Hoc meeting: "Boycott Opponents Uniting," *Oakland Tribune*, September 24, 1971.

245 Quotes of Joseph Simmons on boycott: "Black Backlash Hits Panther Liquor Store Boycott," by Don Martinez, *San Francisco Sunday Examiner and Chronicle*, September 26, 1971; "Oakland Group: Blacks to Fight Panther Boycott," *San Francisco Chronicle*, September 18, 1971.

245 Quotes of Rev. Charles Belcher and Frances Albrier on Cal-Pak boycott: "Black Leaders Hit Panther Demands," *Oakland Tribune*, September 25, 1971.

246 Boycott settlement, including involvement of Ron Dellums: "Pact Ends Boycott of Black Retail Business," by Gayle Montgomery, *Oakland Tribune*, January 16, 1972; "Panthers to Help Store They Picketed," *San Francisco Chronicle*, January 17, 1972.

246 Details of how boycott catalyzed the creation of the New Oakland Committee: Oral biography of Lionel Wilson, contained in the Bancroft Oral History Collection, Bancroft Library, UC Berkeley.

247 Black Panther 1972 Survival Conferences: "Black Panthers Draw Big Crowd," by Dick Halgren, *San Francisco Chronicle*, March 30, 1972; "Panthers' Day-Long Conference," *San Francisco Sunday Examiner and Chronicle*, June 25, 1971.

247 Bert Schneider footing bill for Survival Conferences: *Knockwood*, by Candice Bergen (Ballantine, 1984), pp. 255–256. *Note:* In the book, Bergen gives Schneider the assumed name of "Robin," describing him as the "only white Panther." Printed proof that "Robin" is without question Bert Schneider is available simply by matching descriptions of "Robin" found in Bergen's book with the descriptions found in sources such as *A Taste of Power*, by Elaine Brown (Pantheon, 1993), and *Destructive Generation*, by Peter Collier and David Horowitz (Summit, 1989). In the latter books Schneider's real name is used.

247 Panther candidates for West Oakland Planning Committee: "Model Cities Vote Due," by Bob Distefano, *Oakland Tribune*, August 2, 1972; "Six Panther-Backed Candidates Win," *San Francisco Chronicle*, August 24, 1972.

249 Newton attacking bodyguard and woman who watched Panther children: Interview of Mary Kennedy, Oakland, August 29, 1992.

249 Newton's behavior in the after-hours clubs: Interview with Landon Williams, Berkeley, October 1991; *Destructive Generation*, by Peter Collier and David Horowitz (Summit, 1989), p. 155.

CHAPTER 11

251 Joe Blum on Newton: Interview with Joe Blum, San Francisco, September 9, 1992.

252 David Horowitz's experiences with the Black Panthers: Interview with David Horowitz, Los Angeles, October 6, 1992.

254 Mae Jackson's involvement in efforts to free Johnny Spain: Interview with Mae Jackson, Brooklyn, NY, December 25, 1992.

254 Circumstances of the George Jackson breakout attempt: "Murder Conviction Upset," by Don Wegars, *San Francisco Chronicle*, July 1, 1982; "The Rebirth of the Black Panthers," by Hugh Pearson, *San Francisco Weekly*, April 4, 1990; *Destructive Generation*, by Peter Collier and David Horowitz (Summit, 1989), pp. 42–43.

254 Theory of Newton calling off support for George Jackson's escape attempt and Jackson signing over book royalties to Panthers: Interview with Mae Jackson, Brooklyn, NY, December 25, 1992; interview with David Horowitz, Los Angeles, October 6, 1992.

254 Suspicions of Black Guerilla Family regarding Panther sabotage of George Jackson's escape attempt: *This Side of Glory*, by David Hilliard and Lewis Cole (Little, Brown, 1993), pp. 379–381.

256 Mae Jackson's suspicions of Panther intentions for Johnny Spain and contacting Elaine Wender: Interview with Mae Jackson, Brooklyn, NY, December 25, 1992.

256 Elaine Brown on Elaine Wender and Spain's poems: *A Taste of Power*, by Elaine Brown (Pantheon, 1993), pp. 359–360.

258 Quote of Peter Solomon on experience at Newton's penthouse: Interview with Peter Solomon, Berkeley, July 24, 1992.

259 Seale and Brown 1973 election campaigns: ". . . And a New Bobby," *Newsweek*, April 2, 1973; "Oakland Election Points Up Changing Image of 'Seale, Black Militant,'" *Oakland Post*, April 15, 1973; "Tale of Two Cities" (editorial), *Oakland Post*, April 22, 1973; "Bobby Seale Proposes Pay for Two Hours' Voting Time," *Oakland Post*, April 8, 1973; "Ain't Backing Up Seale Says," by Fran Dauth, *Oakland Tribune*, May 11, 1973.

259 Tom Nash on Seale's campaign: Interview with Tom Nash, Oakland, July 29, 1992.

259 Fritz Pointer incident: "Oakland Attack: College Teacher Beaten in Class," *San Francisco Chronicle*, November 16, 1972.

259 Killing of Anthony Costa by Black Panther: "Panther Charge Now Is Murder," *San Francisco Chronicle*, March 1, 1973.

260 Panther exchange of gunfire at North Oakland gas station: "Shooting in Oakland—2 Arrests," *San Francisco Chronicle*, April 27, 1973.

260 Panther incident with Ike and Tina Turner: "Panthers Say They'll Sue Ike and Tina," *San Francisco Chronicle*, August 1, 1973; "Ike Turner's Version of Oakland Rift," *San Francisco Chronicle*, August 2, 1973.

260 Newton incident at Fratalanza: Interview with Fred Hiestand, San Francisco, July 4, 1992.

261 Departure of Brenda Bay: Interview with Mary Kennedy, Oakland, August 29, 1992; interview with David Horowitz, Los Angeles, October 6, 1992.

262 Party workers wages having to be turned back into the party: Interview with Mary Kennedy, Oakland, August 29, 1992.

263 Things downhill for Seale after 1973 election: Interview with Mary Kennedy, Oakland, August 29, 1992; *A Taste of Power*, by Elaine Brown (Pantheon, 1993), pp. 378–379.

264 Beating and sodomizing of Bobby Seale and expelling from the party: Interview with Mary Kennedy, Oakland, August 29, 1992; interview with David Horowitz, Los Angeles, October 6, 1992; Horowitz also provides written confirmation for the sodomizing in article "Black Murder, Inc.," by David Horowitz, *Heterodoxy*, March 1993. *Note:* Elaine Brown confirms beating *but not sodomizing*, in *A Taste of Power*, by Elaine Brown (Pantheon, 1993), p. 397.

264 Newton incident at Fox Lounge: "Huey Newton Arrested in Brawl," *San Francisco Chronicle*, July 31, 1974; "The Party's Over," by Kate Coleman with Paul Avery, *New Times*, July 10, 1978.

265 Shooting of Kathleen Smith: "Witness Tells of Slaying—and Newton Laughing," by Ed Doughery, *San Francisco Chronicle*; October 26, 1977; "The Party's Over," by Kate Coleman with Paul Avery, *New Times*, July 10, 1978.

265 Comments of Newton that Smith murder was his first nonpolitical one: *Destructive Generation*, by Peter Collier and David Horowitz (Summit, 1989), p. 157.

265 Newton knocking out the glass eye of Lamp Post employee: Interview with Mary Kennedy, Oakland, August 29, 1992.

266 Helen Robinson and Preston Callins incidents: "The Party's Over," by Kate Coleman with Paul Avery, *New Times*, July 10, 1978.

268 Newton fleeing to Cuba and boat capsizing: Interview with Lianna (assumed name—interviewee asked that her real name not be used), San Francisco, June 3, 1992.

CHAPTER 12

269 Garry reporting Newton's reason for fleeing: "The Party's Over," by Kate Coleman with Paul Avery, *New Times*, July 10, 1978; *Destructive Generation*, by Peter Collier and David Horowitz (Summit, 1989), p. 158.

269 Resignation of other Panthers due to Brown's ascendancy and Brown's ascendancy improving image of the Panthers, gaining appointments of important Oaklanders on Oakland Community Learning Center board: Interview with David Horowitz, Los Angeles, October 6, 1992.

270 Huey staying in contact with Brown and others while in Cuba: Interview with Lianna (assumed name—interviewee asked that her real name not be used), San Francisco, June 3, 1992; interview with David Horowitz, Los Angeles, October 6, 1992; "Newton's Life Is on the Line," by Tim Reiterman, *San Francisco Sunday Examiner and Chronicle*, July 17, 1977.

270 Elaine Brown becoming Larry Henson's lover and renting him an apartment: *A Taste of Power*, by Elaine Brown (Pantheon, 1993), p. 405.

270 Brown tooling around Oakland in red Mercedes: Interview with David Horowitz, Los Angeles, October 6, 1992; "The Party's Over," by Kate Coleman with Paul Avery, *New Times*, July 10, 1978.

270 Departure of Gwen Goodloe and alleged drug-related shooting at Learning Center: Interview with David Horowitz, Los Angeles, October 6, 1992.

270 Flores Forbes's denial of drug involvement in Learning Center shooting: Interview with Flores Forbes, New York City, November 6, 1993.

271 Elaine Brown's explanation for the shooting at the Learning Center: "Police Deny Report of Fatal Panther Feud," by Alice Yarish, *San Francisco Examiner*, October 27, 1974.

272 Betty Van Patter's experience with the Black Panthers: Interview with David Horowitz, Los Angeles, October 6, 1992.

272 Second thoughts about Brown's city council campaign by supporters, after questions on Van Patter disappearance: *A Taste of Power*, by Elaine Brown (Pantheon, 1993), p. 413.

272 Elaine Brown's support in 1974–1975 campaign for Oakland City Council: "A Candidate Speaks Up," by Beverly Stephen, *San Francisco Chronicle*, February 25, 1975.

273 Quote of former party member regarding relationship between the party and many powerful people in Oakland's establishment: Interview of former party member requesting anonymity, New York City, December 23, 1992.

273 Assassination of Willie Duke and friend, discovery of body of Wilfred La Tour, and assassination of "Preacherman": "The Party's Over," by Kate Coleman with Paul Avery, *New Times*, July 10, 1978.

274 Brown's increased political clout after 1975 city council bid: "Black Panthers: Now a 'Strong Political Force,'" by Tim Reiterman, *San Francisco Examiner*, July 3, 1977; interview with David Horowitz, Los Angeles, October 6, 1992.

275 Newton's return to Oakland and quote of John George regarding his return: "Black Panthers: Now a 'Strong Political Force,'" by Tim Reiterman, *San Francisco Examiner*, July 3, 1977.

275 Newton stating that charges against him were part of a frame-up: "'Now They Are Trying to Destroy Our Character,'" by Raul Ramirez, *San Francisco Examiner*, July 24, 1977; "Sizing Up the Newton Trial," by Lance Williams, *Oakland Tribune*, January 8, 1978.

275 Panther lawsuit: "Newton's Life Is on the Line," by Tim Reiterman, *San Francisco Sunday Examiner and Chronicle*, July 17, 1977.

275 Newton's release on $80,000 bail and source of money: "'Now They Are Trying to Destroy Our Character,'" by Raul Ramirez, *San Francisco Examiner*, July 24, 1977.

275 Newton moving into home in Oakland Hills provided by benefactors: Interview with Lianna (assumed name—interviewee asked that her name not be used), San Francisco, June 3, 1992; interview with Ron Anderly, San Francisco, September 11, 1992.

275 Newton and state assembly school award incident: Interview with Lianna (assumed name—interviewee asked that her real name not be used), San Francisco, June 3, 1992; interview with Fred Hiestand, San Francisco, July 4, 1992.

276 Newton's reasons for wanting Ph.D.: Interview with Fred Hiestand, San Francisco, July 4, 1992.

276 Newton's return to after-hours carousing and the falling out between Elaine Brown and Larry Henson: *A Taste of Power*, by Elaine Brown (Pantheon, 1993), pp. 496–498.

276 Charges reduced in Fox Lounge and Diane Washington incidents, Preston Collins paid off to forget who beat him: "The Party's Over," by Kate Coleman with Paul Avery, *New Times*, July 10, 1978.

277 Mary Matthews incident: Details of the incident were gleaned from court documents in the case of Flores Forbes, one of the accused gunmen, located at the Contra Costa County Courthouse in Martinez, CA. The Matthews incident is also written about in "The Party's Over," by Kate Coleman with Paul Avery, *New Times*, July 10, 1978.

278 Nelson Malloy incident: "Panthers Sought in Shooting," by Lance Williams, Lloyd Boles, and Pearl Stewart, *Oakland Tribune*, December 7, 1977; "Fugitive Panther Found Shot," by Jerry Roberts, *San Francisco Chronicle*, November 23, 1977; "Secret Flight Home For Wounded Panther," by Jerry Roberts, *San Francisco Chronicle*, December 16, 1977; "The Party's Over," by Kate Coleman with Paul Avery, *New Times*, July 10, 1978.

279 Decline in party support after the attempted murders: "The Party's Over," by Kate Coleman with Paul Avery, *New Times*, July 10, 1978.

280 Resignation of Elaine Brown: "Elaine Brown Resigns as Panther

Chief," *San Francisco Chronicle*, November 23, 1977; "Black Panther Buried Alive," by Lloyd Boles and Pearl Stewart, *Oakland Tribune*, November 23, 1977; *A Taste of Power*, by Elaine Brown (Pantheon, 1993), pp. 501–508.

281 Brown allegedly leaving after being beaten: Interview with Landon Williams, Berkeley, October 1991; "The Party's Over," by Kate Coleman with Paul Avery, *New Times*, July 10, 1978; "Ex-Comrades Return for Tommorrow's Rights," by Bill Snyder, *Oakland Tribune*, August 27, 1989.

281 Mayor Lionel Wilson's resignation from EOC Board of Directors: "Audit of Funds to Black Panthers," by Rick Malispina, *Oakland Tribune*, November 22, 1977.

281 Discovery of EOC improprieties: "Panthers' Public-Paid Jobs," *San Francisco Chronicle*, November 4, 1977; "Audit of Funds to Black Panthers," by Rick Malispina, *Oakland Tribune*, November 22, 1977; "Oakland Audit Assails Panther Accounting," *San Francisco Chronicle*, March 15, 1978; "Oakland to Cut Panther Grant on Juveniles," *San Francisco Chronicle*, March 30, 1978.

282 Firebombing of Pearl Stewart's car: "Arson Fire in Reporter's Car," *San Francisco Chronicle*, March 28, 1978.

282 Pearl Stewart's speculation on the botched assassination: "Black Panther Party Falters," by Pearl Stewart, *Oakland Sunday Tribune*, November 27, 1977.

282 Departure of Phyllis Jackson: "Black Panther Party Falters," by Pearl Stewart, *Oakland Sunday Tribune*, November 27, 1977; "Black Panther Appointee Resigns from Commission," *The Montclarion*, February 15, 1978.

282 Removal of Molly Dougherty from county post: "Panther Backer Ousted," by Lance Williams, *Oakland Tribune*, November 23, 1977.

282 Threats by Newton to *New Times* and Kate Coleman: Discussed in "Behind the Story" segment to chapter containing "The Party's Over," by Kate Coleman with Paul Avery, *New Times*, July 10, 1978, in the book *Raising Hell: How the Center for Investigative Reporting Gets the Story*, ed. by David Weir and Dan Noyes (Addison-Wesley, 1983).

283 Reaction of Joe Blum and son to Coleman-Avery piece: Interview with Joe Blum, San Francisco, September 9, 1992.

283 Santa Cruz bar incident, charges and Newton's various convictions up to 1979: "Huey Newton's Bail Increased by $75,000," by Ed Doughery, *San Francisco Chronicle*, May 20, 1978; "Troubled Life of Huey Newton," *San Francisco Chronicle*, August 23, 1989.

283 Bob Trivors's background and experiences with Huey Newton: Interview with Robert Trivors, Santa Cruz, October 2, 1992.

284 Experiences of Fred Hiestand and his girlfriend with Huey Newton: Interview with Hiestand's former girlfriend (interviewee asked that name not be used), San Francisco, June 3, 1992; interview with Fred Hiestand, San Francisco, July 4, 1992.

286 Outcome of Kathleen Smith murder case: "Witness Tells of Slaying—and Newton Laughing," by Ed Doughery, *San Francisco Chronicle*, October 26, 1977; interview with Tony Serra, September 18, 1992; discussed in "Behind the Story" segment to chapter containing "The Party's Over," by Kate Coleman with Paul Avery, *New Times*, July 10, 1978, in the book *Raising Hell: How the Center for Investigative Reporting Gets the Story*, ed. by David Weir and Dan Noyes (Addison-Wesley, 1983).

286 All information, including the opinions of UC Santa Cruz faculty (except that of Bob Trivors) regarding Huey Newton as a bachelor's degree and Ph.D. student at UC Santa Cruz: *Destructive Generation*, by Peter Collier and David Horowitz (Summit, 1989), pp. 161–162; "Huey Newton Gets Ph.D.," by George Williamson, *San Francisco Chronicle*, June 16, 1980.

286 All quotes regarding Newton's presence as a Ph.D. student at UC Santa Cruz: "Huey Newton Gets Ph.D.," by George Williamson, *San Francisco Chronicle*, June 16, 1980.

287 Description of and quotes from Newton's Ph.D. thesis: From the thesis itself, "War Against the Panthers: A Study of Repression in America," by Huey Percy Newton (copyright 1980).

289 Final meeting between David Horowitz and Huey Newton: Interview with David Horowitz, Los Angeles, October 6, 1992.

291 Woman approaching Newton at Dock of the Bay: Interview with Hiestand's girlfriend (interviewee asked that name not be used), San Francisco, June 3, 1992.

291 Newton's example of revolutionary justice and incident on the veranda: Interview with person who requested anonymity, Oakland, October 7, 1992.

292 Newton's invitation to Middle East: Interview with Hiestand's girl-friend (interviewee asked that name not be used), San Francisco, June 3, 1992; interview with Fred Hiestand, San Francisco, July 4, 1992.

Chapter 13

294 Fate of Bobby Seale and Eldridge Cleaver: "Legacy of Huey Newton's Black Panther Party: Where Prominent Black Panthers Are Now," *Oakland Tribune*, August 23, 1989; *Spitting in the Wind*, by Earl Anthony (Roundtable, 1990), p. 180.

294 Fate of Sheeba Haven: Interview with Sheeba Haven, San Francisco, October 1991.

295 Doctor's opinion of the Panther clinic and closing of the free clinic: "The Party's Over," by Kate Coleman with Paul Avery, *New Times*, July 10, 1978; discussed in "Behind the Story" segment to chapter containing above article, in the book *Raising Hell: How the Center for Investigative Reporting Gets the Story*, ed. by David Weir and Dan Noyes (Addison-Wesley, 1983).

295 Fate of Mary Kennedy: Interview with Mary Kennedy, Oakland, August 29, 1992.

295 Fate of Landon Williams: Landon Williams, Berkeley, October 1991.

296 Autograph incident at the Fairmont Hotel: Interview with Lianna (assumed name—interviewee asked that her real name not be used), San Francisco, June 3, 1992.

296 Incident at the after-hours club: Interview with Fred Hiestand, San Francisco, July 4, 1992.

297 Erica Huggins' role in Panther/EOC and Panther/EOC dealings related to embezzlement charges against Newton in 1982; Interview with Ron Anderly, San Francisco, September 11, 1992; transcripts of "People of the State of California vs. Huey P. Newton," Superior Court of the State of California, County of Alameda, June 23, 1987.

298 Bill Schuford's experiences as principal of Oakland Community Learning Center: Interview with Ron Anderly, San Francisco,

September 11, 1992; transcripts of "People of the State of California vs. Huey P. Newton," Superior Court of the State of California, County of Alameda, June 23, 1987.

299 Departure of Newton's wife: *Destructive Generation*, by Peter Collier and David Horowitz (Summit, 1989), p. 162.

299 Newton's illegal use of EOC New York investment account to pay living expenses: Interview with Ron Anderly, San Francisco, September 11, 1992; transcripts of "People of the State of California vs. Huey P. Newton," Superior Court of the State of California, County of Alameda, June 23, 1987.

300 Search of Newton's home and discovery of weaponry: Typed inventory of items recovered by California Dept. of Justice special agents Ron Anderly and S. A. Wong, located in records of "People of the State of California vs. Huey P. Newton," Superior Court of the State of California, County of Alameda, June 23, 1987.

300 Newton suspected of house burglary: "Huey Newton Sought in Oakland Gun Case," by Clarence Johnson, *San Francisco Chronicle*, November 6, 1986; "Huey Newton Surrenders in Oakland," *San Francisco Chronicle*, November 7, 1986.

301 Newton acquittal on illegal gun possession and quote of Charles Kirk: "Huey Newton Freed in Trial over Guns," by Jill Singleton, *San Francisco Chronicle*, June 26, 1986.

302 Newton ordered back to prison on illegal gun possession charge: "Newton Says He's a Prisoner of the Past," by Marc Sandalow, *San Francisco Chronicle*, March 16, 1987.

302 Changes in Oakland after the election of Lionel Wilson mayor: "Oakland's Reluctant Renaissance," by Kevin Starr, *California Business*, October 1987; "A Piece of the Action," by Tracy Johnson, *California Magazine*, October 1983; "A Question of Force," by John Ross, *The Express*, September 7, 1984.

304 Oakland's drug world in the 1980s: "A Small War in Oakland," by Carla Marinucci and Lance Williams (four-part series), *San Francisco Examiner*, November 25, 26, 27, 28, 1984; "Ex-Drug Dealer Gives Crucial Testimony," by Rob Haeseler, *San Francisco Chronicle*, January 23, 1985; "Conspiracy Trial in Big Heroin Case," by Lance Williams, *San Francisco Examiner*, January 20, 1985; "Drug King Felix Mitchell: Good or Not, He Died Young," by Carla Marinucci and Walt Gibbs, *San Francisco Examiner*, August 31, 1986; "Crack: An Examiner Special Report," by Annie Nakao, John O'Connor, and Lance Williams (two-part series), *San Francisco Examiner*, February 1988; "Crack City U.S.A.," by Mike McGrath, *The Express*, May 19, 1989.

306 BGF involvement with Funktown in Oakland drug dealing: "Funktown Area Named After Whisenton Gang," by Lance Williams, *San Francisco Examiner*, February 14, 1988.

306 Quote of Roosevelt Taylor regarding birth of crack: "Minister Recalls Crack's Early Days," by Lance Williams, *San Francisco Examiner*, February 28, 1988.

307 Daryl Reed said to be largest crack dealer: "Mitchell Kin Inherited Drug Empire, Police Say," by Lance Williams, *San Francisco Examiner*, December 11, 1988.

307 Newton's 1988 San Quentin prison term and protest: "Prison Protest by Ex-Panther Newton," by Torri Minton, *San Francisco Chronicle*, August 24, 1988.

308 Circumstances surrounding Elmer "Geronimo" Pratt's imprisonment: "The Framing of Geronimo Pratt," by John Roemer, *San Francisco Weekly*, February 12, 1992.

308 Circumstances in 1971 murder of Pratt's wife: "Panther Factions Blamed in Killing," *San Francisco Sunday Examiner and Chronicle*, November 14, 1971.

309 BGF members wondering out loud where Newton had been: "Huey Newton Gunned Down in West Oakland: The Final Chapter, Police Suspect Drugs Involved," by Harry Harris, *Oakland Tribune*, August 23, 1989.

309 Newton run-ins with Tyrone Robinson: Police statement of Tyrone Robinson (taken by Robert Chenault and Dan Mercado) and police statement of Derwin Marshall (taken by Robert Chenault and Mike Sitterud), August 25, 1989.

CHAPTER 14

311 Newton arrested in motel freebasing crack and state's charge on one count of embezzlement: Chronology of Newton's troubled life presented in *Oakland Tribune*, August 23, 1989.

312 Strategy of prosecutor in cutting deal with Newton on embezzle- ment charges: Interview with Ron Anderly, San Francisco, Septem- ber 11, 1992.

313 Newton telling reporter that he had tried to drink and drug himself to death: "Huey Newton Talks of Booze and Boredom," by Kitty Butler, *San Francisco Chronicle*, November 5, 1984.

313 Quote of Newton high on cocaine at Schneider residence: *Destructive Generation*, by Peter Collier and David Horowitz (Summit, 1989), p. 164.

313 C. L. Dellums still residing in West Oakland: Oral history of C. L. Dellums, Bancroft Collection, Bancroft Library, UC Berkeley.

314 David Hilliard once living in the Acorns and introducing Huey to crack: *This Side of Glory*, by David Hilliard and Lewis Cole (Little, Brown, 1993), pp. 407–408, 413.

314 Robinson and cohorts' run-ins with Huey Newton: Police statement of Tyrone Robinson (taken by Robert Chenault and Dan Mercado), August 25, 1989; "Newton Slaying Suspect Arrested," by Harry Harris and Paul Grabowicz, *Oakland Tribune*, August 26, 1989.

314 Details of how Newton was killed: From preliminary hearing in "People of the State of California vs. Tyrone Robinson," Superior Court of the State of California, County of Alameda, November 27, 1989.

315 Fire and police department responses to call alerting them to discov- ery of Newton's body: Police statement given by Oakland police officer E. Paulson, August 22, 1989, located in exhibits of "People of the State of California vs. Tyrone Robinson," Superior Court of the State of California, County of Alameda, November 27, 1989.

315 Willie Payne's experiences immediately after Newton's death: Inter- view with Willie Payne, Oakland, July 28, 1992.

316 Quote of Robert Morgan, on seeing Newton's body: "Huey Newton Shot Dead on West Oakland Street," by Lori Olazewski and Rick DelVecchio, *San Francisco Chronicle*, August 23, 1989.

317 Quote of Landon Williams on Huey's death: "Friends and Foes Remember Newton 'Visionary, 'Thug,'" by William Brand and Larry Spears, *Oakland Tribune*, August 23, 1989.

317 Mary Kennedy on Huey's death: Interview with Mary Kennedy, Oakland, August 29, 1992.

318 Comments of Newton family and David Hilliard on Huey's death: "Family and Friends Mourn Huey Newton," by Michael Collier and Harry Harris, *Oakland Tribune*, August 24, 1989.

318 Quotes of Tom Orloff and Elihu Harris on Huey Newton: "Friends and Foes Remember Newton 'Visionary, 'Thug,'" by William Brand and Larry Spears, *Oakland Tribune*, August 23, 1989.

318 Quotes of Cecil Williams responding to Newton being called a thug, and Williams' general comments on Newton's legacy: "Family and Friends Mourn Huey Newton," by Michael Collier and Harry Harris, *Oakland Tribune*, August 24, 1989; "Friends and Foes Remember Newton 'Visionary, 'Thug,'" by William Brand and Larry Spears, *Oakland Tribune*, August 23, 1989.

319 Quotes of Benjamin Hooks, Biko Lumumba, and Charles Garry on Huey: "Family and Friends Mourn Huey Newton," by Michael Collier and Harry Harris, *Oakland Tribune*, August 24, 1989.

320 Police apprehending Tyrone Robinson: "Friend, Relative Led Police to Slaying Suspect," by Harry Harris, *Oakland Tribune*, August 29, 1989.

321 Kiilu Nyasha's response to Newton's death: Interview with Kiilu Nyasha, San Francisco, April 1992.

322 Response of Bob Trivors to Huey's death: Interview with Robert Trivors, Santa Cruz, October 2, 1992.

323 Behavior of mourners at funeral home to view Newton's body: "Mourners Pay Respects to Huey Newton," by Sharon McCormack, *San Francisco Chronicle*, August 28, 1989; "Friends, Family Honor Huey Newton: Mourning," by Jacqueline Cutler, *Oakland Tribune*, August 28, 1989.

323 Quote of Stan Woods on Newton: "Friends, Family Honor Huey Newton: Mourning," by Jacqueline Cutler, *Oakland Tribune*, August 28, 1989.

323 Quotes of speakers at Huey's funeral and details of the funeral: "Slain Panther Eulogized as Hero," by Pearl Stewart, *San Francisco Chronicle*, August 29, 1989; "Newton Laid to Rest, Many Former Black Panthers Attend Rites," by Bill Snyder and Michael Collier, *Oakland Tribune*, August 29, 1989.

AFTERWORD

333 Information on the life of Flores Forbes: Interviews with Flores Forbes, New York City, November 6, 1993, December 9, 1993.

ACKNOWLEDGMENTS

346 Information on Van Patter murder from Tamara Van Patter Baltar: Telephone interview with Tamara Van Patter Baltar, December 18, 1993.

Index

White activists
  alliance of radical, with Pan-
    thers, 149–51
  anti-Vietnam War, 102–4, 144–
    45, 148–49
  E. Cleaver on, 107
  as Freedom Riders, 33–34, 38
  grassroots urban organizations,
    97–98
  idealism of, 99–101
  police confrontations with, 205–
    6
  splintering of radical, 251–52
  support for Panthers by, 157,
    167–68, 190–91, 209–10, 225
  at UC Berkeley, on race and
    civil rights, 48, 50–60, 69–70
  as voting rights activists, 61–68
White Panther Party, 327
Whites for the Defense of Huey
  Newton (WDHN), 153
Wilkins, Roy, 20, 23, 89, 210
  disavows violence, 28
Williams, Cecil, on death of
  H. Newton, 318
Williams, Lance, 282, 306
Williams, Landon, 2, 179, 227
  arrest/imprisonment of, 194, 223
  on death of H. Newton, 317,
    318
  departure from Panthers, 5, 281
  post-Panther life of, 295, 317
  resurrection of Panther newspa-
    per, 330, 331–32
  role of, in Black Panthers, 4,
    173–77, 248
Williams, Ralph, 238
Williams, Robert, 25–28, 35–39, 65

willingness of, to use violence,
    28, 76, 109
Wilson, John, 161
Wilson, Lionel, 246–47
  on death of H. Newton, 319
  as mayor of Oakland, 274, 302
  on Panther corporate board,
    270, 281
Wolfe, Tom, 209
Women, male Black Panther abuse
  of, 158–59, 175–76, 179–80,
    190, 191, 196–98, 225, 227,
    249–50, 265–66, 281n.
Wonder, Stevie, 289
Woods, Stan, on death of H. New-
    ton, 323
Wooten, Tommy, 192
Works Progress Administration
  (WPA), 16

X, Malcolm. *See* Malcolm X

Yale University, H. Newton at,
    227–29
Young, Andrew, 92
Young, Whitney, 89
Young Democrats, 71
Young People's Socialist League,
    71
Young Republicans, 71
Young Socialists Alliance, 71
Younge, Sammy, Jr., 83–84
Youth Delinquency Prevention
  Program, 281–82

Zellner, Bob, 42, 62
Zwerg, Jim, 33